THE FATHERS
OF THE CHURCH

A NEW TRANSLATION

VOLUME 101

THE FATHERS OF THE CHURCH

A NEW TRANSLATION

EDITORIAL BOARD

Thomas P. Halton
The Catholic University of America
Editorial Director

Elizabeth Clark
Duke University

Robert D. Sider
Dickinson College

Joseph T. Lienhard, S.J.
Fordham University

Michael Slusser
Duquesne University

Frank A. C. Mantello
The Catholic University of America

Cynthia White
The University of Arizona

Kathleen McVey
Princeton Theological Seminary

Robin Darling Young
The Catholic University of America

David J. McGonagle
Director
The Catholic University of America Press

FORMER EDITORIAL DIRECTORS

Ludwig Schopp, Roy J. Deferrari, Bernard M. Peebles,
Hermigild Dressler, O.F.M.

Carole Burnett
Cornelia Horn
Staff Editors

THEODORET OF CYRUS

COMMENTARY ON THE PSALMS
PSALMS 1–72

Translated by
ROBERT C. HILL
*The University of Sydney
Australia*

THE CATHOLIC UNIVERSITY OF AMERICA PRESS
Washington, D.C.

Copyright © 2000
THE CATHOLIC UNIVERSITY OF AMERICA PRESS
All rights reserved
Printed in the United States of America

The paper used in this publication meets the minimum requirements of the American National Standards for Information Science—Permanence of Paper for Printed Library Materials, ANSI Z39.48-1984.
∞

LIBRARY OF CONGRESS CATALOGING-IN-PUBLICATION DATA
Theodoret, Bishop of Cyrrhus.
 [Interpretatio in Psalmos. English]
 Theodoret of Cyrus : commentary on the Psalms / Theodoret of Cyrus ; translated with introduction and commentary by Robert C. Hill.
   p. cm. — (Fathers of the church ; 101-)
 Includes bibliographical references and index.
   ISBN 0-8132-0101-2 (v. 1 : alk. paper)
   ISBN 978-0-8132-2767-2 (pbk.)
 1. Bible. O.T. Psalms Commentaries Early works to 1800. I. Hill, Robert C. (Robert Charles), 1931– II. Title. III. Title: Commentary on the Psalms IV. Series.
BS1430.3 .T5413 2000
223'.207—dc21   99-31556

To the memory of
Leonard E. Boyle
of the Order of Preachers
prefect of the Vatican Library

CONTENTS

Abbreviations	xi
Select Bibliography	xiii

Introduction   1

1. Theodoret's exegetical works, including the
   Commentary on the Psalms   2
2. Text of the *Commentary;* short and long forms   4
3. Theodoret's Greek text of the Psalter;
   alternative versions   7
4. *Commentary on the Psalms:* nature, purpose,
   characteristics, and influences   12
5. Theodoret as interpreter of the Psalms; his wider
   thinking on Scripture   18
6. The Christology of the *Commentary on the Psalms*   25
7. Other theological accents   28
8. Moral accents; the spirituality of the *Commentary*   32

COMMENTARY ON THE PSALMS

Preface	39
Commentary on Psalm 1	46
Commentary on Psalm 2	52
Commentary on Psalm 3	60
Commentary on Psalm 4	63
Commentary on Psalm 5	68
Commentary on Psalm 6	73
Commentary on Psalm 7	77
Commentary on Psalm 8	82
Commentary on Psalm 9	87

Commentary on Psalm 10	94
Commentary on Psalm 11	99
Commentary on Psalm 12	102
Commentary on Psalm 13	104
Commentary on Psalm 14	106
Commentary on Psalm 15	111
Commentary on Psalm 16	113
Commentary on Psalm 17	119
Commentary on Psalm 18	123
Commentary on Psalm 19	133
Commentary on Psalm 20	139
Commentary on Psalm 21	141
Commentary on Psalm 22	145
Commentary on Psalm 23	156
Commentary on Psalm 24	159
Commentary on Psalm 25	163
Commentary on Psalm 26	169
Commentary on Psalm 27	172
Commentary on Psalm 28	178
Commentary on Psalm 29	181
Commentary on Psalm 30	187
Commentary on Psalm 31	192
Commentary on Psalm 32	198
Commentary on Psalm 33	202
Commentary on Psalm 34	207
Commentary on Psalm 35	212
Commentary on Psalm 36	218
Commentary on Psalm 37	222
Commentary on Psalm 38	229
Commentary on Psalm 39	233
Commentary on Psalm 40	237
Commentary on Psalm 41	243
Commentary on Psalm 42	248
Commentary on Psalm 43	252
Commentary on Psalm 44	254
Commentary on Psalm 45	259

CONTENTS   ix

Commentary on Psalm 46	268
Commentary on Psalm 47	273
Commentary on Psalm 48	276
Commentary on Psalm 49	281
Commentary on Psalm 50	288
Commentary on Psalm 51	294
Commentary on Psalm 52	304
Commentary on Psalm 53	308
Commentary on Psalm 54	311
Commentary on Psalm 55	314
Commentary on Psalm 56	323
Commentary on Psalm 57	327
Commentary on Psalm 58	331
Commentary on Psalm 59	336
Commentary on Psalm 60	344
Commentary on Psalm 61	349
Commentary on Psalm 62	353
Commentary on Psalm 63	357
Commentary on Psalm 64	361
Commentary on Psalm 65	364
Commentary on Psalm 66	371
Commentary on Psalm 67	377
Commentary on Psalm 68	380
Commentary on Psalm 69	395
Commentary on Psalm 70	404
Commentary on Psalm 71	406
Commentary on Psalm 72	413

INDICES

General Index	423
Index of Holy Scripture	427

ABBREVIATIONS

AB	Anchor Bible, New York: Doubleday.
ABRL	Anchor Bible Reference Library, New York: Doubleday.
ACW	Ancient Christian Writers, New York: Newman.
ATD	Alte Testament Deutsch, Göttingen: Vandenhoeck & Ruprecht.
BASOR	Bulletin of the American Schools of Research.
Bib	*Biblica.*
CCG	Corpus Christianorum Graecorum, Turnhout: Brepols.
DBS	*Dictionnaire de la Bible. Supplément,* IV, Paris: Librairie Letouzey et Ané, 1949.
DS	*Enchiridion Symbolorum, Definitionum et Declarationum,* 34th ed., edd. H. Denzinger, A. Schönmetzer, Freiburg: Herder, 1967.
DTC	*Dictionnaire de théologie catholique* 15, Paris: Librairie Letouzey et Ané, 1946.
EstBib	*Estudios Biblicos.*
ETL	*Ephemerides Theologicae Lovanienses.*
FOTC	Fathers of the Church, Washington DC: Catholic University of America Press.
ITQ	*Irish Theological Quarterly.*
JECS	*Journal of Early Christian Studies.*
LXX	Septuagint.
NJBC	*New Jerome Biblical Commentary,* edd. R. E. Brown et al., Englewood Cliffs NJ: Prentice Hall, 1990.
OCA	Orientalia Christiana Analecta, Rome: Pontifical Oriental Institute.
PG	Patrologia Graeca, ed. J.-P. Migne, Paris, 1857–66.
PL	Patrologia Latina, ed. J.-P. Migne, Paris, 1878–90.
RHT	*Revue d'Histoire des Textes.*
SC	Sources Chrétiennes, Paris: Du Cerf.
StudP	*Studia Patristica.*
TRE	*Theologische Realenzyklopädie,* Berlin: Walter de Gruyter.
VTS	*Vetus Testamentum,* Supplement.

SELECT BIBLIOGRAPHY

Azéma, Y. *Théodoret de Cyr. Correspondance* I, II, III, SC 40, 98, 111, 1955, 1964, 1965.
Bardy, G. "Théodoret." DTC 15 (1946): 299–325.
———. "Interprétation chez les pères." DBS IV (1949): 569–91.
Barthélemy, D. *Les Devanciers d'Aquila.* VTS X. Leiden: Brill, 1963.
Bouyer, L. *The Spirituality of the New Testament and the Fathers.* Eng. trans., London: Burns & Oates, 1963.
Canivet, P. *Histoire d'une entreprise apologétique au Ve siècle.* Paris: Bloud & Gay, 1957.
Clark, E. A. *Women in the Early Church.* Message of the Fathers of the Church 13. Wilmington: Glazier, 1983.
Dahood, M. *Psalms.* AB 16, 17, 17A. New York: Doubleday, 1965–70.
Dorival, G. "L'apport des chaînes exégétiques grecques à une réédition des *Hexaples* d'Origène (à-propos du Psaume 118)." *RHT* 4 (1974): 44–74.
Drewery, B. "Antiochien." *TRE* 3, 103–113.
Fernandez Marcos, N. "Some reflections on the Antiochian text of the Septuagint." In *Studien zur Septuaginta—Robert Hanhart zu Ehren.* Göttingen: Vandenhoeck & Ruprecht, 1990, 219–229.
Guinot, J.-N. *L'Exégèse de Théodoret de Cyr.* Théologie Historique 100. Paris: Beauchesne, 1995.
Halton, T. P. *Theodoret of Cyrus on Divine Providence.* ACW 49. New York: Newman, 1988.
Hill, R. C. *St John Chrysostom's Homilies on Genesis.* FOTC 74, 82, 87. Washington, DC: Catholic University of America Press, 1986–92.
———. "On looking again at *synkatabasis*." *Prudentia* 13 (1981): 3–11.
———. "Chrysostom's terminology for the inspired Word." *EstBib* 41 (1983): 367–73.
———. "Psalm 45: a *locus classicus* for patristic thinking on biblical inspiration." *StudP* 25 (1993): 95–100.
———. "Chrysostom's Commentary on the Psalms: homilies or tracts?" In *Prayer and Spirituality in the Early Church.* Ed. P. Allen. Brisbane: Australian Catholic University, 1998, 301–17.
———. "Chrysostom, interpreter of the Psalms." *EstBib* 56 (1998): 61–74.
———. *St John Chrysostom. Commentary on the Psalms.* Brookline MA: Holy Cross Orthodox Press, 1998.

_____. "Theodoret's Commentary on Paul." *EstBib* 58 (2000): 1–21.
Jellicoe, S. *The Septuagint and Modern Study*. Oxford: Clarendon, 1968.
Kelly, J. N. D. *Early Christian Doctrines*. 5th ed., New York: Harper & Row, 1978.
McCollough, C. T. "Theodoret of Cyrus as biblical interpreter and the presence of Judaism in the later Roman Empire." *StudP* 18 (1985): 327–34.
Mandac, M. "L'union Christologique dans les oeuvres de Théodoret antérieures au Concile d'Ephèse." *ETL* 47 (1971): 64–96.
Quasten, J. *Patrology* III. Westminster, MD: Newman, 1960.
Rondeau, M. J. *Les commentaires patristiques du Psautier (IIIe–Ve siècles)*. OCA 219, 220. Roma: Pont. Inst. Orient., 1982, 1985.
Vaccari, A. "La θεωρία nella scuola esegetica di Antiochia." *Bib* 1 (1920): 3–36.
Viciano, A. "Theodoret von Kyros als Interpret des Apostels Paulus." *Theologie und Glaube* 80 (1990): 279–315.
Wallace-Hadrill, D. S. *Christian Antioch. A Study of Early Christian Thought in the East*. Cambridge: Cambridge University Press, 1982.
Weiser, A. *Psalms*. ATD 14, 15. 5th ed., Eng. trans., London: SCM, 1965.
Weitzman, M. P. *The Syriac Version of the Old Testament*. Cambridge: Cambridge University Press, 1999.
Wilken, R. A. *John Chrysostom and the Jews. Rhetoric and Reality in the late 4th Century*. Berkeley-Los Angeles-London: University of California Press, 1983.
Young, F. *From Nicaea to Chalcedon. A Guide to the Literature and its Background*. Philadelphia: Fortress, 1983.
_____. *Biblical Exegesis and the Formation of Christian Culture*. Cambridge: Cambridge University Press, 1997.

INTRODUCTION

INTRODUCTION

(1) Theodoret, born in Antioch a dozen years after the Second Ecumenical Council had been held in Constantinople in 381, was destined to live in interesting—and theologically tumultuous—times. His life as bishop in Cyrus, "little backwater"[1] though it may have been, was intimately affected by the Third and Fourth Councils, of Ephesus (431) and Chalcedon (451) respectively (not to mention the "Robber Council" of Ephesus in 449 that briefly deposed him), as was his reputation after his death in 466 by the Fifth Council at Constantinople in 553. His exegesis and hermeneutics, the focus of this introduction, fell—if only by dint of birth and upbringing in this center of learning—within the canons of the School of Antioch, whose leading lights he can hardly have known personally. Diodore of Tarsus had died about the time of Theodoret's birth; his pupils John Chrysostom and Theodore of Mopsuestia were then at the pinnacle of their careers, though exercising their episcopal ministry beyond Antioch, the former becoming bishop of Constantinople in 397 (to die in exile a decade later) and the latter bishop of Mopsuestia in Cilicia in 392 until his death in 428. All three great Antiochene exegetes had delivered or composed works on the Psalter,[2] which Theodoret would have come to know at second hand, as he came to know as well works on this spiritual classic from Fathers of the Alexandrian school.

---

1. So Frances Young, *From Nicaea to Chalcedon* (Philadelphia: Fortress, 1983), 267, who also concedes (268 and n. 236, citing Theodoret's *Ep.* 113) that the see had responsibility for 800 parishes.
2. Cf. Diodore of Tarsus, *Commentarii in Psalmos,* ed. J. M. Olivier, CCG 6 (Turnhout: Brepols, 1980); R. Devreesse, *Le commentaire de Théodore de Mopsueste sur les Psaumes (I–LXXX),* Studi e Testi 93 (Rome: Vatican Press, 1939); John Chrysostom, *Expositio in Psalmos,* PG 55.39–498, Eng. trans., Robert C. Hill, *St John Chrysostom. Commentary on the Psalms* (Brookline, MA: Holy Cross Press, 1998).

(2) This introduction to Theodoret's own work on the Psalms will give attention to the following matters:

1. Theodoret's exegetical works, including the *Commentary on the Psalms;*
2. Text of the *Commentary;* short and long forms;
3. Theodoret's Greek text of the Psalter; alternative versions;
4. *Commentary on the Psalms:* nature, purpose, characteristics, and influences;
5. Theodoret as interpreter of the Psalms; his wider thinking on Scripture;
6. The Christology of the *Commentary on the Psalms;*
7. Other theological accents;
8. Moral accents; the spirituality of the *Commentary.*

1. Theodoret's exegetical works, including the Commentary on the Psalms

(3) Though his letters also reveal the degree of his involvement in the civic improvement and social welfare of his diocese, Theodoret devoted much time to writing; he could claim authorship of thirty-five works,[3] interestingly the same number as that of his years as a bishop, and regrettably not all extant. While it is understandable that, in view of the tenor of the times, his dogmatic and controversial treatises attracted particular attention, he wrote also apologetic and historical works, in addition to hundreds of letters. We wonder about his style as a pastor of souls, something not so obvious from the writings on the part of this theologian at his desk by comparison with a preacher like Chrysostom; this dimension would emerge more clearly from the ten *logoi* on Providence delivered to a congregation in Antioch and happily extant, to which he refers in passing in commentary on Ps 68.21.[4]

---

3. *Ep.* 146, ed. Y. Azéma, *Théodoret de Cyr. Correspondance* III, 176 (a letter to "the monks of Constantinople" dated by Azéma in 451).
4. PG 80.1389. Cf. T. Halton, *Theodoret of Cyrus on Divine Providence*, 3: "It is probable that the discourses, if they were more than written exercises, were delivered in Antioch." See also Halton, *loc. cit.,* 162 n. 17, which pro-

INTRODUCTION 3

(4) Theodoret's exegetical output is imposing, and noteworthy for being devoted to the Old Testament primarily, any commentary on the Gospels not figuring and that on the fourteen Pauline Epistles being left possibly till last. The Pentateuch, Historical Books, and Prophets of the Christian Bible, as well as the Song of Songs, all came in for comment, whether in full commentary or—under pressure of failing health—a series of *Quaestiones*. A *Commentary on the Psalms* Theodoret, like so many of the Fathers,[5] did complete, and would like to have begun his exegetical career with this as firstfruits, but was not free (he tells us in its preface):

> It would have been a pleasure for me to do a commentary on the inspired composition of the mighty David prior to the other divine sayings . . . But we were prevented from putting this desire into effect by those who requested from us commentaries on the other divine Scriptures: some required of us clarification of the Song of Songs, others were anxious to have a close knowledge of the inspired composition of the Man of Passion, still others of the work of the divinely inspired Ezekiel, while others were impatient for the predictions of the Twelve Prophets, shrouded in obscurity, to be rendered clear and obvious.

(5) In fact, it was not until well into his mature years that he completed this *Commentary* on "the spiritual harmonies of the divinely inspired David (which) many people frequently call to mind": a letter dated at late 448 claims completion of commentary on "all the prophets, the psalter, and the apostle,"[6] while comment on Ps 18.12–14 about the Lord's acting from heaven to scatter enemies leads Theodoret to refer to invasions of Huns

---

vides a reference to B. Croke, "Dating Theodoret's Church History and Commentary on the Psalms," *Byzantion* 54 (1984): 59–74.

5. Marie-Josèphe Rondeau in her survey of patristic commentaries on the Psalter, *Les commentaires patristiques du Psautier (IIIe–Ve siècles), I Les travaux des pères grecs et latins sur le Psautier. Recherches et bilan,* lists eighteen of them from the Greek Fathers as well as eight major Latin commentators and eight minor.

6. *Ep.* 82, *Correspondance* II, 202. Jean-Noël Guinot, *L'Exégèse de Théodoret de Cyr,* 48–63, finds this evidence for a very late date for the *Commentary* on the Pauline corpus not cogent. A further *terminus ad quem* for the *Psalms Commentary* is his mention of it in the *Quaestiones* on 1 Samuel written towards the end of his life (PG 80.656).

in 434 and of Persians in 441: "This often happens in our time, too: in the wars that just lately broke out he laid waste with hail and fire the savages from the north attacking us. And the Persians recently making war on us from the east, who expected to get possession of our cities without bloodshed, he caught in these snares and prevented their further advance."[7] We thus have grounds for associating the *Commentary on the Psalms* with the years between 441 and 448 when Theodoret had completed two decades as bishop of Cyrus.

2. *Text of the* Commentary; *short and long forms*

(6) Today's reader of this work by Theodoret enjoys the advantage of its rich manuscript tradition, direct and in the catenae, while suffering the limitation of lack of a modern critical text. What is to hand is the eighteenth-century edition by J. L. Schulze that appeared a century later in J. P. Migne's *Patrologia Graeca* 80.857–1998 with a Latin translation by Antonio Carafa. Study of the *Commentary* is further complicated by its survival in two forms, long and short, the latter better attested to by more ancient witnesses, yet the long form being cited by the Palestinian catena and thus in existence since the sixth century. Schulze adopts the short form of the text for his edition, but—without obvious rationale—also incorporates excerpts of the longer form that would puzzle readers did he not acknowledge their inclusion, and that deepen the sense of urgency of need of a critical edition (though, admittedly, what we have enables us to gain a sound general grasp of Theodoret's approach to this well-worked spiritual classic).

(7) On first principles Rondeau gives preference to the short form of the text that we have in PG 80, without having been able to "submit to internal criticism the additions provided by the long form."[8] It is a sage proviso: the reader gains the impres-

---

7. PG 80.978. The thwarted preference of his for initial work on the Psalter possibly reflects his awareness of the priority given it by Theodore and—to judge from textual evidence of youthful inexperience—possibly also by Chrysostom.
8. *Les commentaires patristiques,* 135.

sion that a different spirit—personal, literary, hermeneutical, theological—breathes through the longer form in the excerpts provided by Schulze, and at least one instance suggests not independent tradition but a relationship of dependence on the shorter form. Theodoret in his preface promised his reader(s) that he would "make every possible effort to avoid a superfluity of words," and he generally observes this principle of commentary to a degree of conciseness that can at times approximate to mere paraphrase; so when we note an unusual expansiveness, as in commentary on places like Ps 14.1 and 49.4,[9] we are not surprised to find that the editor has included material from the longer form of the text. Theodoret's unwillingness to write at length on the Psalms extends also to the attention he feels he should give to his readers' personal spiritual development, as we shall see below in section 8; he generally refrains from making such wider spiritual application of a psalm, a restraint resisted by the longer form of the text, as emerges in commentary on Psalms like 54, 55, 60, 63, 64, and 71. We come not to expect a peroration from this theologian at his desk in concluding his commentary on a psalm; so when we find a rare hortatory conclusion, as to Ps 62, it comes from the longer form.

(8) Theodoret strikes one as unwilling to enter into polemic, as flexible rather than dogmatic on debated issues. So when in commentary on Ps 58.4–5 he suddenly and at a tangent to the text launches into snide remarks on "Arians, Eunomians, Macedonians and those that seem to entertain doctrines similar to theirs," and stresses the implications of their positions for baptismal practice, with a mocking pun about *buthizomenos*, "dipping," in place of *baptizomenos*, we find it is from the long form of the text that the carping digression comes. Authorship of psalms and titles Theodoret admitted in his preface to be a matter of some debate, and showed a commendable flexibility in taking a position; the matter surfaces again at the beginning of Ps 73, the first of a block of eleven psalms bearing a title associating them with Asaph, that singer of David's time acknowl-

---

9. It seems more helpful to cite the psalms in the numbering of the Hebrew and modern versions rather than Theodoret's Greek text.

edged by the Chronicler. After further canvassing the various views this attribution raises about authorship, Theodoret remarks, in the Migne text, "Our view, however, as we have often said, is that blessed David wrote them all, which is, in fact, the truth of the matter. Still, let everyone take it as they please: no harm will come from taking it this way or that." The dogmatism of the former ruling (from the long form) does not sit well with the flexibility of the latter concession (from the short form), or with the tolerant spirit of the preface and our impression of Theodoret generally.

(9) The long form of the text is more insistent also in giving a sacramental meaning to psalm verses, as in comment on Ps 60, 66, and 71, as emerges from our notes in those places. It is also less reserved on some doctrinal matters. After the typically concise comment of Theodoret on Ps 67.1 the long form adds:

> Now, he says, *May God have pity on us,* and not only this but also *bless us,* the reason being that he not only blessed us but also had mercy, having saved us by means of his coming from the Virgin; the psalmist says, *may his face shine upon us.* We saw him face to face, of course, but once made man; we saw him presenting no other form but God the Word in person immutably born of the Virgin.

Here we recognize the language of the (future) definition of Chalcedon in 451 (that "triumph of . . . Antiochene Christology," in J. N. D. Kelly's words),[10] particularly with "immutably," ἀτρέπτως, one of the quartet of adverbs the council Fathers employed of the union of natures in Jesus.[11] Theodoret is loath to make reference to Mary, as we shall see, possibly out of regard for the positions of Nestorius.

(10) An instance where comment by the long form of the text seems to betray a later development of the short form arises in comment on Ps 65.6, where the psalmist speaks of the Lord as "girt with his might." Theodoret develops this to present the

---

10. *Early Christian Doctrines,* 341.
11. DS 302. This key term, which appears also at the close of the commentary on this psalm in the short form of the text, is central to Book 1 of Theodoret's treatise on the Monophysites, *Eranistes,* also a work of the 440s like the *Psalms Commentary;* cf. J. Quasten, *Patrology* III, 547.

INTRODUCTION 7

Lord as wearing a belt, ζώνη; but an intrusive comment from the long form evidently misreads the term as ζωή, "life": "You achieve each of these things by employing your ineffable and immeasurable power, which you wear like some belt. Since you are life, in fact, you share it with those who believe in you and arrange for those who are unmoved to be set firm. Since, you see, one who is girt is better equipped for doing whatever one wishes, in figurative fashion he called God's power a belt." Failing availability of a critical edition of Theodoret's text, therefore, there is wisdom in seeing his approach and attitudes better reflected in the short form.

3. *Theodoret's Greek text of the Psalter; alternative versions*

(11) As we shall acknowledge in the next section, we have in Theodoret, unlike Chrysostom commenting on the Psalms to his congregation in the *didaskaleion,* not a preacher but a desk theologian, if we may use the term; the preface to his *Commentary* (Chrysostom's collection having none such) makes that clear. Though clearly having no time for *philomatheis,* scholars interested in unnecessary detail,[12] at his desk he is in a position to refer to as many resources as his exegetical skills allow and he thinks his readers require. This double qualification affects his commentary on the biblical text: how much precision and how great a range of detail could he access and should he communicate? He is given credit for taking textual criticism seriously, unlike Theodore,[13] and it is predictable that he goes about the task more thoroughly than Chrysostom the preacher, who nevertheless puts up a seemingly youthful show of erudition.[14]

(12) What was the Greek text of the Psalter that was before Theodoret at his desk and that he is credited with critiquing? It was obviously the local form of the Septuagint accessible to the ordinary reader; he gives it that name on occasions when comparing it with alternative and also venerable versions in that lan-

12. Cf. his comments on Ps 37.32–33 and Ps 69.4 (and from the longer form of the text, Ps 68.35).
13. So Guinot, *L'Exégèse,* 175.
14. See my "Chrysostom, interpreter of the Psalms," 64–65.

guage (which may not have been his mother tongue) and with a different form of the Septuagint, as in commentary on Psalms 65 and 66. The nature of this Antiochene LXX is still unclear. Jerome, who died about the time Theodoret became bishop, spoke of three forms of the LXX current in his time in Alexandria, Constantinople-Antioch, and "the provinces in between," respectively;[15] the second of these, relevant here, he describes as "another version which Origen and Eusebius of Caesarea and all the Greek commentators call the popular text, and which by most is now called the Lucianic text,"[16] the work of the scholar-priest of Antioch, Lucian, a century earlier. The precise character of this Antiochene recension of the LXX, which Theodoret and Chrysostom are thought to exemplify, is much debated. The claim for its provenance directly from the Hebrew, made for it by the ancients, is thought unlikely in view of general ignorance of that language;[17] Jerome's label "Lucianic" is allowed by some moderns,[18] disallowed as a legend by others, who would prefer to speak of a "texte antiochien" or even Palestinian.[19]

(13) This local form of the Septuagint Theodoret esteemed, if only because of his belief in the inspiration of the seventy translators, as he states in his preface in upholding the antiquity and credibility of the psalm titles (citing without question the authority of the legendary *Letter of Aristeas*). In some cases he would defend its readings of psalm verses against alternatives, aware though he was of the different form of the LXX to be found in the Hexapla, that synoptic tool attributed to Origen of

---

15. *Praef. in Paral.* (PL 28.1324–25).
16. *Ep.* 106.2 (PL 22.838). In view of Lucian's purported Arian associations, it is not surprising that Antiochene commentators like Chrysostom and Theodoret do not attach his name to their text of the LXX.
17. So S. Jellicoe, *The Septuagint and Modern Study*, 160–61.
18. Cf. D. S. Wallace-Hadrill, *Christian Antioch*, 30; B. Drewery, "Antiochien," *TRE* 3, 106. Fernandez Marcos, "Some reflections," speaks of Lucian, Lucianic, and Antiochian recension.
19. Cf. D. Barthélemy, *Les Devanciers d'Aquila*, 126–27; Guinot, *L'Exégèse*, 171–72. K. G. O'Connell would rather place the origins of this revision of the LXX in Palestine, matching Palestinian Hebrew manuscripts from Qumran, and dating back to the late first century: "Texts and versions," *NJBC*, 1092.

INTRODUCTION 9

which Jerome speaks as widely available at one time in Palestine but later becoming defective.[20] Whether or not copies were still freely available in his time, Theodoret can claim in beginning commentary on Ps 24 that the rogue phrase "of one of the sabbaths" in the title he did find in "some copies" (*antigrapha:* other LXX forms?) but "it does not appear in the Hexapla," nor presumably in his *vademecum* copy of the text.[21] Another form of the LXX he cites as "the fifth edition" in commenting on Ps 75.6, perhaps owing this item of information to Symmachus.[22]

(14) Despite the authority he attributes on first principles to the LXX as a basis for commentary, Theodoret has recourse also to the three renowned alternative versions of earlier centuries that came to be associated with the names of Aquila, Symmachus, and Theodotion, perhaps utilizing the Hexapla for this purpose.[23] The extent and manner of this recourse to the alternative Greek versions are intriguing: it has been taken (by Guinot, for example)[24] as an index of the priority he gives to textual criticism, and contrariwise thought to be so mechanical as to be the later addition of a copyist (so G. Dorival on the variant readings in commentary on Ps 119).[25] From the preface, with its note of deference to the LXX, one could get the impression that no alternative version could match "the Seventy"; Aquila's translation of the puzzling rubric found in some psalms, *diapsalma,* as "always" Theodoret declines to accept on

20. Jerome, *Comm. Titus* 3.9 (PL 26.594–95) and *Comm. Ps.* 1.4 (CCL 72, 180).
21. Cf. opening comment on Psalms 31, 65, and 66.
22. In the view of Barthélemy, *Les Devanciers d'Aquila,* 266–70, this was a Palestinian revision of some books in the LXX, owing its name to appearance in the Hexapla as a fifth Greek version. This would seem to be confirmed by his citing a Hexapla LXX to endorse his reading of Ps 74.3 in addition to Hebrew and alternative Greek versions—all available to him in a Hexapla.
23. Chrysostom's *Psalms Commentary* is likewise distinguished for its recourse to these alternative translators, but he never gives them a name.
24. Guinot, *L'Exégèse,* 177–80.
25. "L'apport des chaînes exégétiques grecques à une réédition des *Hexaples* d'Origène (à propos du Psaume 118)," 62. Dorival claims G. Mercati drew the same conclusion about the variant readings in Chrysostom's homilies.

the grounds that "I consider it unjustified to dismiss so many people of such caliber and rely on the opinion of one single person." Yet there are cases where invocation of alternative readings, such as on Ps 1.5, 7.6, and 19.4–6, strikes the reader as mechanical and pointless, giving some color to Dorival's thesis.

(15) More generally, however, citation of alternative versions is evidently deliberate and, in the commentator's view, helpful, as in the debate about the puzzling import of the title to Ps 9. Their rendering of a word or phrase can be given priority, and, in fact, it becomes clear that the version of Symmachus is—almost as rule of thumb—given preference to the LXX as "clearer" basis for comment,[26] even when seeming to the reader to offer no better version. On Ps 42.7, which in the LXX reads, "Deep calls on deep to the sound of your cataracts. All your heights and your billows have passed over me," Theodoret comments:

> Now, living in that land, he is saying, I was given over to a crowd of adversaries, and became like someone drowning in the deep; he calls the ranks of soldiers *deeps*, and likens the extreme size of the crowd to immeasurable waters, and what was done by them to the flood of old which wiped out the whole world. Symmachus translated it more clearly, "Deep challenged deep with a roar of your torrents": you inflicted them, exacting of me a penalty for lawlessness.

But there are also places where the other versions, even the esteemed Symmachus, are declared to be less profound than the LXX or less adequate.[27]

(16) The reason for Theodoret's fondness for alternative Greek translations of a verse may be related to his (rarer) reference to the Hebrew text and the Syriac (*Syrus*) version, probably a form of the Peshitta Bible. Pierre Canivet maintains that Theodoret was bilingual,[28] Syriac his mother tongue, Greek his

---

26. Cf. comment on Ps 17.11, 20.3, 25.8, 27.11, 35.18, 43.4, 49.18, 65.9, 66.17, and 73.22.

27. Cf. comment on Ps 22.1, 30.12, 37.20, 50.23, and 123.4.

28. The term "bilingue," perhaps incautiously taken over, Rondeau uses to imply that Greek and Hebrew were his two languages (*Les commentaires patristiques*, 136). P. Canivet, *Histoire d'une entreprise apologétique au Ve siècle*, 26–27.

written language ("sa langue de culture," in Guinot's phrase);[29] he is less definite about his claim to fluency in Hebrew—and rightly so, to judge from the text of the *Psalms Commentary*. Theodoret's reference to the original language of the Psalms is rarer, more cautious and for that reason less disastrous than Chrysostom's; his familiarity with that related Semitic language, Syriac (a dialect of Aramaic), was sufficient to prevent him from committing some of Chrysostom's solecisms, but not to allow him to recognize those already perpetrated by his LXX text, particularly in psalm titles. Like Chrysostom he accepts the confusion by the LXX of the musical direction for "flutes" (Hebrew *neḥiloth*) in the title to Ps 5 with the verb *naḥal*, "inherit," though we do not get a subsequent discourse on inheritances to the length to which Chrysostom goes. The similar musical direction in the title to Ps 22, "The Deer of Dawn" (apparently a cue to a melody), from *'ayyelet*, "deer," is rendered as "on support at dawn," as though from *'eyalut*, "support"; likewise with Ps 45 the cue "For the Lilies," *shoshanim*, is rendered as "those to be changed," as though from *shanah*. In the title to Ps 46 the word for "maidens," *alamoth*, is read as "on the secrets" as though from *alam*, "conceal." And so on.[30] As well, he frequently fails to recognize cases where the LXX has misread the tense of Hebrew verbs.[31]

(17) With this lack of knowledge of Hebrew the alternative Greek versions (to which he turns in his uncertainty) cannot always help him, Symmachus showing no greater proficiency. It is not the case with him that, in Rondeau's view, he "peut aisément recourir à l'original sémitique," at least with any skill, to solve textual difficulties such as confront him in places like Ps 29.1,

---

29. Guinot, *L'Exégèse*, 195. Weitzman, *The Syriac Version of the Old Testament*, 253, holds that the Peshitta version of the Psalms, along with Pentateuch and Latter Prophets, already existed and had attained authoritative status by around 170. Cf. also J. Joosten, "The Old Testament quotations in the Old Syriac and Peshitta Gospels," *Textus* 15 (1990): 55–76.

30. Cf. our notes to commentary on the titles to Psalms 48, 60, and 69.

31. Cf. note 7 to Ps 27, note 3 to Ps 36, note 2 to Ps 43, note 5 to Ps 45, note 4 to Ps 66, and note 9 to Ps 68. At the close of commentary on Ps 111 he has to take others' word for the fact that this psalm and the next have an alphabetic structure.

30.4–5, and 127.4. And so when he meets such a difficulty in Ps 62.9 he turns for enlightenment not to the original, nor to similar expressions in Scripture (his Scriptural familiarity—strangely for such a prolific commentator—not being of a high order), but to "the other translators." If it is objected that he can quote "the Hebrew" at times, it should also be pointed out that this occurs almost solely in connection with phrases in LXX titles which he is able to recognize are missing from the original (as in Ps 31, 65, 66, 70, and 71); within the body of the psalm it is to Syriac and Hebrew together that he will (on rare occasions) make reference, an easier matter for this speaker of a dialect of Aramaic (as in Ps 41.1, 68.2, 113.1, and 116.9).

(18) In short, it would be a false picture to form of Theodoret at his desk poring over a range of textual resources equally accessible to him. It would seem rather that he made use basically of his Antiochene form of the LXX, and referred to alternative Greek versions available in a copy of the Hexapla, not so much for critiquing his LXX text paleographically as for explicating the many semantically challenging phrases any commentator encounters in the Psalter. This copy of the Hexapla, or another containing also "the fifth edition," offered a parallel Hebrew text sufficient to allow him to note discrepancies in psalm titles (and cross-checked with still further forms, or "copies," of the LXX); occasional reference to the Peshitta Bible on particular passages assisted a further glance at the Hebrew text, which he would otherwise have been struggling to read. His distance from and impatience with the *philomatheis* are therefore understandable in the light of this limited linguistic equipment, which of course has implications for his exegetical and hermeneutical skills, to be commented on below in section 5.

4. Commentary on the Psalms: *nature, purpose, characteristics, and influences*

(19) Evidence assembled above suggests that Bishop Theodoret composed the *Commentary on the Psalms* at the height both of his powers and of his career; hence the reasonable claim that it is "*l'oeuvre classique* of a bishop who regales his people with the

INTRODUCTION   13

knowledge to which he himself has access."[32] The claim has also been made for it that in this, as in his other commentaries, "one finds the same concern for the apostolate, the same desire for clarity, the same scorn for convoluted explanation."[33] Internal evidence certainly establishes that the author had been a bishop for two decades at the time of composition; but the reader also wonders whether it really does betray that episcopal and apostolic *cura pastoralis* implied in these encomiums. In fact, it betrays as little of the pastoral responsibilities of the composer as of his political and social context, apart from passing mention of more recent invasion by Hun and Persian (on Ps 18) and less recent residence in Antioch of Julian the Apostate (on Ps 53). It does not inveigh against the improvident rich at the invitation of Ps 49, as do Chrysostom's homilies on the subject, nor exploit the possibilities for social criticism with references to the poor and needy in a psalm like 72. It is truly the work of a desk theologian, and one not concerned to reflect his own world or even apply to it the psalmist's reflections; the Psalms for Theodoret are, if not exclusively a window onto the psalmist's world, less of a mirror of his reader's.

(20) We have therefore to ask for whom the *Commentary* was intended. The lack of pastoral application of the Psalms, especially in the (more authentic) short form of Theodoret's text, and the odd pejorative comment about the world suggest that the ordinary lay person was not in the composer's sight, though he admits in commentary on Ps 32.6 that David's verses form the pattern of prayer for people in all states of life. In the preface, a feature of this desk commentary, he identifies as particular "students of religion" his fellow cenobites of an earlier time in his life, "those who embrace religious life, and recite [the Psalter] at night and in the middle of the day." They earn his commendation when again he identifies as the bringers of peace to the people, according to Ps 72.3, "those who have embraced the angelic life; . . . acting as ambassadors for human beings, they make divine reconciliation their business." The clergy

32. Rondeau, *Les commentaires patristiques*, 137.
33. G. Bardy, "Théodoret," *DTC* 15, 312.

come in for particular mention in his comment on Ps 45.12, "The wealthy members of his people will entreat your countenance," which he applies first to Christ, then adding, "The priestly order also acts as the Church's countenance in being invested with greater spiritual dignity"—a preference he qualifies in remarking on Ps 34 that, unlike the old covenant, "no longer is the divine nourishment reserved to the priests alone."

(21) The preface leaves one wondering who the intended beneficiaries of the bishop's *Commentary* are: "I wanted to do a commentary on this piece of inspired composition first of all, and offer to discerning investors the profit lying hidden in its depths, so that they might sing its melodies and at the same time recognize the sense of the words they sing, thus reaping a double dividend." He seems to have experienced, whether among lay people or even religious dulled by repetition, what Chrysostom found among his flock, "that those singing it daily and uttering the words by mouth do not enquire about the force of the ideas underlying the words."[34] His commentary, though (as Bardy says) not aiming at convoluted explanation for the *philomatheis*, does have to take account of this cognitive deficiency even among those of consecrated life; his words opening Ps 3 on David's flight from Absalom—"This story, of course, is known to the more studious; but for the benefit of lazier people I shall summarize it"—could be applicable even to them, to judge from Theodoret's own imperfect recall of biblical lore.

(22) Considering the times, it might be otiose for us to raise the point as to whether Theodoret had both women and men in mind in composing his *Commentary*, did he not directly address the issue at the opening. Commenting on Ps 1.1, which both in the Hebrew original and in the LXX translation speaks only of the male, "Blessed the man who did not walk in the counsel of the ungodly," Theodoret formally introduces the question of exclusivity: "Now, no one seeing only a man declared blessed here should think that womankind is excluded from this beatitude. I mean, Christ the Lord in delivering the beatitudes in the mascu-

---

34. At the opening of Chrysostom's commentary on Ps 141 (PG 55.427).

line did not exclude women from possessing virtue: his words include men and women." Not only does his sexual egalitarianism come out in such a backhanded way, however, but before the commentary is finished he lets slip a remark on v. 6 revealing his own exclusivism: "While the work of righteous men (*andres*) continues resplendent, even the evil of godless and unholy people is undone." Women central to some of the biblical narratives, like Sarah and Rebekah in commentary on Ps 37.32–33 and Michal on Ps 59.1, can go nameless, after the manner of the more overtly sexist Chrysostom. Ingrained practice seems at variance with principle, so that we cannot agree that this commentator, with his focus predominantly on David and Christ, has any women readers clearly in mind.[35]

(23) The *Commentary* opens with a preface[36] that immediately engages and impresses the reader as systematic, thorough, reasonably critical, measured (and, in fact, is the only section of the work that many modern commentators know). Theodoret declares the claim the Psalms have on his and any commentator's attention, explaining how only a need to meet urgent requests for guidance on the Song of Songs, Daniel, Ezekiel, and The Twelve prevented him from making a *Psalms Commentary* his first opus. He acknowledges the work of his predecessors, both Alexandrian and Antiochene implicitly, and states frankly that he finds among them two extremes he intends to avoid: undue accent on allegory, where it is Origen (via Eusebius) or (in editor Schulze's view) Apollinaris of Laodicea whom he has in mind, and concentration on the historical background to Psalms in the Jewish manner, where Diodore and Theodore are thought the culprits. His own principles he enunciates: allow for

---

35. Elizabeth A. Clark would concur: "The often repeated assertion that the coming of Christianity benefited women in general is not borne out in our evidence of the period" (*Women in the Early Church*, 156). Patristic commentators were not helped in this regard, Clark observes, by the attitudes of the Scriptures on which they were commentating. Theodoret for one will not labor the point beyond Ps 1.1.

36. A feature that justifies its claim to be "un commentaire au sense précis du terme," in Rondeau's phrase. Chrysostom's homilies on the Psalms—if preached they were—naturally lacked such a feature (see my "Chrysostom's Commentary on the Psalms: homilies or tracts?").

an eschatological sense, whether Christological/messianic or ecclesiological; do not waste words; let the text speak for itself—irreproachable ideals, surely.

(24) He then gives a treatment of some items so as to obviate the need for comment each time they recur in individual psalms. Views on authorship of psalms and their titles and provenance of the latter had varied; in a flexible manner he entertains conservative and liberal points of view, and looks for a majority opinion, if not consensus: "Let the preference of the majority prevail: most historians say the Psalms are David's." On a recurring textual rubric he adopts an independent position, *pace* Aquila, "I take the notation *diapsalma* to indicate an alteration of the melody"—an unusual appreciation of the liturgical dimension of the Psalms, not informing the *Commentary* generally. Though conservative on the question of authorship, he allows their current order to be a matter of historical development: "I am of the view that the divine David himself composed the Psalms, whereas people of a later age fixed their order."

(25) And so to work. He generally relishes a brief discussion of the title to a psalm, allowing him to note variants in the material before him (discussed in the previous section), and providing one factor in his decision on interpretation. He then launches directly into comment on the individual verses of a *text*—not a hymn for singing, as might have been the case with Chrysostom's congregation in the *didaskaleion:* it is text David has left us, either directly written or first spoken by him and then written.[37] Unlike modern commentators influenced by Gunkel or Mowinckel,[38] Theodoret is not interested in any liturgical *Sitz im Leben* of this material, showing no interest in community festival occasions and little in genre; only a verse like Ps 33.2-3 wrings a paraphrase out of him, "All this was performed according to prescribed liturgy: they used lyres, cymbals, drums,

---

37. It may be that he expects his reader to read aloud the verses of the psalm on which he was commenting; on Ps 14.4 he says, "The phrase, Have they no knowledge, all who commit lawlessness, is to be read in declamatory style." But this is an isolated rubric.

38. Cf. A. Weiser, *The Psalms*. Other modern commentaries, by contrast with both Weiser and Theodoret, adopt a linguistic approach, e.g., M. Dahood, *Psalms*.

INTRODUCTION   17

and other musical instruments." He is, however, aware of the early Church's selection of seven Penitential Psalms, and implies also collection of some others, perhaps Psalms of the Righteous Sufferer or suchlike, including Ps 55, of which he remarks, "The psalm is included among the hymns, containing as it does some premonition of the Lord's sufferings."

(26) As good as his word, he is generally brisk and concise in commentary, with none of the periodic flow of preachers like Chrysostom, and no moralizing—something he also leaves to them; he is about teaching, he has told us in the preface, and insists again at the close. Such teaching can at times go no further than mere paraphrase; on Ps 17.4, "On account of the words from your lips I have kept to difficult paths," which would seem to call for some elucidation, he offers his reader only "I performed this difficult and laborious task in obedience to your commands" before moving on. What in particular betrays his relishing the task of commentary on a psalm is the degree of Scriptural documentation he offers the reader; by contrast, psalms he finds difficult or unappealing, like Ps 10, 37, 67, 69, and 73, and the Pilgrim Songs (Ps 120–134) as a block, receive few such references. Elaboration and documentation he can imply are a luxury better left to the idle or inquisitive scholars, *philomatheis;* on Ps 37.32–33, on the Lord's care for the righteous, which he unhappily illustrates by citing Abraham and Isaac emerging unscathed from treatment of their wives we would class as dastardly, he proceeds: "What need is there to list every example? It is easier for the scholars, after all, both to assemble those from the past and to study the recent ones." Brevity is the soul of wit, he implies.[39]

(27) Where that brevity is impaired and the commentary becomes expansive, the reader wonders if in that place Theodoret is the beneficiary of the thinking of his many predecessors along this path. For example, in commentary on Ps 16.5, "The Lord is

---

39. An exception to this reluctance to document his unvarnished commentary is some reference to the natural sciences—zoology, natural history, botany, agriculture—as in commentary on Psalms 29, 58, and 129. Guinot examines such references, as well as Theodoret's interest in geography (*L'Exégèse,* 426–48).

part of my inheritance and my cup," such relative expansiveness on his part sends us to the text of Eusebius,[40] which bears a resemblance to Theodoret that is almost verbatim. It is thought it was especially through the work of Eusebius that Theodoret was able to gain access to the hermeneutics of Alexandria and in particular Origen, and thus to make the critique of it we have seen in his preface. Clearly Theodoret was indebted also to his fellow Antiochenes Diodore, Theodore, and (to a less extent, it seems) Chrysostom. Beyond this unacknowledged dependence, in forty-three places in the *Commentary* Theodoret makes a specific but anonymous acknowledgment of the views of his predecessors, distinguishing among, accepting, or differing from them; Guinot has painstakingly (if provisionally) assigned these views to one or another earlier commentator,[41] the bulk going to Diodore and/or Theodore, a smaller number to Eusebius, and nothing directly to Origen, Didymus, "Athanasius," Apollinaris, or Basil. Clearly, in the composition of his *Commentary*, Theodoret had more on his desk than the biblical text in its various forms, even if he was prepared to identify the latter sources more openly. His readers were the beneficiaries of a rich fare from this commentator (as he himself modestly claims in his brief conclusion), intent though he may have been on teaching more than on pastoral care in other forms.

5. *Theodoret as interpreter of the Psalms; his wider thinking on Scripture*

(28) We have seen that, for all his diligence in assembling a range of textual and scholarly resources for the task of commen-

---

40. PG 23.157–58. It should be noted that we have in direct tradition from Eusebius's *Commentary* only Ps 37 and Ps 51–95.3, the rest from the catenae.

41. *L'Exégèse*, 684–713. The tentative nature of such attribution is illustrated in Theodoret's response to a phrase from Ps 49.2, "Both earthborn people and human beings," where the rejected alternative Guinot can only surmise may be Origen's: "Some called Adam and Eve 'earthborn people' for being formed from earth and not coming from intercourse. But this idea is wide of the truth: he is offering exhortation not to those already dead but to those still living."

tary on this great spiritual classic, Theodoret lacked some of the critical skills we would think desirable in a commentator. A sound knowledge of the language of the original, of course, was not found in many of the Fathers; and lack of it did not prevent him from commenting on a wide range of Old Testament texts—pentateuchal, historical, prophetic, lyrical. Despite this considerable exegetical output—though in view of his and other Fathers' approach to the text we should apply the term exegesis *secundum quid*—his own depth of biblical culture is not above suspicion. In place of a representative grasp of key people in sacred history he shows a fascination for marginal figures, like Sennacherib's lieutenant Rabshakeh and Jonathan's treasonous son Mephibosheth, as in Ps 25, 27, 31, and 52. His recall of the Scriptural texts he uses to document his commentary can send the reader leafing through the Bible to identify what he is loosely recalling: on the first psalm he quotes as though textually exact a collation of Deuteronomic, Johannine, and Isaian texts loosely recalled in different places. He can even be—and frequently is—quite astray in itemizing details of biblical pericopes: on Ps 2 he confuses characters and crowd numbers at Pentecost from Acts 2; on Ps 5 he has Jesus in place of the Baptist quoting Isaiah from Luke 3; on Ps 16 likewise he has Peter in place of Paul addressing the synagogue in Pisidian Antioch; on Ps 36 he confuses the two occasions when David took souvenirs from the unwitting Saul; and so on with a dozen other psalms.

(29) On the positive side he brings to his task as commentator on the sacred text an unwavering conviction of the inspiration of the composer of the Psalms, "the divinely inspired David," an epithet applied also to other biblical authors. They are all responsible as inspired composers, *prophetai,* for producing inspired composition, *propheteia,* a term that he (like Chrysostom)[42] will not apply to New Testament authors, whom he classes "apostolic" or specifically evangelists without denying their inspiration. On the phrase "fountains of Israel" in Ps 68.26 he comments, "Now, it

---

42. See my articles, "Psalm 45: a *locus classicus* for patristic thinking on inspiration" and "Chrysostom's terminology for the inspired Word."

would be right for the inspired (*prophetikos*) books of the Old Testament to be called *fountains of Israel,* because from them we offer hymn singing to God; but . . . in addition to the Old Testament books (*prophetikos*) he regaled us also with the apostolic fountains." In pointing out the correspondence between Ps 33.6 and John's prologue on the world's creation through the Word, he says, "The inspired composition (*propheteia*) of the Old Testament anticipates the Gospel teaching."

(30) Underlying his principle enunciated in the preface of letting the text speak for itself is his Antiochene conviction of the significance of all textual items—a conviction with deep theological roots in a Christology that respects the humanity of the incarnate Word. It is the principle of *akribeia,* precision in the commentator in response to the precision in the text. (We might add: as the text can be precise without being accurate —"accuracy" sometimes being an unfortunate rendering of *akribeia*—so too can the commentator, as Theodoret exemplifies.) For instance, Theodoret finds the first psalm without a title, and observes, "[The Seventy] found this psalm and the one after it without titles and left them without titles, not presuming to add anything of their own to the sayings of the Spirit." Conversely, if a textual detail occurs, it calls for comment: Ps 2.1 reads, "For what purpose did nations rage?" and the omission of the article is noted; on Ps 37.20 it is worthy of a comment that the LXX reads "but" for the "and" of Aquila and Symmachus, each shown to give the verse a different meaning. Helpful though this attention to detail "not idly" recorded in the text may be, one wonders if it compensates for the commentator's inability to engage with the original text of difficult verses, retain proper verb tenses despite the LXX, and appreciate the true significance of psalm titles.

(31) Within the understanding he arrived at, in his unsophisticated manner, of the authorship of the Psalms and the provenance of the psalm titles, as we saw above in section 4, he addressed the question of their classification and the greater challenge of their meaning. In the preface, he briefly classifies them according to topic, theology, and style; and, hoping to avoid extreme hermeneutical positions both Alexandrian and

Antiochene, he sees their meaning as being historical, or generally eschatological, or more specifically Christological.

The psalmist employs not only prophetic discourse but also parenetic and legal discourse as well; sometimes the teaching he offers is moral, sometimes dogmatic; in one place he laments the misfortunes of the Jews, and in another he foretells the salvation of the nations. Frequently, however, it is the Passion and Resurrection of Christ the Lord he is predicting, and to those ready to attend he offers great satisfaction from the variety of inspired composition.

(32) We admire here his flexibility as on other matters, though in all these areas we can be mystified about the basis of decision. He has been credited with a "moderate historicism,"[43] by contrast with Theodore, whose excesses he may have had in mind in his preface; but the reasons for giving one psalm a historical interpretation and another a Christological can be flimsy: absence of a title to Ps 2 is taken as sufficient reason for preferring a Christological sense to a historical, whereas in verses of Ps 7 we feel he is overly keen to apply verses to David's life. The frequent more general eschatological sense, in which the psalmist is seen predicting developments in the early Church and the labors of the apostles, can often take a specifically sacramental bent understandable in this churchman: on v. 7 of the penitential Ps 51, "Purify me with hyssop, and I shall be cleansed," Theodoret remarks at once, "Only the gift of baptism can achieve this cleansing"—an interesting remark for historians of the sacraments of reconciliation.

(33) On one who had completed a commentary on the Song of Songs the figurative language of the Psalms is not lost, and he can show admirable sensitivity to it; even if attached to the literal sense, he is no literalist. On the musical cue "The Deer of Dawn" in the title to Ps 22, which on several scores he fails to grasp correctly, he nonetheless can remind his readers, "Everywhere in Scripture, remember, evil is understood by analogy with darkness." He helps them respond to the figurative expression in Ps 7.9, "God who tests hearts and entrails." But he would not want them to get so caught up in figurative, anthropomor-

---

43. Wallace-Hadrill, *Christian Antioch*, 39.

phic expressions of the Scriptures as to fail in respect for divine transcendence; he warns them of such an expression in Ps 42.9, "Now, *you have forgotten me* means you have not given me a share in your providence: forgetfulness is a human weakness, whereas no such weakness belongs to God." Though he does not employ the term so dear to Chrysostom, *synkatabasis,* he similarly urges them to appreciate this gesture of divine considerateness for human limitations made in the language of the Scriptures. He chooses to take Ps 55 of Jesus' Passion, but warns the reader not to be unaware of the linguistic gesture involved in this:

> But let no one who takes note of the lowliness of the words consider this unworthy of the Incarnation of Christ the Savior. Consider rather that he who did not shrink from gall, vinegar, nails, thorns, spittle, blows, and all kinds of drunken violence, and accepted death at the end would not have spurned lowliness of expression; after all, the terms should reflect the reality.

Chrysostom, whose influence is perhaps detectable here, could not have put it better himself: it is the principle of incarnation that is in evidence here, both by author and by appreciative reader.[44] The medium is not in conflict with the reality, in the person of Jesus or in the Scriptural Word.

(34) In this incarnational principle lay the reason for Antioch's attachment to the literal sense of Scripture (as also for its Christology) and its reluctance to take an allegorical sense. Different levels of meaning could be discerned in a text, especially if Scripture itself suggested this—the old principle of "Scripture interprets itself" (though we never find Theodoret formulating it in those terms, as we do Chrysostom).[45] When commenting on the familiar text of Ps 33.6, "By the word of the Lord the heavens were established," he says, on the authority of John's prologue, "So the face value of the text conveys the surface

---

44. See my "On looking again at *synkatabasis*."
45. PG 55.191 on Ps 45.4, though as a principle it goes back to Origen, says J.-M. Leroux, "Relativité et transcendance du texte biblique d'après Jean Chrysostome," 73: "Le principe n'est pas nouveau; il fait même partie des lois fondamentales de l'exégèse patristique, et on peut le rencontrer en des termes presque identiques dans les écrits d'Origène et d'Augustin."

meaning of this: it was appropriate for the Jews of old. True theology, on the other hand, gives a glimpse of God the Word with the all-holy Spirit making the heavens and the heavenly powers." To the penitential Ps 32 he can give, along with a historical meaning in connection with David's repentance for his sin, a spiritual meaning of Christian sacramental forgiveness. This meaning can become strictly anagogical, especially with New Testament support, as in the case of Ps 24.3, "Who will ascend the Lord's mountain?" which Theodoret sees referring to the heavenly Mount Sion with the encouragement of the Epistle to the Hebrews; and likewise in many other cases.

(35) Allegorical interpretation by Theodoret is rarer. He accepts Diodore's principle in his work on the Octateuch that "we esteem the literal sense as far superior to the allegorical,"[46] though characteristically he practices it more flexibly. Scriptural support for such a sense need only be flimsy: on Ps 45.13–14, "All the glory of the king's daughter is within, in golden tassels, in many colors," he comments, with an implicit reference to 1 Corinthians 12, "Within, he is saying, she has the comeliness of virtue and is resplendent with the manifold gifts of the Holy Spirit. The operations of the divine Spirit, you see, are varied; 'there are varieties of gifts, but the same Spirit.'" Typology, too, is a possible hermeneutic for an Antiochene,[47] again on the proviso of Scriptural encouragement; perhaps a dozen times Theodoret uses this device in the *Commentary*, as on Ps 61.5: "You gave an inheritance to those who fear your name":

It ought to be understood, however, that the words in question contain a foreshadowing of the real inheritance; the real inheritance is eternal life, of which Christ the Lord said to the lambs on his right hand,

---

46. Fragment 93 (so Schäublin, "Diodor von Tarsus," *TRE* 8, 756, though Clavis of CCG acknowledges only 91 fragments, accepting 1–78 as genuine; text found in PG 33.1561–88).

47. Though hardly the "standard method" Derek Krueger implies in his article "Typological figuration in Theodoret of Cyrrhus's *Religious History* and the art of postbiblical narrative," *JECS* 5, no. 3 (1997): 407. Theodoret (and Chrysostom) would be mystified by the statement of F. Young, *Biblical Exegesis*, 152: "'Typology' is a modern construct. Ancient exegetes did not distinguish between typology and allegory."

"Come, you that are blessed by my Father, inherit the kingdom prepared for you before the foundation of the world." The Lord promised to give this inheritance to those who fear him, and he restored the promised land to these people as though in a type.

(36) For an Antiochene, the ability to discern the correct level of meaning in a text required *theoria*,[48] a term which Theodoret employs only as a verb to speak of the process. Clearly, Theodoret grasped Diodore's work on the subject. The reader of the Psalms, while allowing for realization of prophecy in history, could in the perceptive way of *theoria* see its realization also at another level. Ps 46.9 speaks of the Lord bringing wars to an end; some commentators claimed that it referred to the time of Ahaz, but Theodoret looks further to see the benefits flowing from the *pax Romana:* "The verse . . . was thus fulfilled in a historical sense; but if you wanted to understand it in a more figurative way, you would have regard for the cessation of hostilities against the Church and the peace provided them from God, and you would perceive (*theorein*) the realization of the prophecy."

(37) What his Antiochene formation gave Theodoret, in short, if not a range of critical skills for exegesis, was an appreciation of the "inspired Word," *logos prophetikos* (in his frequent phrase), incarnate in the figurative and sometimes lowly language of the psalmist, and a prior if not exclusive esteem for its literal sense—in keeping with an Antiochene Christology and soteriology, of course. While his innate flexibility allowed him to move more freely than his betters from one level of meaning to another, his hermeneutical rationale in so doing is not always clear or well established. If flexible as a commentator, he does

---

48. Cf. A. Vaccari, "La θεωρία nella scuola esegetica di Antiochia," 12: "La essenziale differenza fra teoria e allegoria consiste in ciò, che l'allegoria esclude di sua natura il senso letterale." Theodoret would not be as exclusive as that in his hermeneutics, agreeing rather with Wallace-Hadrill: "It was the practice of *theoria*, insight, which enabled the Christian to see what could not be seen by people living in the old dispensation. It was a recognition that although the age of Law was to be distinguished from the age of Grace, yet both ages were part of the divine strategy, and some degree of continuity was inevitably to be seen running through from beginning to end by those enabled by the Holy Spirit to see it" (*Christian Antioch*, 35).

INTRODUCTION 25

not feel it is proper for him to admit to ignorance (like the best of modern commentators, with all their exegetical skills) before an obscure text like Ps 68; and so he frequently falls to rationalizing in a way we find unconvincing. Eisegesis, too, is not beneath him.

6. The Christology of the Commentary on the Psalms

(38) Christological teaching in this work on the Psalms which is devoted (the preface tells us) to their teaching seems to be influenced by factors touched on already: Theodoret's own disposition, his Antiochene formation, and the times in which he is composing. Flexibility and moderation are terms we have used more than once of his hermeneutical practice: he is not given, it would seem, to extremes, and explicitly endeavors to take a *via media* in commentary. Though in places the text betrays the theological concerns of the age in which he is caught up, he does not allow a polemical edge to color his treatment; snide remarks on "Arians, Eunomians, and Macedonians" and their positions on Trinitarian doctrine and sacramental practice in commentary on Ps 58.4–5 belong to the less authentic long form of his text, as we noted above in section 2.

(39) Antioch, we have just observed in regard to his hermeneutical approach, predisposed Theodoret to take very seriously the humanity of the Word incarnate in both the Scriptural text and the person of Jesus; "moderate historicism," in Wallace-Hadrill's term, could be applied to his attitude to both. He strikes the reader as very comfortable in dwelling on the limitations of Jesus' humanity; above we saw him taking Ps 55 to refer to the Passion, advising the reader not to be daunted by the lowliness of the language in reference to Jesus, the reason being that "the terms should reflect the reality"—the principle of incarnation, and also of soteriology. He repeats the point on vv. 4–5 of that psalm: "It was necessary, you see, for the nature which underwent the Passion to be revealed in this, and the extraordinary long-suffering which he, in his love for us, had for our race; he underwent suffering in the flesh, wishing also in this to be involved in our salvation."

(40) A favorite text beyond the Psalms is Philippians 2.6–7, with its term "form of a slave" occurring frequently as a Christological title in this *Commentary;* after citing it explicitly on Ps 41.1, he adds, "And though having lordship of visible and invisible things, he had nowhere to lay his head, was born of a virgin and through lack of a bed was laid in a manger"—a text which betrays better than some others his acceptance of the *communicatio idiomatum.* If the same text makes some mention of "a virgin," the *Commentary* does not, at least in its shorter form (we noted above), give the prominence to Mary that such a Christology might suggest (were it not for some Antiochene sense of consideration for Nestorius?). If some of these litanies of the limitations of humanity remind one of Chrysostom, there is an echo of Irenaeus in the role given to Jesus of presenting the Father to humankind, as in this comment on Ps 22.24–25, a psalm traditionally (and liturgically) taken Christologically:

Sing praise to the one who proved responsible for this salvation of yours, he is saying, who could not bring himself to overlook your so lowly nature, instead hearkening to you and through my resurrection making your salvation my concern. After this he indicates this equality that as God he has with the Father, adding, *From you comes my praise; I shall confess to you in the great assembly:* as I manifest you to human beings, so too you teach all human beings to offer the same honor to me, saying at one time, "This is my beloved Son."

(41) Evidence presented in section 1 shows that composition of the *Commentary* can be placed in the 440s, and thus after the Council of Ephesus and before Theodoret's deposition at the "Robber Council" of 449. This was also the period of composition of his treatise against the Monophysites, the *Eranistes,* and common Christological features can be detected, it seems, beyond simply the occurrence of a term like ἀτρέπτως that figures in both that work and Chalcedon's definition a few years later. Theodoret had reason to know that trouble still loomed both from continuing Arian ideas of subordination of the Word and from Cyril's inadequate terminology for grappling with them. Hence in giving a Christological interpretation to Ps 45.7 he takes issue with both, employing the Nicene talisman *homoousios* that passed into the Constantinopolitan creed of 381 to put an

end to Arianism, and rejecting Cyril's description of the union of natures as *physike:*

> Thus he was also anointed in the all-holy Spirit, not as God but as human being: as God he was of one being (*homoousios*) with the Spirit, whereas as a human being he receives the gifts of the Spirit like a kind of anointing. Thus he *loved righteousness and hated lawlessness:* this is a matter of intentional choice, not of natural (*physike*) power, whereas as God he has *a rod of equity* as *the rod of his kingship.*[49]

(42) For statements like this Theodoret's theology has been called "fundamentally dualistic."[50] Certainly in this *Commentary* there is a strong impression of a theologian endeavoring to maintain a clear balance in speaking of God the Word made man—an accent eminently understandable in the context of the Monophysite debates. He likes to speak of the nature assuming and the nature assumed,[51] and the distinction could appear at times Nestorian were it not for the currency of views addressed in the *Eranistes* and condemned shortly afterwards at a council for whose convening he can claim some credit. If the *Commentary on the Psalms* exemplifies his "later" theology, it would seem from this explication of Ps 2.6–7 that his "earlier" dualism has not been disowned:[52]

> Now, the verse, *I have been established as king by him,* is expressed in human fashion: as God he possesses his kingship by nature, as human be-

---

49. Cf. Kelly, *Early Christian Doctrines,* 326: "The union between the Word and the humanity He assumed was the result of His free decision and loving favor towards men, and for this reason among others Theodoret objected to Cyril's description of it as 'natural' or 'hypostatic.'" In commentary on Ps 16.11, Theodoret is taking issue with Arius's denial of a rational soul in Jesus and Apollinaris's denial of rational mind and will (cf. Ps 132.6).

50. Young, *From Nicaea to Chalcedon,* 274. Cf. A. Viciano, "Theodoret von Kyros," 288: "Er hebt die *unio hypostatica* nicht genügend hervor. Das gilt auch für die *communicatio idiomatum.*"

51. Cf. Kelly, *Early Christian Doctrines,* 325: "His guiding principles, we should note, were the completeness and distinction of the natures (cf. ἡ λαβοῦσα and ἡ ληφθεῖσα φύσις), and their union in one Person."

52. Cf. Kelly, *Early Christian Doctrines,* 325–26: "Though in his earlier days he was ready enough, like other Antiochenes, to speak of 'the Word' and 'the man,' contrasting 'Him Who assumes' with 'him who is assumed,' he avoided such language once the controversy had made the issues clear."

ing he receives it by election. The fact that as God he possesses power without beginning the same inspired author teaches in the words, "Your throne, O God, is for all ages, the scepter of your kingship a scepter of equity" (Ps 45.6). Now, this psalm blessed Paul says refers to the Son; all the same, as God he possesses kingship and as human being he receives it. Likewise, as God he is called Most High, as human being he is raised on high. David for his part proclaims the divine highness in his cry, "Let them know that your name is Lord, you alone are the Most High over all the earth" (Ps 83.18). Zechariah, too, says to John, "You, child, will be called a prophet of the Most High." Blessed Paul it is, on the other hand, who teaches us the human highness in his words, "Accordingly, God also raised him on high, and bestowed on him the name that is above every name." To be sure, God the Word had the name "only-begotten Son" before the ages as connatural with his condition, yet while still possessing the title of the Son as God, he also receives it as human being.

(43) The reader of this *Commentary* may well find it ironic that a theologian of such temperance and balance should be the object of *odium theologicum* and condemnation. If imbalance, inaccuracy, and diatribe are the fruit of the heat of controversy, Theodoret's measured commentary is well adapted to tracing a middle path, in both biblical interpretation and systematic theology. To apply the term "symmetrical"[53] to this disciplined approach is surely a compliment, even if he is too convinced of the rightness of his position and the wrongness of opposing views to be called evenhanded.

7. *Other theological accents*

(44) One should not gain the impression that in this *Commentary* it is theological debate rather than the meaning of the Psalms that is the commentator's chief concern: Christology

---

53. Cf. K. McNamara, "Theodoret of Cyrus and the unity of person in Christ," 326, though McNamara attributes the term to Alois Grillmeier. In a comprehensive study of a range of views on Theodoret's orthodoxy and of his own statements (from doctrinal works only), "L'union Christologique dans les oeuvres de Théodoret antérieures au Concile d'Ephèse," *ETL* 47 (1971): 64–96, M. Mandac supports the conclusion that Theodoret's Christology is "correcte tout en étant incomplète" (96).

figures because of the interpretation taken in so many psalms, but polemic is not Theodoret's business here. Trinitarian though his theology constantly is, other Trinitarian issues are touched on only in passing; in his comment on Ps 36.9 where Jeremiah also is quoted, he remarks, "We have consequently come to a precise knowledge of the three persons in the one divinity through the inspired words of the Old Testament," where *idiotes* is employed in place of *hypostasis*. We have noted that a sacramental reference is given to particular psalm verses without any developed teaching on the sacraments; the phrase, "The poor eat and will be filled" (Ps 22.26), receives this gloss: "Now, the divine fare and the spiritual teaching we know to be the eucharistic feasting that is immortal, which the initiates have knowledge of."

(45) Mention has been made of Theodoret's imperfect biblical culture in general, besides his exegetical skills. He shows no understanding of Sheol as the abode of the dead; on Ps 28.1, "like those going down to the pit," he comments, "He means, If you keep silence with me and deprive me of your help, I shall immediately be consigned to death, which he called *pit*, since the grave is dug like a pit." In fact, he is unhelpfully vague about the psalmist's eschatological perspective; generally he concedes him a hope of eternal life (a view with which Dahood, on the grounds of debatable Ugaritic support, would concur), as in a gloss to the verse "I may dwell in the house of the Lord for length of days" (23.6): "in saying *for length of days*, that is, always, unceasingly, he relates it to those ages that have no end." Only rarely does he feel the need to limit this atypical Old Testament perspective: "Now, the phrase, *I shall confess to you forever*, refers to the present age," he says of Ps 52.9.

(46) In looking back to human origins he is more secure. Giving no comfort to Pelagian readers, he is in no doubt of the Fall and its consequences. On Ps 16.5 he says, "As soon as the human being was created, he assumed authority over everything and had immortal life; but after the transgression he lost both things, absolute sway and life. In human terms, the Lord made a plea for human nature, asking that they recover both the former life and absolute sway." He examines the question

more fully in commenting on that classic text, Ps 51.5, "For, lo, I was conceived in iniquities, and in sins my mother carried me." He wants to resist the implications of the verse for blaming marriage and procreation as the source of sin; so he remains suitably vague about the "way" or "path" or "currents" by which the sin of the first parents is transmitted to their offspring, saying, "He means that, by having control over our forebears, sin effected some way or path through the offspring. This is also what blessed Paul says: 'Since, you see, sin entered the world through a human being, and through sin death, *because* all sinned,'" where he rightly takes ἐφ' ᾧ in a causal sense (Eve, not Adam, being cited in discussion). He proceeds, steering a careful line between an Augustinian acceptance of impairment of human nature and an unwarranted Pelagian optimism:

> Now, we learn from all this that the force of sin is not part of nature (if this were so, after all, we would be free from punishment), but that nature tends to stumble when troubled by passions; yet victory lies with the mind-set (*gnome*), making use of effort to lend assistance. So he is not, as some maintained, calling marriage in question, or calling the marriage relationship illicit, as some stupidly maintained.[54]

He sees a deadly cycle, progressing from (original)[55] sin to mortality, then to corruption, then to (disordered) passions, then to our own sins; to break the cycle there is need (not of grace, at this place, but) of a firm *gnome* and sound *logismos*.

(47) Bishop of a "little backwater" he may have been, but he has a keen sense of churches other than his own and the Church universal, a theme he often recognizes in the Psalms. In commenting on Ps 48.3, "God is known in its buildings whenever he supports it," he quotes the credal article from Constantinople, used in worship, to bring out ecclesial unity and diversity:

---

54. He has the dualism of Manichees, Marcionites, and Encratites in mind doubtless in upholding the integrity of the marriage relationship against its critics.

55. Original sin is not a term he uses. Guinot, *L'Exégèse*, 702, sees "Athanasius," Apollinaris, and Eusebius also taking the verse to refer to this sin.

INTRODUCTION 31

On the one hand, there is one Church throughout all land and sea; hence we say in prayer, For the holy, single, universal, and apostolic Church, from one end of the world to the other. On the other hand, it is also divided into cities, towns, and villages, which the inspired word called *buildings*. As each city is composed of different houses, and yet is called one city, so there are countless churches that defy numbering, both on islands and continents, but all constitute one by being united in the common harmony of the true teachings.

(48) About the condition of his own church he tells us little if anything; and it may not have been in its regard that he displays a hostility to the Jews ("with their proclivity to malice," he adds in the preface) that is recurring, if far less virulent than in Chrysostom's homilies. There may be a hint of personal and local experience in the suggestion of enforced conversions of Jews and pagans; on Ps 66.3 about God's enemies cringing before him he comments, "This we witness happening constantly: many in thrall to the pagan error are not rash enough to confess it openly, and the Jews, when pressure is brought to bear, sing of the victory of the cross, and the truth of inspired composition is displayed on all sides." The wealth of the Jews does not come in for envious comment;[56] a surface reading of Theodoret's text would imply that it is impiety that irks him in both Jews and pagans. Wallace-Hadrill could be closer to the real reason in suggesting that "a further cause of sensitivity towards Judaism may be found in that fact that the Antiochene Church itself was seen by the rest of the Christian Church as lying too close to Judaism for comfort."[57]

(49) In one place Theodoret can even be quoted in favor of religious tolerance of the Jews in place of any proselytism: on Ps 45.10, "Listen, daughter, take note and incline your ear: forget your people and your father's house," he remarks, "Now, this is in no way relevant to Jews, proud of the piety of their forebears, on whose account they also enjoyed divine providence to the highest degree: Jews he bids follow in the pious ways of their fa-

56. Robert L. Wilken, *John Chrysostom and the Jews. Rhetoric and Reality in the late 4th Century*, 57, suggests this was a factor in the Antioch of that century.
57. *Christian Antioch*, 19.

thers and urges them not to forget their fathers, whereas the Church of the nations had fathers and ancestors that served idols."

(50) He can in a similar vein speak favorably of the advantages of the Jews of the old dispensation, such as the Law, as in comment on Ps 19.7–10 and 55.10–11. But it is also his stated conviction that these advantages have been lost; on the verse "the people he chose as his own inheritance" (Ps 33.12) he comments, "Now, the chosen people, named as *God's inheritance*, was in olden times the Jewish people, but later was the people chosen from the nations and in receipt of the rays of faith." For this displacement theory he develops the same theological justification as Chrysostom:[58] the crucifixion. That heinous deed resulted in the treatment they received (which he outlines in rare historical detail in commentary on Ps 59.12–13) from Caligula, Nero, Vespasian, and Titus, leaving them in the piteous condition he describes in detail as familiar to him: "They are scattered throughout the world, forced to serve the Romans as slaves, and deprived of worship according to the Law; they live far from their celebrated mother city, are bereft of royal care, no longer enjoy priestly attention, and are deprived of the charism of inspiration."

8. Moral accents; the spirituality of the Commentary

(51) As we endeavored to clarify in section 4, the readers for whom Theodoret is writing here may not have been lay people directly but those with some religious or even clerical formation. This may account for the striking absence of a feature that is found in his commentaries generally by Bardy, "le même souci de l'apostolat";[59] it cannot be said to be true of the bishop's *Commentary on the Psalms*. We have noted that a spiritual or even

---

58. New Testament scholar Raymond E. Brown, *The Death of the Messiah*, ABRL (New York: Doubleday, 1994) traces this attitude back to the NT and the early Fathers, quoting Origen on Matt 27.25: "Therefore the blood of Jesus came not only on those who existed at that time but also upon all generations of Jews who would follow afterwards till the endtime" (I, 384).

59. Bardy, "Théodoret," DTC 15, 312.

moral application of psalm verses to the lives of his readers is rare; comment of the type found on Ps 33.3, "Sing to him a new song," is the exception: "It is also appropriate for us to take the words *spiritually;* we can turn ourselves into a fine-sounding and harmonious instrument and sing the praises of God through all our faculties, both of sense and of intellect"—πνευματικῶς here having a generally moral sense. Even rarer—completely absent, in fact—is moralizing on the part of this pastor, as is clear in his treatment of David's sin in that classic penitential Ps 51, where the sin goes unspecified. The most he will bring himself to offer is some listing of vices and virtues, as in developing the moral imperative "Do good" in Ps 34.14:

> Now, what is the summit of good things? *Seek peace, and go after it:* the peaceable person entertains peace towards everyone, not purloining the neighbor's property furtively, not committing homicide, not undermining marriages, not speaking evil, not doing evil, doing favors, showing respect, sharing, lending support, sharing dangers and struggles—such is unalloyed love and genuine friendship.

(52) Such comment on basic moral imperatives is, of course, applicable to all states of life, and as bishop he could hardly deny the validity of them all. We saw him defending marriage in connection with Ps 51.5; and on Ps 25.12, "[The Lord] will legislate for him in the path he has chosen," he says, "Since the ways of living a godly life are many and varied—solitary and communal, in the wilderness and in the city, as private citizens and as soldiers, as kings and artisans, sailors and farmers, and the many other different ways—it was right for the inspired word to claim it is possible to please God in each and every way of life." He can say deferential things about the hierarchy (on Ps 45.12), yet insist on equal access of all the faithful to spiritual goods, unlike the Old Testament priesthood he sees referred to at the opening of Ps 34: "No longer is the divine nourishment reserved to the priests alone; instead, the partaking of divine things is available to those so willing."

(53) Though aware that the work he is commenting on has been, with the Gospels (on which he did not comment, it seems), the principal spiritual guide from the hands of inspired

biblical authors meditated on in Christian tradition, Theodoret hardly sets himself to be an ascetical guru through the dark night of the soul or on the ascent of Mount Carmel. "Mystical" is hardly a word one would associate with his *Commentary* any more than with Chrysostom's, readier though the latter is to apply the Psalms to his listeners' lives. Louis Bouyer recognizes this more pedestrian character as part of an Antiochene protest against Alexandrian mysticism, primarily within monasticism, though "it was the whole orientation of spirituality that was involved." Although running the risk of producing an "asceticism without mysticism" (even without sentiment, if we can take as examples Theodoret's jejune commentary on some of the more moving Pilgrim Songs), in Bouyer's view "the crisis broke out where the mysticism expressed in the forms of thought inherited from Origen proved itself unassimilable. A fervent piety unsatisfied by mere moralism fell by the nature of things into a deceptive 'asceticism,' against which Antiochene spirituality was a healthy reaction."[60]

(54) Underlying these ascetical characteristics remarked on by Bouyer one should discern an incarnational theology favored at Antioch affecting also, we have seen, both Christology and the whole approach to Scripture. Such a theology is less likely to encourage in the spiritual guide flights into mysticism; "feet on the ground" is the more predictable advice. Hence, just as we saw Theodoret resting comfortably with the limitations of the humanity of Jesus and the figurative language of the psalmist (while warning of misconstruing anthropomorphisms), so we find him recommending that his readers ensure a human participation in spiritual development and the process of salvation, and not simply wait for the intervention of divine grace. The balance is as carefully striven for in this area of spirituality as we saw it to be in Christology, and Theodoret's orthodoxy was found wanting—probably without warrant—in both areas at times.

(55) He can say quite baldly, as he does on Ps 32.10, "All people, even if adorned with the works of virtue, stand in need of divine grace," and sees his position in line with Ephesians 2.8. At

---

60. *The Spirituality of the New Testament and the Fathers*, 436, 449.

other times, conversely, he can come out in favor of the priority of virtue and human effort: "You protect those dedicated to you, who have been thought worthy of your affection on account of their own virtue" (on Ps 60.4); it was the *gnome*, not divine grace, that broke the cycle of sin outlined in comment on Ps 51.5, remember. Pastors have been known to stress one aspect rather than a correlative one for didactic purposes; and there are several instances where we see him trying to uphold the correct balance:

He instructs the listener that along with God's loving-kindness our effort is required, too: whether we plead weakness or confusion or God's goodness without contributing what is ours, it is of no benefit to us (on Ps 6.5).

It is impossible for anyone to travel blamelessly the way of virtue without his grace. He works in association with those who have this intent: for the acquisition of virtue there is need of human zeal and divine assistance at one and the same time (on Ps 37.23–24).

(56) For reasons akin to the opposition to their low Christology, Theodoret's spiritual teaching was found deficient along with his fellows' in antiquity, but has been defended despite their "intensified emphasis on individualism."[61] The Pelagians could find little support in this *Commentary; pace* Bardy,[62] its teaching on the Fall and the effects of that primal sin is sound, making no concession to western pessimism about impairment of human nature nor allowing eastern optimism to deny the reality of a deadly cycle of sin, as we saw in the previous section. A criticism of ours might be to the effect that, had he believed his *Commentary* would be available for directing the spiritual lives of laypeople, he could have avoided occasional negative comments

---

61. By Kelly, e.g., *Early Christian Doctrines*, 373, who concedes: "To judge by its leading representatives, Theodore and Theodoret, variants of such [Pelagian] teaching were current in the Antiochene school too, though crossed with an intensified emphasis on individualism." Kelly proceeds to acquit Theodoret in particular.

62. "Théodoret," 323: "On voit sans peine les insuffisances et les lacunes de cette doctrine [of original sin]. Lorsqu'il s'agit de la grâce et de sa nécessité, Théodoret n'est pas moins incomplet." Bardy is not acquainted with the *Commentary on the Psalms* beyond its oft-quoted preface.

about the world in which they worked out their salvation;[63] even his friends the monks of nearby Apamea should not have been prejudiced in that regard.

(57) Clearly, Theodoret is not the ideal spiritual guide, for either laypeople or monks, nor the most original and skillful commentator on a biblical text like the Psalms. His conciseness can be extreme where pregnant sentiments of the psalmist await explication and development, and readers find they themselves have to build the bridge between inspired guidance and daily living. If they can do this, however, they stand to gain much benefit from a commentator who has taken the trouble to be in touch with the best of traditional work on this foundational text and remains firm in his resolve to avoid extreme approaches that would have proved possibly diverting but spiritually irrelevant. The scholars, for whom in any case Theodoret had little time, would find his linguistic and other critical skills deficient as an exegete, while appreciating his hermeneutical restraint and flexibility in the face of disputed issues. Our expectations of this busy pastor perhaps exceed his modest objective of offering his readers "some benefit in concentrated form," as he explains in his preface, so that all who come to the Psalms "might sing its melodies and at the same time recognize the sense of the words they sing." There is, however, more to the Psalms than this, we have to concede, even if in this *Commentary* the spiritual neophyte will not find it.

---

63. Cf. comment on Ps 73.18–20: "He was right to compare (the Babylonians') prosperity to a dream; the unreality of the present life is no different from a dream, after all."

COMMENTARY ON THE PSALMS
1–72

PREFACE

IT WOULD HAVE BEEN a pleasure for me [857][1] to do a commentary[2] on the inspired composition[3] of the mighty David prior to the other divine sayings, especially since the students of religion, both city dwellers and in the country, have all given their attention to this work in particular. Not least of these, however, are those, who embrace religious life, and recite it aloud at night and in the middle of the day;[4] they thus sing praise to the God of all and allay the bodily passions. You see, divine grace mingled benefit with the charm of the poetry, [860] and thus provided human beings with teaching that is both welcome and lovable.[5] You can find most people making little or no reference to the other divine Scriptures, whereas the spiritual harmonies of the divinely inspired David

---

1. The bracketed numbers are keyed to the columns in Migne.

2. Theodoret would have preferred the *Commentary on the Psalms* to be his first essay into biblical interpretation, as it was of his fellow Antiochene Theodore of Mopsuestia; John Chrysostom's also betrays signs of youthful inexperience. The Psalter, of course, was—after the Gospels (strangely missing from his literary profile)—the staple spiritual diet of Christians generally, at least in terms of Scripture. But, as he says, he was obliged to meet demands for commentaries on other books first.

3. As David is an "inspired composer," *prophetes,* so his work—and that of all Old Testament composers—is "inspired composition," *propheteia.* Theodoret therefore insists on the inspiration of David and the other biblical authors.

4. As an erstwhile monk, Theodoret would be aware of the monastic practice of "praying the hours." But, as he says also in commenting on Ps 32, David's verses form the pattern of prayer for people of all states of life.

5. As for Chrysostom (his particular model in biblical commentary, his eighteenth-century editor J. L. Schulze tells us), for Theodoret the Psalms are primarily didactic material rather than, say, celebration in liturgy (not mentioned here as a *Sitz im Leben*); yet he envisages their being sung rather than merely recited, at least by religious. His further statement that people make little reference to the other Scriptures may reflect Theodoret's own insecurity in biblical matters.

many people frequently call to mind, whether at home, in public places or while traveling, gain serenity for themselves from the harmony of the poetry, and reap benefit for themselves through this enjoyment.

(2) This is the reason, then, why I wanted to do a commentary on this piece of inspired composition first of all, and offer to discerning investors the profit lying hidden in its depths, so that they might sing its melodies and at the same time recognize the sense of the words they sing,[6] thus reaping a double dividend. But we were prevented from putting this desire into effect by those who requested from us commentaries on the other divine Scriptures:[7] some required of us clarification of the Song of Songs, others were anxious to have a close knowledge of the inspired composition of the Man of Passion,[8] still others of the work of the divinely inspired Ezekiel, while others were impatient for the predictions of the Twelve Prophets, shrouded in obscurity, to be rendered clear and obvious.

(3) So after it was granted to us by the God of all, who gives insight to the blind, who reveals mysteries, who gives one person speech and makes another deaf and dumb, grants sight to one and makes another blind, that we should complete the commentary on these other divine sayings of his—come now, let us invoke divine grace, which leads the blind (according to the inspired text)[9] by a way they knew not and prepares paths for their traveling with which they were unfamiliar, enables those once deaf to the divine sayings to hear them, and leads those who live in darkness and gloom to enjoy sight; and let us address ourselves to commentary on this inspired composition.

(4) Now, let no one think any the less of our efforts for the reason that others have produced a commentary on this before ours. I have, in fact, encountered various such commentaries: some I found taking refuge in allegory with considerable relish,

6. Chrysostom also complained that congregations could sing a psalm, or at least its liturgical refrain, without understanding the psalm as a whole.
7. These four commentaries are also extant (PG 81).
8. This term for Daniel is found in the Greek version of Dan 9.23 attributed to Theodotion, one of the translators of the OT (with Aquila and Symmachus) in the early Church.
9. Cf. Isa 42.16.

while others make the inspired composition resemble historical narratives of a certain type with the result that the commentary represents a case rather for Jews than the household of the faith.[10] In my opinion, it is for a wise man to shun the extreme tendencies of both the former and the latter: the things that are relevant to stories of the past should be applied to them even today, whereas the prophecies about Christ the Lord, about the Church from the nations, the evangelical lifestyle, and the apostolic preaching should not be applied to anything else, as Jews with their proclivity to malice love to do and contrive a defense for their disbelief.[11] After all, [861] the testimony of the material itself is sufficient to guide towards the truth of commentary those desiring to find it.[12] For precisely that reason our commentary on the prophecy will not involve great labor: study of the text suffices to make it clear. Instead, we shall make every possible effort to avoid a superfluity of words, while offering to those ready for it some benefit in concentrated form. First of all, however, we shall expose the purpose of the Psalms and then come to the commentary.

(5) It is important to realize, of course, that it is characteristic of inspired composition not only to foretell the future but also to recount the present and what has already happened. The divinely inspired Moses, remember, taught us clearly what was created by the God of all very long ago and received existence from him; he got this teaching not from human beings but by the grace of the Spirit. He foretold also events of his time, like the lessons given to Pharaoh, the provision of manna to Israel, and the sharing of meat. He also foretold future events, the coming of Christ the Lord, the scattering of the Jews, the salvation of the

10. Editor Schulze suggests he has in mind Apollinaris of Laodicea and Theodore of Mopsuestia, respectively, as representatives of the extreme approaches mentioned here; others see Origen as the proponent of an allegorical approach. Chrysostom was not averse to finding a historical basis for some Psalms, though this had the effect of curtailing his enthusiasm for commentary and perhaps led him to have some doubts of Davidic authorship.

11. This edge against the Jews can be found in other churchmen in Antioch, of course.

12. We have to admire a commentator who aims to let the text speak for itself, and we shall have to see if the aim is adhered to.

nations. So too with the divine David: he was the first to compose inspired writing after Moses,[13] referring to the benefits already conferred by the God of all and also forecasting what was to come long ages later. He employs not only prophetic discourse but also parenetic and legal discourse as well; sometimes the teaching he offers is moral, sometimes dogmatic; in one place he laments the misfortunes of the Jews, in another he foretells the salvation of the nations. Frequently, however, it is the Passion and the Resurrection of Christ the Lord he is predicting, and to those ready to attend he offers great satisfaction from the variety of inspired composition.

(6) Now, some people claimed that not all the Psalms are David's, but come from other composers as well. Hence, by interpreting the titles in the same way, they attributed some of the Psalms to Jeduthun, some to Ethan, others to the Sons of Korah, still others to Asaph, who they learned from Chronicles were inspired composers. But I for my part have no strong view on these points: what does it matter to me whether all come from him or some come from them, as long as it is clear that they all composed under the influence of the divine Spirit?[14] I mean, we know David was a divinely inspired composer, and Chronicles calls these others inspired composers as well. Now, it is the role

13. An interesting remark. With our knowledge today of the date of the work of the Deuteronomist on the Former Prophets up to and including 2 Kings, we might consider this reflects well on Theodoret's critical sense, shown also here in his categorization of the Psalms according to topic, theology, and style. It is certainly the approach of a thoughtful and systematic theologian at his desk, not a preacher taking Psalms in series and at face value.

14. Theodoret shows his flexibility on matters of authorship of the Psalms and the meaning of the psalm titles (less so their provenance). Diodore of Tarsus, mentor of Theodore and Chrysostom, was prepared to accept that the titles were a later addition; others saw them as original, and even (like Gregory of Nyssa) wrote complete treatises on them. Theodoret notes that the Chronicler makes mention of musicians under David and later (cf. 1 Chron 25), like Jeduthun, Ethan, the Sons of Korah, whose names have crept into the titles. He goes further, though, than the Chronicler in his belief that they were also described as inspired composers, which allows him to adopt a quite liberal attitude to authorship of some Psalms before conceding the majority view. (He discusses the matter again at the opening of Ps 73.)

of an inspired composer to make his tongue available to the grace of the Spirit, according to the sentiment expressed in the Psalms, "My tongue is like the pen of a fluent scribe."[15] Still, let the judgment of the majority prevail: most historians say the Psalms are David's.

(7) Now, since some people declared the titles of the Psalms to be spurious, I think it is necessary [864] to say a few words on this matter, too. It seems to me to be rash to dismiss the titles that were current as far back as the time of Ptolemy,[16] who ruled as king in Egypt after Alexander; all the seventy ancients translated them into the Greek language, as they did all the rest of the divine Scripture. But one hundred fifty years before the translation, that remarkable man Ezra, filled with divine grace, listed the sacred books, which had long been corrupted through the Jews' neglect and the Babylonians' impiety. Now, if he who was also under the influence of the all-holy Spirit renewed the familiarity with these books, and the translators—not without divine inspiration—turned them into the Greek language with great consensus, and in addition to the other divine Scriptures have left us also a translation of the titles,[17] I consider it rash and quite foolhardy to brand them as spurious and accept one's own judgment as more enlightened than the influence of the Spirit. Commentary on the Psalms individually will bring this out more clearly.

(8) They translated the word *diapsalma* differently. Some

---

15. The opening verse of Ps 45, which became a favorite text for many Fathers in dealing with the charism of biblical inspiration. See R. C. Hill, "Psalm 45: a *locus classicus* for patristic thinking on biblical inspiration," *Studia Patristica* 25 (1993): 95–100.

16. Theodoret is taking a less liberal view on the psalm titles than Diodore, who saw them as the work of editors reassembling the Psalter after its loss during the Babylonian captivity; such a loss and need of reassembling did not cross Theodoret's mind. There is thus a critical gap in his chronology and logic. See his opening comment on Ps 27 and Ps 71 for some movement in his position.

17. For Theodoret, Ezra's role in the restoration of Israel and its Scriptures (glorified in a manner compatible with rabbinic tradition, he may not have realized), and the inspiration of the Septuagint translators (on the basis of the legendary *Letter of Aristeas*) are clinching arguments. In fact, it is the Torah alone that figures in both those traditional accounts.

took it as an interruption to the influence of the Spirit, others as a change in biblical composition, others as an alteration of the meter. One, on the other hand, following the translation of Aquila, replaced *diapsalma* with "always," saying it was attached to the previous verse.[18] For example, in the third psalm after the words, "I cried to the Lord with my voice, and from his holy mountain he hearkened to me," we find *diapsalma* inserted. Aquila made the connection this way, "And from his holy mountain he always hearkened to me." In this way he connects it to the preceding verse, making one sentence. For my part, however, since I find that the Septuagint and all the other translators of the divine Scriptures use *diapsalma*, I consider it unjustified to dismiss so many people of such caliber and rely on the opinion of one single person. For this reason I take the notation *diapsalma* to indicate an alteration of the melody. You see, in establishing choirs and offering the singing to God, the mighty David, instead of suiting himself, brought benefit to the people; so it is clear that he made sure the choirs should sing in concert with the instrumentalists as they produced their harmonious sound. Now, even songs have many variations in melody, while lyres and certainly lutes as well play a range of chords; this kind of considerable variation you can notice also with flutes. Accordingly, I think *diapsalma* means, [865] as I said, the alteration in melody. The precise meaning, however, was known by the one who put the particular title in place, and if it was someone else, he received the illumination of the divine Spirit, as did David.[19]

(9) Now, those who read the Psalms studiously should realize

---

18. Chrysostom, for instance, equally aware of diverse translations of the term, but not as well in touch with the Chronicler's mention of Davidic musicians as is Theodoret, fails to see a musical direction in it as in psalm titles, and either simply reproduces *diapsalma* or gets some mileage from Aquila's "always." His lack of Hebrew does not allow him to grapple with the original term *sela'* occurring 71 times in the Psalter.

19. Again we have to admire Theodoret for his balanced judgment on items in the text. After surveying and evaluating a range of possible interpretations, with which he is well acquainted, he makes a firm option for one in the light of the evidence, while allowing for a different verdict. His principal preoccupation is that the divine inspiration of all parts of the text not be impugned.

that these have not preserved the chronological order: some dealing with earlier events have at times been allotted a lower position, while others narrating more recent events, for example, have been placed ahead of them. For instance, Psalm 3 has as its title a reference to Absalom, whereas Psalm 141 is about Saul; to anyone with a knowledge of history it is quite obvious how much earlier is the story of Saul than that of Absalom. Now, I am of the view that the divine David himself composed the Psalms, whereas people of a later age fixed their order.[20]

(10) I made mention of these matters to avoid interrupting my commentary under pressure of writing about them in midstream. Accordingly, let us conclude our preface at this stage, and with God's help address ourselves to commentary on the Psalms individually.[21]

---

20. This, of course, was the consideration that encouraged Diodore to see the psalm titles as secondary, a point Theodoret might have considered. His numbering of the Psalms is that of the Greek, of course, not of the Hebrew or of modern versions.

21. And so we conclude an introduction of "studious" readers to the Psalms that has to be judged systematic, thorough, reasonably critical, and measured, not to mention deeply religious. A preacher like Chrysostom could not offer quite these virtues to his congregation, whose needs admittedly would be somewhat different.

COMMENTARY ON PSALM 1

No title in the Hebrew

LESSED THE MAN *who did not walk in the counsel of the ungodly, take his place in the way of sinners, or rest on the seat of the corrupt* (v. 1).[1] It is easy to grasp from this that in former times the translators of the divine Scriptures who found titles in the Hebrew text turned them into the Greek language. I mean, they found this psalm and the one after it without titles and left them without titles, not presuming to add anything of their own to the sayings of the Spirit.[2]

(2) Some of those who have composed treatises on the Psalms say this psalm contains moral teaching, but to me it seems no less dogmatic than moral. In fact, it includes condemnation not only of sinners but also of the ungodly, and urges constant attention to the divine words; from this we gain benefit that is not only moral but also dogmatic.

(3) Very appropriately did mighty David set forth a beatitude at the beginning of his composition, imitating him who is both his son and his Lord—I mean, Christ the Savior—who began his teaching to the holy disciples with beatitudes: "Blessed are the poor in spirit," he said, "because theirs is the kingdom of heaven."[3] Now, Christ the Lord is son of David in his humanity according to that verse of the holy Gospels, "Book of the genealo-

---

1. Ps 1.1. Whether virtuous women are likewise to be so commended is not a concern of either Hebrew or Greek text. Theodoret, unlike Chrysostom, will not allow this to pass without comment.
2. Naturally, an Antiochene commentator prizes this fidelity of the translator to the text, in line with his school's accent on *akribeia*, precision. For Theodoret, however, the fact is also confirmation of his view of the originality of the titles outlined in the Preface, the reasoning being that if later editors supplied some, they would have supplied all.
3. Matt 5.3.

gy of Jesus Christ, son of Abraham."⁴ But as God he is his Lord and Creator: his own words are as follows, "The Lord said to my lord, 'Sit on my right.'"⁵ [868] So he blesses the person who neither shared the way with the ungodly nor took seriously the counsel of sinners (which he called "taking one's place"), but shunned the abiding contagion of the corrupt. Now, the epithet "blessed" is a divine title; the divine Apostle is witness to this in his exclamation, "O blessed and sole ruler, the King of kings and Lord of lords."⁶ But the Lord God shared this, too, with human beings, as he did other things. After all, he is called faithful: "God is faithful," Scripture says, "and through him you were invited into fellowship with his Son."⁷ And blessed Moses said, "God is faithful; in him there is no wrong."⁸ And he called faithful in turn those human beings who accept his words without reservation. In similar fashion, being God in fact as well as in name, he shared even this appellation with human beings in his munificence, crying aloud, "I said, 'You are gods and all sons of the Most High, yet as human beings you will die.'"⁹

(4) The epithet "blessed," therefore, constitutes the fruit of perfection as far as virtue is concerned. You see, every practice in life looks towards its goal: athletics looks towards olive wreaths, martial arts towards victories and spoils, medicine certainly towards good health and cure of disease, commerce towards amassing wealth and abundance of riches. Likewise, the practice of virtue has as its fruit and goal the beatitude from God. Now, no one seeing only a man declared blessed here should think that womankind is excluded from this beatitude. I mean, Christ the Lord in delivering the beatitudes in the masculine did not exclude women from possessing virtue: his words include men and women. The husband is the head of his wife, remember, as the divine Apostle says.¹⁰ Now, the limbs of the

4. Cf. Matt 1.1, where our received text reads, "son of David, son of Abraham," which would obviously support Theodoret's point less elliptically.
5. Ps 110.1. It will be more helpful for us to cite the Psalms in the numbering of the Hebrew and of modern versions rather than the Greek (and Latin).
6. 1 Tim 6.15. 7. 1 Cor 1.9.
8. Deut 32.4. 9. Ps 82.6–7.
10. Cf. 1 Cor 11.3. What strikes us most about this unusual acknowledg-

body are linked to the head, and when the head is crowned, they share in the glory; in the same manner, too, when we converse with someone and call their head beloved, we are not excluding the body's limbs but are referring to the whole by mention of one part.

(5) Now, it was not idly[11] that he made mention first of traveling, then standing, then sitting; rather, he realized precisely that the reasoning processes, whether casual or intense, experience movement first, then arrest, finally a kind of utter immobility. So he gives the advice neither to allow entrance to any profane thought nor to set about illicit doings. Now, Scripture is in the habit of calling ungodly those who worship no gods or many, whereas it calls sinners those who choose to be partners with lawlessness, or are in love with a wayward life. [869] It calls corrupt those who not only bring ruin on their own heads but also share their ruin with others, like the disease that infects both people and animals that contract it by coming into contact with others already infected. Hence the verse recommends us to avoid association with such people.

(6) Since flight from evil, however, is not sufficient for perfection of virtue, "Turn aside from evil," he says, "and do good,"[12] and blessed Isaiah says, "Put an end to your wrongdoing, learn to do good."[13] Quite appropriately blessed David added, *But his choice is for the law of the Lord, and over his law he will pore day and night* (v. 2). What is required is not merely to abhor the above-mentioned but also to give one's attention to the divine law night and day, to choose what the divine law dictates and to

---

ment of an apparent male bias in Scriptural interpretation is its formality: a writer of the period, a half century after the much more dismissive Chrysostom, deliberately resists such an attitude to include women in his perspective—even if we wonder a little how Jesus can be interpreted to be delivering the Beatitudes with only men in mind. As well, the acknowledgment is not consistently in his mind throughout the *Commentary*.

11. A favorite phrase of Antiochene commentators on the biblical text, noting the purpose of each detail, just as there was commendation for resisting the temptation to supply a missing psalm title. "Precision" is admired in the author, and expected in the commentator.

12. Ps 37.27.
13. Cf. Isa 1.16–17.

guide one's life according to its direction. This, after all, is what the God of all enjoined through Moses in the words, "The words of this law will be at all times in your mouth, and you will ponder them seated or rising, in bed or on the road traveling; you shall hang them from your hand, and they shall be fixed before your eyes."[14]

(7) Then he shows the fruit growing from this: *He will be like the tree planted by the water channels,* he says, in fact, *it will produce its fruit in due season, and its leaf will not fall. Whatever he does will prosper* (v. 3). In other words, the streams from the divine Spirit resemble watering by rivers: just as they cause trees planted near them to flourish, so the spiritual streams are the cause of bearing divine fruit. For this very reason Christ the Lord called his own teaching water: "If any one is thirsty," he said, "let him come to me and drink, and the water that I shall give him will be a spring of living water springing up to life everlasting."[15] And again, "He who believes in me, as Scripture says, rivers of living water will flow from his belly."[16] Likewise to the Samaritan woman, "The person who drinks from this water will be thirsty again, whereas whoever drinks from the water that I shall give him will never be thirsty."[17] In a similar way he says also through the prophet Isaiah, "I shall provide for them as they travel thirstily in the desert; I shall make springs flow in the mountains and rivers on the hills to supply drink for my chosen race, the people I have made my own."[18]

(8) Appropriately, [872] then, blessed David compared the person devoted to the divine sayings to trees growing on riverbanks, ever green, bearing fruit in season. You see, champions of virtue reap the fruit of their labors in the future life; but like a kind of foliage they bear sound hope constantly within them, flourishing and exulting, and by their cheerfulness they overcome the rigor of their labors.[19] They have the generous Lord

---

14. Theodoret seems to have in mind here Deut 6.6–8 and 11.18.
15. Cf. John 7.37; 4.14, loosely collated.
16. John 7.38.
17. John 4.13–14.
18. A loose recall or paraphrase of Isa 43.19–20.
19. Mitchell Dahood, *Psalms,* with his eye ever on Ugaritic encourage-

constantly abetting their enthusiasm: "To those who love God," says the divine Apostle, "all things work together unto good."[20] This is precisely the reason why the blessed David also said, *Whatever he does will prosper.* "By the Lord," he says, "are a person's steps kept straight; he will rejoice exceedingly in his path."[21] Now, it was not idly that he added *Whatever;* rather, it was with great precision:[22] having first condemned every appearance of evil and demonstrated the perfection of the divine laws, he then added, *Whatever he does will prosper,* in the knowledge that such a person at least will have no inclination to do anything opposed to those laws, having his own will so in harmony with the divine law. *His choice is for the law of the Lord,* he said, you recall.

(9) Hence, after exhorting them to virtue and giving them a perfect lesson in sound values, he also prepares the athletes by a lesson in the opposite behavior in the words, *Not so are the ungodly, not so* (v. 4). By the double negative he brings out the contrast more clearly. *Instead, they are like foam, which the wind sweeps from the face of the earth:* whereas the former are watered by the divine sayings, he is saying, are ever green, and bear fruit in season, these people are prostrate under contrary spirits and resemble foam tossed hither and thither by contrary winds.

(10) *For this reason the ungodly will not have a place to stand in judgment, nor sinners in the council of the righteous* (v. 5). The all-holy Spirit details everything with great precision: he did not say, "Ungodly people will not have a place to stand," but *will not have a place to stand in judgment,* as if to say, not in judgment but

---

ment of an eschatological interpretation of the Hebrew text, would approve of the way Theodoret sees reference to eternal life in the psalmist's imagery of rivers and trees.

20. Rom 8.28. Theodoret is content he is demonstrating that this psalm (which we would class a Wisdom psalm) is not simply "moral" but "dogmatic," as he claimed, in that the contrast between the righteous and the wicked is being explored, not merely moral imperatives being urged.

21. Ps 37.23.

22. Precision requires the Antiochene commentator to pick up each item in the text, we noted above; but Theodoret is showing he can be less precise in his recall of Scriptural texts—a failing more understandable in a preacher than in a theologian at his desk.

for condemnation. You see, they do not require convicting, as their ungodliness is patent; rather, they await only the sentence. I mean, they are like murderers caught in the act: the court officials bring them to court not for conviction [873] but to pass sentence on them in keeping with the laws. So too, those in the grip of ungodliness undergo punishment immediately on appearing; they do not come to judgment but receive their sentence. Yet even if they are acquitted of impious teaching while living a life at variance with the law, they will be beyond the conventions of the righteous. Aquila, in fact, gives the translation "council," Theodotion, "assembly," and Symmachus, "congregation."[23]

(11) *Because the Lord knows the way of the righteous, and the way of the ungodly will perish* (v. 6). The righteous Judge, he is saying, knows everything even before judgment, and he needs neither proofs nor refutations. When therefore he is assigning things according to their worth to everyone, he rewards some with commendation and crown, others, however, he sends away to everlasting punishment. The phrase, *the way of the ungodly will perish*, is like those words of the Apostle, "If anyone's work is burnt up, loss will be sustained":[24] while the work of righteous men continues resplendent, even the evil of godless and unholy people is undone.[25]

---

23. Theodoret here, in a throwaway line, nonchalantly includes as a none-too-helpful footnote the alternative versions (of one word!). Unlike Chrysostom, he gives the variants their names, but does not go to the trouble of evaluating them. And as the difference between them is not significant, the gesture seems pointless. See Introduction, section 3.
24. 1 Cor 3.15.
25. Theodoret has been as good as his word in not gilding the lily in his commentary on this first psalm and generally letting the text speak for itself. For all his expressed sensitivity to discrimination against women recipients of the Word, however, his closing reference to "righteous men" (*andres*) seems unnecessarily exclusive.

COMMENTARY ON PSALM 2

No title in the Hebrew

AVING CONCLUDED the first psalm with a reference to the ungodly, he opened the second in turn with this same reference so as to teach us that the aforementioned end of the ungodly lies in wait for both kings and rulers, Jews and Gentiles, who rage against the Savior. You see, in the second psalm he foretells both the human sufferings and the kingship of Christ the Lord;[1] of course, he also emphasizes the calling of the nations and deplores the Jews' failure to believe. I mean, those words, *For what purpose did nations rage?* (v. 1), come from someone deploring and censuring folly. There is no need, however, for a lengthy commentary on our part, as the divinely inspired Peter, chief of the apostles, gave a commentary in the Acts, naming Herod, Pontius Pilate, the chief priests, and scribes kings and rulers.[2] One, you recall, had been sent by the Roman emperor to exercise his command, the other was ruler of the Jews at that time; one had Jewish subjects, the other gentile soldiers. But despite their conspiring together and hatching a tawdry plot for the murder of the Lord, [876] their schemes all came to nothing, as they were unable to consign to oblivion the one crucified by them: on the third day he rose again and took possession of the world.

(2) Very suitably and quite appropriately did he associate the

---

1. Theodoret finds New Testament support for giving this psalm a Christological interpretation. Absence of a title (cf. Ps 3) gives him freedom to forsake a historical reading.

2. He has Acts 4.24–30 in mind, but (once again) he is somewhat astray on details: it is the community to whom Peter and John report that quote vv. 1–2 of this psalm, and in fact they make no mention of chief priests and scribes. The brief reference by them hardly constitutes an adequate "commentary" on the verses.

words, *did they form empty plots,* with the people's role: it was the Jews who made this wicked plot against the Savior. Testimony to this comes from the remark of the sacred evangelists that teaches that "the Pharisees went out and formed a plot to dispose of him"[3] and Caiaphas's exclamation, "It is fitting that one person should die and that the whole nation should not perish."[4] Now, that word *raged* Aquila rendered "were troubled" and Symmachus, "stirs up."[5] It bears on the role of the nations, however, and suggests we understand that when the Jews brought Jesus before Pilate like any despot and repeatedly claimed he should be done away with, he reluctantly passed the death sentence on him for fear that in all likelihood some charge would be fabricated against him if he released him. As blessed Luke said, remember, they spoke accusingly of him, "We found this man perverting the nation and forbidding paying tribute to Caesar and he said he was Christ the King."[6]

(3) *For what purpose did nations rage, and peoples form empty plots? The kings of the earth took their stand, and the rulers came together in concert against the Lord and against his Christ* (vv. 1–2). It does not say "the nations" with the article so that you think all are included,[7] but *nations,* suggesting the sense of something particular. You see, since the Jews took him into custody and handed him over to the nations, accordingly he says, "What was such an important reason and what the cause for the peoples to be stirred up against him and deliver him into the hands of the nations?" The word *raged* is equivalent to "made a pretense."

(4) *Let us break their bonds and thrust away from us their yoke* (v. 3). The person who does not honor the Son, Scripture says,

---

3. Mark 3.6.
4. John 11.50.
5. Dahood, *Psalms* I, 7, in fact, suggests that both the LXX and modern translators have missed this verb's true sense, "forgather." Theodoret betrays some unease about the traditional rendering (arising from Syriac etymology, Dahood informs us), and continues to worry the point.
6. Luke 23.2.
7. Antiochene precision again, noting details of the text like absence of an article (hardly consistently employed in the overall text, in fact) and then rationalizing from this unreliable detail to a condemnation of Jewish skullduggery in the treatment of Jesus.

does not honor the Father either;[8] likewise, along with the Son's they cast aside as well the Father's yoke. Yet it seems to me that the all-holy Spirit in turn urges the faithful to say these words, *Let us break their bonds* (namely, the impious nations') *and thrust away from us their yoke* (the lawless Jews'), and take upon us the easy yoke of the Lord. His, after all, is the call, "Take my yoke upon you, because my yoke is easy and my burden light."[9] Now, the Law itself is called *yoke* by the divine apostles: the divinely inspired Peter says of it in Acts, "Why do you make a trial of God by putting a yoke on the disciples' neck [877] which neither our fathers nor ourselves have managed to carry? Rather, through the grace of the Lord Jesus we believe we shall be saved in the same way as they."[10] To them apply as well the inspired words, *Let us break their bonds and thrust away from us their yoke,* that is, let us prevent our hearts from wishing to be subject to them; let us reject the yoke of the Law; let us consider of no moment the type unless it is understood spiritually; let the shadow be judged to contribute nothing of usefulness unless the mystery of Christ can be discerned in it.

(5) *He who dwells in heaven will ridicule them, and the Lord will mock them* (v. 4). He who was crucified by them and given over to death is in heaven, he has all things in his grasp, and he shows their plans to be vain and futile. His Father, Lord of all things, will inflict a fitting punishment on them.

(6) *Then he will speak to them in his wrath, and in his rage he will confound them* (v. 5). The fulfillment of the story teaches us the interpretation of these words: a Roman army assailed them, plundered the city and burnt down the Temple; most of them were put to death, while those who escaped the slaughter were taken captive and reduced to slavery.[11] Now, it is necessary to

8. Cf. John 5.23.
9. Cf. Matt 11.29–30.
10. Acts 15.10–11. Theodoret may have been aware of the rabbis' reference to the Law as a yoke. To him it is rather type and shadow in view of the reality that is "the mystery of Christ," in Paul's phrase (e.g., Eph 3.4).
11. Theodoret here, too, is adhering to the principles enunciated in his preface, that the psalmist (like Moses) is capable of foretelling the future, even in precise detail. In contrast, modern commentators, like Weiser, see

give attention to the sense here, namely, that two persons are referred to in succession, firstly, Lord and Christ.—Remember, *against the Lord,* he said, *and against his Christ;* then the one dwelling in heaven and Lord.—*He who dwells in heaven will ridicule them, and the Lord will mock them.* Once again he kept the same arrangement.[12]

(7) *But I have been established as king by him* (v. 6). It was necessary to make this point here and then to add *on Sion his holy mountain announcing the Lord's decree* (vv. 6–7). In fact, he rules not only over Mount Sion but over things visible and invisible and over all creation. But on Mount Sion and in Judea he propounded his divine teaching to those who attended; those who accepted it derived streams flowing into the whole world through their obedience to his divine decrees: "Go forth," he says, "make disciples of all nations."[13] Now, the verse, *I have been established as king by him,* is expressed in human fashion: as God he possesses his kingship by nature, as human being he receives it by election. The fact that as God he possesses power without beginning the same inspired author teaches in the words, "Your throne, O God, is for all ages, the scepter of your kingship a scepter of equity."[14] Now, this [880] psalm blessed Paul says refers to the Son;[15] all the same, as God he possesses kingship

---

the verses recited by a king at his enthronement in Jerusalem as the anointed (Christ) of God.

12. The point he is making could be nuanced by consideration of Hebrew parallelism.

13. Matt 28.19.

14. Ps 45.7.

15. Cf. Heb 1.8. The careful and lengthy explication of (what we, but not he, would call) the hypostatic union of two natures in Christ, the Word Incarnate, reminds us that Theodoret's life spans the period between the councils of Constantinople in 381 and Chalcedon in 451 which was marked by much Christological and Trinitarian debate. J. N. D. Kelly takes Theodoret as an example of the middle-ground Antiochene position on these issues, avoiding the extremes of Nestorianism and Cyril's "ill-judged" statements: "His guiding principles, we should note, were the completeness and distinction of the natures (cf. ἡ λαβοῦσα and ἡ ληφθεῖσα φύσις), and their union in one person" (*Early Christian Doctrines,* 325). The distinction between "receiving" and "received" emerges here. See Introduction, section 6 and n. 33 on Ps 22.

and as human being he receives it. Likewise, as God he is called Most High, as human being he is raised on high. David for his part proclaims the divine highness in his cry, "Let them know that your name is Lord, you alone are the Most High over all the earth."[16] Zechariah, too, says to John, "You, child, will be called a prophet of the Most High."[17] Blessed Paul it is, on the other hand, who teaches us the human highness in his words, "Accordingly, God also raised him on high, and bestowed on him the name that is above every name."[18] To be sure, God the Word had the name "only-begotten Son" before the ages as connatural with his condition, yet while still possessing the title of the Son as God, he also receives it as human being. Hence in the present psalm he added the words, *The Lord said to me, "You are my son, today I have begotten you."* Now, no one who believes the teaching of the divine Spirit would apply this verse to the divinity of Christ the Lord.[19] In fact, let us listen in this regard to the God of all speaking through David, "From the womb before the morning star I begot you."[20] So as man he both receives this verse, and as man hears what follows.

(8) *Ask it of me, and I shall give you the nations for your inheritance and the ends of the earth as your possession* (v. 8). As God, you see, he is maker of all things: "Through him everything was made, and without him nothing was made,"[21] and "through him all things were created, things visible and invisible."[22] If he is Lord and Creator of all things, he is Lord and Master of what he created; yet while Lord by nature insofar as he is God, as man he

---

16. Ps 83.18.
17. Luke 1.76.
18. Phil 2.9. Kelly adds, "Though in his earlier days he was ready enough, like other Antiochenes, to speak of 'the Word' and 'the man,' contrasting 'Him who assumes' with 'him who is assumed,' he avoided such language once the controversy had made the issues clear" (*Early Christian Doctrines,* 325–26). The contrast is still obvious here.
19. What may seem a strange caveat corresponds to the gloss on this verse in Heb 5.5, "So also Christ did not glorify himself in becoming a high priest, but was appointed by the one who said to him, 'You are my Son, today I have begotten you,'"—the distinction between "receiving, assuming" and "received, assumed" again.
20. Ps 110.3 [LXX]. 21. John 1.3.
22. Col 1.16.

COMMENTARY ON PSALM 2

also receives the lordship of all things. Since in former times particular care seemed to be lavished only on the Jews—"The people of Jacob," Scripture says, "became the Lord's portion, Israel his allotted inheritance"[23]—and yet were rejected for gaining no advantage from the special care, properly he transfers his care to the nations, without having been uncaring towards them in former times. Thus he fulfilled the oracle of Moses, whose words were, remember, "Rejoice, nations, with his people."[24]

(9) Now, it is possible to discover an appropriate fulfillment for this prophecy, too:[25] the number of the Jews who came to faith were not only the twelve apostles but was as well the seventy disciples, the hundred and twenty whom blessed Peter addressed in assembly,[26] the five hundred to whom he appeared on one occasion after the Resurrection according to [881] the statement of the divinely inspired Paul,[27] the three thousand and the five thousand that the chief of the apostles made his catch through addressing them,[28] and the many myriads of whom the mighty James exclaimed, "You see, brother, what countless numbers of Jewish believers there are."[29] These, to be sure, and in addition to them those of the Jews throughout the whole world who have come to faith he declares a holy people, and through them he takes possession of all the nations, thus fulfilling the prophecy in the words, "Rejoice, nations, with his people."

(10) In addition to this, however, he fulfills also his own prophecy which he made in regard to the Jews in the words, "Now, I have other sheep that do not belong to this fold. Those, too, I must gather; they will hear my voice, and there will be one flock, one shepherd."[30] This, too, he says in the present psalm:

---

23. Deut 32.9 [LXX].
24. Deut 32.43 [LXX].
25. Theodoret's hermeneutical perspective is actively forward-looking, as he suggested in his preface: he will search for New Testament fulfillment of OT texts, even those cited incidentally, as here.
26. Cf. Acts 1.15.
27. Cf. 1 Cor 15.6.
28. Cf. Acts 2.41, 4.4.
29. The attribution of these words to James, admittedly present among the speakers in Acts 21.20, is also wide off the mark.
30. John 10.16.

Ask it of me, and I shall give you the nations for your inheritance and the ends of the earth as your possession. But it occurs to me to lament the faithlessness of the Jews, who though hearing the prophecy that made specific mention of the ends of the earth, and realizing that none of their kings had had such sway, but only Christ the Lord, David's offspring in the flesh, blind the eyes of their mind according to the prophecy that says, "They grope about, as blind people do for the wall, and not as they will do who have the benefit of eyesight."[31] That, of course, is the reason why the inspired word is directed against them.

(11) *You will tend them with an iron rod; you will smash them like pottery* (v. 9). With the Roman Empire, that is, which the prophecy of Daniel refers to figuratively as iron,[32] on account of both its strength and its rigidity, he will smash them like pottery of clay. You see, since they had declined to have him alone as their king and declared in a loud voice, "We have no king but Caesar,"[33] he set Caesar over them as they had requested, and through the Roman army he inflicted punishment for their impiety. If, on the other hand, you think this refers not to Jews but to nations, you should interpret it this way: He will tend the nations with an iron rod, his strong and rigid kingship; and he will smash them like pottery, unmaking and reshaping them through the bath of rebirth, and making them firm through the fire of the Spirit.[34]

(12) After thus foretelling these things in this way, blessed David then urges both kings and subjects to run to the Savior, to embrace his saving laws, and through their guidance and instruction to reap benefit. He says, note, [884] *Kings, now take heed; be instructed, all you who judge the earth* (v. 10). He is king of us all, you see, the one who once was thought to be king of Jews alone. *Serve the Lord in fear, and rejoice in him with trembling* (v. 11), that is, those who exult and rejoice over their salvation ought not rely on his loving-kindness alone, but should be in fear and

---

31. Isa 59.10 [LXX].   32. Cf. Dan 2.40.
33. John 19.15.
34. Theodoret is nothing if not hermeneutically flexible; having opted for a Christological sense (strangely, for an Antiochene, showing no interest in the literal sense of the psalm as a coronation ode), he now allows, briefly, for an ecclesiological/sacramental interpretation.

dread as well of the righteousness linked with it. Scripture says, "If you seem to be standing firm, watch out you do not fall."[35] When, in fact, through fear of the Lord we perform our obligations, we have particular contentment arising from our performance, since our conscience is in fact good and it ensures us the greatest joy. Now, *with trembling* means with compunction, lest delight in God should be changed into delight in the world.[36]

(13) *Take advantage of instruction in case the Lord should be angry and you fall from the right path* (v. 12). Perfection, you see, requires not only the acquisition of knowledge of God; rather, it is necessary as well to pursue the practice of virtue, and then with that to your credit you will travel by the sure path. *Since his wrath is enkindled in a flash. Blessed are all who trust in him.* In other words, at the time of judgment, when your evildoing in the manner of some combustible material ignites the divine wrath like fire, you will be found far from the way of good people, paying the penalty for sins committed in this life. At that time, on the contrary, those who have hoped in him genuinely and consistently will reap the benefit of their hope, beatitude. *Blessed are those who trust in him,* the text goes on to say, note: if the athletes of virtue enjoy beatitude even in the present life, they will surely acquire it more truly on that day when those who have lived in wickedness bring the divine wrath on themselves.

35. 1 Cor 10.12.
36. The obtrusively moralistic tone of these latter sentences may strike us as out of place. However, the editor notes that many manuscripts do not include them.

COMMENTARY ON PSALM 3

A psalm of David when he fled from the presence of his son Absalom.

HIS STORY, OF COURSE, is known to the more studious; but for the benefit of lazier people I shall summarize it.[1] After that double sin of his, the great David encountered many and varied misfortunes. Not only, in fact, were neighboring nations incited to hostility but even his very family was affected by revolt, crime following crime. [885] The intemperance of Amnon was followed by the bloodguilt of Absalom, whose fratricide was followed by the revolt against his father and the rebellion of his subjects.[2] You see, since divine grace was providing for him, none of this overwhelmed David; but with the incidence of that crime of rebellion evil took possession of the place and perpetrated deeds that are the stuff of tragedy, giving rise to a flood of disasters. At that time, accordingly, as he fled from his murderous son and those deployed against him, he wrote this psalm; that is to say, the divine Spirit was at work even in those circumstances, thanks to the ardent repentance practiced by him.[3]

(2) *Lord, why have those who oppress me become so numerous? Many rise up against me. Many say to my soul, "For him salvation does not lie with his God"* (vv. 1–2). Many, in fact, are the enemies of every kind who assail me from all sides; but more numerous are

---

1. Like Chrysostom, who can upbraid his congregation for biblical illiteracy and yet expect them to know recondite details of the text, Theodoret presumes in the reader of a commentary on the Psalms an ignorance of sacred history. Or is it merely an artifice allowing him to set the historical context of the psalm, the title encouraging him to give the psalm a historical interpretation, unlike Ps 2?

2. Cf. 2 Sam 13–17.

3. Like others of the Fathers, Theodoret is in no doubt of divine inspiration of the biblical authors.

those who trouble me by their mockery and their claims that I am bereft of your providence. Yet I know that you would not persist in ignoring me, despite my many failings. On the contrary, you will raise up the one who now humbles himself for the sin he has committed and make him appear stronger than his foes. In fact, he intimated as much by saying, *But you, Lord, are my defense, my glory, you lift up my head* (v. 3). That is to say, I have confidence neither in kingship nor in sovereignty; instead, I trust in you to be my glory, and I expect to be quickly raised up by your right hand.

(3) *I cried aloud to the Lord, and he gave ear to me from his holy mountain* (v. 4). My reason, of course, in offering my prayers to you in all confidence is my knowledge that you grant our requests without delay. Now, the verse is not to be understood as referring to a loud cry but to earnestness of spirit. Thus the God of all spoke to blessed Moses, who said not a word, "Why do you cry out to me?"[4] calling silence a cry on account of the earnestness of his mind. Now, those words, *He hearkened to me from his holy mountain*,[5] are said in accord with the view held once upon a time: it was thought the God of all lived in his dwelling, since he even delivered oracles to the priests from there.

(4) *I lay down and slept; I awoke because the Lord will defend me* (v. 5). Frequently the divine Scripture calls disasters night because those who fall into extreme distress think they are living in a kind of darkness. On the other hand, sleep is associated with nights; so it suggests troubles [888] and release from them at the same time. You see, the words, *I awoke because the Lord will defend me,* mean this, I benefited from divine intervention and so proved superior to the evils that befell me. Hence, *I shall not fear countless numbers of people assailing me all about. Arise, Lord, save me, my God* (vv. 6–7): by your mere presence you succeed in scattering the countless thousands.[6] *Because you have smitten all those*

4. Exod 14.15.
5. As in a previous psalm, this Antiochene with his accent on precision does not cite the verse in precisely the same form as before.
6. As he promised in his preface, Theodoret is not inclined to gild the lily: if he opts for a historical approach to this psalm, he forbears indulging in the kind of moralizing elaboration a preacher—in closer touch with a congregation before him—might be led to add to these verses.

who hate me without cause, breaking the teeth of sinners.[7] Accordingly, make me a sharer in your complete salvation: just as you made those pay the price of their injustice who wrongly made me the butt of their enmity many times—neighbors and foreigners, Israelites and Amalekites, and of course Saul in particular—so now reward me with salvation. The phrase *breaking the teeth of sinners,* that is to say, depriving them of all strength, is by comparison with wild beasts, which when bereft of their teeth are quite undaunting and open to attack.

(5) *Salvation belongs to the Lord* (v. 8). I have no hope in human beings, he says; rather, I expect salvation from you. And not myself alone, but also your people, who are fighting with me. Yet I am distressed also for those who are fighting; after all, they bear the name of your people. So grant the blessing of peace, Lord, to both sides. He intimated as much, in fact, in the words, *May your blessing be on your people.* Blessed Moses, remember, associates peace with blessings,[8] and, even if in history we find blessed David very concerned for the people and even for his parricide son, he was more anxious for peace than for victory against the people.

---

7. The LXX here departs in details from the Hebrew; Dahood further believes the evidence of Ugaritic suggests an optative sense for these verbs, and Theodoret's commentary concurs (Dahood, *Psalms* I, 20).

8. Cf. Gen 26.29; Num 6.22–26.

COMMENTARY ON PSALM 4

To the end, with hymns. A psalm of David.

"O THE END" was rendered by Aquila and Theodotion, "to the author of victory," but by Symmachus, "triumphal." "To the end," however, means that the foretold events will take place a long time afterwards.[1] Now, at the end of the psalm he foretold the resurrection from the dead in the words, *In peace I shall lie down and in the same instant go to sleep because you alone, Lord, have given me grounds for hope* (v. 8). According to the others, by contrast, the present psalm is offered to God, the author of victory, as a triumphal hymn by blessed David after his victory over Absalom. It seems to them, in fact, that the psalm was composed after [889] the conclusion of that war: in the psalm before this, blessed David said, "Many say to my soul, For him salvation does not lie with his God."[2] But in this psalm he says, *Mortals that you are, how long will you be slow of heart? Why do you love futility and search for deceit? Know that the Lord has made his holy one an object of wonder?* (vv. 2–3). Accordingly, in the present psalm he teaches people who are distorted by a lack of belief, who do not hold for a God the one who is provident and governs human affairs, that there is someone who oversees and regulates all things; and he cites particular instances in demonstrating this teaching.

(2) *The God of my righteousness hearkened to me when I called upon*

---

1. Hoist on his own petard, Theodoret is committed—and is struggling—to find some historical significance in the psalm titles, whereas it seems they represent liturgical and specifically musical directions for the leaders (cf. 2 Chron 34.12–13). The phrase, then, that Theodoret discusses is best rendered, "for the conductor," or some such. He is wise enough not to try to resolve the discrepancies in translation by reference to the original—unlike Chrysostom, for whom it proved a minefield.
2. Ps 3.2.

him (v. 1). Learn, he says, from what happened to me, how the God of all gives his attention to human affairs and listens to those who call upon him sincerely; I at any rate had a response to my prayer as soon as I made my request. Now, he put *my righteousness* instead of "my righteous prayer": it was not a mark of prudence for David to testify to his own righteousness and virtue.[3] Yet these words resemble what was spoken by God through Isaiah, "Then you will call and I shall heed you; while you are still speaking I shall say, 'See, here I am.'"[4] *In tribulation you gave me space.* The God of all is in the habit of permitting troubles to come upon his saints, but after exercise and trial he commends the athletes; in fact, in the course of their very trials he provides them with every consolation. That is what the mighty David teaches here, too: In the tribulations themselves I enjoyed your aid and consolation. This resembles what was said by the God of all to the divinely inspired Paul, "My grace is sufficient for you; for my power takes effect in weakness."[5] *Have mercy on me and hearken to my prayer.* Righteous people never have enough of prayer; instead, being in need and taking advantage of goodwill they reap the fruit of prayer and continue offering supplication, realizing as they do the benefit coming from it.

(3) *Mortals that you are, how long will you be slow of heart? Why do you love futility and search for deceit?* (v. 2). From what happened to me, O human beings, learn the regulation of all things, how he supervises human affairs and responds to those sedulously bringing their entreaties and renouncing their vain conceits. *Know that the Lord has made his holy one an object of wonder.* The Lord

---

3. Unlike Chrysostom, who was keen to uphold the place of human effort in the process of salvation, Theodoret is quick to sense a theological problem in predicating righteousness of the psalmist rather than God, and rebukes him. Modern commentators dodge the problem by opting for "vindication" (Dahood) or "salvation" (Weiser), as does a version like the NRSV, "my right."

4. Cf. Isa 58.9.

5. 2 Cor 12.9. The brief exhortation to pray that follows is a rare piece of spiritual direction from this commentator. He does not see his role in instructing his reader on the value of prayer, despite the possibilities the psalm provides, of which a preacher like Chrysostom takes advantage.

will hearken to me in my cry to him (v. 3). You see, he will not simply free me from the [892] troubles that befall me, but will also render me conspicuous and distinguished in victory; this, you see, is the meaning of *made an object of wonder.* He continues without interruption to accept my petitions. Again here he put *holy one* for the faultless person who did no wrong to his opponents but was wronged by them. Now, it was appropriate for him to call unbelievers *slow of heart* for their refusal to recognize God and their unwillingness to discern the divine plan, by comparison with those whose brains are besotted with drunkenness from the fumes rising from their cups, being forced to close their eyes.

(4) *Be angry.* This is to be treated separately, and the rest reads as follows: *and do not sin* (v. 4). Feel anger, he is saying, and impatience when you see those who oppress you unjustly living happily from day to day. But do not add evil to evil by trying to persuade the others that everything happens without rhyme or reason. In fact, you should act in an opposite way to them, calling yourselves to account at night for the sins committed by day. *Repent in bed for what you say in your heart:* since night time is free from external worries and brings peace to our thoughts, he was correct in this verse in bidding us pass in review what was said or done during the day and in obliging us to heal our wounds with the remedy of repentance.

(5) *Offer the sacrifice of righteousness, and put your hope in the Lord* (v. 5). In these words he dismisses as useless the worship according to the Law, and he obliges us to bring the offering of righteousness: the possession of righteousness is more acceptable to God than every sacrifice of a hundred or a thousand beasts—a righteousness, that is, to which is added hope in him. Since many Greeks, Jews, heretics, and holders of false ideas at times give evidence of moderation and righteousness but have no vestige of reverence for God, they reap no benefit from it. Hence the all-holy Spirit urges us through the divine David not only to offer a sacrifice of righteousness but also to put our hope in the Lord. Now, this is also the way Christ our Lord spoke to his disciples: "I am the true vine, you the branches, and my Father is the vinedresser. Every branch in me not bearing

fruit he prunes."[6] He did not simply say "not bearing fruit" but "in me not bearing fruit," that is to say, in accord with my [893] commandments, in accord with my laws, with faith in me, like some you see practicing virtue for human glory apart from confession in him.

(6) *Many say, "Who will show us good things?"* (v. 6). He is hinting at those he called *slow of heart*, fretting at the troubles that come their way and despairing of God's providence, and thus presuming to say this. *The light of your countenance, Lord, has left its mark on us; you have brought joy to my heart.* So while the former think and utter such things, we on the contrary benefit from the radiance of the knowledge of God and are bathed in your light; even in the troubles afflicting us we have sufficient consolation from our hope in you.

(7) *They grew prosperous from the fruit of their grain, wine, and oil* (v. 7). Once more he challenges those who say, *Who will show us good things?*, the kind of people who enjoy the present life and are afflicted with the vice of ingratitude. Now, the thought here is expressed incompletely: *Many say, "Who will show us good things?" They grew prosperous from the fruit of their grain and wine and oil.* And indeed, he says, those who say this enjoy every kind of fruit of the earth (in these three species, you see, vital as they are to mankind, he obviously included other good things). He thus establishes their lack of appreciation of the fact that, though actually holding in their hands God's gifts and enjoying in generous measure his blessings, they presume to say as if in receipt of nothing, *Who will show us good things?*

(8) For my part, on the contrary, enjoying your light and receiving knowledge, *In peace I shall lie down and in the same instant go to sleep because you alone, Lord, have given me grounds for hope* (v. 8). In other words, since I have dismissed all panic and disturbance of mind and have gained relief from them, and have instructed others in reading your wonderful providence in these things, I await death in the hope of resurrection. He called death *sleep* in this verse, note. Now, it was quite appropriate for him to relate hope to the thought of death after treating of

---

6. John 15.1–2, not quite corresponding to our received text.

providence. You see, many people who in this present life fall on hard times and suffer injustice at the hands of their associates come to an end of their days without gaining any relief; so mighty David teaches them not to be annoyed, for the reason that death brings with it hope, and after death the recompense will be made.[7] [896]

7. Theodoret concedes David an eschatological perspective not generally allowed him, and this without the evidence for it from Ugaritic that Dahood adduces. See *Commentary* on Ps 1, n. 19.

COMMENTARY ON PSALM 5

To the end, for the woman receiving an inheritance.
A psalm of David.

HIS IS ALSO THE WAY the others translate the title.[1] So it is clear that the divine word gives the name "heir" in general terms to the Church of God, and in particular to the soul wedded to piety. After all, you can hear Christ saying in the sacred Gospels, "Come, you that are blessed by my Father, inherit the kingdom prepared for you from the foundation of the world."[2] And the divinely inspired Paul says the same thing: "The Spirit bears witness with our spirit that we are children of God, and if children, heirs also, heirs of God and joint heirs with Christ, provided we suffer with him so that we may also be glorified with him";[3] and again, "So you are no longer a slave but a son, and if a son, also an heir of God through Christ."[4] And you can find many other such things in the divine Scripture by which we will be guided and succeed in grasping the sense.

(2) *Give ears to my words, O Lord, understand my cry. Attend to the sound of my prayer, my king and my God* (vv. 1–2). On all sides the Church of God is buffeted by many huge waves, as likewise is each soul that embraces the devout life, but each survives and breasts the billows by constantly invoking the divine aid. This in

---

1. Theodoret is having further trouble with the psalm titles, not helped here by the fact that his LXX text has made an egregious error in reading "inherit" for a Hebrew word meaning flutes (a musical direction again). Other Greek translators do the same, he informs us, probably wondering about the appropriateness of such a title, yet apparently unable to adjust the error. Unlike Chrysostom, he quickly finds a few Scriptural references by way of rationalizing, and moves on. See Introduction, section 5, for a discussion of Theodoret's own grasp of Hebrew.

2. Matt 25.34. 3. Rom 8.16–17.
4. Gal 4.7.

fact is what the inspired word also teaches, instructing us how it behooves us both to entreat and implore the God and king of all; he teaches us in the words, *Give ear to my words, O Lord, understand my cry. Attend to the sound of my prayer.* But *cry* is not to be understood as cry, nor *ear* as ear: the divine Scripture customarily speaks of the God of all in rather corporeal terms, and gives names to the divine activities from parts of the human body:[5] eyes for sight and ears for hearing, and so on in like manner. Now, he calls *cry* the earnestness of those praying and the zealous supplication of their attitude. *Give ear*, on the other hand, stands for this, "Let the words of my prayer reach your ears, listen kindly to my supplication, and carefully attend to the words of my appeal, since I know you are God and king."

(3) *Because I shall pray to you, O Lord; in the morning you will hear my voice. In the morning I shall plead my case to you, and you will take note of me* (vv. 2–3). That is, confident that you will accept my supplication, at the very break of day, shaking sleep from my eyes, surely I plead my case [897] to a king and a lord, presenting my request to you. Now, it is not the privilege of everyone to say to the God of all, *I shall plead my case to you, and you will take note of me.* Instead, it belongs to those who are emboldened, like the great Elijah, to speak from a frankness arising from their way of life, "The Lord lives, in whose sight I stand here today."[6]

(4) *Because you are not a God who wills wickedness. The evildoer will not dwell with you, nor the lawless abide before your eyes* (vv. 4–5). You receive my appeals and cast an eye on my supplication, since you forbid all lawlessness and reject completely those living in sin. After all, you loathe all those embracing a life of lawlessness. This is what she added, in fact: *You hated, O Lord, all the workers of iniquity, you will destroy all the speakers of falsehood. A man of blood and deceit the Lord loathes* (vv. 5–6). He focuses on the list of vices, highlighting everything opposed to the divine will: he not only forbids wickedness, lawlessness, lies, deceit, and homi-

---

5. As an Antiochene, Theodoret has to remind his reader of divine transcendence, and also of divine considerateness (*synkatabasis* in Chrysostom's terminology) for human limitations shown in the concrete language of the Scriptures.
6. 1 Kings 17.1.

cide, but also loathes their perpetrators, unwilling as they are to give a thought to repentance. Now, he indicates in these people at any rate those who have assailed the Church at different periods without managing to have their way, in line with the declaration to the contrary of our God and Savior himself: "The gates of Hades will not prevail against her,"[7] he says, remember, and this is what the psalm also makes clear.

(5) *But I, in the abundance of your mercy, shall enter your house; I shall bow down towards your holy temple in awe of you* (v. 7). In other words, since I enjoy your loving-kindness and am protected by your right hand, I offer you constant adoration in the temple dedicated to your glory, enveloped in awe of you as I always am. I cannot desist from this, you see, trusting as I do in your loving-kindness.[8]

(6) *Guide me in your righteousness, O Lord; because of my enemies direct my path before you* (v. 8). Some copies have "your path before me." Each has a pious meaning. I mean, if our path is directed before God, we will not experience deception; if God's path is directed before us, we will travel it and run enthusiastically towards it. Accordingly, the one receiving the inheritance asks to be guided by God's righteousness, and for her way to be directed and made trouble-free so as to travel easily. Symmachus implied that meaning: for *direct* he said "make level." Now, we hear Christ himself saying in the words of Isaiah, [900] "The uneven ground shall be made level, and the rough ground into smooth ways."[9] And in another psalm blessed David said, "A man's steps are directed by the Lord, and he will greatly delight in his way."[10] Now, the words of the one receiving the inheritance are full of humility: she asks that her way be directed, not thanks to her own righteousness, but because of her enemies' addiction to impiety and their unjust assault on her.

---

7. Matt 16.18.
8. As promised, the commentary is not verbose, and in fact amounts simply to a brief paraphrase. Under the influence of the title, the words are put into the mouth of the Church or the individual soul, not David.
9. Isa 40.4; cf. Luke 3.5, where in fact it is the Baptist who recites Isaiah's words.
10. Ps 37.23.

(7) Then she gives an exposition in detail of their wicked practices. *There is no truth in their mouths* (v. 9). They constantly sully their tongue with falsehood, she is saying. *Their heart is frivolous:* their thinking is in tune with their words, their mind in harmony with their mouth. *Their throat an open grave:* when graves are filled in they keep the stench within, but when opened they release the awful smell. These people are like that, she is saying, spewing out words redolent of utter impiety and evil smells. Now, by these words she suggests blasphemy against God and lewd and licentious speech. *They deceive with their tongues. Judge them, O God* (vv. 9–10). Veiled words are worse than frank ones: by employing deceit they hatch countless problems for their neighbors. *Let them come to grief through their own plotting; by the measure of their own impieties drive them out.* So let them be hauled before your judgment, O Lord, and let them part company with those who plot against us, and learn from experience that they weave spider's webs, and let the penalty fit the crime. *Because they have provoked you, O Lord:* they have stirred up hostilities against you, conducting a campaign against those dedicated to you.

(8) *Let all who hope in you rejoice. They will exult forever, and you will dwell in them* (v. 11). Now, this will fill with joy those who have found faith in you, and will provide them with everlasting delight: not your destroying the others but your showing providence. They are confident, you see, that you dwell and walk about within them, and render them a hallowed dwelling. *Those who love your name will boast of you, because you will bless the righteous, O Lord* (vv. 11–12). In other words, when your servants are regaled with both your blessing and your providence, those who made themselves lovers of your name [901] will glory in your providence, telling of your power. This is also what the blessed Paul says, "Let the one who boasts boast in the Lord."[11] *You crowned us as with a shield of approval.* The divine Scripture calls the favorable will of God *approval;* this is the meaning of the verse, "Lord, you approved of your land,"[12] that is, "You intend-

---

11. 1 Cor 1.31; 2 Cor 10.17; cf. Jer 9.24.
12. Ps 85.1.

ed good things for your land." And in blessed Paul, "According to the approval of his will,"[13] that is, according to his good pleasure. So here he means, "Your good pleasure and your deep affection and love for us have proved a shield protective of victory for us, and a triumphal wreath."

13. Eph 1.9.

COMMENTARY ON PSALM 6

To the end, in hymns, on the eighth. A psalm of David.

THE INSPIRED WORD calls the future condition *eighth*.[1] The present life revolves around the seven days of the week: time begins with the first day and concludes with the seventh, and then returns to the first and in the same fashion progresses to the seventh. So it was appropriate for the divine word to name the age beyond the weekly numbering *eighth*. Now, in this psalm he makes mention of death and judgment—hence his assigning this title as well: he says, *There is no one to remember you in death. In Hades will anyone confess to you?* (v. 5). That is, "The door to repentance is closed to those leaving here, and it is impossible for those who failed to take advantage of the remedy of repentance in the present life to offer to God in the next the confession of sin."[2] Now, the parable of the virgins also gives confirmation of these words: we learned from it that the foolish virgins, with their lamps extinguished, stayed outside the doors of the nuptial chamber, knocking on the doors, but sent

---

1. Even had Theodoret been able to see the title as a liturgical rubric, he might still have had difficulties with the force of this term, which (as also in Ps 12) the LXX correctly translates from the Hebrew. Some commentators see it as a musical direction about octaves on the basis of its occurrence also in 1 Chron 15.21, a book in which liturgical music is given prominence. Mowinckel, on the other hand, denies that the music of the Israelites was based on an octave scale, preferring to note that the number eight plays an important part in many ritual acts. Unaware of all this, Theodoret gives the numeral an anagogical sense.

2. The reasoning here is somewhat elliptical. Apparently aware that in Church practice this psalm was the first of the seven Penitential Psalms, Theodoret reinforces his interpretation of the title from the reference to death in v. 5 and the consequent urgency of repentance in this life. He develops the thought when he arrives at comment on v. 5.

away and excluded from the room. He said to them, in fact, "Go away, I do not know you."[3]

(2) This is the reason, to be sure, that blessed David, after that twofold sin, offers this supplication to God, begging to be healed, because there is no longer any opportunity for the remedy of repentance in the next life. *Lord, do not censure me in your anger, nor discipline me in your wrath* (v. 1). He does not beg not to be censured, but not to be censured in anger, nor does he plead not to be disciplined, but not to suffer it with wrath. Discipline me like a father, he asks, not like a judge; like a physician, not like a torturer. Do not fit the punishment to the crime; instead, temper justice with loving-kindness.

(3) [904] *Have mercy on me, O Lord, because I am weak* (v. 2). Such a verse is appropriate to sinners: under the influence of weakness sin overcomes. After all, if the reasoning faculty within us were not weak, the passions would not rebel; to put it another way, provided the charioteer is firm, and steers and controls the horses skillfully, there is no occasion for bucking. *Heal me, Lord, for my bones are quivering, and my soul is severely shaken* (vv. 2–3). Here he calls reasoning *bones:* since bones are naturally rather dense and support the body, speaking figuratively he gave the name *bones* to reasoning, by which the living being is steered. Disturbance in that faculty, he is saying, ruffled and shook me. Hence I beg to be allowed to enjoy your loving-kindness so as to receive healing through it.

(4) *You, O Lord—how long? Turn, O Lord, rescue my soul, save me for your mercy's sake* (vv. 3–4). The phrase *how long* he does not say by way of censure; rather, being in pain he begs him to be quick with his help. Now, it was appropriate for him to add *for your mercy's sake:* I am not trusting in myself, he is saying, nor do I attribute your help to my own righteousness; instead, I beg to be granted it on account of your mercy. And the phrase *Turn, O Lord* stands for, "Heed me and do not turn your face away from me," by analogy with those who are angry and turn away, unwilling to look at the fallen.

(5) *There is no one to remember you in death. In Hades will anyone*

---

3. Cf. Matt 25.12, not quite the groom's words.

confess to you? (v. 5). For this reason I beg the privilege of enjoying the cure in the present life, since I know that no cure will then be granted those departing this life with wounds, as there is no longer any room for repentance. This was exceptionally sound thinking on the part of the divine David: it is not in death but in life that one recalls God. Likewise, confession and reform do not come to the departed in Hades: God confined life and action to this life; there, however, he conducts an evaluation of performance. And in any case this is proper to the *eighth* day,[4] giving no longer opportunity for preparation by good or bad deeds to those who have arrived at it; instead, whatever works you have sown for yourself you will have occasion to reap. For this reason he obliges you to practice repentance here, there being no practice of this kind of effort in Hades. He says, in fact, "Since the opportunity coming to me for repentance was lengthy, I am afraid death may precede your mercy, there being no room for confession there—hence [905] my request for you to be quick with your mercy." Then he instructs the listener that along with God's loving-kindness our effort is required, too: whether we plead weakness or confusion or God's goodness without contributing what is ours, it is of no benefit to us.[5]

(6) *I grew weary with my groaning, each night I shall drench my bed, flood my bedding with my tears* (v. 6). I am aware of my many and serious failings, yet I continue weeping constantly, deploring the crimes of my own doing. To be sure, the bed that was polluted by my lawlessness I ceaselessly douse with my tears, endeavoring to cleanse it with them; even should I win forgiveness, I shall not cease doing it—such is the force of *each night I shall drench my bed, and flood it.*

---

4. See note 1 for Theodoret's interpretation of this term in the psalm title. One is still uncertain whether the eschatology involved in commentary on these verses is thought by the commentator to be appropriate to the psalmist's listeners or to Christian readers.
5. The relation between grace and human effort became a matter of intense debate in Theodoret's lifetime, especially with the teaching of Pelagius and his disciples. While J. N. D. Kelly admits "an intensified emphasis on individualism" in Antiochene theologians, he defends their attempt to find a balance, such as Theodoret exemplifies here. J. N. D. Kelly, *Early Christian Doctrines,* 373.

(7) *My eye was affected by anger* (v. 7): my very vision was blurred on account of your wrath, Lord. He called the mind *eye* here, note, and hence referred to it in the singular. *I grew old in the midst of all my foes:* the scorn of my foes, he is saying, is worse than anything, it consumes and wastes me, and brings on premature old age.[6]

(8) *Depart from me, all you evildoers, because the Lord has hearkened to the sound of my weeping. The Lord heard my request, the Lord accepted my prayer* (vv. 8–9). Let those who do not see their own iniquities and yet ridicule my failings mock me no longer. I won divine favor, in fact, and am confident that through my entreaties he will overlook my faults and make me a beneficiary of his pardon. *Let all my foes be ashamed and confused; let them be thrown back and quickly put to extreme shame* (v. 10). When you know this, then, cease to fling taunts at me, and rather call your own iniquities to mind, and be filled with shame, alarm, and confusion. The divine judgment, remember, is just and awesome.

---

6. Commentary, we have noted, can be of the briefest.

COMMENTARY ON PSALM 7

A psalm of David, which he sang to the Lord on the words of Hushai, the Benjaminite.

IN FLIGHT FROM HIS NEFARIOUS SON the parricide, the blessed David found an ally in Hushai, who persuaded Absalom not to pursue his father immediately, contrary to the advice of Ahithophel, and instead to get all the people on the move [908] and then to deploy them against his parent. Frustrated and extremely troubled, therefore, for the reason that the advice of Hushai was found preferable, Ahithophel turned to suicide and met his end by hanging.[1] The divine David, in any case, took the opportunity provided by the delay in attack to flee, and gained salvation. This psalm, at any rate, like a kind of hymn or prayer, he offers to God his savior, and provides instruction as well, urging those wronged by anyone to have hope in God and await help from on high, and on the other hand deterring those doing wrong by mention of the just judgment of God.

(2) *O Lord my God, in you have I hoped, save me from all my pursuers and rescue me. Do not snatch my soul like a lion, with no one to redeem me or save me* (vv. 1–2). Trusting in no human help, he is saying, and instead holding fast by myself to hope in you alone, my prayer is to win your consideration. I am afraid that my adversaries will like a wild beast assail me, and finding me bereft of your providence utterly destroy me.

(3) *O Lord my God, if I have done this* (v. 3). Then he teaches in a clearer manner what he means: *If there is wrong on my hands.*

---

1. Cf. 2 Sam 16–17. Again succinctly, and without upbraiding his readers for lack of acquaintance with sacred history, as Chrysostom does, or also like him embroidering the narrative in a manner at odds with the Deuteronomic historian, Theodoret presents a neat summary of the relevant chapters. He is not interested in entertainment.

And to show what kind of wrong he means here, he adds at once, *If I have repaid evil for evil, let me then end up empty handed before my foes. Let the foe then hunt down my soul and seize it, trample my life into the ground and bury my glory in the dust* (vv. 4–5). There are many species of virtue, not only temperance and prudence but also fortitude and justice.[2] So at this place he does not give evidence of the pinnacle of virtue in his own case; rather, that although he scarcely wronged his enemies, he suffers unjust banishment on their account. Not only was I not the first to offend, he says, but at no stage did I presume to take vengeance on those who wronged me: though often having Saul in my power, I did not exact penalty for his unjust hostility. For this very reason, Lord, I beg you, in your clear understanding of the whole story, to give a fair judgment in my favor, and if ever I commit anything of the like, to deprive me of your care (he says, note, *Let me then end up empty handed before my foes*), and to subject me to those hostile to me so as to deprive me not only of the glory and kingship you gave me but even hand me over to a foolish death. This is what he meant, after all, in saying, *Let him bury my glory in the dust.*

(4) *Rise up, O Lord, in your wrath; be exalted in the boundaries of my foes* (v. 6). While Symmachus read [909] "in fury" and Theodotion, "in anger," Aquila at any rate read by contrast "in haste."[3] So he begs the just Judge no longer to employ his longsuffering but his just verdict, and impose punishment on the wrongdoers. He used, *Rise up,* instead of, "Show no further longsuffering"; it is like, "Rouse yourself! Why do you sleep, Lord?"[4] and, "Rise up, Lord, help us":[5] it is time not for loving-kindness but for righteous anger. Accordingly, impose a boundary on my foes, curtailing their lawless forays. *Awake, O Lord my God, in the*

---

2. As from a moral textbook, he reels off the four cardinal virtues.

3. It is surely this mechanical, unevaluative, inconsistent citing of variant translations that leads to the suggestion that not the commentator but a later copyist has added the inconsequential datum. Or does Aquila's accent on haste (in a rare term not known to the LXX) support his comment about the expiration of long suffering? See Introduction, section 3.

4. Ps 44.23.

5. Cf. Ps 3.7, where Theodoret read instead "save me." His recall is less than perfect (for an Antiochene).

command you gave: You gave orders for the wronged to be assisted; so what you bade be done for the others, O Lord, do now and give me a share in your turning the scales.

(5) *An assembly of peoples will surround you; over it return on high* (v. 7): once this providence of yours has become clear, everyone will offer their hymns to you and will address you as God Most High insofar as you survey all things and for wrongdoers you make the punishment fit the crime. *Return on high* means, "Being by nature Most High yet unknown to many people, show what you are through care for the wronged." Then, in inspired fashion: *The Lord will judge peoples:* he judges not only my case but also that of the whole human race. *Judge me, O Lord, according to my righteousness and according to the innocence within me* (v. 8). In these words the divine David has not left a testimony to his own righteousness: we hear him protesting the opposite, "Because I acknowledge my lawlessness, and my sin is always before me"; and, "I said, 'I shall declare my lawlessness against myself to the Lord,'"[6] but he calls it justice in the matter before us. I committed no wrong, in fact, he is saying, against Absalom, or Ahithophel, or those arrayed in battle with them against me. So I beg to be judged in the light of this righteousness and innocence, and not in the light of the faults previously committed by me. I ask for a judgment on these current grounds, and not for a payment of penalty at this time for other sins.

(6) *Let the wickedness of sinners be brought to an end, and you will direct the righteous* (v. 9). For *brought to an end* Symmachus put "completed." If the wickedness of those addicted to vice is shown to be futile, the disciples of virtue will more zealously make its way their choice. *God who tests hearts and entrails.* [912] Help for me is justified from the God who saves the right of heart. He uses the term *entrails* here for thoughts: since the entrails arouse the appetites of the abdomen, and from there our thoughts in turn give rise to desires, in figurative fashion he called the thoughts *entrails*.[7] So the one who understands the hidden thoughts of people's mind, he is saying, will provide me

6. Ps 51.3; 32.5.
7. As befits one who in the preface decried as one extreme in previous commentaries a proclivity to allegorical interpretation of the Psalms,

with help that is called for inasmuch as doing this is his custom; after all, he invariably avenges the wronged. From this point he proceeds to terrify those addicted to wickedness by giving a glimpse of the punishments due, and he foretells the fate of Ahithophel. *God is a righteous judge, strong and long-suffering, who does not give free rein to his wrath every day.* Instead, he also shows loving-kindness, by which he bears people's faults for a longer time. For whenever he sees people not reaping profit from it, he gives them further opportunity with the addition of threats, putting the punishments off; but if they scorn the opportunity and persist in sinning, he immediately brings on their ruin in keeping with justice. What this involves he indicated through what follows.

(7) *If they are not converted, he will wield his sword; he bent his bow, and had it at the ready. With it he prepared means of death* (vv. 12–13). These are not words of punishment, note, but of threat: he said *wield*, not inflict; *bent his bow*, not fired the arrow. And to teach us against whom he will fire the arrows, he immediately attached the words, *He made his arrows into flaming shafts*, that is, those taking combustible material of sin, building with wood, hay, and stubble, as the divine Apostle says,[8] will be struck with these fiery arrows.

(8) *Lo, he gave birth to iniquity* (v. 14). Ahithophel, author of that wicked attitude, *conceived distress and brought forth lawlessness*: leaving no extremity of wickedness untried, he armed the lawless son against the father who had done him no wrong.[9] *He dug a pit, excavated it, and fell into the depths he had made. His trouble will come back on his own head, and on his own crown will descend his wrongdoing* (vv. 15–16). He will be caught in his own snares, he is saying, from his own efforts receive his just deserts, and be snared in the nets he laid for catching others.

Theodoret holds to a literal—but not literalist—interpretation and so is able to appreciate the figurative language employed by the psalmist.

8. 1 Cor 3.12–15.

9. Though that other extreme in interpretation that he wishes to avoid is excessive attachment to Jewish history such that the Psalms are reduced to "historical narratives," Theodoret evidently feels that this psalm's title allows him to apply individual verses to this sorry incident in David's life.

(9) *I shall confess to the Lord in keeping with his righteousness, and sing to the name of the Lord* [913] *Most High* (v. 17). I have won God's wonderful providence, and shall sing praise of his beneficence constantly, recounting the justice of his judgment.[10]

---

10. Though at the opening Theodoret claimed the psalm had something to say to anyone else wronged besides the psalmist in the precise historical situation, far from taking this opportunity to moralize, he has hardly applied it to the lives of his readers, and closes abruptly where we might have expected a moral peroration.

COMMENTARY ON PSALM 8

To the end, on the winepresses. A psalm of David.

OU NEED TO RECALL that in every psalm where the Septuagint put "To the end" Aquila and Theodotion gave the rendering "to the author of victory" and Symmachus, "triumphal." Accordingly this triumphal psalm is offered to God, the author of victory, who brought about the undoing of the hostile and avenging devil, and at the end liberated human beings from his tyranny.[1] It is to the churches, however, that he gives the name "winepresses,"[2] since the Lord is called a vine as well: he said in the sacred Gospels, "I am the true vine."[3] Now, by harvesting this vine the believers make the mystical wine. Yet this represents in particular an accusation against the Jews' infidelity: they had heard of a number of winepresses, and knew clearly that one particular winepress was cited—or, rather, not a winepress but a wine vat, "He dug a wine vat in it, and waited for it to yield grapes, but it yielded thorns,"[4] Scripture says.

---

1. The psalm titles, which Theodoret does not recognize as rubrics, are giving him continuing trouble. With more than a casual citing this time of variant versions of the first phrase, he manages an improbable justification of both his own (the Septuagint's) and theirs.

2. He is then faced with the problem of the second phrase; even modern commentators admit ignorance of the force of Gittith in the original, possibly referring to a musical instrument. The ancients, however, with their poor grasp of Hebrew (including Theodoret, *pace* Rondeau), saw the word Gat, "winepress," in this term—which resulted in further rationalizing. He does not really explain what he means in regard to the churches being called winepresses.

3. John 15.1, encouraging Theodoret to hazard a brief allegorical gloss before taking a different tack. In fact, he seems to be threshing about to get a clue from this puzzling title as to the direction he should take in his commentary.

4. In this quandary, he at least lights on an occurrence of "wine vat" in Isa 5.2. But he soon abandons this tack, too.

They refused to admit that ancient ways had come to an end and the grace of the New Testament had come into view, summoning everyone to salvation. For this very reason, no longer in accordance with the ancient Law do the priests press the fruit of people on one altar; instead, throughout the whole earth and sea altars are erected in numbers beyond counting. The eighty-third psalm teaches this more clearly. Also bearing a title about winepresses, it made reference to many altars: "How lovely are your dwelling places, Lord of hosts! My soul longs and faints for the courts of the Lord"; and shortly after, "Your altars, Lord of hosts."[5] Now, the eighth psalm, entitled "On the winepresses," foretells salvation of the world and teaches God's care for people, and predicts the Incarnation of the Only-begotten.[6]

(2) *O Lord our Lord, how wonderful is your name in all the earth! Because your magnificence is exalted above the heavens* (v. 1). The word *how* in this case does not indicate comparison but extent:[7] Your name, O Lord, is glorified in song by all extraordinarily, he is saying, and they all name you as maker of heaven and earth. The phrase, you see, *your magnificence is exalted* [916] *above the heavens*, suggests this: Everyone knew that you are in control of heaven and earth and all things; he always enjoyed magnificence, of course, but it was not always known to human beings. The blessed Habakkuk also foretells such things: after saying, "God will come from Teman, and the Holy One from the mountain of shadows," he added, "his virtue covered the heavens, and the earth was full of his praise."[8] And when he appeared in person to Jacob, he replied to his enquiry about his name, "Why do you ask my name? It is awesome."[9]

(3) *Out of the mouth of babes and sucklings you have perfected*

5. Ps 84.1–2, 3.
6. So finally, clutching at these straws, Theodoret decides to give the psalm a Christological bent, and sees it dealing with the Incarnation (ἐνανθρώπησις).
7. An Antiochene commentator like Theodoret or Chrysostom may be misled by psalm titles and his own ignorance of Hebrew, but he can always come back to his staple skill, seizing on minute details of the language.
8. Hab 3.3.
9. Cf. Gen 32.29, loosely recalled and expanded, and not clearly relevant—but at least the commentator is doing more than paraphrase.

praise on account of your enemies so as to destroy enemy and avenger (v. 2). Now, what most of all demonstrated your power was that through men who failed to master human wisdom and who give the impression of the simplicity of unweaned children you destroyed that most wicked of tyrants. He is always hostile to you, his God, and deceives human beings on account of the hostility to you, and again like some avenger he exacts penalty for his deception of them. Thus, after causing Ahithophel to say those dreadful things, he dispatched him to a death at his own hand;[10] likewise, after supplying Judas with the means of betrayal, he gave him the noose as a reward for his obedience.[11] And it is possible to learn the truth of the prophecy from history: in the sacred Gospels, to the Jews annoyed at the children's carrying olive branches ahead of him and saying, "Hosanna in the highest! Blessed is he who comes in the name of the Lord," Christ the Lord replied, "Did you not read, 'Out of the mouths of babes and sucklings you have perfected praise'?"[12] So even those children condemn the ungrateful people of the Jews for being enemy and avenger like the devil: they always transgress the divine Law and behave at variance with God's directions; and further, on the pretext of upholding the cause of the Lawgiver, they crucified Christ the Lord, branding him an enemy of God and transgressor of the Law.

(4) *Because I shall see the heavens, the works of your fingers, moon and stars which you have put in place* (v. 3): even the elements are sufficient, he is saying, to demonstrate your magnificence, O Lord—sky, earth, moon, sun, both the order and the beauty of them. Providence, which reaches to lowly [917] human beings, however, proclaims your ineffable loving-kindness to a greater degree. *What is man, after all, for you to be mindful of him, or the son of man for you to have regard for him?* (v. 4). Now, this has to do not with creation but with providence: he did not say "for you to form" but *for you to be mindful and have regard*. Elsewhere, on the

10. Cf. 2 Sam 17.23.
11. Cf. Matt 27.5.
12. A miscellany of Matt 21.9; Luke 19.38; Matt 21.16. Theodoret's recall of Scripture, we have noticed, is less than precise—especially for a desk theologian.

other hand, he deplores with greater clarity the lowliness of our nature: "Man was made like futility, his days pass away like a shadow";[13] and again, "Man is like grass, his days like a flower of the field blossoming: a wind passed over him and he will not survive, nor will a trace of him be recognized any longer."[14] And you can find countless other such remarks in the divine Scripture to restrain human conceit. In this verse, accordingly, the inspired word expresses loud amazement, *What is man for you to be mindful of him, or the son of man for you to have regard for him?* After all, it is not simply that you brought them into being, but that you presented them with a privileged existence, you continue to keep them in mind and keep an eye on those badly disposed.

(5) *You have brought him a little lower than the angels* (v. 5). Here he adverted to the sentence following the Fall: by his mortality he was brought lower than the angels. *With glory and honor you crowned him, and appointed him over the works of your hands* (v. 6). Now, it was after the Incarnation of our God and Savior that our nature received these privileges: "By grace it is, in fact, that you have been saved," as the divine Apostle says, "and he raised us up with him and seated us in the heavenly places through Christ Jesus."[15]

(6) *You put all things under his feet, sheep and all cattle, and also the beasts of the field, birds of the air and fish of the sea, the creatures that travel the ways of the seas* (vv. 6–8). And this is a precise demonstration of your loving-kindness and power, he is saying, imbuing the lowly nature of human beings with wisdom so that they might have control over not only the land creatures but those that fly and that swim and that do both, use their skills to hunt those in the heights and in the depths, and keep under control those that pass through the air and those hidden in the water.

(7) You have therefore regaled all human beings with a common lordship over these creatures. But when the divine Word assumed our human first-fruits, declared it his own temple, named it his own flesh, and achieved the ineffable union, he

---

13. Ps 144.4.
15. Eph 2.5–6.

14. Ps 103.15–16.

took his seat above every principality, authority, [920] and domination, and every name which is named, not only in this age but in the age to come; he put everything under his feet, not only sheep and all cattle but all creation, visible and invisible. The divine Apostle witnesses to this in his explicit cry, "But we see Jesus, who was made a little lower than the angels, crowned with glory and honor on account of the suffering of death"; and a little above, he says, "putting all things under his feet";[16] and in the letter to the Corinthians, "But when it says, 'All things are put in subjection,' it is clear that this does not include the one who put all things in subjection to him."[17] Uncreated nature alone, you see, is separate from this subjection as something free. The nature, which receives existence from it, however, is subject whatever it be—visible or invisible—to Christ the Lord, both as God and as man. Such is the honor human nature received from the God of all. Hence, as a conclusion he used the same verse as at the beginning: *O Lord our Lord, how wonderful is your name in all the earth!*

16. Heb 2.9, 2.8.
17. 1 Cor 15.27.

COMMENTARY ON PSALM 9[1]

To the end, on the son's secrets. A psalm of David.

HILE SYMMACHUS READ "a triumphal ode on the son's death," Aquila read "to the author of victory on the son's youth," and Theodotion, "on the son's prime." By being in agreement, then, in making mention of the son, all of them teach us that this psalm also contains a prophecy of Christ the Lord's victory over death: having bravely and vigorously conquered sin without giving death any occasion for capture, he brought to an end its dominion.[2] Now, the Septuagint called this mystery *secret* since it escaped the notice of everyone including the apostles themselves.[3] The evangelist is witness to this frequent statement of the Lord to them, "See, we are going up to Jerusalem, and the Son of Man will be handed over to be crucified, and they will kill him, and on the third day he will rise"; and the evangelist added, "And this was hidden from their eyes."[4] Hence blessed Paul also calls out, "We speak of God's wis-

---

1. The long psalm which the LXX retains as one, our (Masoretic) Hebrew text has divided, in defiance of its original alphabetic structure.

2. This time, like Chrysostom on this psalm, Theodoret seems deliberate in citing the ancient variants, and in so doing reveals again his uncertainty about its relation to the original. Modern commentators regard Muth Labben in the title as a technical term, perhaps a cue to the melody from a song beginning thus, as occurs with other phrases. The ancients, on the other hand, practiced popular etymology on it, coming up with references to death, secrets, and son, and having to find corresponding elements in the body of the psalm.

3. The two words, despite popular English usage and some unfortunate translations of the Bible, are not synonymous: for Paul the mystery of Christ is God's whole plan (*oikonomia* being close to it in meaning), at the summit of which comes the death and Resurrection of Jesus—a design found weak and foolish by some, and in fact not clear until the New Testament. See note 12 on *Commentary* on Ps 22.

4. A precis of Luke 18.31–34.

dom, hidden in mystery, which none of the rulers of this age understood; had they known it, after all, they would not have crucified the Lord of glory."[5] [921] And again, "the mystery hidden for ages and generations."[6] It was proper, therefore, for the Septuagint to call the Son's death a *secret.*

(2) *I shall confess to you, O Lord, with all my heart, I shall recount all your marvels. I shall rejoice and be glad in you, I shall sing to your name, O Most High* (vv. 1–2). It is characteristic of the perfect to dedicate their whole heart to God and to consecrate their whole mind to him. "You shall love the Lord your God with your whole heart," Scripture says, "with your whole soul, with your whole strength, and with your whole mind."[7] Those who divide their thoughts between mammon and God, between Christ and gold, between the present and the future life, cannot truthfully say, *I shall confess to you, O Lord, with all my heart.* The inspired author, however, foresees what is to come with the eyes of a prophet, and does not only confess with his whole heart but also recounts all his marvels. He makes the listeners sharers in the hymn singing, and wishes only to sing the praise of his benefactor and to have as the basis of his satisfaction not wealth or influence, not bodily health or strength, but the remembrance of God. *I shall rejoice and be glad in you,* he says, note. In similar terms in another place, too: "I remembered God, and was overjoyed";[8] and elsewhere, "Rejoice in the Lord, and be glad, you righteous ones";[9] and again, "Let the hearts of those seeking the Lord rejoice."[10]

(3) *When my enemies turn backwards, they will lose their strength and vanish from your sight* (v. 3). Symmachus translated it this way: "I shall sing to your name, O Most High, as my enemies are turned backwards, stumble and vanish from your sight." In oth-

---

5. 1 Cor 2.7–8, telescoped, not without some damage to the syntax. For the Pauline corpus "wisdom" is another synonym for "mystery," along with words like purpose, will, plan (cf. Eph 1.1–10). *Pace* Theodoret, secrecy is not the keynote of the term in Paul's thinking. (In the plural, the term has a different sense, of the rites of pagan religions, which Theodoret employs below on v. 5.)

6. Col 1.26.
7. Luke 10.27; cf. Deut 6.5.
8. Ps 77.3 [LXX].
9. Ps 32.11.
10. Ps 105.3.

er words, beholding my opponents worsted, put to flight, then captured and suffering complete overthrow, I shall sound your praises and continue singing of your favors. Now, it is in regard to human nature that the inspired author is going into this detail, for the reason that he has been freed from the devil and has received liberty, thanks to divine grace. This psalm, in fact, is not recited by the Savior in person, as some suspected, but rather with him in mind as benefactor of the benefits received, as the words themselves teach.

(4) *Because you were responsible for my judgment being fair* (v. 4). By what means? *Seated on your throne as the righteous judge.* What verdict did he give? [924] *You rebuked the nations, and the godless perished; you cancelled his name forever and ever* (v. 5). You could not bring yourself, he is saying, to ignore any longer human nature reduced to such evil servitude by the harsh tyrant; instead, like some judge seated on a lofty throne and an awesome tribunal you inflicted such an awful punishment on him that his memory was consigned to utter oblivion. Now, this part at any rate, *You rebuked the nations, and the godless perished,* has this sense: Through the sacred apostles and the heralds of truth after them you offered to the nations the divine teachings, and when they received them and were rid of error, the godless perished, deprived of people to worship him in ignorance. Thus Barnabas and Paul upbraided the people of Lycaonia attempting to offer sacrifice, shouting at them, "What are you fellows doing? We are human, just like you, converting you to God away from these futile practices."[11] In similar terms blessed Paul upbraided the Galatians: "O foolish Galatians! Who has bewitched you? It was before your eyes that Jesus Christ was publicly exhibited on the cross."[12] Likewise the Corinthians: "It is actually reported that there is sexual immorality among you, and of such a kind as is not recorded even amongst the nations."[13] So he rebuked the nations, and the godless perished, and his name was can-

11. Acts 14.15, omitting an important phrase.
12. Gal 3.1.
13. 1 Cor 5.1. Despite the length of this psalm in its undivided form, Theodoret is developing a relish for commentary lacking in earlier psalms, the amount of Scriptural documentation being one index of this.

celled forever and ever. The godless rites were completely extinguished, in fact, and consigned to utter oblivion, with the result that no one alive today knows the mysteries of godlessness.

(5) *The enemy's swords failed utterly, and you destroyed cities* (v. 6). In other words, he was stripped of his own weapons, having no supporters of his godlessness; instead, those who appointed themselves his instruments have now changed sides and taken up the fight against him. With the overthrow of godlessness practiced in them in former times, the cities took on the building up of true religion; it would have been impossible for them to develop true religion had not they overthrown godlessness first. This is what the divine Apostle also said, "The grace of God has appeared bringing salvation to all, teaching us to renounce godlessness and worldly lusts, and live with self-control and godliness in this life,"[14] and so on. Likewise, each person is not risen with Christ before accepting a share in his death; hence the divine Paul also says, "For if we have been united with him by [925] a likeness of his death, we shall certainly be united with him by a likeness of his Resurrection"; and again, "If we died with him, we shall also live with him."[15] This is the way he also overthrew godlessness of his enemies and built up true religion.

(6) *The memory of them has disappeared resoundingly, and the Lord abides forever* (vv. 6–7). That person, he is saying, suffered a terrible end obvious to all and extremely notorious; that is what *resoundingly* means, after all, by analogy with the collapse of houses in some earthquake, creating an awful din. Our God and Lord, on the other hand, he is saying, enjoys everlasting power and his kingdom is indestructible. *He established his throne in judgment; he will judge the world in righteousness, he will judge peoples in rectitude* (vv. 7–8): not only did he demonstrate his peculiar power in the present life, but even in the life to come he will show his fearsome judgment, dispensing justice to everyone and rendering to each their due.

(7) *The Lord became a refuge for the needy, a help at the right time, in tribulations* (v. 9). The phrase *at the right time* Aquila rendered

---

14. Cf. Titus 2.11–12.
15. Rom 6.5, 6.8.

as "in time" and Symmachus, "opportunely." The phrase teaches us, however, that he concerned himself with our salvation at the appropriate time: he calls human nature *needy* on account of the great poverty that is lawlessness. Blessed Paul teaches us the appropriateness of this moment: "When we were infants, you see," he says, "we were enslaved to the elemental spirits of the universe; but when the fullness of time arrived, God sent his Son, born of a woman, born under the Law, to redeem those under the Law so that we might receive adoption as children."[16] *Let those who know your name hope in you because you did not forsake those seeking you, O Lord* (v. 10). For *hope* Aquila and Symmachus said "will trust," using the indicative instead of the imperative. In other words, once this salvation is won by you, he is saying, those learning that you are creator and God will place their hope in you.

(8) *Sing to the Lord dwelling in Sion* (v. 11). The inspired author said this according to the ancient belief of the Jews, whereas we have learned on the contrary from the apostolic teaching that it is a heavenly Sion: "You have come to Mount Sion," Scripture says, "and to the city of the living God, the heavenly Jerusalem."[17] *Announce his exploits among the nations.* [928] For *exploits* Symmachus said "devices" and Aquila, "alterations";[18] in fact, a drastic alteration of circumstances took place in reality: ancient enemies became friends, those distant became close, slaves became sons, those ignorant became knowledgeable, those in darkness came to be in light, the dead in hope of life, the poor became heirs of the kingdom of heaven, Jews came to be far away and Gentiles close at hand, sons became dogs, dogs sons. In short, the Savior's devices took on a divine seemliness: the gift of immortality was given through mortality, life through death, honor through dishonor, blessing through curse, salvation through a cross—these are the devices, these the exploits of

---

16. Gal 4.3–5.
17. Heb 12.22.
18. Theodoret in these verses is briefly adverting to the alternative versions, not just mechanically, but as preferable to his LXX, and he proceeds to comment on and develop them—irrespective of what the Hebrew original may imply.

our God.[19] *Because he who looks for blood remembered them, he did not forget the cry of the poor* (v. 12): the one who observes everything and seeks out precisely what has happened, he is saying, saw the slaughter committed by the devil through deceiving human beings, and went to the aid of the wronged. This is the meaning, in fact, of *he did not forget the cry of the poor:* by *cry* here he means not prayer or petition but the hardship coming from sin, the cause also of untimely deaths, laments, and disasters.

(9) *Have mercy on me, O Lord, see my humiliation by my foes* (v. 13): this was the kind of cry of lament and wailing, as though containing some petition about the troubles besetting him. *You who lift me up from the gates of death so that I may sing all your praises* (vv. 13–14). This, he is saying, is the summit of good things, freedom from destruction, an end of death; enjoying it we shall ever sing of your favors. *In the gates of the daughter of Sion we shall rejoice in your salvation.* He calls the heavenly city *Sion* as blessed Paul taught; by its *gates* he refers to the churches everywhere on earth, through which the believers enter it. So let us rejoice in them, he says, dancing in the hope of resurrection, and celebrating the provider of these good things.

(10) After mentioning the end of death, he rightly added, *Nations are stuck fast in the ruin they made, their foot caught in the snare they hid. By making judgments the Lord is known; by the works of his hands the sinner is caught* (vv. 15–16). He calls *nations* here [929] the column of demons: by devising the saving cross they fell from their tyrannical rule: *their foot was caught in the snare they hid,* and *by the works of his hands the sinner is caught.* Now, if the preceding words are understood of the unbelieving nations that did away with the triumphant apostles and martyrs, this too is the way we shall find the truth of the inspired composition: it was through their murder, to be sure, that the proclamation of godliness was confirmed, and by dying they gave life to a greater number than they caught in their lifetime. *By the works of his hands the sinner is caught,* and *by making his judgments the Lord is known,* that is, by managing wisely and righteously.

---

19. The greater degree of engagement with the material Theodoret is showing, as we remarked in note 13 above, is even manifesting itself in rhetorical patterns.

(11) *Let the sinners be sent off into Hades, all the nations who give no thought to God. Because the poor will not be forgotten in the end, the perseverance of the needy will not be lost forever* (vv. 17–18). The former, he is saying, lacking faith in the divine message, will be brought down to Hades as quickly as possible and consigned to death, nor will they inflict a chance injury on those pursued by them: *the perseverance of the needy will not be lost forever,* because "the one persevering to the end will be saved"[20] and "Blessed are the poor in spirit, because theirs is the kingdom of heaven."[21]

(12) Then, seeing from afar with prophetic eyes the heralds of godliness driven off by the ungodly, he says in the manner of a suppliant, *Rise up, O Lord, do not let man prevail; may the nations be judged in your presence. Appoint them a lawgiver, O Lord, let the nations know they are human* (vv. 19–20). It would be right for anyone to ask Jews what kind of lawgiver the inspired author here asks to be given. The mighty Moses, after all, who in the dim and distant past had been appointed instrument of divine lawgiving, reached the end of his life, and "no other lawgiver has arisen since him."[22] Now, if no other lawgiver has come to light, appointed either for the Jews or for the nations, it remains to be understood that Christ the Lord has been declared Lawgiver for nations, who cries out in the sacred Gospels, "It was said to the ancients, 'You shall not kill,' but I say to you, 'Anyone angry with his brother without reason will be liable to judgment.' It was said to the ancients, 'You shall not commit adultery,' but I say to you, 'The one looking after a woman to lust after her has already committed adultery with her in his heart' ";[23] and all the rest likewise. So the inspired author pleads for this man's lawgiving to be provided for [932] the nations so that they may abandon the way of life of savages and realize they are human beings. "Man," the inspired author says, "though in a position of honor, did not realize it; he was compared with mindless cattle and became like them."[24] Hence he says here, too, *Let the nations know they are human.*

20. Matt 10.22.
21. Matt 5.3.
22. Cf. Deut 34.10.
23. Cf. Matt 5.21–22, 5.27–28.
24. Cf. Ps 49.12.

COMMENTARY ON PSALM 10[1]
(IN THE HEBREW)

WHY, O LORD, DO YOU STAND far off? *Why do you look down on us in good times and bad? When the godless acts disdainfully, the poor person is inflamed; they are caught up in the schemes they have devised* (vv. 1–2). You, O Lord, seem to stand at a distance and not to notice human affairs, not assisting the wronged, whereas from discouragement, as if from some fire, the wronged are consumed on seeing the arrogance of the wrongdoers. Now, most appropriately did he apply *inflamed* to the discouraged: they are like people set on fire, and they utter a groan from their mouth like a sort of smoke. And harm will come to them from their discouragement, he is saying, since instead of putting their minds to seemly thinking they are in two minds about your providence—this is what is meant by *they are caught up in the schemes they have devised*.[2] He instructs us in the reason for this by adding, *Because the wicked is confirmed in the desires of his heart, and the wrongdoer is praised* (v. 3): despite committing countless crimes, they win praise from their cronies.

(2) The *sinner provoked the Lord in the intensity of his wrath* (v. 4). This part is to be kept separate, and then the added phrase, *He will not seek it out*, as if to say, *He provoked the Lord by saying, "He will not seek it out."* That is, motivated by frenzy and rage, as if no one was watching, he proceeds to every kind of lawlessness, not believing the judge will seek out their crimes. Then he says it

---

1. Our Hebrew text at this point interrupts the long psalm which the LXX (more correctly) treats as one to begin a new psalm; and it is probably more helpful to conform our numbering to the Hebrew and modern versions. Theodoret, of course, gives no indication of the break.

2. This clause in the Hebrew and modern versions seems to refer rather to the godless. Other references also seem to be applied differently by the commentator on his text.

more clearly: *God is not before his eyes.* The unbeliever and the sinner never keeps God before his eyes; instead, each day and at every moment he soils and sullies his paths, not believing there is any judgment. Well, what is the reason for this? *His ways are profaned at every moment. Your judgments are kept from his view* (v. 5): he completely despises your laws; he spends all his time in lawlessness. The unbeliever, in fact, belittles and vilifies the commands of God. *He will gain dominion over all his foes.* Yet even in doing such things he will prosper.

(3) Then he depicts the extraordinary degree of his conceit: [933] *He said in his heart, in fact, "I shall not be moved from one generation to the next, suffering no harm"* (v. 6). Symmachus rendered this more clearly, "I shall not be overturned from one generation to the next, nor shall I come to any harm." He takes advantage of this boldness, and believes he will suffer no trouble as though free from all forms of evil. *His mouth is full of cursing, bitterness, and deceit; under his tongue lies trouble and hardship* (v. 7): he hatches plots and concocts crimes, and passes his life in schemes against the needy. The trouble is fruitless and the hardship without gain: apart from this he does not move his tongue at all.[3] *He lies in hiding with the rich under cover, intending to slay the innocent* (v. 8). Seated in meetings and councils, he devises ambushes and wiles for the guiltless. Those abounding in godlessness live ever in pretense: they lie in wait for the innocent, and the rich in particular waylay the needy. The devil acted in stealth in seeking to kill Christ, remember, God alone having clean hands and being pure in heart.

(4) *His eyes are on the needy; he lies in wait under cover, like a lion in its den. He lies in wait to snatch the poor by luring him; he will humiliate him in his trap* (vv. 8–9). As the lion moves its eye hither and yon in search of its prey, so he gives thought night and day to plans of rapine and greed, and yet *he will stoop and fall* (v. 10).

---

3. The text of the *Commentary* in its present state has some inconsequential statements like this of which the editor is uncertain. Of course, it is also true that it has been a long psalm (in the LXX) and quite repetitious, and the commentator is desperate to say something new. Theodoret does not afford himself the luxury of a lengthy digression such as a preacher like Chrysostom might.

Like a lion in his lair ever in waiting to strike, so too did the devil in the synagogue of the Jews, as though in his den, hunt Christ, thinking him a mere man. *So as to have dominion over the needy:* when he prevails over everyone, the mouth of death will by no means be avoided; rather, like everybody else he will be consigned to the grave. So the enemy thought he had dominion over the apostles and even over the martyrs; when therefore he seemed to have prevailed over everyone, then he was crushed and fell—*will stoop,* indicating the crushing. *He said in his heart, "You see, God has forgotten. He turned away his face from ever looking at it"* (v. 11). Now, the ungodly tries his hand at all this against the needy of God, deceiving himself and nourishing the thought that God is not on guard. At any rate, *he said in his heart, "God has forgotten. He turned away his face from ever looking at it."* Impious words and godless thoughts will do him no good; instead, it will emerge from the facts themselves that he observes human affairs as the ruler of all.

(5) Greatly distressed by these impious words, [936] the inspired author once again turns his treatment into a prayer in the words, *Rise up, O Lord my God, let your hand be uplifted; forget not your needy ones forever* (v. 12). When the needy and those living in sin claim by their actions that God has forgotten, teach them by experience that you have not forgotten nor turned away your face, but that you are showing care for the wronged. Even more vexed by their blasphemies he added, *Why did the godless one provoke God? He said in his heart, after all, "He will not require an account"* (v. 13). Even if he had these thoughts countless times, however, you are looking: this is the way it is to be taken—in other words, There is no one to require an account, no matter whom I swallow, says the devil.[4]

(6) *You are looking, because you perceive hardship and anger so as to give him into your hands* (v. 14). This was the way Symmachus also made the distinction, note: "You see because you watch labor and provocation"; and Aquila, "You saw because you gaze on hardship and provocation." Even if those living in impiety claim countless times, he is saying, that you are not looking at

---

4. Another doubtful and inconsequential element in the text.

human affairs, we know that you are studying and considering their crimes, and requiring due penalty of them. *The poor, after all, is left in your care, you were a help to an orphan.* Hence I implore you, *Break the arm of the sinner and evildoer* (v. 15). Now, it will happen, provided you decide to seek out his sin: if it happens, he will depart immediately and be consigned to ruin, which is what he indicated in saying, *His sin will be looked for, and will not be found* on account of the sin itself, though Symmachus said it more clearly, "His godlessness will be looked for, and he will not be found"—that is, once it is looked for and brought to light, he perishes.

(7) *The Lord is king forever, and forever and ever* (v. 16): since the impious said, "He does not seek nor look," rightly does the prophetic [937] word teach that he will reign, and not simply reign, but forever and ever. Now, it is proper for a king to care for his subjects. *You will perish, nations, from his earth,* addicted as you are to crime, unreceptive to the saving message. *You hearkened to the longing of the needy, O Lord, your ear attended to the readiness of their heart* (v. 17). Symmachus, on the other hand, said "the proposal of readiness." I know precisely, he is saying, what the needy long for, and what proposal they have.[5]

(8) Then he teaches this more clearly: *To judge in favor of orphaned and humbled* (v. 18): each wronged person longs for this, he is saying. *So that a human being may not go further in boasting on the earth:* with the punishment of those guilty of godlessness and crime, it will be of the greatest benefit for all other people to have them in view and not venture to emulate them. Now, the inspired author did not simply attach this to the present psalm; instead, it was from his wish to show first the condition of human nature in olden times and the fact that the only-begotten Word of God became incarnate in the fullness of time and applied various remedies to our wounds.[6] In any case, he teaches

---

5. Not for the first time does Theodoret incline in his commentary to the alternative reading; Symmachus in particular can be preferred to the LXX.
6. Theodoret has resisted developing a Christological interpretation at length in commenting on this psalm, adverting only casually to the treatment meted out to apostles and martyrs. The signs are that he has found the psalm heavy going, with its unvaried accent on the malice of the wicked;

in addition to this that the God of all will consign to worse chastisement on the day of his second coming those prepared to accept no advantage from his beneficence.

---

even Scriptural documentation is notably absent, and (partly because of the state of the text) some comments are puzzling. Unlike a preacher on the text, this desk theologian has resisted the temptation to moralize, and true to his principles he does not believe in length for its own sake.

COMMENTARY ON PSALM 11

To the end. A psalm of David.

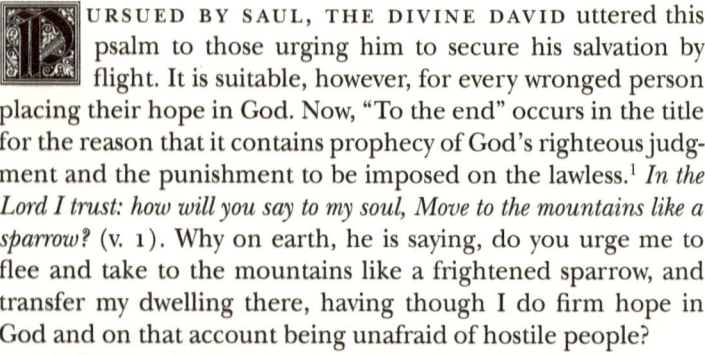URSUED BY SAUL, THE DIVINE DAVID uttered this psalm to those urging him to secure his salvation by flight. It is suitable, however, for every wronged person placing their hope in God. Now, "To the end" occurs in the title for the reason that it contains prophecy of God's righteous judgment and the punishment to be imposed on the lawless.[1] *In the Lord I trust: how will you say to my soul, Move to the mountains like a sparrow?* (v. 1). Why on earth, he is saying, do you urge me to flee and take to the mountains like a frightened sparrow, and transfer my dwelling there, having though I do firm hope in God and on that account being unafraid of hostile people?

(2) *Because, lo, the sinners have bent the bow,* [940] *they have prepared arrows for the quiver to shoot in the dark at the upright of heart* (v. 2). Now, some linked this to the preceding verses,[2] but what follows does not allow it: he adds, *Because what you completed they laid low* (v. 2). Now, from this we learn that the inspired author directed his words to God, employing a petition and teaching that both the arrows and the spears of the enemies were in readiness, and their purpose was to make use of lairs and ambushes against us as though on some dark and moonless night; by the *dark*, you see, he referred to the secrecy and furtiveness of the plot, the term suggesting a moonless night. He also spoke of *upright in heart,* not testifying to his own elevated virtue but

---

1. A rationalizing comment made necessary by Theodoret's failure to recognize the titles as liturgical directions. He arrived at this meaning for the phrase at its first occurrence on Ps 4.

2. Theodoret is credited with acquaintance with and even reliance on the work of earlier commentators (see Introduction, section 4) and we shall shortly note his dependence; Guinot sees the hand of Diodore in this case. But, as we have seen from his preface, he can have his own views.

knowing that he had never done anything to harm Saul, and instead had consistently dealt with him with the greatest good will. *Because what you completed they laid low:* far from seizing kingship, he is saying, I was elected by your grace. But they take up arms in defiance of your choice, and strive to undo me.

(3) *But what did the righteous man do? The Lord is in his holy temple, the Lord, his throne is in heaven. His eyes behold the world, his gaze examines the sons of men. The Lord examines the righteous and the godless* (vv. 3–5). So while they practice their evil ways against me, you, the righteous Judge, seated on your heavenly throne and making your own special appearance in the Temple on earth, view the whole world, though sufficient for you is a mere glance of your eyes to learn about all human affairs. You know precisely the doings of the righteous and the unrighteous, and you measure out repayment for work done. Now, it must be acknowledged that he refers to eyes, eyelids, thrones, and other such things in rather bodily fashion to teach human beings divine realities from human things, giving the names of human faculties to the divine operations.[3] *He who loves unrighteousness hates his own soul.* He who loves his soul hates unrighteousness, whereas he who is well disposed to the latter brings ruin on his soul, drawing down divine wrath, about which the inspired word goes into details.

(4) *Because on sinners he will rain down snares, fire and sulphur, and blast of a storm* (v. 6).[4] From what had happened previously in the region of Sodom he forms a description of the punishments; the Lord reigned down on those cities fire and sulphur from heaven from the Lord, remember.[5] So here too he threatened

---

3. An Antiochene could not let pass without comment and instruction the highly anthropomorphic expression of these verses. Characteristically, Theodoret is pithy even on such matters, whereas Chrysostom would spell out the risk to divine transcendence in such linguistic accommodation, or *synkatabasis*.

4. For the "snares" of the LXX Dahood suggests the Hebrew could better be rendered "bellows" (Dahood, *Psalms* I, 70). Theodoret is strangely silent on what must have been alternative offerings from the other ancient translators on this difficult reading, for which Chrysostom cited one such variant obviously reading the similar Hebrew form for "charcoals" (PG 55.143; see De Montfaucon's note there).

5. Cf. Gen 19.24.

these things, not as though on the point of inflicting them altogether, but through them indicating the manifold [941] punishments. *The portion of their drinking cup:* they assigned themselves these things, he is saying, by choosing lawlessness. Now, he gives the name *drinking cup* to the punishment, as also in another psalm, "In the hand of the Lord there is a cup of wine, full of a strong mixture," and a little later, "All the sinners of the earth will drink it."[6] This drinking cup blessed Jeremiah was ordered to offer to the nations.[7]

(5) *Because the Lord is righteous, and loved righteous deeds; he saw uprightness before his eyes* (v. 7). These things the Lord of all inflicts on those living in sin, he is saying; for he is a fount of righteousness, and directs everything by use of his uprightness like some rudder.[8]

6. Ps 75.8.
7. Jer 25.15.
8. In keeping with his principles, Theodoret has not exploited the historical reference some find in the psalm (of which Chrysostom seemed unaware, preferring—with his fascination for the fate of the righteous sufferer—to anticipate Theodoret's view that the sentiments suit anyone in a similar plight).

COMMENTARY ON PSALM 12

To the end, on the eighth. A psalm of David.

HIS PSALM RETAINS the same sense: he upbraids those employing deceit and, while promising friendship, betraying him to his enemy Saul and disclosing to him where he was living. It bears the title "on the eighth" for the reason that it mentions God's righteous judgment, which the righteous Judge will carry out after the seventh day, as we said before.[1] The reason it is also entitled "To the end" is that there will be a prophecy at a later stage.

(2) *Save me, Lord, because there is no holy person left, because truth is esteemed little among sons of men* (v. 1). My request is to enjoy salvation from you, O Lord, since regard for truth is in danger of being snuffed out, with everyone, you might say, suffering from distrust in one another. Then he describes more clearly what they are up to: *Everyone spoke lies to their neighbor* (v. 2): they pretend friendship and perform the actions of enemies. *Lying lips in their heart and evil spoken in the heart:* they talk to each other deceitfully, he is saying. Some use their lips to direct falsehood into their neighbor's heart, others return the compliment.

(3) Then on this account he threatens them with punishment: *The Lord will destroy all deceitful lips, every boasting tongue* (v. 3). Now, what form does the boasting take? [944] *Those who say, "We shall give free rein to our tongue. Our lips are our own. Who is our master?"* (v. 4). They cannot bear, he is saying, to keep their words in conformity with their nature, nor are they prepared to have regard for the divine laws; instead, with mouths agape they heedlessly utter whatever occurs to them, scornful of divine long-suffering and giving no thought to their falling under the lordship of God. Pharaoh was like that, and so he said, *"I do not know the Lord."*[2] Rabshakeh was like that, presuming to say, *"Do*

---

1. Cf. note 1 on Ps 6.   2. Exod 5.2.

not let your God deceive you, trusting in him for the deliverance of Jerusalem from my hand."[3] Nabuchodonosor was like that, striking fear into those noble children and not afraid to say, *"Who is the God who will deliver you out of my hands?"*[4] Still, even they paid the penalty for their audacity, and those of whom the inspired word speaks will pay the due penalty.[5]

(4) He indicated as much in adding, *For the sake of the hardship of the poor and the groaning of the needy I shall now arise, says the Lord; I shall place them in safety, I shall deal faithfully with them* (v. 5). I shall not ignore them in their weeping and groaning that result from the crimes committed against them; instead, shaking off my long-suffering like a sleep I shall make their salvation obvious and illustrious. Symmachus in fact rendered it thus: "I shall arrange salvation in a visible position." Teaching us that what has been said will really be true, the psalmist added, *The Lord's sayings are pure sayings, silver tested in the furnace, proven in the ground, purified seven times* (v. 6). He put *seven times* instead of "many times," this being customary with the divine Scripture.[6] *You, O Lord, will protect us, and defend us from this generation and forever* (v. 7): guarded by your grace we shall not only escape the wiles of the present generation, but shall also be provided with everlasting salvation.

(5) *The godless roam around; you prospered sons of men in your loftiness* (v. 8). Those addicted to impiety, then, forsaking the divine path, wander this way and that, endeavoring to outflank and as it were besiege more reasonable people. You, on the contrary, when you make your appearance from the loftiness of your nature, judge those assailed by such people to be worthy of your care, at one time consoling them in tribulation, and a little later regaling them with complete salvation. [945]

3. Cf. 2 Kings 18.29–30, loosely recalled.
4. Dan 3.15.
5. The biblical parallels are brief and to the point, and if obscure in at least one case, the reader is expected to recall the context (even if the commentator seems unsure of the text in another case).
6. Chrysostom, also an Antiochene, would not have let this detail escape him, but would hardly have been content with the bare acknowledgment, instead finding reasons and further examples to embroider the point. Not Theodoret, despite the brevity of the commentary overall.

COMMENTARY ON PSALM 13

To the end. A psalm of David.

HE MIGHTY DAVID DIRECTED this psalm also to himself, not in fact when pursued by Saul but when under attack from Absalom. The incident involving Saul, remember, was before the sin, and for that reason he spoke with great confidence, whereas the incident involving Absalom was after the sin, and hence his words were mixed with weeping and groaning. *How long, O Lord? Will you forget me forever?* (v. 1). He called the delay in assistance *forgetting:* his request is not to be forgotten forever, that is, not to be completely bereft of divine providence. *How long will you turn your face away from me?* By analogy with people who are angry and refuse to look at those who have offended them, he used this expression. Hence a little later he says, "Look at me, and have mercy on me,"[1] not taking *face* to mean face, or *turning away* to mean turning away; rather, he frames his language in human terms once more.[2]

(2) *How long shall I hold counsels in my soul, pangs in my heart day and night?* (v. 2).[3] I am constantly worn out night and day, mulling over my thoughts again and again, at one time hoping to enjoy your loving-kindness, at another wondering if my mind will hold, at another surrendering my firmer hope. *How long will my foe be exalted over me?* It is appropriate to apply this also to ourselves when under attack from the devil, and to call on divine help unceasingly: the divine David was distressed to see his enemies more powerful.

---

1. Not quite the psalmist's words, in fact.
2. This reminder about the concreteness of the language of poetry, implying a risk to divine transcendence, he had to give at the end of the previous psalm.
3. Dahood has to have recourse to Ugaritic to deal with the phrase the Hebrew and LXX render "hold counsels," suggesting instead "place doubts" (NRSV, "bear pain").

(3) *Look at me, hearken to me, O Lord my God, give light to my eyes lest I sleep in death* (v. 3). By night I am overwhelmed by my problems, in the grip of discouragement like a kind of sleep. But if the light of your assistance shines, it will disperse the darkness of trouble and put an end to the sleep of discouragement. If, on the other hand, you delay your help, I am afraid the sleep will turn into death, as the distress becomes stronger than my resolve. *In case my foe should ever say, "I prevailed over him." Those distressing me will rejoice if I falter* (v. 4). Do not make me appear an object of satisfaction to my adversaries: this would be the most grievous of griefs for me.

(4) *But I hoped for your mercy* (v. 5). It is clear also from this that he uttered this psalm after the sin: he relies not on his righteousness [948] but on mercy, and says it is in this that he trusts: *My heart will rejoice in your salvation.* Now I have hope in your mercy, and enjoying salvation I shall be rid of my despondency and make music with complete satisfaction. He added this, in fact: *I shall sing to the Lord my benefactor, and the name of the Lord Most High I shall celebrate in song* (v. 6). Even though I do not understand your ineffable nature, nevertheless your name suffices to bring me to my knees and prompt me to song and to a request for all proper assistance: I believe I shall attain it, even though simply calling upon your name.[4]

---

4. It is a powerful psalm, an eloquent if brief cry for help amidst distress, but dispatched quite tersely by Theodoret in keeping with his promise not to gild the lily, no single Scriptural reference being made beyond the psalm. Chrysostom, interestingly, was also relatively brief in his commentary, though not resisting the obvious parallel with the distress of the Paul of 2 Corinthians, a soul mate of his.

COMMENTARY ON PSALM 14

To the end. A psalm of David.

HIS PSALM ALSO REFERS us forward "To the end," since it forecasts the future. Now, this is its theme: Sennacherib, king of the Assyrians, made war on Judah at that time and took possession of many cities, some by surrender, some by siege. Hoping to get the better of Jerusalem as well, he sent Rabshakeh to Hezekiah, who ruled the Jews at that time, employing blasphemies and impious words against God: "Say to Hezekiah," he said, "Do not let your God, in whom you trust, deceive you into thinking he will rescue Jerusalem from my hand. Where is the god of Hamath and Arpad? And where is the god of the city of Sepharvaim? Surely they were unable to rescue them from my hand for the same reason that the Lord will not rescue Jerusalem from my hand?"[1] While that was his advice, Hezekiah scorned his mighty force and the frenzy of his words, and relying on his own godliness he invoked divine help and immediately felt the benefit of it. The righteous Judge, you see, loathed the impiety of the one and accepted the piety of the other, and with a single angel annihilated one hundred and eighty-five thousand Assyrians, put the others to flight, and provided the besieged with unexpected salvation.[2]

1. Cf. 2 Kings 18.29–30, 18.32–35. The incident of Sennacherib's challenge to the God of Hezekiah mediated through Rabshakeh, evidently a favorite locus of Theodoret's, had been briefly referred to in a comment on Ps 12. But here, despite his professed unwillingness to present the Psalms as the story of the Jews, he goes into it at greater length, yet without adverting to the Christian application of vv. 1–3 in Rom 3.10–12. Could this historical association of the psalm have been a reason why Chrysostom's extant *Commentary* breaks off after Ps 13?
2. Cf. 2 Kings 19.35, which recounts the annihilation, not the flight; the grisly assassination of Sennacherib recorded in the following two verses would have been grist to Theodoret's mill, one would have thought.

(2) *The fool has said in his heart, There is no God* (v. 1). The opening of the psalm matches closely the words of Sennacherib and Rabshakeh:[3] they claimed Hezekiah was deceived, as though God was not the defender of Judah. Now, the company of Sennacherib indulged in corrupt practices, or, to be precise, a corrupt way of life, such that God did not find among them even one interested in virtue: everything took a turn for depravity. Why? Will not his very works [949] bring to knowledge of the power of God those who consume and devour his people like bread? All will come to know through experience the one fighting against them; fear will strike them from a source they did not expect. I mean, who would have thought they would be destroyed by an angel? That God cares for the Jews? Those who mocked the counsel of poor and lowly Hezekiah for trusting in God rather than arms will realize that the one who made himself dependent on God enjoyed a hope that was not disappointed. After all, who else than God would both save those remaining in Sion and bring back those then in captivity so that the joy would be shared by the twelve tribes who took their name from the patriarch Jacob as their root and origin, who enjoyed the new name of Israel, with the result that they were named after him as Jacob and Israel?

(3) So much for the historical sense; let us examine the more subtle spiritual sense. *They became corrupt and loathsome in their pursuits; there is no one who does good.* Their corrupt life, he is saying, was the basis and root of their godlessness: since they had given themselves over to intemperance and a savage way of living, they expelled from their minds the remembrance of God; instead, they adopted the frenzy of their leader as his subjects.[4] Some people utterly deny the divine, and profess that God is not

---

3. At this point, the text is supplemented from individual codices to the extent that the treatment is much more expansive than we have come to expect of Theodoret.
4. While briefly the text departed from the historical theme as Theodoret explored a spiritual sense, from this point on the comment adopts a speculative tone and periodic style in regard to the nature of non-belief that contrasts with his commentary on previous psalms and on the almost identical Ps 53 (see notes there). Comparison with the commentary of Eusebius at this place reveals a relationship between the two.

the origin of things but that the name is without force and devoid of any substance. Others, on the other hand, give the name gods to what are really not, while rejecting the only one that is. Still others concede in word that he exists, but do not actually come up with evidence of his care for things on earth or his scrutiny of human affairs. They have thus all been caught up in the one doctrine of atheism, presuming there is no God. For they did not presume to admit as much in what they say: they all had within them natural instincts and natural inklings in the direction of admitting to knowledge of God—hence their not presuming to deny it with their lips. Instead, they pretended to know there was not one God but actually gods beyond number. In their hearts, at any rate, they persuaded themselves that there is absolutely no God, being quite foolish and stupid as they were; but proof of their atheistic belief were the actions performed by them, the tree being known by its fruits, after all. So sometimes in their very deeds and the rest of their life they corrupted their entire soul by the body itself, surrendering it to complete ruin, as in the case of men lusting after men and corrupting themselves with all kinds of lawless and unmentionable behavior, and thus being loathsome. So how could it be other than obvious that, despite their subscribing in words to gods beyond number, and [952] despite claiming to know and confess by their lips the God who rules all, there is no single true understanding of God alive in their heart, that is, in their mind? Before the coming of our Savior, therefore, the whole of life was in fact like this. Now, to the atheist is the name *fool* most accurately applied in truth and nature: if the fear of God is the beginning of wisdom,[5] lack of fear and denial of him would be the opposite of wisdom.

(4) *The Lord looked down from heaven on the sons of men to see if there is anyone who is intelligent or seeks after God. All went astray and at the same time proved useless; there is no one who does good, there is not even one* (vv. 2–3). Of course, the one who dwells in heaven and looks after the lowly did not watch over those who do and

5. Cf. Ps 111.10; Prov 1.7. The rare Scriptural reference indicates perhaps the return of Theodoret to the commentary, thence conducted in the terse, piecemeal style we have come to expect of him.

say such things; instead, he made a precise examination even of their very thoughts, and saw all who were caught up in the same way in impiety and the lawless way of life. This resembled the words spoken to Abraham: "The cry of Sodom and Gomorrah to me has increased, and their sins are exceedingly great; so I shall go down and see if they are absorbed in the way the cry coming to me says."[6]

(5) *Have they no knowledge, all those who commit lawlessness, who eat up my people like a meal of bread? They did not invoke the Lord. There they were gripped with fear where there was no fear* (vv. 4–5). You were unwilling, he is saying, you who devour them, to acknowledge this; so you will learn through practical experience itself that my people will not be easily taken by you, nor will you consume them like some bread for eating, since you despise my providence—which is what is meant by *They did not invoke the Lord.* For this reason, you who speak boldly and fear no one will experience fear and dread and take to flight, even though no one alive is there to terrorize and pursue you—which is what he indicates by *There they were gripped by fear where there was no fear.* Now, the phrase, *Have they no knowledge, all those who commit lawlessness,* is to be read in declamatory style.[7] The verse, on the other hand, *The Lord looked down from heaven on the sons of men to see if there is anyone who is intelligent or seeks after God,* he depicted in human fashion, to show that he sent down punishment from heaven on the Assyrians: it is clear [953] that the God of all is present everywhere and holds in his control the circle of the earth and those who dwell in it like locusts, according to the inspired author's statement.[8]

(6) *Because God accompanies the generation of the righteous. You confounded the purpose of the poor one, but the Lord is his hope* (vv. 5–6). Now, the Lord of all does this on account of Hezekiah's

---

6. Gen 18.20–21.
7. Unlike Chrysostom's congregation, which evidently sang the psalms even in the classroom where his sessions took place, for Theodoret's readers here the psalms are to be read, aloud—though he recommends somewhat more than usual expression for this challenging phrase. In his preface, on the other hand, he spoke of the psalms being sung.
8. Cf. Isa 40.22.

virtue and the generation piously tended by him, whom you impious lot despised as worthless, and you mocked his firm trust in me—which he called *purpose*, meaning intention. He nevertheless clung to hope in me like a sacred anchor, and in fact attained the salvation he hoped for: the psalmist even added as much: *Who will give from Sion the salvation of Israel?* (v. 7). Now, this inspired statement has a double reference: it forecasts not only the salvation affecting the besieged at that time but also the saving manifestation of our Savior occurring there many ages later. *When the Lord averts the captivity of his people, Jacob will rejoice and Israel be glad:* since the ten tribes had already been enslaved, and in fact many cities of Judah as well, he prays for them to attain the same salvation and receive their freedom. There will then be, he is saying, greater joy for the people having the double name: they were given the name not only of Jacob but also of Israel, inheriting the title assigned their forefather by God.[9]

9. The conclusion repeats material offered in the text of the commentary on v. 1, reinforcing the impression of supplementary material there. The absence of reference to alternative versions is also a distinguishing feature of this *Commentary*.

COMMENTARY ON PSALM 15

A psalm of David.

INCE THE PSALM BEFORE THIS also prophesied salvation for the inhabitants of Jerusalem, and forecast the return of those already made captive, it is right for him to introduce exhortation in this psalm and propose a way of life proper for them to live who are under God's command and enjoying such wonderful assistance. So he casts his words in the form of question and answer: *Lord, who will abide in your dwelling? And who will dwell on your holy mountain?* (v. 1). Who is worthy, O Lord, to take his place in your Temple [956] and live his life in your city? How should these people conduct themselves? What pursuits should they follow? He calls the Temple God's *dwelling*, note, and Jerusalem his *holy mountain*.

(2) Having asked the question, he receives this reply: *He who walks blamelessly and performs righteousness* (v. 2). It is necessary, he is saying, for such a one to rid himself of evil and be free of all blame, and to practice every virtue studiously. Here he calls the ultimate virtue *righteousness*, note, and is keen to outline its forms. *Speaking truth in his heart, he did not deceive with his tongue nor do evil to his neighbor* (vv. 2–3): he must keep free of falsehood not only his tongue but also his mind, and also be rid completely of the double deceit so that on their part no harm results to their neighbor. Now, it was very logical for him to make mention first of the heart, then of the tongue, and then of the deed: word precedes action; and thinking, word. *He did not level a reproach against his neighbor.* And even if some should fall foul of a calamity, it would not be proper to ridicule or take advantage of them, but rather to share their discouragement in keeping with the apostolic law bidding us weep with those who weep.[1]

1. Rom 12.15.

(3) *In his eyes every evildoer is despised* (v. 4). If, on the other hand, someone chooses a lawless life, let him consider such a person thrice unhappy, even should he profit from favorable winds to enjoy the utmost prosperity. You see, since he chose not to level a reproach, he was right to add this, teaching the difference between good and evil men,[2] *whereas he honors those who fear the Lord*. Now, it is a pious act to respect all those who place great store by God's things and grant them all veneration and esteem. *Who makes an oath to his neighbor without breaking it. He did not lend his money at interest or take bribes against the innocent* (vv. 4–5). Let practice bear out their oaths, and avarice not sully their affluence, usury being a form of this. On the contrary, let a judge be incorruptible, and deliver the verdict uninfluenced by bribes, bribery being the destroyer of justice.

(4) *He who does these things will never be moved.* Now, the prize for this virtue is constant enjoyment of divine aid, abiding in many good things and awaiting eternal life.[3] This is no less applicable to us than to the ancients: since we have lived by a new law in addition to the old, we have attained also greater grace.

---

2. Despite his disclaimer in commenting on the exclusive language of the opening verse of the first psalm, Theodoret can fall into the same habit himself.

3. Theodoret seems to be presuming an eschatology in the psalmist more expansive than is normally credited him.

COMMENTARY ON PSALM 16

An inscription for David.

HERE HE FORETELLS THE PASSION and Resurrection of the Lord [957] and the salvation of those believing in him. Now, the title suggests victory as well as death: a column is not set up on graves only, but is raised also for victors, and is inscribed to teach those unaware of it about the victory. The title about the "inscription" has this meaning, for example.[1]

(2) *Protect me, Lord, for in you have I hoped. I said to the Lord, You are my Lord* (vv. 1–2). The psalm is spoken in the person of the Savior, but is spoken from the viewpoint of his humanity,[2] as are also many other such statements that we find in the sacred Gospels. Such a one is this, "Father, if it is possible, let this cup pass from me; yet not as I want but as you want";[3] and, "I go to my Father and your Father, my God and your God."[4] This is the way we find him praying constantly and bending his knees. Now, that this belongs to human nature and not to divinity, which is in need of nothing, the Apostle clearly teaches; he says as much in the Epistle to the Hebrews: "In the days of his flesh he offered up prayers and supplications with a strong cry and tears to the one able to save him from death, and he was heard for his reverence. Although Son, he learnt obedience from his sufferings, and being made perfect he became the cause of eternal salvation for all who obey him."[5] What was made perfect, however,

---

1. Theodoret's estimate of the sense of this term corresponds to that of modern commentators, who also allow an etymological connection in Hebrew with "gold," encouraging Luther's version, "a golden jewel."
2. Another expansive comment on these verses signals a relationship with the work of Eusebius; Theodoret's own principles would hardly permit such a lengthy and developed Christological excursus, one would think.
3. Matt 26.39.   4. Cf. John 20.17.
5. Heb 5.7–9.

was not God the Word perfect from eternity, but the form of the slave, which was made impassible, incorruptible, and immortal. It is therefore this that he says the Lord did in the days of his flesh, when he had a mortal body; all these things, for example, are human, not characteristic of God. So in this psalm also he asks this way to be protected, and is protected by himself: while he asks as a human being, as God he grants the request, his own Father of course being pleased and cooperating. That verse, at any rate, *I said to the Lord, You are my Lord,* is consistent with "I go to my God and your God."

(3) *Because you have no need of goods from me:* you are without need, and do not require human righteousness; rather, whatever good anyone does he is helped to do, whereas it is of no benefit to you. Now, Symmachus rendered it differently, "Any good that is mine is not independent of you." All the abundance of good things, he is saying, comes to me from your grace.[6] Yet each of these has a pious sense: we enjoy the good things from God, and he does not need our righteous behavior, yet he requires it of us for our benefit. [960] *The Lord has shown his wonders to the holy ones in his land, because all his wishes are in them* (v. 3). Here he hints at the apostles and those who have come to faith through them: he says God's marvels have become obvious to them, since, he says, they have fulfilled all my commands.[7]

(4) *Their weaknesses were multiplied, later they accelerated* (v. 4). Many assaults were launched from all sides, he is saying—from mobs and rabble-rousers, kings and generals. Yet they speedily overcame them all because they finished the course and reached the winning post. Now, this resembles the apostolic saying, "Whenever I am weak, then I am strong."[8] *I shall not assemble their assemblies of blood, nor make mention of their names on my lips.* But those who rose up against them I shall consign to punish-

---

6. The version of Symmachus, which corresponds more closely to modern versions and attracts Theodoret, signals his resumption of the commentary, also prompting him to assert the priority of divine grace to human effort.
7. Versions ancient and modern have difficulty with these verses; Dahood sees not apostles being referred to, but Canaanite and Phoenician deities. Theodoret's customary brevity limits the damage of his option.
8. 2 Cor 12.10.

ment, and hide their memory in oblivion so that even their very names will be unknown to anyone.

(5) *The Lord is part of my inheritance and my cup* (v. 5). It is proper to recall what was said in the second psalm: in human fashion once again the Father said to him, "Ask it of me, and I shall give you nations for your inheritance, and the ends of the earth as your possession."[9] And in the sacred Gospels he himself said to his Father about the apostles, "Father, those you gave me were yours, and you gave them to me; none of them perished except the son of perdition."[10] But just as he speaks here in human fashion with his exhortation to accept the kingdom, so elsewhere he shows that he himself is Lord of all: "My sheep hear my voice, he says, I know them and they follow me, and I give them eternal life"; and again, "But I have other sheep that are not of this fold; them I must also bring, and they will listen to my voice, and there will be one flock, one shepherd."[11] Of course, in the present psalm he speaks in human fashion, *The Lord is part of my inheritance and my cup,* calling the kingdom of the nations *inheritance,* while calling the death he endured for us *cup.* [961] That is the way he spoke in the sacred Gospels, too, remember: "Father, if it is possible, let this cup pass from me,"[12] as if to say more clearly, The Lord is part of my Church, which is my inheritance, whereas he himself is also part of my cup, that is, he himself having become part of death. *You are the one to restore my inheritance to me.* He did not say, the one to give, but *the one to restore my inheritance to me:* as soon as the human being was created, he assumed authority over everything and had immortal life; but after the transgression he lost both things, absolute sway and life.[13] In human terms the Lord made a plea for human nature, asking that they recover both the former life and absolute sway.

(6) *Cords fell out for me among the finest; my inheritance, after all,*

---

9. Ps 2.8. The resemblance to Eusebius here is almost verbatim (see Introduction, section 4).
10. John 17.6, 12, loosely recalled.
11. John 10.27–28, 16.
12. Matt 26.39.
13. Theodoret is definite about the Fall and its effects.

is the finest for me (v. 6). On account of this inheritance, he is saying, I was the subject of the current schemes. He calls the schemes *cords,* note, and similarly says in another psalm, "Cords of sinners ensnared me, and I did not forget your Law."[14] So he means, For the sake of this finest inheritance and thanks to the salvation, I am exposed to the current schemes. *I shall bless the Lord who gave me wisdom; even until night my entrails brought me to my senses* (v. 7). Yet with the Lord giving me wisdom, and by calling upon my clearest thinking, I shall survive the night of suffering. He called the darkness of temptations *night,* note. Now, let no one think it inappropriate that Christ the Lord is given wisdom according to his human nature, after hearing the divinely inspired Luke saying, "And Jesus advanced in wisdom and in divine and human favor."[15] And listen to him saying again that when he was trembling with emotion and sweating drops of blood an angel came and supported him.[16] Now, if he stood in need of angelic assistance to give evidence of what the form of a slave was like,[17] much more presumably was he given wisdom by the divinity dwelling within him. Being human and God, after all, he was given wisdom as a human being whereas he was the fount of wisdom as God.

(7) *I had the Lord in sight ever before me, because he is on my right lest I be moved. Hence my heart rejoiced and my tongue was glad; further, my flesh will rest in hope. Because you will not abandon my soul in Hades, nor will you allow your holy one to see corruption. You made known to me paths of life; with your presence you will fill me with joy, with delight at your right hand forever* (vv. 8–11). It is superfluous for us to interpret this, since the divinely inspired Peter received a revelation from the Father, from the Son, [964] and from the

14. Ps 119.61.   15. Luke 2.52, loosely recalled.
16. Cf. Luke 22.43.
17. Cf. Phil 2.7, Theodoret having a likeness for this term, "the form of a slave," used also above. As well, not only does he explain to his readers the figurative language of the Psalms, but he keeps reminding them that they also speak "in human fashion" of the divinity, as Chrysostom would remind his listeners of the *synkatabasis* involved. And occasionally, as here, he has to intervene at somewhat greater length (though still briefly) to establish the necessary balance in speaking of the hypostatic union in cases where he gives a psalm a Christological interpretation.

Holy Spirit, and in former times gave an interpretation of it. In addressing the Jews, remember, and giving this public witness in their midst, he spoke in these terms: "Men, Brothers, I can say to you with assurance regarding the patriarch David that he died, was buried, and his tomb is with us to this day. So being a prophet, and knowing that God had sworn an oath to him that from his loins the Christ according to the flesh would rise, he saw the future and spoke of his Resurrection, that is, his soul was not abandoned in Hades nor would his flesh see corruption."[18] And again, "While David died after serving his own generation and saw corruption, the one whom God raised did not see corruption."[19] These things ought to be brought to the attention of those presuming to give a full interpretation, including the Jews, of course;[20] they contain a patent refutation of their stupidity, after all. So at this place, too, Christ the Lord in human fashion says, "Constantly supported by the divine nature, I am in the midst of my saving passion and find gladness in the hope of resurrection. My soul, you see, will not be abandoned in Hades, nor will my flesh suffer natural corruption: I shall achieve a rapid resurrection and return to life, giving all people a glimpse of this path."

(8) *With your presence you will fill me with joy, with delight at your right hand forever.* Since he had said approaching his Passion, "My soul is sorrowful to the point of death,"[21] it was right for him to use these words to recall the Resurrection, teaching that in place of that discouragement he will be in unceasing joy, having become immune to suffering, to change, to death, even in his human nature. As God, you see, this was always the case, and of course even in his human nature once formed in the womb it was easy to provide him with this. But he allowed the nature he had assumed to travel through the sufferings so as by these

---

18. Acts 2.29–32, loosely recalled.
19. Acts 13.36–37, where in fact Paul is the speaker, not Peter.
20. Theodoret is not above directing the incidental shaft in the direction of the Jews of his day, for reasons suggested in Introduction, section 7; but with his characteristic brevity he does not allow himself the lengthy digressions that Chrysostom did in commenting on the Psalms.
21. Matt 26.38.

means to loose the sway of sin, put a stop to the tyranny of the devil, undo the power of death, and provide all people with the basis of a new life. So as man he assumes both incorruption and immortality. This psalm refutes the folly of Arius, of Eunomius, and of Apollinaris: the former ones said God the Word assumed a body without a soul, whereas Apollinaris called the body that was assumed ensouled though denying it a rational soul; [965] I do not know where he found his doctrine of these two souls—the divine Scripture nowhere teaches it.[22] Yet the all-holy Spirit through blessed David made undisguised mention of a soul, thus giving clear refutation of each heresy.

22. Arius in the first half of the fourth century had developed a "Word-flesh" Christology in which the Word united himself to a human body lacking a rational soul, himself taking the place of one. This Christology characterized also a new radical Arianism developed by Eunomius of Cyzicus in the middle of that century known as Eunomianism. Antioch generally, on the other hand, always stressed the two natures in Christ, a dualist or "diophysite" emphasis that irked Apollinaris of Laodicea late in that century (just before Theodoret's time), who denied a rational mind and will to Christ, teaching that "the divine energy fulfils the role of the *psyche* and the *nous*," (quoted by Kelly, *Early Christian Doctrines,* 292), the latter meaning to him (on a Platonic, not Scriptural, basis) the rational soul. Gregory of Nyssa also dealt with this teaching in his dictum, "What has not been assumed cannot be restored; it is what is united with God that is saved" (Ep. 101.7).

COMMENTARY ON PSALM 17

A prayer of David.

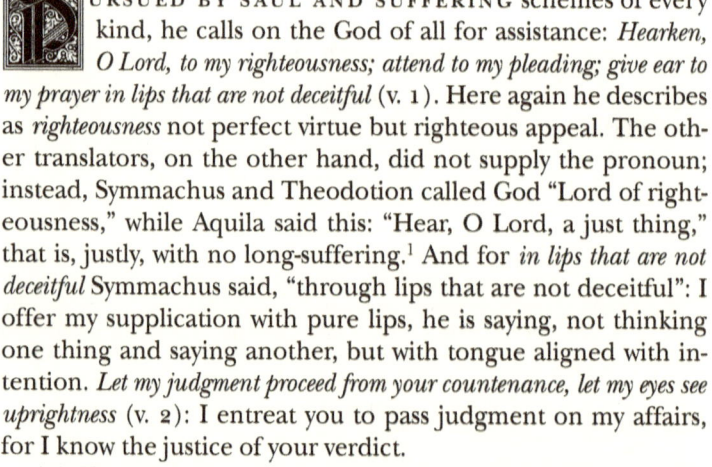URSUED BY SAUL AND SUFFERING schemes of every kind, he calls on the God of all for assistance: *Hearken, O Lord, to my righteousness; attend to my pleading; give ear to my prayer in lips that are not deceitful* (v. 1). Here again he describes as *righteousness* not perfect virtue but righteous appeal. The other translators, on the other hand, did not supply the pronoun; instead, Symmachus and Theodotion called God "Lord of righteousness," while Aquila said this: "Hear, O Lord, a just thing," that is, justly, with no long-suffering.[1] And for *in lips that are not deceitful* Symmachus said, "through lips that are not deceitful": I offer my supplication with pure lips, he is saying, not thinking one thing and saying another, but with tongue aligned with intention. *Let my judgment proceed from your countenance, let my eyes see uprightness* (v. 2): I entreat you to pass judgment on my affairs, for I know the justice of your verdict.

(2) *You tested my heart, you came to me in vision by night, you examined me by fire, and no wrong was found in me. There was no way my mouth spoke of people's doings* (v. 3). Here he teaches us that, though many times having Saul in his grasp, he refrained from doing away with him, and instead rendered good for evil; hence he recalled even the night in which he did this, when by night he saved the sleeping Saul from death and allowed no one to deal him a lethal blow. Now, in figurative manner he calls the

---

1. As he did on the opening of Ps 4, where he rebuked David for claiming righteousness for himself (see note 3 there), Theodoret is chary about a repetition of the phrase here, noting how the other versions avoid it by omission of "my" (modern translators like Dahood finding linguistic grounds for opting for "vindication" in both places, the NRSV going in Aquila's direction). Chrysostom (extant only on Ps 4, not here) showed no such concern about the presumption that worries Theodoret.

disasters *nights* on account of the gloom of discouragement, as likewise he refers to the testing as burning: *you examined me by fire,* he says, *and no wrong was found in me.* In other words, just as you would test gold of some sort, you found me unadulterated, O Lord: so far be it from me to harm the enemy that I even [968] kept my tongue free of abuse against him, and what he continues to do I refrained from mentioning.

(3) *On account of the words from your lips I have kept to difficult paths* (v. 4): I performed this difficult and laborious task in obedience to your commands.[2] *Perfect my steps in your tracks lest my steps be shaken* (v. 5). So I beseech you that my purpose not be frustrated; this would happen if I were to enjoy your aid. He gave the name *steps* to the thrust of his behavior, note. *I cried out, and you hearkened to me, O God* (v. 6): it was not idly that I used those words, but with experience of your loving-kindness, as you heard me calling frequently. *Incline your ear to me, and hearken to my words: Let your mercies be objects of wonder, since you save those who hope in you* (vv. 6–7). So accept my entreaty, move many tongues to songs of praise: those who behold the wronged enjoying mercy at your hands will sing of your providence. You accustomed those believing in you to reach out for assistance. *From my adversaries at your right hand protect me, Lord, as the apple of your eye* (v. 8). He gave the name *adversaries at the right hand* of God to those opposing him, and rightly so: he had been anointed by God and on his initiative received the royal calling. So he says, "Those involved in battle against me are ranging themselves against your decision"; his prayer is to enjoy such protection as does the apple of the eye, which has eyelids as a kind of rampart and eyelashes for a palisade; it also has eyebrows as mounds, conducting the stream of sweat to the temples and warding off from the faculty of sight any harm from that source. This is the kind of care he asks to gain.

(4) *Shelter me in the shelter of your wings from the gaze of the ungodly who afflict me* (vv. 8–9). Once more by the use of another figure he asks to be afforded assistance: he heard also the

---

2. The commentary is becoming as cryptic as the verses commented upon; one wonders how helpful its readers have found it.

mighty Moses saying, "Spreading its wings, it took them, [969] and lifted them up on to its back."³ And the Lord said to Jerusalem, "How often did I desire to gather your children together in the way a hen gathers her brood under her wings, and you refused?"⁴ Now, he gives the name *wings* to the rapidity and sureness of his own providence, the movement of wings being very effortless.

(5) *My foes surrounded my soul. They hemmed in their fatness; their mouth uttered arrogance* (vv. 9–10). Some people gave the name *fatness* to prosperity and good health, but I prefer to speak thus of kindliness and brotherly love. What follows confirms this: shutting off all natural benevolence and giving no room for thoughts of loving-kindness, they utter lofty and extravagant remarks, but set up for me snares and traps of all kinds. *They cast me out and at that moment encircled me; they set their eyes to bring me to the ground* (v. 11). They drove me out from my country and in turn run hither and yon in their desire to lay hold of me; instead of wanting to keep uprightness in view, they have the eye of their mind set in another direction. This was the way, in fact, that Symmachus rendered it: "They set their eyes to slope down to the ground."⁵ *They came upon me like a lion ready for the prey, like a lion cub lurking in ambush* (v. 12). Setting aside natural reason, they are like wild beasts hankering after food, looking around for it, and suddenly leaping on it.

(6) *Rise up, O Lord, anticipate them, and trip them up. Rescue my soul from the ungodly, your sword from foes of your hand* (v. 13). Impede their attack, O Lord, with impediments you know of—this is what he means by *trip up*, by analogy with those who furtively bring down people running. On the other hand, free me from their scheming, applying your sword against them. This is in fact the way Symmachus put it, "For your sword, O Lord, from few of the soil": by your rule, he is saying, you dispatch human beings to death; you [972] said, remember, "You are soil, and to soil

3. Cf. Deut 32.11, where (in the song of Moses) the Lord is compared to the eagle with its young.
4. Luke 13.34; Matt 23.37.
5. As often, it is the version of Symmachus that Theodoret prefers to his LXX text.

you shall return."⁶ *Sow confusion in the ranks of those who live this way; let their belly be filled with what is hidden* (v. 14). Even if it is a simple thing for you to dispatch to death, I still beg that they be dispersed in their lifetime, their evil conspiracy be defeated and they taste the punishments you have stored up. This, too, is what in the Song of the mighty Moses God himself said, "Lo, is not all this laid up with me and sealed in my treasures? I shall repay on the day of retribution, at the moment their foot slips."⁷ *Their sons were sated, they left their remnants to their infants.* Symmachus translated it this way, "Their sons will be sated, and will leave their leftovers for their infants": I know that you will inflict the right penalty not only on them, he is saying, but also on their sons, on their progeny who imitated their parents' wickedness. Now, "they will be sated" implies they will share the evil to the point of satiety.

(7) *As for me, in righteousness I shall appear in your sight, I shall be satisfied in the appearance of your glory to me* (v. 15), that is, to your Son: whereas they will pay such penalties, I for my part shall revel in the good things stemming from your righteous providence, enjoying a wonderful experience of your beneficence.⁸

6. Gen 3.19.
7. Deut 32.34–35.
8. Modern commentators like Dahood have recourse to linguistic data to make sense of these verses. Small wonder, then, that Theodoret fails to make them sound convincing.

COMMENTARY ON PSALM 18

To the end. To David, the servant of the Lord, what he said to the Lord, the words of this song, on the day the Lord rescued him from the hand of all his foes and from the hand of Saul. And he said.

THE TITLE IS CLEAR; no interpretation is required. The sense of this psalm is contained also in the history of the kings.[1] Now, the sound values of the inspired author call for our admiration: despite enduring such schemes on the part of Saul, he did not number him among his foes; instead, he distinguished him from his enemies and did not mention him as hostile. "To the end" occurs because it contains also a prophecy of the calling of the nations and the alienation of the Jews, which happened a long time after.

(2) *I shall love you, O Lord. The Lord is my strength, my steadfastness, my refuge, my rescuer. My God is my helper, and I shall hope in him,* [973] *my protector, horn of my salvation, my defender* (vv. 1–2). The inspired author repays favors with love: this is the only way the one who was well-treated can repay God. In the beginning God required it by law: "You shall love the Lord your God with your whole heart, with your whole soul, and with all your might."[2] But service to the beloved follows on love: "Love bears everything," remember, "believes everything, hopes everything, endures everything; love never disappears."[3] Now, the blessed David promises to love God, not because he had not done this perfectly to that point but because he could not bear to have satiety of love. Then he gives names to the divine favors, and composes a list of names for the list of good things he had attained: he calls God *strength* as though he had a share in it, *stead-*

1. Cf. 2 Sam 22. 2. Deut 6.5; Luke 10.27.
3. 1 Cor 13.7–8.

fastness as if being made steadfast against his enemies, *refuge* as though having God as a wall and stout rampart, *rescuer* as though freed from adversaries by God, *helper* as though having gained assistance from that source, *protector* as one turned champion at the right time, *horn of salvation* and *defender* as though saved by his providence. Now, he used *horn of salvation* by analogy with animals that ward off enemies with their horns. (The meaning of *horn* can also be kingship, however: "He will give strength to our kings," remember, "and he will exalt the horn of his Christ," referring to the kingship of his Christ.)[4]

(3) *In praise I shall call upon the Lord, and shall be saved from my foes* (v. 3). Here we learn to give thanks for favors conferred, and to ask in turn for what is needed: by doing this, he says, I shall be stronger than my adversaries. Then he describes all the kinds of enemy incursions: *Death's pangs encircled me, and torrents of lawlessness threw me into confusion. Pangs of Hades surrounded me, death's snares caught me unawares* (vv. 4–5). By *death's pangs* and *pangs of Hades* he refers to deadly perils: just as pangs accompany birth, so the greatest perils are associated with death. Now, he calls the unjust and unexpected assaults of the foe *torrents of lawlessness:* just as a torrent that receives the currents of water flowing from this direction and that strikes suddenly, so too did Saul and the other enemies inflict their assaults. He called the stealthy attacks *death's snares:* [976] what a snare is to the animals, an ambush is to those under attack; each stratagem is characterized by hidden injury.

(4) *In my tribulation I called upon the Lord, and cried out to my God. The Lord heard my voice from his holy temple; my cry before him will reach his ears* (v. 6). Although beset by so many calamities, I spurned all human assistance and invoked divine aid, and hope did not disappoint me: immediately my prayers were answered. The *temple* he refers to here was not the one made by hands, that one not having been built at that stage, Solomon constructing it later; rather, he used this name of heaven.

(5) *Then the earth was moved and began trembling, and the foundations of the hills were shaken, they were moved, because God was en-*

---

4. 1 Sam 2.10, from the Song of Hannah. (The editor suggests that a copyist has placed this comment here in error.)

raged with them. In his anger smoke arose, and fire flamed from his face, coals were kindled by him (vv. 7–8). Now, he included all these things, not because they happened altogether in this way, but because they were thought of this way in faith. God being the one who not only punishes but also terrifies human beings, he often did such things, causing terror with thunder claps, din, earthquakes, and fire. Wanting to terrify Israel also in this way, he showed Mount Sion flaming with fire. So in these ways the present inspired author also made mention of the punishment inflicted on the enemies, and teaches other people as well not to do the same lest they suffer the same.

(6) *He bent down the heavens and descended; thick gloom was under his feet. He mounted cherubim and flew on wings of winds. He set darkness as his concealment, his tent around him* (vv. 10–11). Once more here he describes God's manifestation, instilling appropriate terror in the listeners. Yet we understand neither descending nor ascending of the divine nature: the divinity is uncircumscribed, present everywhere, embracing all things.[5] In these ways, however, we learn the difference in the provisions made: sometimes he appears to human beings in a milder fashion, sometimes more magnificently. But there are also times when in his desire to instill fear as well he reveals something surprising and novel. So that verse [977] *He bent down the heavens and descended* let us take to mean that he made his own manifestation clear. *Thick gloom was under his feet* suggests the invisibility of his presence; *mounting the Cherubim* and *flying on the winds*, the rapidity of his appearance; *he set darkness as his concealment*, our inability to see his nature; *his tent around him*, the light encircling him—hence also blessed Paul's remark, "It is he alone who has immortality and dwells in inaccessible light."[6]

(7) *Waters of darkness in clouds of air. In the distant splendor before him the clouds pass by* (vv. 11–12). Just as the air turns dark with the density of clouds and then sends out flashes of lightning, he is saying, so the God of all, though invisible, emits rays of light visible to the mind, and with punishing fire punishes those ad-

---

5. Another reminder by this Antiochene to his reader of the anthropomorphisms of the psalm, not to be taken in literalistic fashion.
6. 1 Tim 6.16.

dicted to wickedness. He made this clear, note, by adding, *Hail and coals of fire. The Lord thundered from heaven, and the Most High uttered his sound. He fired arrows and scattered them; he multiplied his lightning flashes, and alarmed them* (vv. 12–14). This often happens in our time, too: in the wars that just lately broke out he laid waste with hail and fire the savages from the north attacking us. And the Persians recently making war on us from the east, who expected to get possession of our cities without bloodshed, he caught in these snares and prevented their further advance; some he put to death, others he sent off as reporters of what had occurred.[7]

(8) *The fountains of the waters appeared, and the foundations of the world were revealed, at your rebuke, O Lord, at the blast of the breath of your rage* (v. 15). This happened in our time in many regions: the earth was moved and broke open, an immense gap appeared in the highest mountains, and water gushed out in waterless places. Now, the ruler of all does this, giving evidence to human beings of his power of retribution, and teaching them that he has the power to inflict ruin on all in a flash; yet he applies instead his loving-kindness, and puts off the retribution and awaits their repentance.

(9) *He sent down from on high and took me; he drew me out of the flood of waters* (v. 16). And to teach what in figurative fashion he calls *waters* he added, [980] *He will deliver me from powerful foes and from those who hate me, because they were too strong for me* (v. 17). In an obvious manner, he is saying, he showed to my enemies his care for me; he said so by remarking, *He sent down from on high and took me*, that is, he convinced everyone that he provided assistance for me from heaven. Now, he thought me deserving of this providence on seeing the strength of the enemies: *they were too strong for me*, he says. *They forestalled me on the day of my misfortune* (v. 18). Here he seems to me to touch on the revolt of Absalom after the sin had been committed: by *misfortune*, which

---

7. A rare reflection by Theodoret of current events, providing a *terminus a quo* for the dating of the work (see Introduction, section 1). At the time of this war in 441 Theodoret would have been in his late forties. The *Commentary on the Psalms*, therefore, does not betray the signs of youthful inexperience that characterize Chrysostom's work on them.

Symmachus calls "hardship," he means the soul's weakness, on account of which the sin was committed.

(10) *The Lord became my support; he brought me out into a wide space* (vv. 18–19). When I was pushed down and cast headlong, he is saying, the Lord lifted me up, and turned my constriction into space, which means he granted me life instead of the expected death. He says this also in another psalm, "I was pushed hard and turned backwards so as to fall, and the Lord lifted me up."[8] *He will rescue me because he wants me.* I hope that he will grant me the same help in the future, and I shall be stronger than my adversaries, even if they have far greater power. *The Lord will repay me for my righteousness, and for the purity of my hands he will repay me. Because I kept the ways of the Lord, and did not forsake my God for impiety. Because all his judgments are before me, and his decrees have not failed me* (vv. 20–22). It is not unfair for him to show providence for me, he is saying; rather, it is because he understands my purpose and knows that it is my concern to keep all his commandments. In other words, after revealing great care shown him by God, he shows the fairness of this to urge the listeners to virtue and teach them that it is not possible for us to attain this unless we practice true regard for God. The inspired author, you see, did not wish to reveal to everyone the list of his own virtuous actions, but to propose how it is possible to enjoy the divine providence.

(11) *I shall be guiltless in his sight* (v. 23). How is it possible to achieve this? *I shall keep myself from my lawlessness.* Refraining from the evil I did, he is saying, I shall prove guiltless in the future. Thus the mighty David, [981] after being forced to mention his own virtuous actions so as to demonstrate the fairness of God's providence, could not bear to conceal the iniquity he had committed. *The Lord will repay me for my righteousness and for the purity of my hands before his eyes* (v. 24). When I prove completely guiltless, he is saying, then precisely is the time I shall attain the perfect good. The God of all has all things in view, after all, and for good deeds—he called them *purity of hands*—and pious intention he makes recompense.

8. Ps 118.13.

(12) Then he teaches this same thing more clearly: *With a holy one you will be holy, and with an innocent man you will be innocent; with a chosen one you will be chosen, and with a crooked one you will turn about* (vv. 25–26). You adjust your recompense to people's attitudes, O Lord: to the holy you provide what holiness deserves, to the guiltless and those free from sin what is fitting, to the chosen and perfect what is perfect, while to those straying from the right path and traveling in the opposite direction you ensure their finding the due end of their journey. How and in what fashion? *Because you will save a lowly people and you will lower the eyes of the haughty* (v. 27). Those who adopt a restrained outlook or are humbled by circumstances you will deem worthy of salvation and render illustrious, whereas those of haughty demeanor and slaves of conceit you will oblige to fall to the earth and have a thought to their natural lowliness.

(13) *Because you will light my lamp, O Lord, my God, you will shed light in my darkness* (v. 28). Since he often called tribulations *darkness*, he rightly gave the name *light* to freedom from them. Now, I enjoy this providence at your hands, he is saying; since the lamp that gets the true light—this is the name he gives the form of a slave[9]—is mine and will be formed from my loins. He says this also in another psalm, "There I shall raise up a horn for David, I prepared a lamp for my Christ."[10] *Because in you I shall be rescued from temptation, and by my God I shall vault a wall* (v. 29): every scheme and every ambush—he calls the ambush *temptation* and *wall*—I shall escape through your grace. *O my God, his way is faultless* (v. 30): you direct everything rightly, and for that reason I have confidence. *The sayings of the Lord are proved by fire:* now, this [984] I learnt from your trustworthy sayings—*proved by fire*, as I said before,[11] means tested and freed from falsehood. *He is the protector of all who hope in him:* not I alone, however, but also all who have this hope in him will enjoy the same help.[12]

---

9. We noted Theodoret's fondness for this term from Phil 2.7 for Christ in commentary on Ps 16.
10. Ps 132.17.
11. Cf. comment on Ps 17.3.
12. Commentary on the latter verses in this long psalm is becoming telegraphically brief, not much beyond simple paraphrase.

(14) *For who is God except our Lord, and who is God except our God?* (v. 31). There is no other God, you see, one responding to one person's request, another to another's. *The God who girded me with strength and made my path flawless* (v. 32): strengthened by his power, I shall hasten to travel the straight path. *He furnished me with feet like a deer's, and set me on the heights* (v. 33). In other words, just as he gave the deer the natural ability to trample on the fierce arrows, so he rendered me stronger and superior to the enemy. *Training my hands for war* (v. 34): lifting them in prayer, I prevail over my adversaries. *He set my arms as a bronze bow:* hence he caused my arms, like an unbroken bow of bronze, to fire the arrows against the enemy. *You gave me a protection of my salvation, and your right hand supported me; your instruction guided me to the end, and your instruction itself will teach me* (v. 35): you instructed the sinner, and lifted up the fallen; to the extent that the sin is evil you gave your teaching, and you deemed him worthy of salvation.

(15) *You gave my steps room under me, and my footprints were not weakened* (v. 36): in the constriction of tribulation you gave me the space of comfort, by which I was refreshed and persevered up to the present. For *gave room* Symmachus said, "broadened." [985] *I shall pursue my foes and lay hold of them; I shall not desist until they fail. I shall cause them distress, and they will not succeed in standing firm; they will fall under my feet* (vv. 37–38): strengthened in this way by your providence I hope to prevail over all my adversaries, and not desist until I bring them all into subjection again, which was what he suggested in saying, *they will fall under my feet.*

(16) *You girded me with strength for war, you put all those assailing me under my feet* (v. 39): you granted me bravery and strength, whereas you handicapped the onset of the enemies. This is what happened in the case of Goliath and Saul: the former wasted the time for action in empty words, and he brought him down with a sling; the other was disabled by sleep, and he easily got away from him. In this way he also escaped the schemes of the inhabitants of Gath.

(17) *You made my foes turn their back on me* (v. 40), that is, you put them to flight: those fleeing normally turn their back. *And*

those who hated me you destroyed—Saul, Ahithophel, Absalom, and countless others. *They cried out, and there was no one to save them; to the Lord, and he did not hearken to them* (v. 41). When the foreigners called on their own gods for assistance, they did not enjoy providential care from them: Saul, Absalom, Shimei, and the other enemies of the Israelites did not have God as their ally.[13] *I shall beat them as fine as dust before the wind, I shall grind them like dirt of the streets* (v. 42): they will become completely ruined and invisible, your grace at work in me.

(18) *You will deliver me from strife with the people* (v. 43). Here he forecasts the Jews' frenzy against the Savior and the salvation of the nations. His advice is to have nothing to do with their strife. *You will appoint me as head of the nations.* Admittedly, we do not know David ruled over the nations; so through the one born of him according to the flesh the prophecy is fulfilled. You see, the one born of David according to the flesh and also named David according to the divine Ezekiel[14]—I mean Christ the Lord—ruled over all the nations: as God he exercises eternal lordship over all, and after the Incarnation he receives the willing service of those believing in him. [988] *A people whom I did not know served me, on their ear's hearing of me they served me* (vv. 43–44). He makes this prediction in the person of Christ the Lord. Now, he says, Those who had never accepted lawgiver or prophet of mine were easily called and obeyed, and loved my service.

(19) *Foreign sons were false to me; foreign sons grew old, and went limping from their paths* (vv. 44–45). Now, those who were called sons and were enrolled in the ranks of sons made themselves foreign by proving ungrateful for favors done, limping in respect of the faith and abandoning the path of godliness. Thus God said through the prophet Jeremiah, "How did you turn into bitterness to me, a foreign vine, whereas I planted every vine to be genuine and fruitful?"[15] One shows its true cultivation, one proves their ingratitude. Now, for they *grew old* and *limped* Symmachus said "will be dishonored" and "shamed." The

---

13. A hasty reference, in which Saul, Absalom, and Shimei do not fit into the group of "foreigners" and "enemies of the Israelites."
14. Cf. Ezek 34.24, 37.24.
15. Cf. Jer 2.21.

outcome proves the prophecy: they are full of dishonor, seen to be loathsome to everyone.

(20) *The Lord lives! Blessed be my God; let the God of my salvation be exalted* (v. 46). After mentioning the disputation of the Jews, he hints at the Passion and the Resurrection, which follows the Passion. Since the Jews are accustomed to call the crucified one a corpse, for his part he shouts out, *The Lord lives! Blessed be my God; let the God of my salvation be exalted*—and not only *lives* but has even ascended to heaven and proffers salvation to those wanting it. *The God who gives me vengeance and subdued peoples under me, my rescuer from my wrathful foes. From my adversaries you will raise me up and from an unrighteous man rescue me* (vv. 47–48). You, therefore, who are at work long periods later, will rescue me, too, from those warring against me unjustly, and will render obedient the people you subjected to me.

(21) *Hence I shall confess to you among nations, O Lord, and sing to your name* (v. 49): through the nations that will be called a little later, I shall sing to you in all the churches throughout the whole world. Now, it is possible to see the outcome of this prophecy: in all cities, villages, fields, borders, mountains, hills, on land and sea, in the inhabited world and the deserts, the divinely inspired David sings praise to God in pious mouths.

(22) [989] *Magnifying the salvations of the king, and showing mercy to his anointed, to David and his seed forever* (v. 50). In other words, You who anointed me king not only save me but make me illustrious. Not only me, however, but also my children you will deem worthy of this providence, and you will forever preserve the luster for my seed. Now, if we take this in regard to the Jews, the prophecy is borne out: up to the captivity the line of David continued in kingship, but after return from there only Zorobabel ruled and did not leave heirs to his rule. So if the prophecy is true—as of course it is true, the Spirit of truth revealing it—it remains to understand the seed of David, who has eternal luster, as Christ the Lord, born of David according to the flesh, who enjoys everlasting kingship and glory; he enjoyed this before the ages as creator and God, but received it again as a human being at the end of the days. Hence also through the divinely inspired Ezekiel the God of all said, "I shall give to them

David as their king," and again, "David the king in their midst."[16] Now, he called him David as sprung from the loins of David according to the flesh. Blessed Isaiah also calls this out: "There will be the root of Jesse arising to rule nations, and in him nations shall hope."[17] Acquainted with this, blessed Matthew began the evangelical history in this way, "Book of genealogy of Jesus Christ son of David."[18]

16. Cf. Ezek 37.24; 34.24.
17. Cf. Isa 11.10.
18. Matt 1.1. As he stated in his preface, Theodoret is reluctant to give the psalm an exclusively historical or spiritual interpretation, concluding with a little of each.

COMMENTARY ON PSALM 19

To the end. A psalm of David.

WE LEARN THREE KINDS of divine laws from blessed Paul.[1] One unwritten kind he said was given to human beings in creation and nature: "From the creation of the world," he says, "his invisible attributes have been understood and espied in created things"; and again, "For when the Gentiles, who do not have the law, practice the obligations of the law instinctively, despite having no law they are a law to themselves."[2] He says another law was provided in writing through the mighty Moses: "The Law was added because of transgressions," he says, "ordained through angels in the hand of a mediator."[3] He knew also a third one imposed after these, the law of grace: "For the law of the Spirit of life," he says, "has set me free from the law of sin and death."[4] Blessed David in this psalm [992] teaches human beings the harmony between these, following the same order: firstly, the one the creator preaches in creation; then the one given through Moses, instilling a greater knowledge of the creator to those willing to attend; after that, the law of grace, perfectly purifying souls and freeing them from the present destruction. This in fact is the reason the psalm also refers us "to the end," naming the New Testament in the end.

---

1. This psalm, with its abrupt movement from natural lyricism to praise of law after the opening six verses, leads modern commentators to admit an unhappy conjunction of two disparate compositions (Weiser refuses to take them both together) or, like Dahood, to see a Canaanite work in the opening part. Theodoret, not disposed to be so critical, arrives at an appealing synthesis of law natural and positive in the psalm as a whole—probably not of his own invention.

2. Cf. Rom 1.20, 2.14.   3. Cf. Gal 3.19.
4. Rom 8.2.

(2) *The heavens tell of the glory of God, and the firmament announces work of his hands* (v. 1). Even the visible beauty and magnitude of the heavens are alone sufficient, he is saying, to proclaim the power of the creator: if you observe a most mighty and magnificent building, you admire the builder; and if you see a skillfully and beautifully designed ship, you think of the shipwright; and at the sight of a painting the painter comes to mind. Much more, to be sure, does the sight of creation lead the viewers to the creator. It was also logical for him to mention heaven and firmament in the teaching of Moses: that one first mentioned the making of heaven, then described the creation of the firmament, which in turn he called heaven of heavens, the text says. Now, let the plural form "heavens" surprise no one: it is usual for Scripture to use it in the singular in some cases and in the plural in others. Blessed David uses it in the singular: "Heaven belongs to the Lord of heaven";[5] and again, "Who covers heaven in clouds."[6] But he likewise uses it in the plural: "Praise him, heavens of heavens,"[7] he says, though the same meaning is had by "Heaven belongs to the Lord of heaven": the heaven that is visible is like some kind of roof prepared for the earth, whereas the higher one stands in the same relation to it as the latter does to the earth. Hence it is called heaven of heaven, and they are named heavens of heavens. Now, it is possible to see amongst us also the double usage in connection with cities: we also call Tarsus Tarsoi, though it is one city, and Thebe Thebes, the same city; likewise, the ancients spoke both of Mycene and Mycenae, though aware they were giving a plural form to one city. In this case, however, in my view it is not an idle reference, but due to those who try to count several heavens.

(3) *Day to day belches forth speech, and night to night proclaims knowledge* (v. 2). That is, the ordained succession of night and day illustrates the boundaries set by the creator, [993] which inanimate creation refrains from infringing. With regard for human beings' needs, you see, day and night both wax and wane,

---

5. Ps 115.16 [LXX]. Discrepancy in morphological details was grist to an Antiochene's mill, of course.
6. Ps 147.8.
7. Ps 148.4.

sharing the time with one another and repaying the debt to one another, and thus illustrate the providence conferred on them. The words, *belches forth speech, proclaims knowledge, tells of glory* teach us that the visible things are inanimate, being a kind of mask that teaches everyone to be led from visible things to the invisible God and to offer singing to him. *There is no speech nor word, their voices are not heard. Their utterance went out to all the earth, to the bounds of the world their messages* (vv. 3–4). Symmachus translated this more clearly: "Night announces knowledge to night, not in speech or words, their voices are not heard, but their sound went out to all the earth"—or according to Aquila, "their norm." That is, by putting forth neither words nor verbal expressions but the norm, and demonstrating their own order, they summon all land and sea to the divine singing.

(4) *In the sun he set up his tent, and he emerges like a bridegroom from his chamber. He will rejoice like a giant to run the race; his emergence is from heaven's zenith and his course to heaven's zenith* (vv. 4–6). The three translated this, too, more clearly.[8] *In the sun he set up his tent,* he is saying, in them—that is, in the heavens. The mighty Moses taught this, too: "God made the two great lights, and set them in the firmament of heaven for illuminating the earth."[9] The divine David said the same thing, that he set the tent in the heavens for the sun so that it might travel on them and resemble in beauty a bridegroom emerging from a chamber with great finery, and in speed some giant running with great force and strength, with nothing getting in the way or endeavoring to hinder his progress. This is the way the sun also rises in the east, traverses the sky in one day [996] and arrives at the west, sharing its warmth with every living thing: *There is nothing concealed from its warmth.* He made mention of *warmth* in place of light to show its force to be greater than man-made light in that it is possible for things at a distance to enjoy the warmth; the man-made light can do this only for things coming close to it, whereas the sun shares its heat along with light by emitting its rays from a distance. This is also sufficient to reveal

8. An aside like this—though not really typical—would support the view that evidence from alternative versions was a later insert.
9. Cf. Gen 1.16–17.

the creator to human beings, yet by way of help he also gave the Law, which was capable of correcting those in error.

(5) *The Law of the Lord is faultless, correcting souls; the testimony of the Lord is reliable, giving wisdom to the simple. The judgments of the Lord are right, gladdening the heart; the command of the Lord is clear, giving light to the eyes. The fear of the Lord is pure, abiding forever; the decrees of the Lord are true, completely justified, more desirable than heaps of gold or precious stones, and sweeter than honey or honeycomb* (vv. 7–10). He calls the Mosaic Law *Law, testimony, judgments, command, decrees*: this is what the Law calls itself, saying in one place, "These are the judgments and the decrees the Lord gave to Moses," and elsewhere, "You will keep the Law of the Lord your God and observe his commandments."[10] It is called *Law* in that it regulates and prescribes the best way of life, *testimony* in testifying against sinners and highlighting the punishment for transgression, *judgments* in teaching what is right, forbidding what is wrong and declaring virtuous people righteous, *command* in commanding what is to be done and giving orders authoritatively, *decrees* in revealing the divine verdicts and teaching what goods the observant will enjoy and to what punishments the transgressor will be consigned.

(6) So he means that the *Law* of God, being free of every fault, corrects people's souls and makes them faultless; the *testimony* gives wisdom to the immature and simple by frightening them; the *judgments* gladden the heart by revealing the basis of judgment; the *command* gives light to the mind's eye, teaching what constitutes service to the God of all. While piety and the *fear* of God, in suggesting observance of these, [997] procure enjoyment of the eternal goods, it was right for him to speak of the fear of God as *pure*—that is, free from blame—for the reason that human fear is blameworthy, being synonymous with dread. Now, he called the decrees *true* and *justified* on account of their conferring on people both honors and warranted punishments. In conclusion, he said these are worth more than gold and precious stones and sweeter than honey—not to all human beings,

---

10. Two statements in the style of Deuteronomy, approximating to places like 6.1 and 7.11. Theodoret, we saw, can be inexact in his recall of the Scriptures.

however, but to those truly human, whose life is not comparable with the brute beasts, in the words of the same divinely inspired author.[11]

(7) *Your servant in fact will keep them* (v. 11). Be clearer in teaching what benefit comes from it: *abundant the repayment for keeping them.* A wonderful reward, he is saying, is laid up for those choosing to keep them. And because he claimed to keep the decrees of God, calling to mind human weakness and considering the arrogance of the claim, he immediately added, *Who will understand faults? Purify me from my hidden ones* (v. 12): even if I intend with great enthusiasm to keep God's commands, I am dragged down by natural weakness to many faults against my will; some faults I commit in ignorance, some when overcome by the onset of circumstances. And even if I avoid sin in deed, thoughts fill me with every defilement. Hence I beseech you, who are able to purify me, and I cry out, *Purify me from my hidden ones.*

(8) *Spare your servant from hostile beings* (v. 13): not only do thoughts encircle me, but the column of the demons also besets me; some devise plots without, some conspire within. Now, he was right to call them *hostile* for being adversaries and enemies, and totally opposed to relationship with us. *If they do not gain dominion over me, then I shall be faultless and shall be purified from serious sin. My mouth's utterances will meet with favor, and my heart's attention is completely in your direction* (vv. 13–14). I long to enjoy your help in eluding their schemes and presenting my soul to you completely free of blame. On receipt of pardon from you for my past failings, may I offer to you everlasting hymn singing, giving my unwavering attention to your sayings. In these words, of course, he foretells the New Testament, [1000] the grace of baptism, and the gift of the all-holy Spirit, thanks to which the believers receive forgiveness of past sins, and with help sufficient for the future they prevail over the onset of passions, schemes, and wicked spirits.

---

11. Cf. Ps 32.9. Theodoret has really warmed to these verses on the Law under its various synonyms. Like Chrysostom, his anti-Jewish attitudes do not extend to the advantages of the Old Testament people of the psalmist's time.

(9) To this he adds, *O Lord, my helper and my redeemer.* By way of supplying a denouement to the psalm, he called him *Lord* in so far as he is maker and creator, and *redeemer* in so far as he frees us by the regeneration of all-holy baptism from our former perdition, redeems us from enslavement to the demons, and bestows on us incorruptibility and immortality. The psalm includes both former and latter subjects: it instructs us firstly on creation and providence; in the middle, on the Law; and finally, on grace.[12] It says, *Who will understand faults? Purify me of my hidden ones, O Lord, and spare your servant from hostile beings,* and *O Lord, my helper and my redeemer.* Now, the New Testament provides these goods.

12. In defiance of modern commentators, who are unable to accommodate the psalm's shift in focus (although Dahood on morphological grounds has to concede one author for the whole), Theodoret on theological grounds has succeeded in showing a unity and defensible movement of thought—even if on first principles he would admittedly be reluctant to question the form of the material bequeathed to him.

COMMENTARY ON PSALM 20

To the end. A psalm of David.

WHEN IN FORMER TIMES Sennacherib invaded Judah and dispatched a huge army commanded by Rabshakeh to besiege Jerusalem, he sent written word to Hezekiah full of every blasphemy and impiety.[1] On receipt of this letter, blessed Hezekiah, a man adorned with utter godliness, invited the prophet Isaiah to intercede for him, hastened to the divine Temple, opened the letter, and showed it to God, revealing the enemies' impiety, and beseeching him on account of the blasphemy committed to demonstrate to the Assyrians his peculiar force. Many generations previously, blessed David prophesies this, illuminated by the all-holy Spirit, and recites the present psalm,[2] showing the people praying with the king and asking for his supplication to be accepted.

(2) *The Lord hear you in the day of tribulation, the name of the God of Jacob protect you! Send help from the holy place, support you from Sion!* (vv. 1–2). When the remarkable Hezekiah ran to the divine Temple, you remember, clutching the blasphemous letter, they pray that his supplication be accepted and he gain help from that source. He called the Temple *holy place* here. [1001] *May the Lord remember all your sacrifice, and your holocaust be enriched* (v. 3). Since also in time of peace he gave attention to divine worship, they are justified in recounting this of him, beseeching the God of all to take account of the king's godliness, remember his many rituals of all kinds and in turn give peace so that he may placate him with further sacrifices. That phrase *may your holo-*

---

1. That incident again from 2 Kings 18–19 that Theodoret has several times before thought to supply a theme for psalms. Here he somewhat dramatizes the bare narrative of receipt of the letter and response to it.

2. Singing on the part of Old Testament psalmist or Christian believers is not emphasized by Theodoret. At least he is consistent about the divine inspiration of the biblical authors.

caust be enriched. Symmachus in fact rendered this way: "and may he make your offering greater," that is, giving the security that comes from peace, may he give you the opportunity to placate him with further sacrifices.[3]

(3) *May the Lord grant you your heart's desire, and implement your every purpose* (v. 4). We beseech the righteous judge, he is saying, to grant a response appropriate to your purity of soul. *We shall rejoice in your salvation, and be magnified in the name of the Lord our God. The Lord fulfill all the requests of your heart* (v. 5): when you receive the requests, we shall share the joy, becoming the cynosure of all eyes, thanks to the power of God. *Now I know that the Lord saved his Christ, he will hear him from his holy heaven* (v. 6). We have learnt from the events themselves, he is saying, that our king trusted in God and will win salvation; offering supplications in the Temple below, he receives help from on high. In fact, after he showed him praying below, he shows him being helped from on high. *In sovereignties the salvation of his right hand:* the greatest force for salvation is the power of his right hand, which he extends to those approaching him. Now, once more he said *right hand* in human fashion, referring to the divine operation in this way.

(4) *Some rely on chariots, some on horses, whereas we shall call upon the name of the Lord our God. They were entangled and fell, while we got up and stood straight* (vv. 7–8). They trusted in horses and chariots, he is saying, and enjoyed no benefit from them, but were caught up in unseen entanglements and collapsed. We by contrast invoked divine assistance and won salvation in visible manner, and emerged superior to the adversaries, as if the enemies had been stricken down with fear. *Lord, save the king; hear us on the day we call upon you* (v. 10): having enjoyed such support, therefore, we beg that we ourselves and our king may share in it unceasingly, Lord.[4]

---

3. Not for the first time does Theodoret find that the rendering of Symmachus throws light on an obscure phrase; he had in fact already turned it in this sense, and now acknowledges his debt.

4. Brief paraphrase has returned in place of the expansiveness and original synthesis distinguishing the commentary on the previous psalm. Is it that, like Chrysostom, Theodoret feels his style cramped when dealing with historical material?

COMMENTARY ON PSALM 21

To the end. A psalm of David. [1004]

AFTER THAT FAMOUS and illustrious victory and the unseen destruction of the Assyrians, blessed Hezekiah fell ill. Learning from the prophet Isaiah that he would die, he appeased God with his hot tears and gained release from the illness, and received a promise of fifteen years of life. Once again, therefore, the divine David wrote this psalm in the person of the people, singing the praise of God for the king's health.[1]

(2) *Lord, in your power the king will be glad, and will rejoice exceedingly in your salvation. You have given him his heart's desire, and did not deprive him of the request of his lips* (vv. 1–2). Being powerful and loving, he says, you received our king's prayer favorably, and granted him all his requests—or, rather, you gave him gifts beyond his requests, as he said further: *Because you anticipated him with blessings of goodness, you set on his head a crown of precious stone* (v. 3): without being asked you awarded kingship to him, adorning his head with the royal crown out of your peculiar generosity.

(3) *He asked life of you, and you gave him length of days forever* (v. 4). He received what he asked, the psalmist is saying, and gained life for which he longed. The word *forever*, you see, indicates also the future life prepared for the saints, which is indestructible.[2]

---

1. Modern commentators differ as to the occasion of the psalm, generally seeing it relating to military victory. Theodoret, while resembling this approach in connecting it to the incidents of 2 Kings 20, differs from them in focusing on Hezekiah's recovery from illness—and, as before, keeps his commentary very brief.

2. We have noted Theodoret's readiness to credit the Old Testament with an eschatology generally considered typical rather of New Testament thought—Dahood being a notorious exception, and in his commentary endorsing comments like these of Theodoret.

Thanks to your salvation his glory is wonderful; you endowed him with glory and magnificence (v. 5): you not only granted him salvation but also made him illustrious and exalted, and as well a cause of wonder both for the amazing death of the enemies and for the sun's moving backwards. Now, this became so well known everywhere on land and sea that the king of the Babylonians sent gifts to those who once upon a time gave gifts to the Assyrians, suspecting that it was on account of Hezekiah that the sun did this or had it done to it, prompted by the sign of the Assyrians' death.[3]

(4) *Because you gave him blessing forever; you will gladden him with joy in your presence* (v. 6). He will be famous in all generations, the psalmist is saying, and on everybody's lips for the great degree of [1005] confidence he enjoys with you. Symmachus in fact put "before your presence" for *in your presence;* so his meaning is that he will have joy and constant satisfaction by winning your presence, that is, your favor. Now, his trust in you was responsible for this: the psalmist said as much by adding, *Because the king hopes in the Lord, and by the mercy of the Most High he will not be moved* (v. 7): by enjoying your grace he is stronger than those at war with him, yet he enjoys it through trusting not in any human being but in your hope.

(5) *Let your hand be found on all your foes; may your right hand find all those who hate you* (v. 8). Symmachus said this more clearly: "Your hand will lay hold of all your foes; your right hand will find all those who hate you." Now, these words are consistent with the theme: the king's trust in your hope was not idle but arose from his knowledge that your right hand is stronger than all the enemies and will both lay hold of the swiftest and succeed in undoing the strongest. *Right hand* and *hand* once again mean "operation." *Because you will set them like a baking pan of fire at the time of your appearance. The Lord in his wrath will confound them and fire will consume them. You will destroy their fruit from the earth and their seed from the sons of men* (vv. 9–10). It is easy for you to ignite

---

3. Not quite the drift of the text of 2 Kings 20, where the gift is almost a mere customary gesture like the proverbial bunch of flowers, and where the Deuteronomist's emphasis falls rather on Hezekiah's consequent folly in boasting to the Babylonians of his wealth.

them like a baking pan and to destroy them like inflammable material—and not only them but also their progeny (he called them *seed* and *fruit*)—so that all memory of them is blotted out. Now, the phrase *at the time of your appearance* means at the time of your wrath, when you think fit for it to happen and judge the moment for punishment appropriate.

(6) *Because they directed evils against you* (v. 11): since they wagged their tongue against you, and employed blasphemous words. *They devised plans, which could not succeed in practice.* While some of the copies have *succeed,* Symmachus put it this way: "They considered impractical ideas." Now, in this he foretells the [1008] blasphemous remarks of the Assyrian: "Do not let the God in whom you believe deceive you into thinking he will deliver Jerusalem from my hand."[4] In connection with these words he says, "They considered impractical ideas," or they considered *plans, which could not succeed in practice,* expecting to prevail over the true God like the idols.

(7) *Because you will put them to flight* (v. 12). Symmachus, on the other hand, has this: "Because you will turn them about": as they flee the angel's blow,[5] you will rout them and force them to turn their backs so that as they depart they may broadcast what has happened. Now, the inspired author cited this in prophetic mode, as something not yet realized. *In your remnants you will prepare their countenance.* Some claimed this is a case of metathesis, and understood it this way: In their remnants you will prepare your countenance, that is to say, On both those apprehended and those fleeing you will inflict punishment. It is possible, on the other hand, by employing the same structure to approximate to the same thought, *In your remnants you will prepare their countenance:* It will be simple and easy for you to inflict on them the punishments remaining to you: you will be able to turn around, stop, and punish those fleeing, turning their backs, and believing they have escaped death.[6]

---

4. Cf. 2 Kings 18.29–35.
5. Cf. 2 Kings 19.35.
6. Theodoret has not given up easily on this obscure verse, which in the original contains more than one *hapax legomenon:* he recognizes its obscurity, considers an amended reading, but insists on finding an acceptable

(8) *Be exalted, O Lord, in your power; we shall celebrate and sing of your sovereignties* (v. 13). Not for being lowly is God exalted, nor does he receive what he does not possess; instead, what he possesses he reveals. So it was right for the psalmist to say, *Be exalted, O Lord, in your power:* your exaltation is revealed in your ineffable power, which we shall continue to celebrate and sing, recounting your marvelous works.

---

meaning in the text as it stands. Unlike Chrysostom, he shows no willingness to cite Hebrew at his reader, let alone go further back to Ugaritic, like Dahood.

COMMENTARY ON PSALM 22

To the end. On support at dawn. A psalm of David.[1]

HIS PSALM FORETELLS the events of Christ the Lord's Passion and Resurrection, the calling of the nations and the salvation of the world. Now, the title, *To the end. On support at dawn,* suggests as much: *To the end* occurs for you to consider the plan achieved by him at the consummation of the ages; [1009] *support at dawn* means manifestation of our Savior, which like daybreak illumines those seated in darkness,[2] the Lord being true light. Now, when the light rises, it results in daybreak, and at its appearance darkness is dissolved and with it the devil's gloom. Everywhere in Scripture, remember, evil is understood by analogy with darkness.[3] Some people, on the other hand, say *support at dawn* means the moment of the Savior's Resurrection. The psalm, then, moves along those lines: more faith is to be placed in the sacred apostles' and the Savior's own clear adoption of the psalm's opening than on those essaying a contrary interpretation.[4]

1. The LXX and therefore Theodoret have difficulty also with this title, not understanding it as a direction for the musicians. While the Hebrew once again seems to be citing a well-known air, rendered by NRSV as The Deer of the Dawn, the LXX errs further in mistaking *'ayyelet,* "deer," for *'eyalut,* "support." The fact that Symmachus concurs (though Theodoret looks for support neither from Hebrew nor from alternative versions) would have encouraged him to follow suit.
2. Cf. Luke 1.79.
3. Theodoret we have seen sensitive to the figurative language of the Psalms and of Scripture generally, and ready to remind his readers of it briefly—but never tempted to be carried away into flights of allegorical fancy.
4. Though the text is a little uncertain at this point, he seems to be weighing up diverse interpretations of which he is aware and (without reference to the language of the original, of course) coming down in favor of the one arising from New Testament usage as far as he understands it. At

(2) *O God my God, attend to me: why have you abandoned me?* (v. 1). Now, it was while fixed to the wood that the Lord uttered this cry, using the very language of the Hebrews, "Eli, Eli, lema sabachthani?"[5] So how could the testimony of truth itself be found inadmissible? He says he has been abandoned, however, since, despite no sin having been committed by him, death prevailed after receiving authority against sinners. So he calls *abandonment* not any separation from the divinity to which he was united, as some suspected, but the permission given for the Passion: the divinity was present to the form of a slave in his suffering and permitted him to suffer so as to procure salvation for the whole of nature. Of course, it was not affected by suffering from that source: how could the impassible nature suffer? It is Christ the Lord as man, on the contrary, who speaks these words, and since he was the firstfruits of human nature,[6] it is on behalf of all of nature that he utters the words in what follows: *The words of my failings are far from saving me.*

(3) Now, you should know that none of the other translators mentioned the *failings:* Aquila said "my roaring," Symmachus, "my lamentations," Theodotion, "my cry." Lest by depending on the other translators here, however, we should seem to be contesting different versions of the psalm laboriously, we shall use the version of the Septuagint. In dealing with this verse, in fact, it too did not claim to apply the psalm to the Lord: how could you [1012] say of a person who was not a sinner, it objects, *The words of my failings are far from saving me?* Let it therefore heed John's loud cry, "Behold the lamb of God, who takes away the sin of the world,"[7] and the divinely inspired Paul's words, "For

---

the close of the commentary he will give a firm rebuttal of Jewish insistence on referring the psalm to David's life.

5. Matt 27.46.

6. Cf. 1 Cor 15.20. Being under pressure of New Testament usage to see the psalm referring to Jesus, Theodoret finds himself also required to deal with the Christological implications both of the Passion and of ambiguous statements in the psalm; and so willy-nilly the commentary becomes expansive.

7. John 1.29. Theodoret could have taken the soft option of an alternative version that suppressed the theologically difficult "failings" of the LXX. Instead, he adopted it, and with the support of NT statements found another way of dealing with the theological problem.

us he made him to be sin who did not know sin so that we might become righteousness through him,"[8] and again, "Christ redeemed us from the curse of the Law by becoming a curse for us."[9] So just as the one who was a fount of righteousness assumed our sin, and the one who was an ocean of blessing accepted a curse lying upon us, and scorning shame endured a cross, so too he uttered the words on our behalf. After all, if he willingly submitted to chastisement prescribed for us—"Chastisement of our peace is upon him,"[10] the inspired author says—much more is it the case that it was on our behalf that he employed these words in our person, crying out, *The words of my failings are far from saving me:* do not have regard to the faults of nature, he is saying, but grant salvation in view of my sufferings.

(4) And since he dealt with the passion in human fashion and frequently prayed at the time of the Passion, "Father, if it is possible, let this cup pass from me," and in his distress he said, "My soul is sorrowful to the point of death,"[11] it was right for the psalm also to predict it in the words, *O God, I shall cry to you by day, and you will not hearken to me, by night, and not to my folly* (v. 2). Or, according to the others, "by night, and there is no silence": despite my crying out unceasingly night and day and not bearing to keep silent, you do not hear, but instead give me over to suffering. All the same, I know the mystery of the design, as the phrase suggests, *not to my folly:* I have come to realize that, far from it being without purpose that you delayed granting my request, you designed some marvelous saving reality stemming from my suffering.[12]

(5) *You, however, the praise of Israel, dwell in the holy place* (v. 3). This is the most baffling thing of all, he is saying, that despite your dwelling in this holy body the Passion is carried out. Now, he calls him *praise of Israel* in being praised and celebrated by his own attendants, the other translators in place of *praise* putting "hymn." *Our Fathers hoped in you* (v. 4). He shows the benefit of

8. 1 Cor 5.21.   9. Gal 3.13.
10. Isa 53.5 [LXX].   11. Matt 26.39, 38.
12. Theodoret is perhaps evoking here the Pauline statements of the way of salvation that is the *mystery* of Christ, that defies human logic but is in keeping with the divine design or *economy*, such as "the plan of the mystery," of which Eph 3.9 speaks. See note 3 on *Commentary* on Ps 9.

the hope, *they hoped and you rescued them:* they cried to you and were saved, they hoped in you and were not put to shame. Indeed I am clearly aware, he is saying, that all our fathers trusted in your help and were not disappointed in their hope, they called to you for assistance and enjoyed your providence.

(6) [1013] *But I am a worm, not a human being, reproached by man, scorned by the people* (v. 6). But I am like a worm, he is saying, seen to be worthless and become a laughingstock. Now, some claimed that by *worm* is suggested also the birth from a virgin, as it is not by intercourse that it comes into existence; but I believe only lowliness is indicated here by *worm,* to judge from what he goes on to say: *At the sight of me they all turned up their nose at me, they muttered under their breath and shook their head, He hoped in the Lord, let him rescue him, let him save him because he wants him* (vv. 7–8). This is what is set forth in the sacred Gospels: "Many shook their heads and said, He saved others, he cannot save himself."[13] The other brigand said, "If you are the Son of God, save yourself and us."[14] Indeed this verse, *He hoped in the Lord, let him rescue him, let him save him because he wants him,* can be found in the sacred Gospels.

(7) *Because you are the one who drew me out of the womb, my hope from my mother's breasts. On you I was cast from the womb, from my mother's womb you are my God* (vv. 9–10). Blessed Isaiah also prophesied this; after saying, "The virgin will conceive and bear a son, and they will give him the name Emmanuel," he added, "He eats curds and honey before knowing good and evil, he declines evil in choosing the good."[15] So blessed David, in the person of Christ the Lord, says, You both formed me in the womb and in turn brought me forth from there; still suckling and pulling on my mother's breast, I rested my hope on your care. *Do not keep your distance from me, because tribulation is nigh, because there is no one to help me* (v. 11): at that time even a band of the disciples abandoned him.

---

13. Matt 27.39–42, loosely recalled. Theodoret is no stickler for putting words in the mouth of the right speakers.
14. Luke 23.39, loosely recalled: at least Theodoret avoided the common mistake of calling these brigands thieves.
15. Cf. Isa 7.14–16 [LXX].

(8) Then he forecasts the forms of tribulation. *Many young bulls surrounded me, fat bulls encircled me. They opened their mouth at me like a lion striking and roaring* (vv. 12–13). Now, he calls *bulls* the priests and scribes, entrusted with ruling the people and given to great audacity; *young bulls* those under them, calling them *fat* because reveling in the good things supplied by him. This was the way the mighty Moses also prophesied: "Jacob ate his fill, the beloved kicked up his heels, he grew fat, bloated, and obese, and [1016] abandoned the Lord who made him."[16] Blessed Hosea actually likens him to a frisky heifer: "Like a rebellious heifer Ephraim rebelled." Now, he gave that name to the people: "This was the way with Ephraim, a heifer trained to love contention,"[17] that is, quarrelsome and contentious. He gives the name *contention* not to conquest, note, but to contentiousness. And to show the humiliation that came afterwards, he added, "But I shall tread on the beauty of her neck": I shall lower her haughty neck and impose the yoke of slavery. So the psalm describes in advance the attacks of the chief priests, the scribes, and the Pharisees, who in imitation of the audacity of bulls and the frenzy of lions hemmed in Christ the Lord.

(9) *All my bones are poured out like water* (v. 14). He gives the name *bones* to the sacred apostles, since he also calls the Church *body*, and the bones are the strength of the body, the body's looseness and fluidity being supported by them. Now, at the time of the Passion everyone was scattered, dispersed hither and yon like water. *My heart was melted like wax in the midst of my belly, my strength is dried up like a potsherd, my tongue sticks to my throat. You have brought me down to the dust of death* (vv. 14–15). All this happened at the time of the Passion: the heart was dissolved by fear like wax by fire, and strength gave no evidence of its former energy; the tongue remained quite immobile as well. The inspired evangelists teach us that he was often questioned but gave no reply. He was consigned to the tomb after the Passion, which the psalmist called *dust of death*, the buried being covered in dust.

(10) *Because many dogs surrounded me, a mob of evildoers encir-*

16. Deut 32.15.
17. Hos 4.16, 10.11.

cled me (v. 16). After the Jews he makes mention of an army from the nations; they handed him over to them, remember. Hence the inspired composition even keeps to the order of events. Now, it was right for him to name the former *bulls* and the latter *dogs:* one group were subject to the Law, even if they openly transgressed the Law, while the other were impure in terms of the Law. The Lord spoke in those terms also of the Canaanite woman: "It is not right to take the children's food," [1017] he said, "and give it to the pups."[18] Nevertheless, after the Passion those former *dogs* took on the status of sons through faith, whereas those who once had enjoyed the care shown to sons received the name of dogs for raging against the Lord like very dogs. Blessed Paul cries out about them, "Beware of the dogs, beware of the evildoers. Beware of mutilation."[19] The inspired word therefore called them *dogs: a mob of evildoers encircled me.*

(11) Then he describes the deeds perpetrated by them: *They dug my hands and my feet, they numbered all my bones* (vv. 16–17). This is obvious and clear even to the most contentious: we hear in the sacred Gospels the Lord himself saying to his holy disciples, "Look at my hands and my feet for proof that I am here in person."[20] And he actually showed Thomas the marks of the nails and the blow of the spear.[21] Now, *they numbered all my bones* suggests, In crucifying me they stretched me out so that it would be easy for anyone wishing to do so to get to know even the number of my bones. *Whereas for their part they stared and scrutinized me,* that is, mocking and jeering at me. *They divided my garments among them, and on my clothing cast lots* (v. 18). Now, this, too, the story of the sacred Gospels clearly teaches us.[22]

18. Matt 15.26. Having taken the difficult option of defending the relevance of v. 1 to Jesus without altering the text, Theodoret is now encouraged to find later verses even following "the order of events" of his life and Passion. He chooses not to mention that Aquila and Theodotion read "hunters" for "dogs."

19. Phil 3.2. Theodoret is as restrained as are the Gospels in evoking these colorful Old Testament testimonies to the Passion of Christ; he has no wish to exploit them for effect.

20. Luke 24.39.

21. Cf. John 20.27.

22. Cf. Matt 27.35, a point simply made without the elaboration of, say, sacred art.

(12) *But you, O Lord, do not keep your help at a distance from me; have an eye to my support. Rescue my soul from a sword, my single possession from the grasp of a dog; save me from a lion's mouth and my lowliness from unicorns' horns* (vv. 19–21). Since I have no human help, he is saying, may I receive your support and be rescued both from them and from the one who works through them like a dog and an attacking lion. Now, he gives the names *lion, dog,* and *unicorn* to the one with the power of death, in the Apostle's phrase[23]—that is, the devil, who attacked him at the time of the Passion like a wild beast, inflicting death. The Lord had also said this in the sacred Gospels: "Now is the judgment of this world, now the ruler of this world will be driven out"; and again, "The ruler of this world is coming, and [1020] he will find nothing in me."[24] Yet despite finding nothing he was looking for—he was looking for the follies of sin—he shamelessly and most unjustly handed him over to death, whereas the latter did not shrink from the injustice in his purpose of doing away with the death common to all.

(13) *I shall tell of your name to my brothers, I shall sing to you in the midst of the Church* (v. 22). From this it is clear that he was uttering these things in human fashion in so far as he was enduring in human fashion, too, what he was uttering. I mean, he calls *brothers* those believing in him. It is as man that he has them as *brothers,* however: as God he is their Master and Lord, whereas as man he is called also their *brother.* He is Only-begotten and Firstborn; one title belongs to him as God and Lord, whereas the other belongs to him as man. In other words, as God he alone is begotten and is called Only-begotten, while as man he is also called Firstborn: the Apostle is witness to this in his words, "In order that he might be firstborn among many brothers."[25] So he says this, *Telling it to my brothers, I shall sing to you through them,* to ensure they compose this hymn; then he fulfils the promise.

23. Cf. Heb 2.14.
24. John 12.31, 14.30.
25. Rom 8.29, supplied as though an afterthought, to qualify his previous assignment of this title. Once again Theodoret is anxious his readers are crystal clear about the hypostatic union in Jesus; psalm expressions are not as precise on this topic as he would like.

(14) *You who fear the Lord, praise him; all the descendants of Jacob, glorify him. Let all the descendants of Israel stand in awe of him* (v. 23). Since, you see, the church was composed both of Gentiles and Jews, he roused both to hymn singing, the latter by naming them after their forebear, both Jacob and Israel, the former on the basis of virtue as a sufficient ornament in place of race. This was also the way Jews who came to the Law from the Gentiles were named; the story of the Acts teaches us this, too: in a public address the divine Apostle said, "Men of Israel, and those amongst you who fear God."[26] *Because he did not despise or abhor the prayer of the poor, nor turn his face from me; when I cried to him he hearkened to me* (v. 24). Sing praise to the one who proved responsible for this salvation of yours, he is saying, who could not bring himself to overlook your so lowly nature, instead hearkening to you and through my resurrection making your salvation my concern.

(15) After this he indicates the equality that as God he has with the Father, adding, *From you comes my praise; I shall confess to you in the great assembly* (v. 25): as I [1021] manifest you to human beings, so too you teach all human beings to offer the same honor to me, saying at one time, "This is my beloved Son, in whom I am well pleased; listen to him,"[27] at another, "I have glorified you, and will glorify you again."[28] This is the way he made the revelation of himself to Peter, likewise to Paul, likewise in turn through them to human beings: he called the *great assembly* that which reaches to the ends of the earth. *My vows I shall pay before those who fear him.* The *vows* he speaks of here are not prayers but promises: the Law also knew that distinction, "Should you make a vow to the Lord,"[29] that is, If you promise something to God. So after previously promising to compose a hymn through those believing in him, here he teaches more clearly that he will

---

26. Cf. Acts 13.16.
27. Matt 17.5. Theodoret's statement of Jesus' role as making the Father clear to human beings reminds one of Irenaeus's better known "The glory of God is the human being fully alive" (*Adversus haereses* 4.7, which refers, of course, to the Incarnate Word as the prime analogue).
28. John 12.28, adapted.
29. Deut 23.21.

impose a limit on the promises so that those meditating on the divine sayings may learn the truth of what is said through the events themselves. Now, in mentioning *assembly* he necessarily makes a prophecy about it, forecasting the calling of all the nations: he calls them *needy* in not having had in former times the riches of godliness but being in thrall to the penury of ignorance.

(16) *The poor eat and will be filled, and those who seek him out will praise the Lord* (v. 26)—not everyone (the Gospel was not obeyed by everyone, after all), but those who gave way to the divine desire: these for the reason of their hunger and thirst he said would be satisfied by enjoying the immortal fare. Now, the divine fare and the spiritual teaching we know to be the eucharistic feasting that is immortal, of which the initiates have knowledge.[30] *Their hearts will live forever:* though clad in a yet corruptible body, they are refreshed by the hope of resurrection and look forward to eternal life. *All the ends of the earth will remember and will be converted to the Lord* (v. 27). That was well put, *will remember,* because though receiving their existence from God they forgot the one who created them. *All the ends of the earth,* to be sure—not one nation or even two, but countless numbers of all those in the world will run to him, and will enthusiastically receive the rays of the knowledge of God. *All the clans of the nations will bow down before him.* And to teach that the lordship is God's own and not another's, he went on: [1024] *Because kingship is the Lord's, and he rules the nations* (v. 28): God is not only God of Jews, as they believe, but maker of the whole human race. This is the way the Apostle also spoke: "Or is he the God of the Jews only, and not also of the nations? Of the nations also, to be sure, since God is one, and he will justify the circumcision on the basis of faith and the uncircumcised through the same faith."[31]

(17) *All the prosperous of the earth ate and adored him, all who go down to the earth will be prostrate before him* (v. 29): those who eat and are filled, giving thanks for the immortal fare, will give the

---

30. Writing at his desk, and not speaking in church in a liturgical situation, Theodoret does not make frequent reference to the sacramental life of his readers.

31. Rom 3.29–30.

adoration due to God to the one who became provider of these things. Since in the first half of the verse he mentioned only the prosperous in so far as they had become like that through that divine fare, he was right to add, *all who go down to the earth will be prostrate before him.* After the resurrection from the dead, you see, they will offer this adoration to God, some willingly, some unwillingly, some by desire, some through fear, according to that apostolic saying, "Every knee will bend to him, in heaven, on earth, and under the earth, and every tongue confess that Jesus Christ is Lord, to the glory of God the Father."[32] *My soul will live for him, and my descendants will serve him* (v. 30). Now, *descendants* of Christ the Lord are those who have been reborn through the washing of regeneration and have received the grace of adoption. Hence he said that his soul would live for him, but not that it would serve—rather, that the descendants would serve; the nature assumed was united to the divinity assuming, and shared the same glory and honor.[33]

(18) *The generation to come will be reported to the Lord, and will report his righteousness to the people to be born, whom the Lord made* (vv. 30–31). Not about this generation do I speak, he is saying, in terms of which I, David, make this prophecy, but about the one to come and the people to be born, whom the Lord of all himself set up. So he prophesied all this. For my part, however, I deplore the stupidity of the Jews on the score that, though in constant contact with the divine utterances, they do not take in the truth that is so clearly obvious in them. Instead, they declare the psalm refers to David,[34] taking him to be the one crying out, *The generation to come will be reported to the Lord, and will report his righteousness to the people to be born,* [1025] *whom the Lord made. All the*

32. Phil 2.10–11.
33. Again Theodoret's anxiety that psalm statements should not obscure in his reader's mind the distinction of natures in Jesus and his equality of status. Cf. notes 15 and 18 on *Commentary* on Ps 2.
34. Theodoret in his preface disapproved of commentators' excessive reference of psalms to Jewish history, yet he has shown himself quite ready to make this reference in psalms not coercively encouraging the commentator to do so. Probably because of the New Testament evidence of Jesus' own use of this psalm, however, he has invested much Christological attention in it, and is unwilling to leave it to the Jews.

ends of the earth will remember and be converted to the Lord, and all the clans of the nations will bow down before him. All the prosperous of the earth ate and adored him: we see none of this happening to David or to any of his successors. Only Christ the Lord, on the contrary, who is of David according to the flesh, God the Word who became man, who though of David's line took the form of a slave; he filled all earth and sea with the knowledge of God, after all, and persuaded those who were once in error and offered adoration to idols to adore the true God instead of false gods.

(19) Let us leave behind words addressed to the Jews, however, and proceed to our current concern and the commentary on the remaining psalms.[35]

---

35. Unlike Chrysostom, from whom, incidentally, we do not have an extant commentary on this psalm, Theodoret does not exploit at length this occasion for highlighting Jewish error in interpretation, and moves on— not without a compliment to the Jews for their reading of Scripture. He is also no doubt aware he has already exceeded his normal length of commentary.

COMMENTARY ON PSALM 23

To the end. A psalm of David.

HE PRESENT PSALM IS SUNG in the person of the nations rejoicing in his shepherding them. They actually describe the mystical feast, which the one shepherding them set before them. *The Lord shepherds me, and nothing will be wanting to me* (v. 1). It has the same sense as what was commented on before: having said in the psalm before this, "The needy eat and will be filled, and those who seek him out will praise the Lord," and again, "All the prosperous of the earth ate and adored him,"[1] here he suggests the provider of such food, and calls the feeder shepherd. This in fact is the name Christ the Lord also gave himself: "I am the good shepherd, I know my own, and I am known by my own."[2] It is also what he called himself through the prophet Ezekiel.[3] So here, too, all who enjoyed the saving food cry out, *The Lord shepherds me, and nothing will be wanting for me:* this shepherd regales those shepherded by him with enjoyment of good things of all kinds.

(2) *He settled me in a green pasture* (v. 2). After calling the provider of the good things a shepherd, it was right for him also to use figurative language in mentioning the sheep's food. Now, he calls *green pasture* here the sacred teaching of the divine sayings: first he rears us in word, and then offers us the more mystical food. *Near restful water he reared me.* He hints at the water of rebirth, in which the baptized person longs for grace and sheds the old age of sin and is made young instead of being old.[4]

---

1. Ps 22.26, 22.29.
2. John 10.14—not the form of the received text.
3. Cf. Ezek 34.
4. Though on this psalm, for all its attractiveness to modern readers, he is not as expansive as on the preceding, he does give a sacramental and catechetical interpretation to some verses. He seems here to be referring to

[1028] *He corrected my soul; he guided me in paths of righteousness* (v. 3). He let me share in these things, he is saying, firstly freeing me from error, and causing me to tread the right way. *For his name's sake.* Now, all these things are gifts of his generosity: it was not due to our virtue that we enjoyed them.

(3) Having therefore such an ally and champion, I shall not dread even the gates of death, but shall despise death altogether. He added as much, in fact: *For even if I travel in the midst of death's darkness, I shall fear no evil, because you are with me* (v. 4). To this he adds more: *Your rod and your staff comforted me:* with one he supports my weakness, with the other he guides towards the right way. You would not be wrong, however, to apply this to the saving cross:[5] by its seal and remembrance we are rid of the hostile demons and guided to the true path. This is the meaning of *Your rod and your staff comforted me:* the cross is assembled from two rods, with the upright staff confirming and directing those who believe in him and strengthening those who are weak, and using the crossbar as a rod against the demons.

(4) *You laid a table before me in opposition to those distressing me; you anointed my head with oil, your cup inebriates me like finest wine* (v. 5). This is clear to the initiates and requires no comment: they know the spiritual oil with which the head is soothed, the inebriation that strengthens without disabling, and the mystical food which the one turned bridegroom applies to us by way of shepherding.[6] Now, with these good things you equipped me, he is saying, while the adversaries were distressed and afflicted, because those who were once self-serving underwent such a great transformation. *Your mercy will closely follow me all the days of my life so that I may dwell in the house of the Lord for length of days* (v.

---

the stages of initiation of (adult) catechumens and possibly also to the structure of the Eucharist in terms of liturgy of Word and liturgy of Eucharist.

5. Theodoret is able to move quickly through this psalm because he is not giving it more than a generally Christological meaning; but at this point he feels emboldened to risk a brief (and probably not original) sally into allegory.

6. Again he gives (succinctly) a sacramental interpretation to items in the text, familiar to those who had experienced the rites of initiation, particularly confirmation and Eucharist.

6). Now, providing these good things is your ineffable lovingkindness, not awaiting our request but closely following us like fugitives, anticipating our needs, giving us a share in salvation, providing residence in the divine dwellings, one in the present life, one in the future. This he indicated [1029] in saying *for length of days,* that is, always, unceasingly; he relates it to those ages that have no end.[7]

7. Again (without solid textual encouragement, it would seem) he sees the psalmist's perspective as eternal—a view with which Dahood sympathizes, who sees in the psalm a description of the Elysian Fields: "The psalmist is quietly confident that Yahweh is his shepherd, who will guide him through the vicissitudes of this life to the eternal bliss of Paradise." Not all commentators share this view.

COMMENTARY ON PSALM 24

A psalm of David.

IN SOME COPIES I FOUND "of one of the sabbaths," but it does not appear in the Hexapla.[1] So as not to leave even it without comment, however, you need to know that it means the Lord's Resurrection, after which all land and sea received the rays of the knowledge of God. This is the prophecy the psalm makes, too, and in addition to that the Lord's ascension to heaven.

(2) *The earth is the Lord's, and its fullness; the world, and all who dwell in it* (v. 1). You see, since the Jews had the idea that he was Lord only of Palestine and his providence reached only them, being their God only, it was right for the inspired word to teach that he is Lord of the whole world. He is its Lord, however, not by wresting authority nor by depriving anyone else of lordship, but by personally creating it and leading it from non-being into being. *He founded it on seas, and established it on rivers* (v. 2). Now, through this he shows not only creation but also providence: the earth being naturally arid, he endowed it with appropriate moisture, on the one hand embracing it beyond its bounds and in between by mighty oceans, and on the other causing the largest rivers of the greatest possible abundance and of course springs to rise in the midst of the continents, the former constantly crossing them and the latter gushing forth.

---

1. For this rogue item Theodoret claims to have consulted the *Hexapla Biblia*, or six-columned Old Testament, that Origen had pioneered as a collection of original text with a range of Greek versions, including LXX and the alternatives Theodoret has been seen quoting (see Introduction, section 3). It could be, however, that he looked only at Symmachus, who in fact does not include it, whereas Aquila has some form of it, as does the form of the LXX occurring in an edition like Rahlfs'. Modern commentators ignore it as not original. Good Antiochene that he is, Theodoret could hardly "leave even it without comment," which—off the cuff—it duly gets.

(3) After demonstrating in this way God's lordship and also forecasting the nations' acknowledgment of him, the psalmist offers an exhortation about virtue, framing his discourse in the form of question and answer: *Who will ascend the Lord's mountain?* he asks, *and who will stand in his holy place?* (v. 3). Now, he calls *mountain* here not the earthly one of Sion, but the heavenly one, of which the blessed Paul gave us a glimpse in the words, "You have come to Mount Sion and the city of the living God, the heavenly Jerusalem."[2] Since he had previously taught, you see, that the God of all is maker and creator, it was right for him to show the way leading to it and give a reply to the question.

(4) *He who is stainless in hand and pure of heart, who has not received his soul for vanity's sake nor sworn deceitfully to his neighbor* (v. 4). It is appropriate, he is saying, for him who desires to ascend that mountain both to [1032] purify his soul of idle thoughts and to keep his hands away from such pursuits. He put *hands* in place of pursuits, and by *heart* he implied desires: with the latter we form our intentions, and by the former we put them into action. Now, it behooves such a person not to hanker after anything shifty and corrupt, which he called *vanity*, Ecclesiastes speaking of it this way, "Vanity of vanities, all is vanity."[3] And since deceit and breaking of oaths are associated with avarice, he is right to forbid them along with it, *nor sworn deceitfully to his neighbor.* Then he shows the fruit of these virtuous actions: *Such a person will receive blessing from the Lord, and mercy from God his savior* (v. 5). Now, it was quite appropriate for him to associate mercy with blessing: even what are thought rewards are given to human beings only on account of divine loving-kindness. I mean, all the righteousness of human beings is not nearly sufficient for gifts bestowed by God, and certainly not for those yet to come, which even surpass human imagining.

(5) *This is the generation of those seeking the Lord, seeking the face of the God of Jacob* (v. 6). Those choosing to live by these counsels,

2. Heb 12.22. Theodoret has no qualms about admitting an anagogical sense here when Scripture has already supplied it.
3. Eccl 1.2. Dahood in fact sees this term in the Psalms often denoting idols, whereas Theodoret's following comment implies the notion of idle greed.

he is saying, in fact long to see the one who prescribes virtue, as once upon a time he also awarded the mighty Jacob an appearance of himself. Likewise in the eleventh psalm, in speaking of a different generation, which was given over to every evil and wickedness, the inspired author entreated God in the words, "You, Lord, will protect us, and defend us from this generation and forever."[4] But here he forecasts the opposite: *This is the generation of those seeking the Lord.* You see, after the Incarnation of our God and Savior, all land and sea believed in the divine message, forsook their ancestral gods, and are seeking out the God of Jacob. Thus, after prophesying the salvation of the world, he then teaches those who had come to faith that Christ the Lord not only loosed the power of death and rose, but also went up to heaven. I mean, since the twenty-first psalm contained the prophecies of the saving sufferings and the inspired account of the salvation of the nations, it was right for him once again here to make mention of the nations, prophesy their acknowledgment of God, describe in advance the Lord's ascension, [1033] and show us the choirs of angels, some preceding Christ the Lord and others making enquiry from on high in their wish to learn the meaning of the marvelous vision.[5]

(6) *Lift up your gates, rulers; be lifted up, eternal gates, and the king of glory will enter. Who is this king of glory? A Lord mighty and powerful, a Lord powerful in war. Lift up your gates, rulers; be lifted up, eternal gates, and the king of glory will enter. Who is this king of glory? A Lord of powers, he is the king of glory* (vv. 7–10). Let no one wonder, I ask you, on hearing of the ignorance of the invisible powers: they have neither advance knowledge nor complete knowledge—only the divine nature has that knowledge. Angels and archangels, on the other hand, and the other companies of the invisible powers know as much as they are taught, for which reason the divine Apostle also, speaking of them, said, "So that to the Principalities and Authorities in the heavenly places the wisdom of God in its rich variety might now be made known

4. Ps 12.7.
5. Theodoret is really developing at length here an anagogical sense to this verse which modern commentators have little difficulty seeing as part of an entrance rite for worshippers coming into the Temple.

through the Church."⁶ Now, if they came to learn the divine wisdom more precisely through the life of the Church, there is nothing out of order for the powers on high to be ignorant even of the mystery of Christ's ascension when they see the human nature and do not perceive the divinity concealed in it.

(7) Should you not concede this, however, accept the solution contained in commentary on the present psalm: by question and answer he developed the explanation of moral virtue by saying, *Who will ascend the Lord's mountain, and who will stand in his holy place?* and with the question so posed he supplied the answer, *He who is stainless of hand and pure in heart* and so on. Regard this, too, as a similar figure of speech, and believe the questioners are not speaking in ignorance, but through this proclamation of the one ascending are teaching all human beings his lordship. Hence the powers in reply say he is king of glory in that he receives glory from all and has the true and lasting kingship. Now, they call him also *a Lord mighty and powerful in war:* he destroyed the harsh tyranny of the devil and dissipated the deceit of the demons who are subject to him. *Eternal gates* are bidden open up as though never admitting human nature before. [1036] In fact, no human being had ever passed through them; but when God the Word became human and took up our firstfruits, he both led the way up to heaven and took his place at the right hand of majesty in the highest places, above every principality, authority, dominion, and every name that is named, not only in this age but also in the age to come. Now, the great Elijah was taken up, not into heaven, however, but as though into heaven⁷—hence the former question and answer, some inquiring and some replying and learning that the Lord of the powers himself is the king of glory—that is, he is maker and creator of angels and archangels, and of all nature invisible and created.

---

6. Eph 3.10. By wanting to give the psalm a Christological meaning and taking this section in reference to the ascension, Theodoret feels he runs the risk of not convincing his readers, and will try another tack. Modern commentators like Weiser simply see the verses reflecting "the representation of the theophany in the Temple which was dramatized in the cult."

7. To make this point, Theodoret has to elude the statements to the contrary in 2 Kings 2.1, 2.11, but he cannot afford to debate the question further.

COMMENTARY ON PSALM 25

To the end. A psalm of David.

THIS PSALM HAS THE FORM of a prayer; this is the reason, to be sure, as makes sense, that the title does not give a name to the psalm. Some historians, however, claimed it forecasts the captivity, and interpreted it as spoken by people of that time, focusing only on the end, *Redeem Israel, O God, from all its troubles* (v. 22). For my part, on the contrary, I believe this psalm was composed by blessed David when he sustained many assaults from enemies.[1] This is surely the reason he makes mention of former and recent sins, and begs to be rid of them. He also introduces an exhortation useful for people, however. Now, the present psalm is particularly suited to those called from the nations, and follows on closely the one that preceded it.

(2) *To you, O Lord, I lifted up my soul. O my God, in you I trusted, may I not be put to shame forever, nor may my enemies ridicule me* (vv. 1–2): beset on all sides by countless adversaries, I offer you my soul, Lord, and depend on your help, praying that I not live constantly in disgrace and be gloated over by the enemy. *Let all those who wait for you in fact not be put to shame. May those who break the Law for no reason be confounded* (v. 3). I have a sufficient basis for hope, he is saying, in those who already believe in you and enjoy your aid: you are in the habit of showing care for them, while confounding those given to lawlessness. Now, it is appro-

---

1. Theodoret recognizes the genre of the psalm, and resists the tendency (visible also in Chrysostom, though this psalm also is missing from his extant *Commentary*) to relate many Psalms to the Babylonian captivity and return. He is also perceptive enough to see that such an interpretation rests shakily on the final verse; had he been able to consult the Hebrew, he would have noted also that v. 22 is not formally included in the structure of this alphabetic psalm.

priate to point out that it is not the sinners but those breaking the Law for no reason who he said were covered in shame: not everyone errs [1037] in the same fashion, some coming to grief from a particular circumstance or natural weakness, others exulting in their transgressions and contemplating further ones.

(3) *Make your ways known to me, Lord, and teach me your paths. Guide me in your truth, and teach me that you are the God who is my savior; I waited for you all day long* (vv. 4–5): my prayer is first to discern your ways, and get to know the paths leading to you so as constantly to travel your true way free of error. Then I beg to learn from experience that you are my Savior: I am in constant expectation of loving-kindness at your hands. He put *all day long* in place of "always," note: he wants to teach that he does not have this attitude in one case while in another he entertains a different one. *Be mindful of your compassion, O Lord, and your mercies, because they are from the beginning. Do not call to mind my youthful sin and ignorance; remember me in your mercy* (vv. 6–7). You always govern people gently and with loving-kindness, he is saying, and now I beg that I may enjoy this goodness, and that you remember your loving-kindness, not my sin, and in remembering me you practice compassion, not justice. In those expressions what he was asking for was this: According to your great mercy remember me; remember not my sin but me in loving fashion. Now, the verse *Do not call to mind my youthful sin and ignorance* has this sense (he is referring, in fact, to the people in Egypt): I worshipped idols there; remember not those sins but your loving-kindness, by which you had mercy on the ignorant at that time by applying loving-kindness. *For the sake of your goodness, O Lord:* my prayer is to be granted this, not from my own worthiness but from your loving-kindness.

(4) *Good and upright is the Lord* (v. 8). It was not without purpose, he is saying, that I used these words, but in my knowledge that the Lord is not only righteous but also loving. Now, the divine Scripture teaches us this everywhere—for example, "I shall sing of your mercy and judgment, O Lord";[2] and "Merciful, compassionate, and righteous is the Lord, our God shows mer-

---

2. Ps 101.1.

cy";[3] and "God is a righteous judge, strong and longsuffering, not venting his wrath each day."[4] *Hence he will legislate for sinners in the way. He will guide the gentle in judgment, he will teach the gentle his ways* (vv. 8–9). Symmachus rendered it more clearly: "Hence he will give sinners a glimpse of the way":[5] [1040] employing goodness he does not immediately punish sinners, but both gives them a glimpse of the right way and also teaches them the law of repentance; and those practicing gentleness and simplicity he teaches to discern the nature of things, and causes them to know all his dispensations lest their simplicity prove an occasion of ignorance and cause them great harm.

(5) He next gives a glimpse of the nature of the ways spoken of: *All the ways of the Lord are mercy and truth for those who seek out his covenant and his testimonies* (v. 10). In other words, those constantly reared on the sacred Words have a precise knowledge from them that all the dispensations of God our Savior are tempered with mercy and truth: to some, who repent of sins committed, he extends mercy and pardon; others unconquered he proclaims and crowns as champions of virtue, giving his verdict with truth, while admittedly on those caught up in lawlessness and not taking advantage of repentance he inflicts punishments in terms of the standard of truth. *For your name's sake, O Lord, have mercy for my sin, for it is grave* (v. 11). I beg you therefore to have mercy for my sins, he is saying, not on account of my prompt repentance, but for the name you have for loving-kindness and because I rested my hope in your name.

(6) *Who is the person who fears the Lord? He will legislate for him in the path he has chosen. His soul will repose in good things, and his descendants will inherit the earth* (vv. 12–13). He proceeds from there, offering profitable advice and promising all kinds of providence to those who fear the Lord. Since the ways of living a godly life are many and varied—solitary and communal, in the wilderness and in the city, as private citizens and as soldiers, as

3. Ps 116.5.
4. Ps 7.11.
5. Symmachus, whose version here does not strike one as a conspicuous improvement on the LXX, frequently wins Theodoret's vote—though in fact he has not cited alternative versions for a while.

kings and artisans, sailors and farmers, and the many other different ways—it was right for the inspired word to claim it is possible to please God in each and every way of life: *Who is the person who fears the Lord? He will legislate for him in the path he has chosen,* that is to say, in that life, which he has chosen to live, he will give laws suited and appropriate to him. That was the reply the divine John the [1041] Baptist gave to the tax collectors asking what they should do, urging them to take nothing more than was prescribed, whereas he urged the soldiers not to extort money from anyone but be content with their pay, that is, the rations assigned them.[6] Likewise the divine Apostle imposed appropriate laws on slaves and masters, children and parents, wives and husbands.[7] Accordingly, the inspired word promised those who had kept these laws a life of good things for their soul and blessing for their descendants. *His soul will repose in good things, and his descendants will inherit the earth.* Since, you see, a large family is most desirable for the Jews, as is also bequeathing inheritances, and in fact this very thing is very dear also today to those embracing the common life, he also promotes the practice of virtue by these promises.

(7) *The strength of the Lord is in favor of those who fear him, and he will reveal his covenant to them* (v. 14). Symmachus and Theodotion rendered this more clearly: "The mystery of the Lord is for those who fear him, and he will reveal his treaty to them." Now, it is possible to hear the Lord himself speaking through the prophet Isaiah in the words, "My mysteries are for me and for mine": he reveals them not simply to all but to those who fear him, and gives a glimpse of the purpose of his divine sayings. But according to the Septuagint, *The strength of the Lord is in favor of those who fear him,* which renders them unconquered and

---

6. Cf. Luke 3.12–14. Theodoret in his preface made particular reference to monastic recitation of the Psalms, and in the course of his *Commentary* he has little to say about the life of Christians generally, something we would expect more from a preacher to his mixed congregation. But here at least he acknowledges the diversity of states of life, all of which may be "ways of living a godly life," and admits "it is possible to please God in each and every way of life."

7. Cf. Eph 6.1–9; Col 3.18–4.1.

stronger than the enemy.[8] *My eyes are always turned to the Lord, because he is the one who will pluck my feet from the snare* (v. 15). Once again by *eyes* here he means those of the mind, which he said he keeps in God's direction in the sense that he knows clearly that through his care he will escape the schemes hatched by his foes.

(8) *Have regard for me and have mercy on me, because I am alone and poor* (v. 16). *Alone* the rest rendered "solitary," but he means, I am bereft of all help—hence my prayer is to gain your support. Now, very pitiable was his statement, *Have regard for me and have mercy on me:* regard my isolation and my being besieged by my foes, he is saying; seeing me like this you will have mercy. *The tribulations of my heart have been multiplied; rescue me from my difficulties.* See [1044] *my humiliation and my hardship, and forgive all my transgressions* (vv. 17–18). I am beset by many sufferings from every quarter, he is saying; accordingly, balance this humiliation and oppression of mine against my iniquities, grant me forgiveness and allow me pardon.

(9) *Note how my foes have been multiplied and hate me with an unjust hatred* (v. 19). If I do not seem deserving of loving-kindness despite my struggling with so many troubles, at least take account of the unjust hostility of my enemies and give me a share of loving-kindness: I have sinned against you by breaking your commandments, whereas they have no charge against me and still make war on me unjustly. *Guard my soul and rescue me; do not put me to shame, because I called upon you* (v. 20): even if I broke some of your laws, nevertheless I did not separate myself from your providence—hence my prayer is to be rescued from the enemy and protected. *Innocent and upright people stayed close to me because I waited for you, O Lord* (v. 21). This is typical of virtue: despising the assemblies of vile people while having as associates and friends those who respect equality, adopt upright ways, and stay clear of vice.[9] This, in fact, is what the inspired author

---

8. The commentary at this point is complicated by textual difficulties in the original, in the LXX, and in the verse from Isa 24.16; as well, Theodoret's editor suggests he is misquoting Symmachus. Brevity is certainly a virtue amidst such confusion.

9. We do not find Theodoret frequently formulating his principles of

claimed to have done, considering himself to be serving the Lord by this way in particular.

(10) *Redeem Israel, O God, from all its troubles* (v. 22). Prayer offered to God befits a king: it is appropriate for one appointed to rule to exercise complete care of his subjects. This is surely the reason that blessed David offered prayer not only for himself but also for a people entrusted to him, especially as the salvation of the one who reigns wisely and well constitutes the welfare of the whole people. The verse implies something else as well, however. Israel was divided, in the time of Saul, of Mephibosheth,[10] and of Absalom. Consequently, if I were to enjoy your aid, he is saying, and prove stronger than my adversaries, Israel itself would obtain peace by putting an end to civil strife and would revel in your good things.

---

spirituality, or even of morality, beyond paraphrasing the Psalm text. Here by contrast he essays a brief definition of patterns of virtuous behavior.

10. It is interesting that Theodoret does not make great play of the dominant figures in sacred history, like Abraham, Moses, and Solomon, in the manner of a Chrysostom; but some marginal figures seem to take his fancy, like Sennacherib's lieutenant Rabshakeh and here that Mephibosheth who betrayed David's kindness to side with the treacherous Absalom but was pardoned (2 Sam 9.16, 9.19, and 9.21).

COMMENTARY ON PSALM 26

A psalm of David.

N MY VIEW the divine David uttered this psalm also with himself in mind, and I believe it precedes the one before it. I mean, that one [1045] referred to a sin, and a sin of gravity: "Have mercy for my sin, for it is grave,"[1] it said, whereas here he surveys the forms of his own virtue. Hence I consider he is employing these words when pursued by Saul and forced to live among foreigners; seeing their involvement in impiety, superstition, and every kind of lawlessness, he shunned their assemblies and the feasts celebrated in honor of the demons.

(2) Now, the interpretation of the verses teaches us this more clearly: *Judge me, O Lord, because in my innocence I have kept to the straight and narrow, and by hoping in the Lord I shall not fail* (v. 1). Though adopting simplicity and working no harm against Saul, he is saying, and yet driven out so harshly, I appeal to you, O Lord, to act as judge of the justice of my cause: I know you are God, I placed my hopes in your providence, and I am confident I shall not fall into the hands of my pursuers. *Test me, O Lord, and try me; use fire to test my entrails and my heart* (v. 2). It is clear from this that the psalm is prior to the sin: he is looking forward to risky trials like a person of simple and innocent life, with no

---

1. Ps 25.11. Theodoret probably feels it a bold remark to suggest on the grounds of subject matter that the Psalms are not following a chronological order here. He would like to see them all as David's work, and would not be content to join scholars like Mowinckel in seeing the Psalter as the culmination of many stages of compilation such that "the last redaction of the Psalter may have displaced this or that psalm from its original place in one of the minor collections," a critical judgment supporting the tentative commentator of earlier times.

experience of sin. Now, it is his thoughts he calls *entrails* and *heart*, as we have often mentioned.²

(3) *Because your mercy is ever before my eyes* (v. 3): I beg to be tested like gold put to the fire since I have confidence in your mercy, and I await help from that quarter. Depending on that, *I took delight in your truth*. Then he surveys the forms of the delight: *I did not sit with the council of futility, nor would I go in to join the lawless. I hated an assembly of evildoers, nor would I take my seat with the ungodly* (vv. 4–5). Now, to such a degree was I mindful of your service, he is saying, that even when in the presence of impious and lawless people I shunned their assemblies and their harmful gatherings. By these expressions he suggests life among the foreigners with whom he was forced to dwell on account of flight, without being able to bring himself to share impiety or lawlessness with them.

(4) *I shall wash my hands among innocent people, and shall move around your altar, O Lord, so as to hear the voice of your praise and describe all your marvels* (vv. 6–7): while, then, I deeply abhor their superstition, I long to see your altar, O Lord, to give ear to your melodies and teach the ignorant the magnitude of your wonders. [1048] Now, the verse *I shall wash my hands among innocent people* resembles what was done by Pilate who, not wishing to share in the Jewish bloodguiltiness, washed his hands to show in action his shunning the affair.³ So, being innocent and having nothing in common with them, he is saying, I confidently wash my hands as well.

(5) *O Lord, I loved the decoration of your house and place of habitation of your glory. Do not destroy my soul along with ungodly people, and my life with men of blood, whose hands are stained with iniquities, their right hand filled with bribes* (vv. 8–10). For *decoration* Symmachus put "temple," and for *men of blood*, "bloodstained men."

2. He has indeed frequently drawn his readers' attention to the figurative expression of the Psalms.

3. Cf. Matt 27.24. Theodoret is not prepared to admit there is a certain implausibility in his interpretation of the psalm as an expression of David who, while being in foreign parts, can still speak of moving about the Lord's altar. He might also have thought more about crediting Pilate with commendable renunciation of involvement in Jesus' death, we may add. Brevity and brisk movement forestall a critical rejoinder.

Be quick, he is saying, to release me from life with these people, O Lord, longing as I do for your house, which is resplendent with your grace, lest I perish along with the impious, the blood-stained, those who give bribes and betray justice. With these words he shows them once again to be what they are. Now, it was the tabernacle he called *house*, the divine Temple not yet being built; hence he added, *place of habitation of your glory.*

(6) *In my innocence I have kept to the straight and narrow; redeem me, O Lord, and have mercy on me. My foot stood on level ground* (vv. 11–12): while associating with them in the meantime, I adopt the simplicity of faith and cut myself off from all evil; if I fixed my feet to the level ground of godliness, I stood fast and firm for the time being. I pray, however, I may hold my ground to the end; but this will only happen provided I am freed from residing with them. *In churches I shall bless you, Lord.* From this in particular we have come to the very clear understanding that the psalm was uttered with David himself in mind: he promised to sing and give praise in all the churches of the world through the writing of the Psalms, foreseeing with prophetic eyes the transformation of the world. The prophecy was fulfilled: on all land and sea mighty David praises in song the beneficent God through pious mouths.[4]

---

4. The singing of the psalms (which he sees composed in writing, *syngraphe*) in the churches of his day is for Theodoret the clinching argument that David composed this psalm in his own person.

COMMENTARY ON PSALM 27

A psalm of David, before he was anointed.

FOUND THIS TITLE not in the Hexapla but in some copies. Despite this, from that fact some people took occasion to reject all the titles as lacking authenticity:[1] how is it possible, they ask, for David, who was not yet anointed and had not [1049] received the grace of the all-holy Spirit, to write inspired psalms, especially as he was young at the time, was minding sheep and not running the kingdom, and was not pursued by some adversaries? They ought to understand, on the contrary, that the history of the Kings says David had been anointed twice, or rather three times: first, in Bethlehem by the prophet Samuel;[2] secondly, in Hebron by the tribe of Judah after the removal of Saul;[3] and thirdly, by all the tribes after the death of Mephibosheth.[4] Now, this is what it says about the second anointing: "David inquired of the Lord, 'Should I go up to one of the cities of Judah?' The Lord replied, 'Go up.' David asked, 'To which should I go?' He replied, 'To Hebron.'" Then the historiographer added by way of explanation of where he had gone, "The men of Judah came, and there they anointed David king over the house of Judah."[5] And in turn regarding the

---

1. Theodoret has addressed the more general objection to the authenticity of the psalm titles in his preface; here he sees his task only to reconcile discrepancies in chronology if this psalm is to be inserted into David's life story. The implication that inspiration for biblical composition also comes with anointing and appointment as king is interesting, too.
2. Cf. 1 Sam 16.13.
3. Cf. 2 Sam 2.4.
4. Cf. 2 Sam 5.3. See also note 10 on *Commentary* on Ps 25, on David's interest in marginal figures like Mephibosheth, whose mention here is in fact anachronistic.
5. 2 Sam 2.1, 2.4. The Deuteronomist is not referred to by Theodoret as a *prophetes*, an inspired composer, but as a *historiographos*, just as Chrysostom

third anointing thus: "All the tribes of Israel came to David at Hebron"; and a little later, "King David made a covenant with them at Hebron in the sight of the Lord, and they anointed David king over all Israel."[6]

(2) So it is clear that he uttered this psalm before accepting the second election, and before the conduct of affairs was openly entrusted to him. So when pursued by Saul, he used these words at the time he came to the priest Abimelech, prayed in the tabernacle of God, received the blessing of the holy loaves, and escaped the hands of his enemy.[7] Now, he refers to this in the psalm itself: *Because he hid me in his tabernacle in the day of my troubles* (v. 5). At that time also Doeg the Idumean, who was tending the royal mules there, reported David's flight to Saul;[8] hence in the psalm he says, *Unjust witnesses rose up against me* (v. 12). Commentary on individual verses, however, will teach us this more clearly.

(3) *The Lord is my light and my salvation: whom shall I fear? The Lord is the protector of my life: whom should I dread?* (v. 1). Enlightened by you, he is saying, and illumined by the light you shed on my mind, I scorn all my enemies together.[9] *When evildoers pressed upon me to devour my flesh, those who distressed me and my foes them-*

---

likewise used the term *syngrapheus* (a term Theodoret will employ in opening commentary on Ps 29).

6. 2 Sam 5.1, 5.3.

7. Cf. 1 Sam 21.1–6. In quoting v. 7 of the psalm as a reflection of this incident, of course, Theodoret's argument turns upon the tense of the verb—future in the Hebrew, not past (as often in the LXX). He actually adverts to that possibility in quoting and developing Aquila's version of v. 6 below.

8. Cf. 1 Sam 22.9. It is interesting that Theodoret has gone to considerable trouble to research the sequence of events to justify the psalm's title (not found in our Hebrew) and its ascription to David at a particular point in his life, this time getting all the Scriptural quotations correct (the LXX, perhaps by a Freudian slip, putting "mules"—lit. "half-asses"—where the Hebrew has "servants" in this final verse). He then proceeds to his more usual indicator, the subject matter of particular verses.

9. Perhaps in haste after the lengthy historical introduction, the commentator sweeps over this moving verse almost without comment. Generally speaking, a true spiritual director would probably pay more attention to such pregnant sentiments and less to historical discrepancies and linguistic oddities (see note 15 below).

selves fainted and fell (v. 2). I am not disappointed in my hope, he is saying, so confident am I of your aid: those who stole an advantage over me in their pursuit like wild animals [1052] and their attempts to make a meal of me while still alive, far from doing me any harm, were themselves the victims of total destruction. Now, history teaches that this happened often: once or twice when hunted by Saul he escaped the net—or, rather, if he had wanted to, he could have destroyed his pursuer. Instead, he gave evidence of his characteristic sound values, whereas the other man paid the penalty for his wickedness among foreigners. So these words are a prophecy of what would come to pass. *If a fortress were constructed against me, my heart would not fear; if war broke out against me, I would still hope* (v. 3). Having such wonderful experience of assistance, he is saying, even should two or three times the number of enemies try to attack me, I would brave the difficulties, armed with this hope.

(4) *One thing I asked of the Lord, this shall I seek, to dwell in the house of the Lord all the days of my life, to behold the charm of the Lord and visit his holy temple. Because he hid me in his tabernacle in the day of my troubles, he kept me in hiding in his tabernacle, he set me high on a rock* (vv. 4–5). Now, having enjoyed such beneficence, he is saying, I seek from my benefactor not wealth or influence, royalty or glory, but constant attendance in the divine temple, contemplation of the divine beauty there, and inspection of everything happening in accordance with law. I have a feeling of benefit, in fact, having already secured salvation from that source and escaped the hands of my pursuers. This the mighty David both asked for and received from the munificent God: he brought back the divine Ark, erected another, more wonderful tabernacle, and assembled the different choirs of singers; you could gain a more precise knowledge of this from the books of Chronicles.[10] Now, the phrase *One thing I asked of the Lord* refers to "one grace"; this is the way to understand it.

---

10. Theodoret showed in his preface that he was aware of the liturgical detail provided by the Chronicler, though it did not affect his view of the psalm titles. He has passed over vv. 4–5 rapidly, focusing on his historical study of David on the run, and neglecting phrases not bearing on this, like "he set me high on a rock," as also the anachronism involved in speaking of

(5) *Now see, he lifted my head above my foes; I circled about and sacrificed in his tabernacle a sacrifice of praise and outcry* (v. 6). Here there is a change of tense, which is what Aquila also taught: in place of *he lifted my head* he put "my head will be lifted up"; so he is suggesting that he will reign and will prevail over his adversaries, and he who is now encircled will encircle them; he will offer to God, not the sacrifices prescribed by law in the tabernacle, but the sacrifice of praise which in all the churches throughout the world he offers night and day through those who believe in God. Some copies, on the other hand, have "a sacrifice of praise and [1053] outcry,"[11] but this has the same meaning: "outcry" is a warlike noise, made by the more audacious group against the more timid. Hymn singing occurs in the same fashion: it is the sound of those in good spirits who are singing praise to God. Scripture says, "Is there anyone of good spirits among you? Let them sing praise."[12] *I shall praise and sing to the Lord.* It is clear from this that there has been a change of tense from what was said before: he promises to sing praise and to offer the hymn.

(6) *Hearken, O Lord, to the cry I utter; have mercy on me, and hearken to me* (v. 7). He asks for mercy, not opposed to justice but quite in keeping with it.[13] *My heart said to you, I shall seek the Lord* (v. 8): I did not employ words devoid of truth; instead, I applied myself with mind in keeping with the words. *My face shall seek you out:* what I have done is not adequate, but I shall continue working at it in the future as well. *I shall seek your face, O Lord:* do not repel me in my longing, therefore, nor deprive me of what I long for.[14] *Do not turn your face from me, and do not avert in anger*

"the divine temple" at this stage—a problem he had acknowledged in comment on Ps 26.8.

11. The text could be defective here.

12. Jas 5.13. Theodoret is hardly fulsome in his encouragement to his readers to indulge in singing the psalms; we have seen him thinking of the psalmist, too, as a writer.

13. Theodoret, as brisk as ever, has obviously not picked up the shift in tone at this point that leads some modern commentators to suggest the psalm "consists of two parts which differ from each other in mood and subject matter," and even to print the two halves separately, as does Weiser.

14. Theodoret has not found the verse any more susceptible of easy commentary than modern commentators have.

from your servant (v. 9). He phrased this by analogy with angry people, who turn away from those approaching and endeavor to take a different direction. *Be my help, do not dismiss me, do not abandon me, O God my Savior.* For *do not dismiss me* the other translators said "do not cast me off"; the Septuagint, after all, has taken this term from secular culture, "Go to the dogs!" being a phrase from a certain fable adopted as an insult by the ancients.[15] *Because my father and my mother abandoned me, whereas the Lord accepted me* (v. 10). Pursued by Saul, you see, he was forced to live at a distance from his parents; but, he says, you suffice for me in place of them all, Lord.

(7) *Guide me in your way by law, O Lord, and lead me in the right path* (v. 11). In place of *Guide me by law,* Aquila and Theodotion said, "Illuminate," whereas Symmachus has, "Give me a glimpse of your way." Since I am forced to live at a distance from my own kin, he is saying, become for me in your own person both lawgiver and guide, giving me a glimpse of the path leading to you.[16] *On account of my foes. Do not hand me over to the souls of those harassing me.* [1056] These words spring from a humble spirit: he means, I am unworthy of salvation, yet since I have in no way wronged those hostile to me, I am driven out wrongly—so do not hand over the wronged man to those doing him wrong. *Because unjust witnesses rose up against me, and injustice gave false testimony against itself.* Aquila put it more clearly, "False witnesses objected, and injustice was unmasked." For their part, he is saying, they employed calumnies against me, whereas I suffered no outrage from that source owing to your help; instead, it rebounded on the unjust, and the shafts dispatched in my direction by them rebounded in turn on them. Now, this is taken from colloquial usage: we normally say of schemers, who fail to cause

---

15. Though not alert to the psalm's change of tone, as a fellow poet would be, Theodoret can inform his readers of the derivation of this rare verb found in secular usage and based on the insult, meaning literally "To the ravens!" and similar to contemporary jibes like "Go to the dogs!" or "Be hanged!" Likewise on v. 12 he suggests the psalmist is borrowing a phrase from colloquial usage.

16. Again it is noticeable that Theodoret is prepared to accept an improvement on the LXX reading from Symmachus, less so the other versions.

harm, "They hurt themselves, not me." Thus blessed David also claimed, *Injustice gave false testimony against itself.*

(8) *I believe that I shall see the goodness of the Lord in the land of the living* (v. 13): I shall not only be stronger than my enemies in the present life, but shall also have enjoyment of the good things I look forward to. Then he offers encouragement to everyone: *Wait for the Lord* (v. 14). And how would this be possible? *Play the man, let your heart be strengthened, and wait for the Lord.* The mind adorned with virility, he is saying, and by means of it getting the better of the onset of misfortunes, is strengthened and gains the victory, and awaits the divine promises, to which it becomes the heir, the body also cooperating. Now, he calls the life looked forward to *land of the living* in so far as it is separated from death and free of corruption and sadness.[17]

---

17. Once again without qualms Theodoret accepts the eternal perspective of the psalmist, something Dahood has to establish on the basis of a parallel from Ugaritic to his version, "land of life eternal." Again he neglects to add the disclaimer about the exclusive language of the Psalms that he made on Ps 1.1.

COMMENTARY ON PSALM 28

A psalm of David.

E SINGS THIS PSALM in the person of those who have come to faith in Christ, and with entreaty he calls on Christ for assistance. As well, it contains a rebuke for the Jews' folly and a prayer for separation from their hand, or rather any part with them. *I cried out to you, O Lord, do not keep silence with me, O my God, lest in your silence with me I become like those going down to the pit* (v. 1). The psalm was spoken by David when he was pursued by Saul and was the object of schemes on the part of those who seemed to be friends but betrayed him and tried to reveal his whereabouts to Saul, [1057] like Doeg[1] and the Ziphites[2] and many others in addition to them. This psalm, on the other hand, and in fact the psalms before it as well are suited to everyone encountering calamities of this kind: like blessed David it is possible for the person intent on persevering both to petition God and thereby to secure his providence.[3] He used *cried out* in fact not of sound but of enthusiasm and intense, zealous prayer, whereas *do not keep silence with me* he took by analogy from people called on by some but refusing to make any reply. Hence he means, If you keep silence with me and deprive me of your help, I shall immediately be consigned to death, which he called *pit*, since the grave is dug like a pit.[4]

---

1. Cf. 1 Sam 22.9.
2. Cf. 1 Sam 23.19–20.
3. It is rare that Theodoret gets beyond the historical background of the psalm, the occasional linguistic feature, a possible theological clarification, and the customary brisk paraphrase, to suggest (even briefly, as here) that the readers may find the sentiments of the psalm relevant and even helpful in their own situation. It is psalm as window rather than as mirror that interests him, unlike many a spiritual director.
4. While we have seen Theodoret ready (against the general tenor of Old Testament thought, *pace* Dahood) to understand the psalmist as looking

(2) *Hearken, O Lord, to the voice of my entreaty, when I entreat you, when I lift my hands to your holy temple* (v. 2). Though the Temple was not yet built, he gives the name *temple* to the tabernacle in which he prayed, distant from it in body but directing his mind there. Likewise also when blessed Daniel in Babylon prayed, he opened the windows facing Jerusalem,[5] not under the impression that God was confined there but from his knowledge that the divine manifestation occurred there. *Do not drag me away with sinners, and with workers of iniquity do not destroy me, those who talk peace with their neighbors but in whose hearts is evil* (v. 3). The prayer of blessed David is to have no truck with those who practice duplicity: he calls abhorrent those who say one thing but mean another.

(3) This is surely the reason he also wishes that they reap a due reward for their exploits, saying, *Repay them, O Lord, according to their works, and according to the wickedness of their exploits. Repay them for the works of their hands; grant them their due repayment* (v. 4). Let no one think, however, that the righteous person is cursing his enemies: the words are a mark not of cursing but of a just verdict. *Grant them their due repayment,* he says, meaning, May they fall foul of their own schemes, which they hatch against one another. This is said also in the seventh psalm, "Their trouble will come back on their own head, and their wrong will come down on top of them."[6] Then he teaches the reason for the retribution: [1060] *Because they did not understand the works of the Lord and the works of his hands* (v. 5). Now, they committed these things, he is saying, because they had no wish to learn either the divine word or work. *Hence you will destroy them and not build them up.* In other words, destruction of a useless building is of some advantage to the wicked builders. From this it is clear that he uttered the previous remarks in prophetic fashion, not to curse them but to prophesy the future: he did not say, "destroy" but *you will destroy and not build up again.*

---

forward to life beyond the grave, he shows here no understanding of OT acceptance of Sheol as the destination of the dead—a destination that, in John McKenzie's words, "is not a form of survival but a denial of survival; all come to Sheol and the good and evil of life cease there" (*NJBC,* 1313).

5. Cf. Dan 6.10.
6. Ps 7.16.

(4) Then, enjoying divine revelation again and perceiving at a distance the coming help, he moved his tongue to hymn singing:[7] *Blessed be the Lord because he hearkened to the sound of my petition. The Lord is my help and my protection* (vv. 6–7). And to show the reason for the prompt assistance, he added, *Because my heart hoped in him, and I was helped and my flesh grew strong again:* the hope placed in him proved for me the source of this providence. Hence I am freed of this ill treatment owing to flight, I am reinvigorated and I flourish, and good health has returned along with good cheer. *I shall willingly confess to him,* that is, I offer him the hymn not under duress but willingly. Elsewhere he speaks this way, too: "I shall willingly sacrifice to you,"[8] and again, "May the willing sayings from my mouth be pleasing, O Lord."[9]

(5) *The Lord is the strength of his people, and is protection of the salvations of his Anointed* (v. 8): I sing his praises as a good Master, generously providing both king and people with strength, might, and salvation.[10] He calls himself *Anointed* as king: this name was common to kings, prophets, and priests. *Save your people, bless your inheritance, shepherd them, and raise them up forever* (v. 9). So share this blessing and salvation with your people, he is saying, by directing, shepherding, and rendering them mightier than their enemies. The prayer for the people befits the king as well: it is also admirable about mighty David that though pursued also by the people, who waged war on him along with Saul, he offered supplication on their behalf to God. He foresaw their future conversion, you see, and had regard not for the injustice but for the servitude to come.

---

7. Though not betraying a sense of disjunction here, as do those modern commentators who see the psalm falling into two parts, related or unrelated, Theodoret at least notes the shift from lament and appeal to a hymn of praise.

8. Ps 54.6.

9. Ps 119.108 [LXX].

10. Theodoret probably notes the odd plural form "salvations" in his text; but unable to throw light on it (it is, Dahood suggests, a royal plural in the Hebrew) he is wise enough not to open up a fruitless inquiry; even alternative versions are not invoked.

COMMENTARY ON PSALM 29

A psalm of David, of a tabernacle procession.[1] *[1061]*

DID NOT FIND THIS TITLE in the Hexapla either but in some copies. Taking a lead from it, some historians judged that blessed David uttered this psalm when he brought back the Ark. But the psalm's verses have no such meaning: the psalm prophesies different things. Yet the prophecy it contains is twofold, one relevant to King Hezekiah, the other to the king of us all, who by dissipating the error of the idols illumined the world with the rays of the knowledge of God. For my part I shall be brief[2] in speaking of the prophecy referring to Hezekiah, but at greater length of our prophecy as being of greater relevance to ourselves.

(2) When the admirable Hezekiah prevailed over the Assyrians and was rejoicing in the surprising character of the victory, he bade the people make a response to God in sacrifices, offer hymns and praise to him, and conduct the prescribed worship in his holy court.[3] The Temple was not accessible to everybody, entry to it being for the priests alone. Then the psalmist teaches the reason for this, suggesting by mention of voice and thunder that the blow from the Assyrians was divinely inflicted, referring

---

1. This reading of the title, found in the LXX (though editor Schulze has *exodou* in Theodoret's text in place of *exodiou*), Weiser takes as grounds for thinking the psalm was sung on the last day of the Feast of Tabernacles. The ancient commentators show less interest in *Sitz im Leben*.

2. This, of course, was a policy enunciated by Theodoret in his preface, of speaking συντόμως of historical matters—as of most things. In fact, he does leave the historical reference quickly in his wake.

3. Once again Theodoret is referring a psalm to the reign of Hezekiah and his troubles with the Assyrians under Sennacherib, with probably the Chronicler's account in mind, which characteristically includes Hezekiah's attention to Temple worship—but *before* mention of the miraculous slaying of the Assyrians (cf. 2 Chron 32.21–23).

in figurative fashion to the multitude of the enemy as *flood of waters*.⁴ Then in turn he calls them *cedars*, implying their height and density, and says they are smashed to pieces, whereas the beloved people are compared with unicorns in that they worship one God and through him destroy the countless hosts of attacking opponents. But he cut them down and scattered them like a flame, he is saying, and struck the battalion bereft of God, and the place that resembled a coppice for the density of those camped in it he left bare of inhabitants. On the other hand, he cured us of our bout of deer-like timidity, and made us hold our ground instead of taking to flight. This is surely reason enough for everyone to run together to the temple and offer him the response of hymns: after freeing us of these impediments he will be responsible for our once more building and inhabiting what was outside the ramparts [1064] and destroyed by the enemy as if by a tidal wave. You see, having as we do an eternal king, who has also allowed us to prevail and granted us peace, we shall easily put all to rights.

(3) The fact, therefore, that the present psalm refers to blessed Hezekiah the commentary has demonstrated; but since the Old is a type of the New, come now, let us bring substance to the shadow and show the similarity: in one case a pious king, here Christ, the teacher of piety; there a people obedient to the one, here a people saved by the other; there war and destruction of Assyrians, here revolt and overthrow of demons. Accordingly, the grace of the Spirit bids the sacred apostles preach salvation to the nations and offer the believers to God. He calls the apostles *sons of God,* as bearing the title brothers of Christ ("Tell my brothers," he said, "that I am going before you into Galilee"),⁵ and those who had come to faith from the nations *sons of rams* as sprung from irrational parents.

4. A modern commentator might account for these elements in the psalm on the basis of its pagan origins, as a Phoenician hymn praising the weather god, in Frank Cross's view in "Notes on a Canaanite Psalm in the Old Testament," *BASOR* 117 (1950): 19–21. "Virtually every word in the psalm can now be duplicated in older Canaanite texts," maintains Dahood (*Psalms* I, 175).

5. Matt 28.10. While this Scriptural reference is apposite, the following foray (of the LXX originally) into zoology springs erroneously from a con-

(4) *Bring to the Lord, sons of God, bring to the Lord sons of rams. Bring to the Lord glory and praise, bring to the Lord glory for his name; worship the Lord in his holy court* (vv. 1–2). You who are entrusted with the divine message, he is saying, and are called sons of God, bear the divine message everywhere with all enthusiasm, transform those reared on nonsense into rational people, and offer them first to God; then through them present the worship and the hymns, celebrating the benefactor in the divine dwellings. This resembles what was said by the Savior to the sacred apostles, "Go, make disciples of all the nations, baptizing [1065] them in the name of the Father and the Son and the Holy Spirit."[6] The psalm in fact immediately after those words made mention of the sacred waters: *Voice of the Lord on the waters, the God of glory thundered* (v. 3). Now, the verse forecasts the voice emanating from heaven at the Jordan, "This is my Son, the Beloved, in whom I am well pleased."[7] He called it *thunder* as coursing to the whole world through the sacred Gospels; he called the pair of apostles "Sons of thunder"[8] on account of the voice of their extraordinary divine theology. *The Lord on many waters:* not only did the Jordan receive this grace, but the mystery of baptism was performed on all land and sea, the divine epiclesis sanctifying the nature of the waters.[9]

(5) From this he prophesies the power imparted to the apostles: *Voice of the Lord in power; voice of the Lord in majesty* (v. 4). The narrative of the Acts also teaches us things in harmony with this: we learn from there how at his ascension Christ the Lord addressed his holy disciples in the words, "Stay in this city until you

---

fusion of similar forms in the Hebrew. Dahood is more to the point: "In Canaanite mythology the *bn ilm*, 'the sons of El,' are minor gods [not rams] who form part of the pantheon of which El is the head" (*Psalm* I, 175). Rondeau's compliment to Theodoret—"un pasteur cultivé qui, bilingue, peut aisément recourir à l'originale sémitique" (*Les commentaires patristiques,* I, 136)—is overly generous.

6. Matt 28.19.   7. Matt 3.17.
8. Mark 3.17.

9. In adopting a spiritual sense for the verses, Theodoret is led by the mention of water to speak in terms of the sacrament, or mystery, of baptism, in which rite the invocation, or epiclesis, of the Spirit occurs as in other sacraments of the Church's liturgy.

have been clothed with power from on high."[10] Ten days later on the feast of Pentecost, "There came a sound from heaven like that of a violent wind blowing, and it filled the house where they were seated; divided tongues appeared among them, as of fire, and rested on each one of them."[11] Now, he gives the name *voice* to the grace of the Spirit filling the apostles with power and might, and rendering puny men magnificent. Then he shows what they achieved when empowered by this voice: *Voice of the Lord shattering cedars; the Lord will shatter the cedars of Lebanon* (v. 5). Now, he signals through these words the overthrow of the idols: since the idols' precincts in ancient times were on high places, providing no fruit to their worshippers, he likened them to *the cedars of Lebanon,* which though lofty do not naturally bear edible fruit.

(6) *He beat them to powder like the calf of Lebanon* (v. 6). He often calls Jerusalem *Lebanon:* "Open your doors, O Lebanon, and let the fire consume your cedars."[12] Now, the *calf of Lebanon* is the one made by them [1068] on Horeb: "They made a calf on Horeb," Scripture says, "and worshipped the cast image";[13] but Moses the lawgiver shattered it and beat it to powder. So in similar fashion he says all the idols of the world will be beaten to powder and rendered futile. *And the beloved like a son of unicorns.* Now, the people who believe, freed from that error and called beloved for that reason, will be invincible and unconquerable in being rid of polytheism and worshipping one godhead.

(7) *Voice of the Lord who flashes a split of flame* (v. 7): the choir of the sacred apostles received the grace of the all-holy Spirit in forms of fire, and were illuminated but not burnt. In the future life, however, the twofold operation of fire will be divided, illu-

10. Luke 24.49. Theodoret has at least the author, if not the book, right.
11. Acts 2.6.
12. Zech 11.1. Even allowing for the obscurity of the two parts of the book of Zechariah, Theodoret's comment is strange, as this oracle is in fact thought to be one describing the desolation of Judah's vanquished enemies. If the geography got the better of him, no wonder the difficult verb in the verse also proved too much.
13. Ps 106.19—but what is the association of the Horeb calf with Lebanon? If only because of its Canaanite origins, the psalm is difficult for a commentator of any age.

minating the athletes of virtue and incinerating evildoers—hence he uses the word *fire*, and the punishment of the lawless is called darkness because its illuminating power is not visible there. *Voice of the Lord who shakes the wilderness; the Lord will shake the wilderness of Kadesh* (v. 8). Symmachus, on the other hand, said not *shaking* but "delivering," and Aquila, "giving birth." Now, Isaiah also prophesies about this wilderness, "Rejoice, parched desert; let the desert rejoice and flower like a lily."[14] He calls the nations *wilderness* for being once upon a time bereft of God; but while the divinely inspired Isaiah said they would flower, blessed David said they would be in labor and give birth. This occurs in Isaiah in other places as well: "Rejoice, O barren one who does not bear; burst forth and cry out, you who are not in labor, because the children of the desolate woman are more numerous than of the one with a husband."[15] This is the wilderness the Lord is shaking, *shaking* suggesting God's appearance; he will cause it to give birth to salvation according to the prophecy that says, "For fear of you, O Lord, we conceived, were in labor, and gave birth to a spirit of your salvation, a spirit which you wrought on the earth."[16] For this reason he calls it *Kadesh*, that is, holy: that is the way to translate *Kadesh*.[17]

(8) *Voice of the Lord furnishing deer; it will bring woods to light* (v. 9). It is the nature of deer to scorn reptiles,[18] and this facility the Lord gave also to the sacred apostles: "I have given you the authority to [1069] walk on snakes and scorpions, and over all the power of the foe."[19] Empowered by this word, they drove out the deceitful demons of the world and exposed the weakness of

---

14. Cf. Isa 35.1.   15. Isa 54.1.
16. Isa 26.17–18 [LXX].
17. The authority with which Theodoret delivers this piece of Semitic science has already been undercut by his version of v. 1, of course.
18. To judge from many modern versions, which speak here of oaks whirling, the LXX would seem to have committed the error again of confusing similar forms. By reference to Job 39.1, however, Dahood thinks the option for "deer" may be correct. Theodoret bypasses the linguistic argument to find something in natural history to justify the rendition, if still needing to draw the longbow. (He seems to have forgotten he opened the psalm by taking the deer as a symbol of timidity.)
19. Luke 10.19.

the idols; the prophetic word predicted this, *Voice of the Lord furnishing deer, it will bring woods to light.* This in fact is baffling, that by means of deer he overcame the multitude of wild beasts of all kinds, confuted the hollow knowledge of philosophers by means of the unlettered, and abolished the tyranny of the devil by means of fishermen. Now, he called *woods* the idols' precincts as being utterly fruitless; these are the kinds of woods or coppices that the best woodcutters are accustomed to chop down, leaving the earth bare of them, and they plant fruitbearing trees and sow seeds of edible crops. The cultivators of the world did this, too: pulling up the idols' precincts by the roots, they planted the divine churches in their place. *Hence in his temple everyone says Glory,* moved to hymn singing by this amazing magnificence.

(9) *The Lord dwells in the flood, the Lord will be enthroned as king forever* (v. 10): he will build a world that is inundated with the torrent of iniquity, will restore it, and will make it a new creation. Hence blessed Paul also cries aloud, "If anyone is in Christ, he is a new creation."[20] Now, after doing this, he is saying, he will not allow impiety to have a place any longer, but will reign forever. *The Lord will give strength to his people, the Lord will bless his people with peace* (v. 11). Through this he also prophesied the rebellions of the ungodly, the victory of the triumphant martyrs, and the peace provided to the churches afterwards. *The Lord will give strength to his people,* that is, in time of war, and *he will bless his people with peace* by concluding the long war.

20. 2 Cor 5.17. The commentator has had to struggle with this antique poem, whose pagan origins resist easy transposition to the world either of Hezekiah or of the apostolic church. Lacking a familiarity with Hebrew or Canaanite forms, he has had to fall back on natural history or mere rationalizing, as he does not have the sureness of touch or familiarity with the Scriptures such as Chrysostom demonstrates.

COMMENTARY ON PSALM 30

A psalm for singing at the re-consecration of the house.
To the end. Of David.

LESSED DAVID DID NOT BUILD the divine Temple, nor do the verses of the psalm fit the builder. So by *re-consecration of the house* he refers to the restoration of human nature which Christ the Lord accomplished by accepting death on behalf of us, destroying death and giving us hope of resurrection. This psalm as well, however, refers to blessed Hezekiah: after destruction of the Assyrians [1072] and cure of his illness, he celebrated a great feast, as was appropriate, giving thanks to God for both granting them salvation and liberating his holy Temple from the fire of the enemy. Consequently, since the celebrations resembled a festival of re-consecration, it was understandable that it also got this title.[1] It should be realized, however, that it is applicable to Hezekiah as a type, but to all human nature in reality: just as he gave admission to lofty thoughts (as the story of the Chronicles taught),[2] received the sentence of death but by divine grace secured his life, so Adam, the first parent, who had built up pretensions to becoming God and

---

1. Theodoret's approach to the psalm's title is predictable. He notes that the contents do not bear on the building of the Temple—not David's work in any case—and is encouraged by the phrase "At the end" to give them a predominantly spiritual meaning. But, as before, he is prepared to find a historical reference to the story of Hezekiah, and loosely (cf. note 3 to *Commentary* on Ps 29) cites 2 Chron 32.22–23 in regard to an occasion when the psalm may have been employed for Temple re-dedication. Modern commentators, of course, feel much freer in seeing the title introduced later for such a ceremony as in the time of the Maccabees after the desecration by Antiochus (so Weiser).

2. Cf. 2 Chron 32.25, though the illness and cure is detailed more fully in 2 Kings 20. Theodoret conducts here an exercise in typology—or two, forward and reverse: Hezekiah's reversal of fortunes is seen as type both of human nature in general and of Adam.

formed lofty ambitions against his maker, was consigned to death but by divine loving-kindness attained resurrection.

(2) *I shall extol you, Lord, because you have supported me, and have not let my foes rejoice over me* (v. 1). By taking up our firstfruits,³ the Lord thus endowed all of nature with salvation, and did not allow the hostile and inimical demons to be gleeful. *O Lord my God, I cried to you, and you healed me. Lord, you brought my soul up from Hades, you saved me from the ranks of those going down into the pit* (vv. 2–3). We hear this from the viewpoint of human nature. I mean, the verse *I cried to you and you healed me* is applicable to Hezekiah as far as the obvious sense goes, but not to human nature in this sense: human nature did not beseech God and look for reprieve from destruction; rather, it constantly fell to wailing and weeping, with death in view and no expectation of resurrection.⁴ Accordingly, the psalmist made mention of the tears and laments that occur with the sick and dying to show the ineffable loving-kindness of God in return for prayer in that, without being invoked, and seeing only the wailing, he took pity on what was happening and gave a reprieve from death, death being called *pit* here, too.⁵

(3) *Sing to the Lord, you his holy ones, confess to the memory of his holiness. Because there is wrath in his anger, and life in his will* (vv. 4–5). He was right to assign the hymn and the confession of favor to the holy ones: since he gave the gift of resurrection to all human beings, and not all were worthy of the favor, appropriately he consecrated the worthy ones for hymn singing. Now, the other distinction he made was just right as well, attributing *wrath* [1073] to *anger,* giving the name *wrath* to instruction,⁶ and at-

---

3. Cf. 1 Cor 15.20.
4. Theodoret is continuing to develop his distinction of senses in the psalm—in reference to the plight of Hezekiah in a literal sense, and to the plight of human nature in a spiritual sense. He resists any temptation to develop the latter in the direction of moralizing, as a preacher like Chrysostom might.
5. Cf. note 4 to *Commentary* on Ps 28 on Theodoret's undeveloped understanding of OT thinking on Sheol.
6. Editor Schulze suggests that the LXX and other translators have made a rod for their own back here by reading Hebrew *rogez,* "excitement, wrath," for *rega',* "moment" (with Jerome and the NRSV) or "tranquillity" (which Dahood extends to mean "life eternal"); others suggest the LXX is reading

tributing *life* to *will:* he wishes the former, to be sure, not the latter, which is something we bring on ourselves, after all: "God did not make death," Scripture says, "and finds no satisfaction in the destruction of the living; he created everything for existence, in fact, and the generations of the world are wholesome."[7] And we also hear him saying through the prophet Ezekiel, "Surely I do not wish the death of the sinner as much as his being converted to me and living?"[8] *Weeping will last till evening, and joy till morning.* Now, things turned out like this both in the case of Hezekiah and in the case of the salvation of everyone: after the Assyrians applied those awful threats and moved the city to weeping, they sustained the blow at night, and in the morning they filled with good cheer those whom they had forced to weep. The divine Isaiah brought Hezekiah the sentence of death in the evening, and towards morning brought him in turn the good news of life.[9] And it happened likewise in the case of the salvation of everyone: the sacred apostles and the believers along with them lamented the Passion of the Lord, but towards morning the women came and brought the joy of the Resurrection.

(4) *Now, I said in my prosperity, I shall not be moved forever* (v. 6). Adam had hopes for this, too, while living in paradise before the deception, as did Hezekiah after conquering the Assyrian: the book of Chronicles teaches us this clearly when it says the heart of King Hezekiah was lifted up.[10] *Lord, by your will you provided my power in beauty; but you turned your face away, and I was disturbed* (v. 7). This too is applicable both to Hezekiah and all of human nature. He enjoyed the divine providence on account of virtue and prevailed over the Assyrians, and in turn when bereft of the divine favor he fell victim to disease and was affected by fear of dy-

---

the right form but giving it a different meaning. Theodoret, of course, is not in a position to rule on these possibilities, and simply falls to rationalizing his received text, which is apparently identical to that of his other available versions.

7. Wis 1.13–14.
8. Ezek 18.23.
9. Reference to the relevant biblical passages (cf. note 2) shows that Theodoret is forcing the facts somewhat to make his point about times of day. The Resurrection accounts support him more closely.
10. Cf. 2 Chron 32.25.

ing. Adam, too, in the garden was adorned with the beauty of virtue, and was proof against destruction; but when deprived of the divine providence through the Fall, he experienced the turmoil that comes from living. Now, Symmachus put it very clearly, "Lord, in your good pleasure you fixed power in my forefather," so that it would be clear that human nature in person is saying this to Christ the Lord, who awarded it the great gift of life.[11]

(5) [1076] *I shall cry to you, O Lord, and make my petition to my God. What good is there in my blood, in my going down to destruction? Surely dust will not confess to you or proclaim your truth?* (vv. 8–9). Blessed Hezekiah also employed these words, as the fourth book of Kings and the inspired composition of the divine Isaiah teach.[12] Human nature also cried out to God, of course, although not in every case, nevertheless through the holy ones, using words like this, It is right to sing hymns to you as creator, and to give thanks in words for your favors. This belongs to the living: how could those who have dissolved into dust and ashes and lost their bodily function manage to sing of your kindnesses?

(6) *The Lord heard and had mercy on me, the Lord became my helper. You turned my lamentation into joy for me. You rent my sackcloth and clad me in joy so that my glory might sing to you and I might feel no compunction* (vv. 10–12). Clad in sackcloth, Hezekiah offered prayer to God against the Assyrians, and human nature put on the guise of grieving. Even today some foolish people in their bewailing the dead are wrong to sit about in sackcloth and have no wish to give ear to the inspired words that cry out unmistakably, *You rent my sackcloth and clad me in joy, and turned my lamentation into joy for me.* I mean, just as Hezekiah was filled with great joy on receiving the promise of the fifteen years,[13] so it is right for us on receiving the hope of resurrection not to mourn the

11. In using Adam as an antitype of Hezekiah, as it were, Theodoret has referred several times to the Fall, and so would give little encouragement to the Pelagians, despite accusations against Antiochene theologians like him; his eastern optimism also comes through, however, the sin being accompanied by the promise of life.
12. Cf. 2 Kings 20.3; Isa 38.18.
13. Cf. 2 Kings 20.6. It is rare for Theodoret to make some application of the psalmist's thinking to the lives of his readers, such as the proper Christian response to death, as here.

dead but to await joyfully that wonderful outcome. Now, the verse, *so that my glory might sing to you and I might feel no compunction,* Symmachus rendered thus: "so that glory might praise you and not keep silence," that is, In response to this beneficence it behooves us to sing your praises constantly and celebrate those who have attained such glory, at no time keeping silence. Compunction encourages silence; accordingly, the Septuagint put *compunction* in place of silence.[14] Now, Hezekiah attained glory once such a countless number sustained a divine blow on his account and the sun turned back;[15] we, on the other hand, have a basis of high repute in the evidence given by the God of all of his great affection for us: "God so loved the world," Scripture says, "that he has given his only-begotten Son so that all who believe in him may not perish but have eternal life."[16] *O Lord my God, I shall confess to you forever:* not only in the present life but [1077] also after the resurrection I shall offer hymns to you, constantly recounting your extraordinary and ineffable gifts.

---

14. It is also rare to see Theodoret, after comparison of the relevant readings, explicating Symmachus but preferring the LXX as more profound (Dahood also commending it, though—perhaps inadequately—taking it to mean "lest I be absorbed in grief").

15. Cf. 2 Kings 20.11.

16. John 3.16. Commentary on this psalm has enabled Theodoret to demonstrate a carefully balanced process such as he foreshadowed in his preface, allowing for some reference to Old Testament and New Testament history as well as to the spiritual life in general. His hermeneutical thinking on matters such as the literal sense of the text, a fuller sense, and typology has also emerged more clearly than in most cases.

COMMENTARY ON PSALM 31

To the end. A psalm of David, of departure.

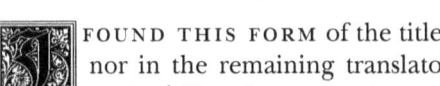 FOUND THIS FORM of the title neither in the Hebrew nor in the remaining translators, but in some of the copies.[1] Now, in my view it touches on Uriah: it says in the body of the psalm, *I said in my departure, I am driven from your sight* (v. 22), that is, After my sin I expected to be deprived of your providence. This psalm is likely to have been spoken by blessed David at the time of being pursued by Absalom; commentary on the verses teaches this more clearly.

(2) *In you, O Lord, I hoped; let me not be forever ashamed* (v. 1). The sin covered me in deep shame, he is saying, but I pray this may not long remain with me owing to my confidence placed in you. *In your righteousness rescue me and snatch me away.* Do not fix your eyes on my sin, he is saying, but on the lawlessness of my pursuers: by applying this righteous verdict you will free me from the calamities besetting me. *Incline your ear to me, speedily snatch me away* (v. 2): heed my prayer and give me prompt help.

(3) *Become a protector God for me and a house of refuge; save me, because you are my might and my refuge* (vv. 2–3). He said this also in the seventeenth psalm,[2] indicating God's manifold care. *My might*, however, Aquila and Symmachus rendered as "my rock." Now, it is likely that the Old Testament term agreed with that in

---

1. For all Rondeau's confidence in Theodoret's grasp of Semitics, one finds it hard to envision him poring over a range of material that included the Hebrew text. As his usual alternative versions do not contain the intriguing word, it must be in variants of the LXX that he finds it; and we wonder about the number of these at his disposal (a modern composite LXX text like Rahlfs' includes this *ekstaseos*). See the discussion of the nature of Theodoret's text in Introduction, section 3.

2. Ps 18.2, which however does not have this unusual construction, "a protector God"; the resemblance is rather to the opening verses of Ps 71, a fact Theodoret does not recall when making comment there.

the Gospels, which gives a glimpse of the prudent person building the house on the rock, which the force neither of winds nor of rain and floods ruined on account of its stability.[3] *For your name's sake you will guide me and nourish me.* Symmachus, on the other hand, put "protect" for *nourish,* meaning, You will accord me providence of every kind on account of your name, in which I trusted. Now, through all the verses occurring here, at any rate, we learn the measure of his prudence: his appeal for divine assistance is made on the basis not of his own virtue [1080] but of God's name and of God's righteousness and because he hoped in him.

(4) *You will draw me out of this snare which they have hidden for me, because you are my protector, O Lord* (v. 4). By this he indicated the plot of Ahithophel, which he put into operation against him, as we have spoken about previously.[4] *Into your hands I shall entrust my spirit; redeem me, O Lord, God of truth* (v. 5): after frequently encountering many disasters I was freed from them by your aid—hence I entrust my soul to your providence. He calls providence here once again *hands. You hated all those who paid constant attention to futile things* (v. 6). So they did not trust in you, he is saying, but relied on their own futile reasoning. You, on the contrary, ignore such people completely.

(5) *For my part, on the other hand, I hoped in the Lord. I shall be glad and rejoice in your mercy* (v. 7): even in the midst of disasters I call on your help, and enjoying it I attribute the cause of good things to your loving-kindness. *Because you took note of my humiliation, you saved my soul from distress. You have not confined me in the hands of foes; you set my feet in open spaces* (vv. 7–8). Instead, relying on thoughts like this I was not thwarted: when I oftentimes encountered enemies' wiles and snares, and fell into the nets set for me, I escaped the hunters. He said this: *You have not confined me in the hands of a foe.* Now, history teaches that though often overtaken by Saul and actually confined in the cave, he escaped

---

3. Matt 7.24–25. For Theodoret the Old Testament expression (literally, the *logos prophetikos,* or the word that is inspired, a term not applied to the work of NT composers like the evangelists and Paul) is in harmony with the New Testament. See Introduction, section 5.
4. Cf. Ps 7.1.

the hands of that man, and at another time the people of Gath by feigning madness.[5]

(6) *Have mercy on me, O Lord, because I am in distress; anger has upset my eye, my soul, and my stomach* (v. 9). Symmachus put it this way: "My eye is disturbed with anger." In other words, having provoked you to anger by sin, I must constantly weep, and in fact my soul is filled with distress and alarm. Now, he gave the name *stomach* to the recesses of his thoughts: it was his thoughts that were disturbed, not his stomach. [1081] *My life is wasted with pain, and my years with groans* (v. 10). I have consumed all my life, he is saying, in pains and tears. *My strength has failed in poverty, and my bones are disturbed:* indigence and the lack of necessities have wasted my body. Now, history also records this indigence: "Shobi son of Nahash the Ammonite and Barzillai the Gileadite offered wheat, barley, meal, beans, lentils, and some other things to David and the people, because they said that the people were in need and were worn out with starvation in the wilderness."[6]

(7) *By comparison with all my foes I became a severe reproach even to my neighbors and a fright to my friends* (v. 11). While my foes enjoy good cheer, he is saying, I am a laughingstock and a joke to my neighbors and the terror of my acquaintances. And to teach this more clearly he added, *Those who set eyes on me in public avoid me:* they are afraid to associate with me lest they fall foul of my foes. *I have been lost to the heart like a dead man, I have become like a vessel mislaid* (v. 12). Everyone has given me up for lost, he is saying, like a vessel mislaid or a corpse occupying a tomb. He brought out the degree of forgetfulness by reference to the worthless vessel: just as when lost it vanishes from the memory of the losers for reason of its worthlessness, he is saying, so too am I in their estimation like someone non-existent and have become deserving of no esteem.

(8) *Because I heard the criticism of many huddling together* (v. 13):

5. Cf. 1 Kings 24; 21.
6. Cf. 2 Sam 17.27–29. If we were in any doubt of the historical reference of the psalm, this verse (slightly abbreviated in terms of donors and donations) really pins it down. As we have noted, Theodoret has a fascination with quaint detail in the Scriptures.

I say this not by way of conjecture but hearing with my own ears their reproaches. Now, in this he is suggesting also the abuse of Shimei.[7] *As they assembled together against me they plotted to take my life. But I hoped in you, O Lord; I said, You are my God, my lot is in your hands* (vv. 13–15): so while they gathered together and plotted my death, I knew you to be my God and ruler. He says, *my lot is in your hands,* or as the rest say, "my times are in your hands," that is, You allot to each as you will faintheartedness and exhilaration, and in turn you reverse these as you please; he calls "times" or *lot* the changes in circumstances—[1084] wealth and poverty, slavery and lordship, peace and war, and likewise the other things of this kind. *Rescue me from the hand of my foes and those pursuing me.*

(9) Then he shows the form of the redemption: *Lord, let your face shine upon your servant; save me in your mercy* (v. 16): when you make your appearance, gloom is immediately lifted. *Lord, let me not be confounded, because I called upon you. Let the ungodly be put to shame and cast down to Hades* (vv. 16–17). From this we learn that the sin is very different from impiety; hence the mighty David beseeches that he be freed from the shame caused by the sin, but those addicted to impiety be sent in shame to their death. *Let the lying lips become mute that speak iniquity against the righteous with arrogance and contempt* (v. 18). Here he forecasts the death of Ahithophel who, though friend and adviser to David, uncovered the ancient plot and used his words to the detriment of the one who had done him no wrong.[8] Now, the psalmist was right to call that counsel *arrogance and contempt* since he egged on the son to murder his father.

(10) *How great the extent of your goodness, O Lord, which you have laid up for those who fear you* (v. 19). Once again he uses *how* not by way of comparison but for effect. Hence Aquila and Symmachus rendered it thus: "What great good is yours, which you have set aside and hidden for those who fear you." Now, the verse has this sense: You hide the rewards and prizes for those

---

7. Cf. 2 Sam 16.5–13.
8. Cf. 2 Sam 15–17. Though finding this psalm suited to application in a generally spiritual sense, Theodoret keeps supplying, almost mechanically, the odd reference to David's life.

who fear you, O Lord, many and great and marvelous though these are, and instead you allow them to struggle with sweat and tears. Yet there comes the time when you reveal the rewards, giving cheer to the athletes: he added this, *You accomplished it for those who hope in you in the sight of the sons of men.* Then he described in detail the providence in their favor: *You will keep them in hiding in your presence away from the disturbance of people. You will shelter them in your tabernacle away from contentious tongues* (v. 20). Your appearance suffices, he is saying (he calls it *presence*), for them to be freed from all human disturbance and commotion, [1085] and to conceal them as though admitted to the precincts of some tabernacle, and render them invisible. He personally enjoyed this providence when pursued by Saul: though caught up in the midst of perils, he won salvation. Likewise the great Elisha fled the Syrians encircling him by casting a haze on their eyes.[9] And you could find many similar things in the divine Scripture.

(11) *Blessed be the Lord because he has marvelously shown his mercy to me in a city surrounded* (v. 21). Symmachus, on the other hand, put it this way: "Blessed be the Lord who is baffling in his mercy to me as in a city enclosed": he surrounded and enclosed me in his habitual loving-kindness, he is saying, as the inhabitants encircle a city with a strong rampart. *But I said in my departure, I am driven from the sight of your eyes; hence hearken to the sound of my appeal when I cry out to you* (v. 22). I thought that on falling into sin, he is saying, I was far from your care; but you took account of my humble words and did not despise me in my need. Now, he rightly called his sin *departure:* after treading the way of righteousness he left it and turned aside; but he stumbled and fell foul of bloodthirsty brigands. This very thing reveals David's virtue: he was not in the habit of sinning, but departing a little from his chosen course he suffered that awful slide.

(12) From this point he switches his treatment to exhortation, giving an insight into divine loving-kindness and providence from the events of his life. *Love the Lord, all you his holy ones, because the Lord looks for truth, and repays those who are guilty of*

9. Cf. 2 Kings 6.

extraordinary arrogance (v. 23). It behooves you all, he is saying, who have chosen the course of treading the divine way to love the ruler of all ardently, who uses truth like some norm and punishes those who let pretense get out of control. He did not simply say, *who are guilty of arrogance* but *who are guilty of extraordinary arrogance.* This too, you see, is sufficient to reveal the divine goodness: he puts up with those who adopt somewhat greater presumption, but those whose heads are swollen and are exorbitantly haughty he consigns to appropriate punishments. *Be bold, and let your heart grow strong, all you who hope in the Lord* (v. 24). Aware of this, then, you who pass through the present life with divine hope strengthen your souls with bravery [1088] and heed the directions of the pilot, traveling wherever he leads. This is also suitable advice for us, who find encouragement in hope.[10]

10. Theodoret, as we have had cause to remark, does not see himself as pastor or spiritual director; application of a psalm's teaching is at best perfunctory.

COMMENTARY ON PSALM 32

For David, of understanding.[1]

HIS PSALM HAS THE SAME SENSE: it was uttered amid those awful calamities after the sin. Looking forward, however, with inspired eyes to the grace of the New Testament and to the forgiveness accorded the believers through all-holy baptism, he declares them blessed for actually receiving forgiveness of sins effortlessly.[2] He says in beginning the psalm, *Blessed are those whose iniquities are forgiven and whose sins are covered over. Blessed the man of whose sin the Lord takes no account and in whose mouth there is no deceit* (vv. 1–2): I was wasted with constant grieving and weeping on account of the sin, and for that reason fell foul of manifold disasters; so I class as enviable and blessed those who by the Lord's loving-kindness receive forgiveness of sins effortlessly. To them, in fact, he exercises such generosity as not only to forgive them but also cover over their sins so that no trace of them remains.

(2) *Because I kept silence, my bones grew old from my crying aloud all day* (v. 3). When he committed that awful sin, he had recourse to the remedy of repentance not at once but after Nathan's re-

---

1. Unlike the ancients, modern commentators are content to see the term *maskil* as denoting one type of psalm, somehow related to the root *skl;* Mowinckel can then deduce that "a *maskil* thus probably indicates the cultic poem as the outcome of a supra-normal 'wisdom' and 'insight' as to the way in which the deity ought to be worshipped and influenced; originally the word probably also sought to express that the song was filled with active power and was particularly 'effective' in use." Theodoret's LXX, of course, is thinking not of genre but of semantics.

2. Perhaps it is because this psalm, Augustine's favorite, is the second of the seven Penitential Psalms of the early Church that Theodoret immediately admits a spiritual dimension to it along with the historical reference he accords it, namely, the "effortless" remission of sins achieved in baptism.

proof.³ Accordingly he shouts this aloud at this point. Since on receipt of the blow he did not at once show the wound to the physician but kept silence in an endeavor to conceal it, he grew old crying aloud and denouncing the sin. *Because day and night your hand was heavy upon me* (v. 4): I mourn and howl, smitten with censure and retribution of all kinds. He used that statement, *your hand was heavy upon me,* by analogy with those striking with the hand and persisting in it at length. *I was reduced to distress with a thorn being fixed in me.* Far from your censure of me being unfair, he is saying, it is quite justified: sin is the cause of my troubles, something I gave rise to like a bunch of grapes, and I am constantly stung by it. He spoke of sin, note, as *a thorn* [1089] and as a useless growth, grown as it were to sting him.

(3) *I made the sin known, and did not hide my lawlessness. I said, To the Lord I shall confess my sin against myself, and you put away the impiety of my sin* (v. 5): at first on sinning I kept silence, but afterwards I have been accusing myself day and night, and have gained great benefits from the accusation with your granting me forgiveness of the sins. Now, we should remark that he did not say, "you forgave my sin" but *the impiety of my sin,* that is to say, You did not punish my transgression as it deserved; instead, you made allowance for the enormity of the sin and applied treatment with measured censure. History teaches this, too: when David said, "I have sinned against the Lord," Nathan replied, "The Lord has put away your sin, you will not die."⁴ He did, however, threaten to fill his house with calamities of all kinds; here too likewise, *You put away the impiety of my sin:* immediately after perpetrating such things, he is saying, I should have been consigned to death according to the law, but you applied your loving-kindness and did not so consign me, keeping my treatment to moderate censure.

---

3. Cf. 2 Sam 12. In commentary on this psalm and the previous one, Theodoret has spoken gravely of "the (awful) sin" of David, and made the connection with Uriah, but goes into no further detail of the adultery with Bathsheba narrated in 2 Sam 11—an incident a preacher like Chrysostom would have exploited for effect with his congregation. Theodoret strikes us as very modest by comparison.
4. 2 Sam 12.13.

(4) *For this every holy one will pray at the right time* (v. 6). By *the right time* he means the living of the New Testament by which on all land and sea believers honor God with David's hymn singing. So here the psalmist prophesies this and says to the Lord, Not only do I entreat you over this sin, but also everyone throughout the world who is a recipient of the knowledge of God will offer this prayer on my behalf. It is likely, you see, that in some way or other we utter David's sentiments and adopt his words in singing the praises of God.[5] *Even in the rush of mighty waters they will not approach them.* Symmachus, on the other hand, rendered it this way, "Every holy person will pray about him, finding the opportune moment, lest mighty waters become a flood and approach him": those who offer zealous entreaty to you will enjoy providence of all kinds, and so even if encountering diverse calamities flooding about them like water they will be superior to them and emerge stronger than the troubles.

(5) *You are a refuge for me from the onset of tribulation;* [1092] *my joy, rescue me from those surrounding me* (v. 7). After saying this about the sin, he begs to be delivered from the evils besetting him as a result of it, and actually gains a response: the Lord says to him, *I shall give you understanding, and instruct you in the way you should travel; I shall fix my eyes on you* (v. 8). When you turn aside and approve of error, he is saying, I shall lead you back to the straight and narrow and impart to you knowledge and familiarity with it, and I shall allow you to share in the former benevolence. He said, *I shall fix my eyes on you* by analogy with those kindly disposed to someone, wanting constantly to gaze upon them: just as those angry with them seem to turn their face away from them, so they indicate their favor by attentiveness. Hence the inspired author said elsewhere as well, "Turn to me and have mercy on me"; and again, "Do not turn your face away from me."[6] And God himself through the prophet Jeremiah, "Turn back to me, and I shall turn back to you."[7] Here the inspired word urges, on the one hand, those in the grip of lawless-

---

5. We recall Theodoret's statement in the preface about the universality of the practice of praying the Psalms.
6. Ps 25.16, 27.9.
7. Jer 15.19.

ness not to imitate the irrationality of brute beasts and, on the other, the righteous always to maintain God's joyfulness.

(6) He puts it this way: *Do not be like horse or mule that have no understanding. Keep their jaws under tight muzzle and rein if they do not come near you* (v. 9). I urge you, he is saying, not to imitate their irrationality; but if you do not obey, accept rein and muzzle like them. In this way he indicates his censure; hence he added, *Many the scourges of the sinner* (v. 10). After introducing this further proposition about sinners in this way, he shifts his attention to a different group: *Mercy will envelop those who hope in the Lord.* All people, even if adorned with the works of virtue, stand in need of divine grace; hence [1093] the divine Apostle also shouts aloud, "By grace you are saved through faith; this is not of your doing—it is God's gift."[8]

(7) *Rejoice in the Lord and be glad, you righteous ones, and boast, all you who are upright in heart* (v. 11). So let no one rejoice in their own achievements, but rather exult in God and find satisfaction in that. This is in keeping with the apostolic statements, "Let the one who boasts boast in the Lord,"[9] and "If you seem to be standing, take care not to fall."[10] Hence he also bids us teach in a spirit of gentleness: "Keep yourself in mind in case you, too, are tempted."[11]

---

8. Eph 2.8. Chrysostom could never have left this unqualified statement of the gratuity of grace pass without saying, as he does on Ps 111, "Faith is not sufficient if a way of life in keeping with faith is not forthcoming." Brevity has its advantages.
9. 2 Cor 10.17.
10. 1 Cor 10.12.
11. Gal 6.1.

COMMENTARY ON PSALM 33

NO TITLE IN THE HEBREW. The Septuagint mentioned this in translating the psalm: Do not look for a translation of the title, it says; we found no title.¹ Now, this psalm was spoken by blessed David with a view to the question of the remarkable Hezekiah, but is framed as if coming from Hezekiah in person encouraging the people to hymn singing in the wake of the surprising victory and destruction of the Assyrians.

(2) *Rejoice in the Lord, you righteous ones* (v. 1). In many places Aquila has "praise" for *rejoice;* Symmachus likewise rendered it "Praise becomes the upright":² it is appropriate for those who acknowledge God and are freed from error to sing praise to God constantly. Then he teaches also how it behooves them to conduct their hymn singing: *Confess to the Lord with a lyre, sing to him with a ten-stringed harp. Sing him a new song, sing a beautiful song to him with full voice* (vv. 2–3). Now, all this was performed according to prescribed liturgy:³ they used lyres, cymbals, drums, and other musical instruments. *Full voice* is a triumphant shout, raised against the fugitives by the victors. It is also appropriate for us to take the words spiritually;⁴ we can turn ourselves

---

1. Did Theodoret read such a rubric in his form of the Septuagint, or is he merely expatiating on the significance of the absence of a title for his reader? In fact, at least some forms of the LXX (with some Hebrew manuscript encouragement) do have a title, "For David," which in Aquila is preceded by "A psalm."

2. As the LXX (like the Hebrew) is in no doubt that this is the second half of v. 1, it seems more likely that editor Schulze has erred in punctuation than that Theodoret has attributed the clause to Symmachus alone.

3. It would be nice to have from Theodoret some further insight into liturgical practice of his time, such as the singing of the psalms; but he is treating them as text for commentary, not the stuff of living worship.

4. Theodoret often reminds his readers that the psalmist proceeds by analogy, and that the reader ought therefore be aware of the figurative use

into a fine-sounding and harmonious instrument and sing the praises of God through all our faculties, both of sense and of intellect.

(3) *Because the word of the Lord is upright, and all his works in faithfulness* (v. 4). [1096] The Lord of all rules everything righteously, he is saying, and he set before us the insight[5] into his works, encouraging us to believe and not to pry into how they occurred. *The Lord loves mercy and judgment* (v. 5): what is done by him he bids everyone accept unquestioningly and without demur, though taking care of life and adorning it with mercy and judgment. *The earth is full of the Lord's mercy.* It behooves us to imitate the Maker, he is saying: just as he administers mercy in his arrangements and has pity on the wronged, so too is it necessary for us to administer judgment to the unjust and mercy to the wronged. Our loving Lord administered judgment against the Assyrians, whereas he accorded us loving-kindness and longsuffering. After recounting the unfolding of divine providence in this way, he transfers his attention to creation, and teaches how after creating everything he rules everything and cares for it as his own doing, not others'.

(4) *By the word of the Lord the heavens were established, and by the breath of his mouth all their power* (v. 6). Effort and time on the part of workers was not required: a word was sufficient for creating on his part; he said, Let a firmament be made, and so it was; Let lights be made in the firmament of heaven, and so it was.[6] So the face value of the text conveys the surface meaning of this: it was appropriate for the Jews of old. True theology, on the other hand, gives a glimpse of God the Word with the all-holy Spirit

---

of language, as also of a Christological interpretation he himself gives to whole psalms. He does not often admit the words can be taken πνευματικῶς as here; the word has a moral sense for him, and he is reluctant to adopt that relationship with his readers.

5. For Theodoret it is possible to achieve a θεωρία into the works of the Lord; Diodore and Chrysostom will use this term to speak of finding a fuller sense in Scripture—something Theodoret (without use of the term) will in fact proceed to do in commenting on the next verse, where he sees theologians delving below a "surface meaning" of a text taken "at face value"—adequate for Jews of old—to find a fuller meaning of the Word's activity.

6. Cf. Gen 1.6–7, 1.14–15.

making the heavens and the heavenly powers.⁷ The inspired composition of the Old Testament anticipates the Gospel teaching:⁸ as the divinely inspired John, the son of thunder, taught the whole world, "In the beginning was the Word, and the Word was with God, and the Word was God; all things were made through him, and without him was made not one thing that was made,"⁹ so blessed David proclaims in the words, *By the word of the Lord the heavens were established, and by the breath of his mouth all their powers.* Now, he does not attribute to God the Word the creation of the heavens and to the all-holy Spirit the making of the powers; rather, he says God the Word and the Holy Spirit made former and latter. Some said the *powers* of heaven are the heavenly [1097] lights, others the unseen powers.¹⁰ The second strikes me as the truer: in giving us a glimpse of God the creator, he would not have made mention only of visible creation.

(5) *Collecting the waters of the sea like a flask, putting the deeps in storehouses* (v. 7): he has all the nature of water confined in determined places as in some treasuries; some he draws to the upper air whenever he wishes, and collects in the clouds as in some flask. Hence he says, "He brings the clouds up from the end of the earth";¹¹ and again in another place the divine Scripture says, "Who summons the water of the sea, and pours it out on the surface of all the earth."¹² *Let all the earth fear the Lord, and let all the inhabitants of the earth tremble before him. Because he spoke, and they were made; he commanded, and they were created* (vv. 8–9). Having mentioned the heavens and the unseen powers, and then

---

7. The word *power* is in the singular in Theodoret's text of this v. 6, as also in the versions of Aquila and Symmachus, though he proceeds to comment on it in the plural to develop his point.

8. As we have mentioned before (see note 3 on Ps 31), for Theodoret as for Chrysostom there is a harmony between *propheteia* (OT inspired composition) and the NT authors, the evangelists and Paul (not that they are not inspired, but they are writing in the wake of the Word's enfleshment). See my "Chrysostom's terminology for the inspired Word."

9. Cf. John 1.1, 1.3.

10. Theodoret, whose commentary shows the influence of previous Psalm commentators from both Antioch and Alexandria, is not unaware of alternative interpretations, as of alternative versions of the text. The former interpretation is that of Diodore and Theodore, Guinot tells us, the latter that of Eusebius.

11. Ps 135.7.   12. Amos 5.8.

the substance of the waters, he highlights as well the land in their midst and its inhabitants, teaching that they are his creation, and recommending fear and trembling before the creator and obedience to his bidding. For *tremble* Symmachus said, "reverence," you see, and Aquila, "will shudder," transposing the world's reverence to the time to come: people demonstrated it, not when he composed these words, but after the Incarnation, Passion, and Resurrection of Christ the Lord.

(6) *The Lord frustrates nations' plans, sets aside peoples' thoughts, sets aside rulers' plans. But the plan of the Lord abides forever, thoughts of his heart from age to age* (vv. 10–11). The words have a twofold interpretation: he not only frustrated the plans of the Assyrians, Sennacherib and Rabshakeh, and showed the power and truth of his own plan, but also thwarted the rebellions of the nations throughout the whole world against the apostles, and made the might of his own power obvious to everyone. The inspired word hinted at this: *thoughts of his heart from age to age,* the mention of the two ages teaching both what happened then and what would come later.[13] *Happy the nation whose God is the Lord, the people he chose as his own inheritance* (v. 12). One should declare blessed, he is saying, not those priding themselves on their wealth, [1100] but those trusting in God and enjoying aid from him. Now, the chosen people, named as *God's inheritance,* was in olden times the Jewish people, but later was the people chosen from the nations and in receipt of the rays of faith: "Ask of me," the psalmist says, "and I shall give you nations as your inheritance and the ends of the earth as your possession."[14]

(7) *From heaven the Lord looked down, he saw all sons of men. From his ready abode he looked on all the inhabitants of the earth* (vv. 13–14). He said this also in the thirteenth psalm, making the same inspired statement.[15] After saying *looked down,* in case any-

13. So, as often, Theodoret sees the psalmist's text as *promise* achieving double *fulfillment*—in later Old Testament times and in New Testament times as well.
14. Ps 2.8. Such a statement of the displacement of the Jewish people from the position of privilege and election would in Chrysostom have prompted a lengthy polemic, whereas it is simply stated as fact by Theodoret.
15. Cf. Ps 14.2.

one thought he was ignorant of what people are up to, he added opportunely, *He forms their hearts individually, he understands all their deeds* (v. 15). I said the God of all looks down, he is saying, not as ignorant and anxious to learn, but as judging and sentencing: how could the one who made the soul be ignorant of its movements? He put *hearts* for "reason," you see.

(8) *A king is not saved by great power, nor will a giant be saved by his excessive strength. Worthless a horse for salvation, it will not be saved by its excessive power* (vv. 16–17). We have come to know through experience that one should trust not in strength of body, nor in bravery of spirit, nor in speed of mount, nor in number of subjects: Sennacherib abounded in all of these, all to no avail, and instead he suffered ruin. So show what is to be done, O prophet. *Lo, the eyes of the Lord are on those who fear him, who hope in his mercy, to rescue their souls from death, to sustain them in famine* (vv. 18–19). Godliness is the provider of all goods, he is saying: it draws down divine providence, and is an obstacle to the onset of death and need, while bestowing the abundance of good things. Now, it is likely that at the time of that awful siege the besieged experienced a shortage of necessities, then were liberated from that calamity by the overthrow of the enemy.

(9) *Our soul waits for the Lord, he is our help and our protector, because our heart rejoices in him, and we hoped in his holy name* (vv. 20–21): enjoying such good things, therefore, we have firm hope in God, and we shall always look forward to help from him; he has granted us [1101] current prosperity as well. Then after saying *because we hoped in his holy name,* his prayer is to receive mercy commensurate to his hope; he says, in fact, *May your mercy be shown to us, O Lord, as we have hoped in you* (v. 22). Now, this is the extreme expression of rashness, and presumptuous in the view of people of our time: whose hope reaches such a degree as to be bold enough to say, Measure your mercy by my hope? Yet the Lord taught this even in the sacred Gospels: "The measure you use will be the measure applied to you."[16] Consequently, let us acquire hope that is perfect and sincere, and keep the rest of our life in accordance with our hope, so as to reap much mercy.

16. Matt 7.2.

COMMENTARY ON PSALM 34

For David, when he altered his appearance in the presence of Ahimelech, and he dismissed him, and he got away.

HE DIVINE DAVID PERCEIVED Saul's abrasive and envious attitude, and relying on advice from the admirable Jonathan he took to his heels and reached the city of Nob.¹ So when he was there in the company of the priest Ahimelech he concealed his flight and said he had been sent by the king on a certain urgent business. Looking for loaves, he found only those assigned to the priests and took them, the priest giving them to him contrary to the Law; food like this, you see, was assigned to the priests only. The sacraments of grace, however, were foreshadowed, and the door of divine liberality opened to the faithful in advance: no longer is the divine nourishment reserved to the priests alone; instead, the partaking of divine things is available to those so willing.² The mighty David at that time also took the sword of Goliath, which he dedicated to God as the firstfruits of that skirmish.

(2) Now, Scripture called Ahimelech Abiathar as though having two names.³ So when as a fugitive he did not inform the priest of his flight but said he was carrying out some royal busi-

---

1. Commentators ancient and modern agree the psalm title refers to the flight of David from Saul, when he reached Nob where Ahimelech (misnamed Abiathar, his son, by Mark at Mark 2.26) was priest, and then Gath, city of King Achish (both incidents recounted in 1 Sam 21). Theodoret thinks the contents support the former reference; moderns prefer to see the psalm simply as an individual's prayer of thanksgiving—and in fact our commentator soon ignores the historical situation.

2. Though Theodoret's own introduction to commentary is directed to debating the more appropriate historical reference, he takes time to offer this liberal comment about the end of clerical exclusiveness in approach to the sacraments, at least the Eucharist. See note 10 below.

3. It is probably to Mark's retelling of this incident, where father and son are confused, that Theodoret is referring here, seemingly not aware the

ness, he is said to have "altered his appearance," as though not adopting his normal truthfulness but taking on an attitude different from normal. Some commentators, on the other hand, have supplied a different occasion for the psalm, saying David altered his appearance when he entered the presence of Achish: fearful of the foreigners' scheming, he feigned madness and secured his salvation by this means. But the psalm's verses bear no relation [1104] to this occasion, suiting instead what I have said, as with God's help will be demonstrated forthwith.

(3) *I shall bless the Lord at every moment, praise of him always in my mouth* (v. 1). Both in flight and in pursuit, when my lot is fair and when it is foul, I shall praise my Lord. *In the Lord will my soul be commended* (v. 2): he made me illustrious in turn, and will bring me to the fore. *Let the gentle hear and be glad. Magnify the Lord with me, and let us exalt his name together* (vv. 2–3). He is not prepared to raise his voice in song alone; instead, he wants those who share his gentleness to share also the hymn singing. Then he gives an insight into the reason for thanksgiving: *I sought out the Lord, and he heeded me, and from the midst of all my tribulations he rescued me* (v. 4). I besought him, he is saying, and was made proof against calamity.[4]

(4) *Approach him and be enlightened, and your faces will not blush* (v. 5): whoever approaches him in faith receives rays of intellectual light. The mighty Moses, too, was likewise made resplendent in his visible features, as David already remarked, "The light of your countenance, Lord, has left its mark on us."[5] Having thus exhorted people of like mind, he proposes himself to them as a model: *This poor man cried out, and the Lord hearkened to*

---

two are distinct people, having troubles enough with Scriptural details when these are not confused. (The Greek manuscripts give this Ahimelech a range of names, including Abimelech, which Dahood thinks could have been the Semitic name of the Philistine king of Gath, and which was the name of the Philistine king in Gerar in Gen 26.1.)

4. As though guiltridden for his lengthy introduction, he is now brisk and terse in commentary even by his standards. Alternative versions are not offered; so we are left to presume, for example, that in v. 10 none of the Greek translators took the option (shown in NRSV) of the metaphor of "young lions."

5. Ps 4.6. Moses in fact did not rate a mention in commentary on that psalm.

him, and saved him from all his tribulations (v. 6). Learn from my experience, he is saying, to trust in the God of all: though lowly and a mere shepherd, he accorded me his personal providence, and rendered me superior to my enemies.

(5) *An angel of the Lord will encamp around those who fear him, and will rescue them* (v. 7). The Apostle's words are also consistent with these, saying as he does about the angels, "Are they not all spirits in the divine service sent to minister to those destined to inherit salvation?"[6] Likewise the blessed Jacob said in prayer, "The angel who rescues me from all evils."[7] Likewise the patriarch Abraham said to his remarkable servant, "The Lord God will send his angel before you, and you will take a wife for my son Isaac from there."[8] Likewise blessed Zechariah says, "The angel talking in me."[9]

(6) [1105] *Taste and see that the Lord is good. Blessed is the man who hopes in him* (v. 8). After saying, *Approach him and be enlightened,* he recommends also *Taste.* Learn from experience, he is saying, the goodness of the Lord: you will gain blessedness from it. It should be understood, however, that while the obvious sense of the words applies to the Jews of old, the meaning hidden in the depth of the text, at any rate, suggests the grace of the divine sacraments: through all-holy baptism true illumination is acquired by those who approach it, and the taste of the life-giving food palpably manifests the goodness of the Savior. I mean, what could give us such a clear insight into his loving-kindness as Cross, Passion, and death occurring for our sake, and his becoming food and font together for his own sheep?[10]

---

6. Heb 1.14.   7. Gen 48.16.
8. Cf. Gen 24.7.
9. Zech 1.9. Is it the mention of angels that Theodoret warms to, prompting him to a battery of Scriptural texts not unworthy of Chrysostom in his pulpit?
10. Once again it is the sacramental dimension he sees in the text that leads Theodoret to distinguish levels of meaning. As at the beginning of this Psalm we noted this bishop insisting on the declericalization of divine beneficence, so he speaks eloquently (if with characteristic conciseness) of the experience of "tasting the goodness of the Lord" in the sacraments of initiation, baptism, and Eucharist, "food and font together." (Does the "together" suggest the reception of both sacraments on the one occasion by "those who approach," the adult catechumens? Confirmation is not men-

(7) *Fear the Lord, all you his holy ones, because those who fear him want for nothing. Wealthy people felt poverty and hunger, whereas those who seek out the Lord will not suffer lessening of any good* (vv. 9–10). This, too, is in harmony with what was said above: he exhorts those who have already received sanctification through baptism to blend love with fear, and to look for abundance of good things from the Lord alone. Wealth, after all, is subject to many changes: the person who is wealthy today is shortly transformed into a state of penury. The Jews of old, though enriched with God's care, *felt poverty and hunger* through failing to believe, whereas the believing nations received the abundance of good things from God.

(8) *Come, children, listen to me, I shall teach you fear of the Lord. Who is the person who chooses life, who loves to see good days?* (vv. 11–12). After proposing a carefree life as a kind of desirable and longed for prize, he urges them to the contest: *Keep your tongue from evil, and your lips from speaking guile. Turn away from evil, and do good; seek peace, and go after it* (vv. 13–14). First he dissuades from evil, then he bids them practice the forms of virtue. In the first place he bids them purify the tongue, as a member prone to fall, from all guile and wickedness; and he associates the lips with the tongue as cooperating in the same actions in response to its movements. In the second place he forbids the practice of evil: *Turn away from evil.* Then he prescribes good action: *Do good.* Now, what is the summit of good things? *Seek peace, and go after it:* the peaceable person entertains peace towards everyone, not purloining the neighbor's property furtively, [1108] not committing homicide, not undermining marriages, not speaking evil, not doing evil, doing favors, showing respect, sharing, lending support, sharing dangers and struggles—such is unalloyed love and genuine friendship.[11]

(9) Then he goes on to show the fruit of this: *The eyes of the Lord are on the righteous, and his ears open to their appeal* (v. 15). Those who do this, he is saying, are regarded by the Lord God,

---

tioned as a separate rite of initiation in these texts.) A theology that relates sacraments of initiation to the Paschal Mystery of Jesus also appeals.

11. Theodoret does not often expatiate on moral principles; so it is enlightening to see him here listing the chief vices and virtues in his view.

and when they request good things they gain their requests. Then he confirms what he said from its opposite: *But the face of the Lord is on evildoers, to destroy remembrance of them from the land* (v. 16). He sees also those guilty of the opposite, he is saying, and pronounces a sentence of total destruction against them. *The righteous cried aloud, and the Lord hearkened to them; he rescued them from all their tribulations. The Lord is near to the contrite of heart, and he will save the humble in spirit* (vv. 17–18). The Lord is present to the righteous, he is saying, and gladly receives their prayers, but he is especially caring for those who show restraint in their attitude, calling these *contrite of heart*. He said this also in another psalm, "A contrite and humbled heart, O God, you will not despise."[12]

(10) *Many are the tribulations of the righteous, and from them all the Lord will rescue them. The Lord protects all their bones, not one of them will be broken* (vv. 19–20). While he allows them to descend into the arena of tribulations, he comes to their assistance and renders them superior to the calamities besetting them, confirming their resolve and making it strong. He called their resolve *bones*, note: just as the rest of the body is carried by the bones as its support, so the soul reaps the fruit of salvation through its resolve. *Wickedness means death for sinners, and those who hate the righteous will come to grief. The Lord will redeem the souls of his servants, and all who hope in him will not come to grief* (vv. 21–22). So whereas the lovers of virtue will enjoy such wonderful goods, those addicted to wickedness will meet a fitting end to their life; a wicked life will have a wicked end. Those choosing the service of God, on the contrary, and resting on hope in him will attain salvation from him, as becomes those refraining altogether from breaching the laws set down by him.[13]

12. Ps 51.17.
13. There has been no sense in the commentary that Theodoret has felt, or even adverted to, the formal limitations of the acrostic form of this psalm; he has not felt bound to respond to the implication, voiced by Dahood, that "the reader and the exegete must accordingly take into account the formal element and its logical consequences." Further, since David—not to mention Ahimelech—soon dropped from sight, Theodoret has hardly lived up to his promise of justifying the historical reference he supported against the (more likely) option.

COMMENTARY ON PSALM 35

A psalm of David. [1109]

LESSED DAVID UTTERED this psalm likewise when pursued by Saul. He mentions also Doeg's wickedness, who personally reported to Saul what happened with Ahimelech the priest, and was responsible for that awfully great slaughter.[1] He mentions also the Ziphites and the others who betrayed David to Saul,[2] as the verses themselves will teach.

(2) *Judge, O Lord, those who wrong me, war against those who war against me* (v. 1). The order of the words is impressive, befitting the righteous man's prayer: he first asked the God of all to judge, then to impose the sentence of punishment. *Take up weapon and shield, and arise to help me. Brandish a sword, and engage those pursuing me* (vv. 2–3). After mentioning war, of necessity he detailed as well the types of weapons, frightening those addicted to wickedness by the outline of weaponry: God did not use such weapons in punishing the wrongdoers; instead, he needed but a word for extreme punishment. *Say to my soul, I am your salvation:* your word is sufficient to me for salvation. Since the inspired author had mentioned weapons, you see, it was right for him to teach that God does not need such instruments: by word alone he punishes the one and benefits the other.

(3) *Let those who seek my life be ashamed and fearful, let them be turned backwards, and let those who devise evil for me be confounded* (v. 4). Let them fail in their blood-curdling plots, he is saying, and let shame be the fruit of wickedness for them. *Let them be like*

---

1. Cf. 1 Sam 22.9–10, 18–19.
2. Cf. 1 Sam 26.1. Again there is the opening relation of the psalm to historical events, the promise that the verses will bear this out, and the subsequent failure to redeem the promise in the main. This insistence on staying with a historical base sits strangely with a commentator who lamented it in others in his preface.

foam before the wind, with an angel of the Lord distressing them (v. 5). He had this also in the first psalm, "Not so are the godless, not so; instead, they are like foam, which the wind sweeps from the face of the earth."[3] *Let their way be darkness and sliding, with an angel of the Lord pursuing them* (v. 6): put them to flight, entrusting the pursuit to the unseen angels. This is the way we also find the Assyrians exterminated by an angel,[4] and the way the exterminator destroyed the firstborn of the Egyptians.[5] Now, he calls stumbling *darkness and sliding:* both those who limp and those who suffer sliding stumble.

(4) To show the righteousness of the prayer, he added, [1112] *Because they hid their destructive snare for me without cause, rashly they reproached my soul* (v. 7). They employ unjust schemes against me, he is saying. Now, for *reproached* Symmachus said "undermined," hinting at the ruin prepared secretly. *Let a trap fall on him of which he is ignorant, and let the prey he hid take him; in that trap he will fall* (v. 8). May they fall foul of their own planning, he is saying, and trip their own nets; may they be the victim of unforeseen hunting, which is what is meant by *a trap of which he is ignorant.*

(5) *My soul will rejoice in the Lord, it will delight in his salvation. All my bones will say, Lord, Lord, who is like you?* (vv. 9–10): I shall gain satisfaction and joy in your good things, Lord, and through all my limbs I shall cry out that you alone are God. The phrase *who is like you?* has the sense, You alone are God, having power over all. *Rescuing the poor from the hand of those stronger than he, and the poor and needy from those despoiling him:* you do not allow the needy to be hemmed in by the more powerful; instead, the latter you suppress and come to the aid of the former.

(6) *Unjust witnesses rose up against me, questioning me on matters I had no knowledge of* (v. 11). I was subjected to calumny, he is saying, accused of crimes I had not planned. When Saul under the

---

3. Ps 1.5. In both places Theodoret's text seems to read "foam," χνοῦς, not "dust," χοῦς.
4. Cf. 2 Kings 19.35.
5. Cf. Exod 12.23, 29. In thus envisioning a bloody end for the psalmist's adversaries, Theodoret has none of the misgivings he later voices about the curse in v. 26.

influence of envy, remember, suspected him of plotting a coup and for that reason maintained a state of war, the slanderers (whom he calls false *witnesses*) took occasion not to desist from spreading calumny against him. Some of these were Doeg, the Ziphites, and many others in addition to them. *They repaid me evil for good, and sterility for my soul* (v. 12): I disposed of Goliath when he was boasting and vaunting himself against the whole people, I often took up arms against foreigners, and with my inspired playing I rid him of demonic frenzy, yet he does not cease from warring against me, aiming to consign me to death and oblivion (calling oblivion *sterility* for the reason that remembrance is kept by the children). Hence the God of all [1113] says through the prophet Isaiah, "Do not let the eunuch say, I am dry wood, because the Lord says this to his chosen eunuchs, In my house I shall give them what I please, a remarkable place within my walls, a good name, better than sons and daughters."[6]

(7) *On my part, by contrast, I wore sackcloth when they were in trouble, and I humbled my soul with fasting, my prayer will be directed to my lap* (v. 13). From this we learn how troubles are to be dealt with:[7] wrapping myself in sackcloth, he is saying, and wasting with my fast, I offered supplication to God, and I received the fruits of petition. The phrase, *my prayer will be directed to my lap*, means, In prayer I received what I requested from God, and I filled my lap. *I was pleased as though for a neighbor, for our brother; I was humbled as though sorrowful and downcast* (v. 14). I performed the complete ritual, he is saying, as though for a real brother, and displayed the same humility as someone grieving and lamenting, not bringing myself to take pride in my virtuous acts. History teaches us this, too: when Saul said in that place, "Is that you, my son David?" he replied, "I am your servant, my lord king"; and again, "Why does my lord the king chase after me like a dead dog or a single flea?"[8]

---

6. Cf. Isa 56.3–5.
7. Theodoret can sense that this psalm, which deals with the plight of the righteous sufferer in general, has potential for pastoral care; but he keeps resisting the temptation to follow that line out of respect for the historical situation he finds below the surface.
8. Cf. 1 Sam 26.17–18 and 24.14 collated.

(8) *They gloated over me and gathered together; scourges were piled on me, and I did not understand* (v. 15): they attacked me in force, expecting to destroy me, and beset me of a sudden, trying to take me unawares. The phrase, *scourges were piled on me, and I did not understand*, Symmachus rendered thus: "Strikers gathered against me, and I was unaware." *They were rent asunder, and had no regrets.* Disappointed in their hopes and thwarted, he is saying, they did not repent of the evil schemes they formed, but set about the same things again. *They made attempts on me, they sneered at me with sneers, they gnashed their teeth at me* (v. 16). [1116] They followed every avenue in their wish to vent their spleen, he is saying: sometimes they tried to hunt me down by the use of deceitful words, at other times they chewed noisily like a lion and roared.

(9) *Lord, when will you take note?* (v. 17). Now, he says this not by way of accusation but out of a longing for help. When will you appear, he is saying, and assist the wronged? *Restore my soul from their evildoing*: render my soul proof against their machinations. *Rescue my solitary life from the lions.* After saying above, *they gnashed their teeth at me*, gnashing being typical of lions, it was right for him also to call them *lions*, accusing them of savagery and ferocity of attitude. For *my solitary life* Symmachus said "my solitude," that is, deprivation of all human help. *I shall confess to you, O Lord, in the great assembly, I shall praise you in a mighty people* (v. 18). For *in a mighty people*, on the other hand, Symmachus said "in a multitudinous people." Now, this was prophecy, and prophecy that had a fulfillment: on all land and sea the divine David sings to God also through the believers, the churches throughout the world being called *great assembly* and *multitudinous people*.[9]

(10) *Let those who hate me unjustly not rejoice over me, those hating me without cause and winking their eyes* (v. 19). Here once more he mentions those egging Saul on, pretending friendship but acting the part of enemies. He said it even more clearly in what follows: *Because they spoke words of peace to me, but devised deceit in anger* (v. 20): by employing friendly words, they endeavored to conceal their anger as though in some land, their mind full of

---

9. Again Theodoret finds the version of Symmachus preferable for commentary to his LXX text.

deceit.[10] *They opened wide their mouths towards me, saying, Aha, Aha, our eyes saw it* (v. 21): when they perceived that I detected their scheming, they then unmasked their hidden hostility, loudly gloating over my calamities.

(11) *You have seen, O Lord; do not be silent, O Lord, do not keep your distance from me. Awake, O Lord, attend to my judgment, O my God and my Lord, for the sake of my just cause* (vv. 22–23): you are judge, O Lord, [1117] you have an eye for everything, and nothing escapes your inspection; do not pass over what has been done, nor leave me bereft of your providence, but make your judgment and give your verdict quickly. This is also what the following words indicate: *Judge me, O Lord, according to your righteousness, O Lord my God, and let my foes not gloat over me. Let them not say in their hearts, Aha, Aha, in our soul, nor say, We swallowed him* (vv. 24–25): if you delay your judgment, O Lord, they will once more jeer, and will make my pangs an occasion of good cheer and consider my bad luck their success.

(12) *Let those who rejoice in my troubles be ashamed and afraid at the same time; let those who exalt themselves over me wear shame and reproach* (v. 26). Shame is fitting for those who mock their neighbor; hence the inspired author calls it down on their arrogance and boasting. *Let those who wish justice for me rejoice and be glad, and those who wish his servant's peace say always, May the Lord be magnified* (v. 27): may those who wish good things for me and long for my peace continually rejoice and be glad, and on seeing me attain this may they sing your praises as the Lord. *My tongue will ponder your righteousness, your praise all day long* (v. 28): enjoying your providence, I shall meditate on your commandments night and day, shall constantly sing of your favors. For *all day long* in fact Symmachus said *every day,* this way suggesting the constancy.

(13) While the psalm had this ending, therefore, I beseech those reading it not to incur even the slightest harm from the prayer of the righteous man nor make it the occasion for curses

---

10. The obscure v. 20b contains a *hapax legomenon,* which Dahood renders "the oppressed in the land," reflected also in the version of Symmachus but not in the LXX. Theodoret cites the text of the LXX, but his commentary bears marks of the difficult original, probably through reference to Symmachus.

against one's enemies, but realize that the inspired author was adopting the way of life sanctioned by the Law, not by the Gospels. Now, the Law speaks plainly of loving the neighbor and hating the enemy. By contrast Christ the Lord, to show virtue in its perfection, said, "It was said to those of old, You shall love your neighbor and hate your enemy, but I say to you, Love your enemies and bless those who persecute you."[11] [1120] The divine Apostle also said something in harmony with this, "Bless and do not curse."[12] Looking at this difference, therefore, realize what is in keeping with the Law, and what with grace. In particular, it was not to deliver a curse that David said this; rather, in inspired fashion he foretold what would clearly come to be.[13] Now, for proof that in keeping with the Gospel requirements even he did not take vengeance on those who wronged him, listen to him saying, "If I repaid in like fashion those rendering me evil, let me then end up empty-handed before my foes. Let my foe then hunt my soul down, apprehend it, trample my life in the ground, and bury my glory in the dust."[14] And he did not say this without doing it: he put his words into practice, and the actions are clearer than the words. Twice when he had his enemy in his hands, remember, he not only did not do away with him but even forbade those anxious to do away with him; when he fell in battle, he wept bitterly over him, and the one who brought word of his death he dispatched for exulting and boasting of the execution. Now, I was obliged to recount these events because of those who boast and quote the case of the divine David so that they may have the best values of David as a beneficial model.

11. Matt 5.43–44, loosely recalled.
12. Rom 12.14.
13. This codicil about cursing has some puzzling features. The imprecation in v. 26 is quite mild; more extreme examples earlier in the *Commentary* (e.g., Ps 21.9–12, Ps 31.17) passed without comment. Further, the reasoning is inconsistent: David's curse is first admitted, and blamed on life under the Law as opposed to the Gospel, and then denied and reinterpreted as mere prophecy, and his conduct towards Saul cited in defense. We shall see Theodoret later coping with a real cursing psalm, with which through his inability to recognize a range of genres in the Psalter he will have greater difficulty, as did Chrysostom.
14. Ps 7.4–5.

COMMENTARY ON PSALM 36

To the end. Of David, the servant of the Lord.

HEN THE DIVINE DAVID had Saul in his power, he not only did not do away with him but even prevented those attempting to do away with him. At daybreak on a mountain ridge he made his complaint to Saul, accusing him of the injustice of hostility, letting him know that though he found him asleep at night, he did not do away with him as an enemy but saved his life as a benefactor. He showed him the corner of his cloak, the water jar, and the spear, which he had taken, as proof of the truth of his words. To this Saul replied in words tinged with benevolence, adopting the guise of friendship; to his words he also added oaths, feigning repentance. That was the time, therefore, that blessed David spoke this psalm,[1] directing an accusation against those addicted to evil, and proclaiming the providence of God extending through all situations. In his words he mingled theology and prophecy; for this reason the title "To the end" directs the reader further.[2]

(2) *The lawbreaker speaks within himself with a view to sinning* (v. 1). The one nurtured on evil, he is saying, thinks no one per-

---

1. In fact, Theodoret is conflating two separate occasions, narrated in 1 Sam 24 (of the piece of cloak taken in the cave in the wilderness of En Gedi) and 1 Sam 26 (of the spear and water jar taken on the hill of Hachilah, which were shown to Abner, not Saul)—neither at daybreak. If the reader was not expected to check the text for accuracy, we wonder if Theodoret was aware of the discrepancies.

2. This time Theodoret allows the psalm a more general application, which he styles *theologia* (a term he used in connection with the apostles James and John "on account of their extraordinary divine theology" in commentary on Ps 29.3), whereas the psalm's New Testament reference justifies its being styled "prophecy" and explains (in his view) that part of the psalm title. Modern commentators, on the other hand, see it as a miscellany of different elements—Wisdom, hymn, and lament.

ceives his soul's hidden plans: he put *speak* to mean "consider" or "suspect." *There is no fear of God* [1121] *before his eyes.* Now, this is responsible for such insensibility: not dreading the Lord who sees everything. *He was not honest with himself about the discovery and hatred of his lawlessness* (v. 2). He so distracts himself, he is saying, and banishes the fear of God from his own sight that his lawlessness, which in fact is obvious, is seen and discovered by everyone, and hence attracts loathing. He has given himself unswervingly to lawlessness. Now, he adopts this ignorance so willingly that he is not prepared to assess what he has done or loathe his evil exploits.

(3) *The words of his mouth were lawlessness and deceit; he had no wish to understand and do good. In bed he plotted lawlessness, he took every path that is not good, he did not abhor evil* (vv. 3–4): he uses words devoid of truth and composed of deceit; instead of wanting to come to an understanding of what is decent, by night he hatches wicked schemes against his neighbor, and by day he puts his plans into effect. Now, the cause of this is that he does not loathe and turn away utterly from the forms of vice. He put *they did not abhor evil* for "did not loathe": the divine Scripture sometimes calls the idols loathsome, sometimes abhorrent. Aquila, on the other hand, rendered it "they did not repudiate," Symmachus, "they did not reject," and Theodotion, "they did not drive out."

(4) *Lord, your mercy is in heaven, your truth extends as far as the clouds, your righteousness like God's mountains* (vv. 5–6): so while those people turn their hand to such things as though no one were watching, you, Lord, possess immeasurable mercy, incalculable truth, and righteousness comparable to the highest mountains. Now, your truth comes to human beings through the inspired authors as though through some clouds, regaling them with saving rain. *Your judgments are like the great deep:* possessing such wonderful truth and righteousness, why you show longsuffering I do not know; your judgments resemble the impenetrable depths. That is to say, just as the bottom of the sea is beyond human vision, so an understanding of your judgments is beyond our grasp.

(5) [1124] *You will save human beings and cattle, Lord.* And the

reason for this? *How you extended your mercy, O God!* (v. 7): your loving-kindness reaches even to the cattle, and you nourish not only human beings but also what was made with the human being in mind, doing favors for human beings through them. *The sons of men will hope in the shelter of your wings.* The content takes on a prophetic character with the change that takes place after the Incarnation of our Savior: he did not say "hoped" but *will hope*.³ *They will be intoxicated with the rich fare of your house, and you will give them to drink of the flood of your delicacies* (v. 8): human nature will take refuge in you, perceiving the wealth of good things springing up in your house. Now, in this he is suggesting not only the streams of divine teaching but also enjoyment of sacramental nourishment,⁴ likening the supply of such wonderful goods to a flood—firstly, the fact that it was not given to human beings from the beginning, and then his exhorting all human beings to come forward and drink, not from an everflowing river but from a flood, and one that flows at a particular time. I mean, those who do not come forward in the present time will not enjoy the sacred streams after the exile here.

(6) After showing that the wealth of good things is naturally everflowing but becomes a flood for the divine dispensations, he added opportunely, *Because with you is a fountain of life* (v. 9). Now, here he clearly reveals to us the mystery of the holy Trinity: he called the Only-begotten Word of God a *fountain of life*. This is the name, too, remember, God personally gave himself through the prophet Jeremiah: "They have forsaken me, a fountain of living water, taken their leave and dug for themselves

---

3. Though we have noted before that the Greek translators had difficulty with the force of tenses in the Hebrew, and it is therefore inadvisable for Theodoret to build his argument on morphology, he is suggesting here that the psalm has a fuller sense when read in the light of the Incarnation, which transforms previous events and texts. This, we have suggested, is the understanding that leads Fathers like Chrysostom and Theodoret (and the creeds) to style Old Testament authors alone *prophetai;* the New Testament authors are composing from a different standpoint.

4. Again Theodoret shows that his spirituality is sacramental as well as Scriptural (though admittedly this is a false antithesis, justified only perhaps by a *Commentary* like Chrysostom's that is silent on the latter, verbose on the former). The New Testament enjoys an advantage in this regard, he says, the flood occurring only then.

cracked cisterns incapable of holding water."[5] So he says this fountain is in the presence of the Father, according to the following Gospel teaching: "I in the Father and the Father in me."[6] *In your light we shall see light:* illumined by the all-holy Spirit we shall perceive the rays of your Only-begotten; Scripture says, "No one can say Jesus is Lord except by the Holy Spirit,"[7] and "God revealed to us through his Spirit." We have consequently come to a precise knowledge of the three persons in the one divinity through the inspired words.[8]

(7) [1125] *Extend your mercy to those who know you, and your righteousness to the upright of heart* (v. 10): so give an unfailing share of your gentle and righteous care to those thought worthy of the knowledge of God and choosing to put good into practice. He said both things about the same people, you see, making a distinction on the basis of individual characteristics: he does not say some know him while others are upright of heart, nor that he requires mercy for some and righteousness for others; rather, he defined mature virtue in terms of true teachings and good actions, and promised those practicing it mercy and righteousness.

(8) *May the foot of arrogance not come my way, and a sinner's hand not move me. All evildoers fell there; they were thrust out, may they never stand* (vv. 11–12). The phrase, *All evildoers fell there,* Symmachus rendered thus: "Where evildoers fall, they are thrust out and will be unable to stand." Now, the prayer of the inspired author is to respect the bounds of nature, and not be diverted from the straight and narrow by the schemes of lawbreakers, knowing as he did where the opposite way leads: those who fall into that extreme, he is saying, will then never succeed in rising up and running in the other direction. The words in the sixth psalm bear on them: "Because in death there is no one to remember you: rather, in Hades who will confess to you?"[9]

5. Jer 2.13.
6. John 14.10.
7. 1 Cor 12.3, 2.10.
8. Theodoret is satisfied to have established that Old Testament inspired authors, the psalmist and Jeremiah, have taught about the Trinity (using *idiotes* and not *hypostasis* for a person of the Trinity).
9. Ps 6.5.

COMMENTARY ON PSALM 37

A psalm of David.

O NOT VIE WITH EVILDOERS, *nor rival those committing iniquity* (v. 1). The divine David learned from experience the vast number of goods gentleness brings,[1] and the fact that a grievous end befitting their life awaits those addicted to injustice and practiced in arrogance. This he learned from his dealings with Saul and Absalom, and with the others who perpetrated similar things to them. So he offers all people an exhortation, urging them to take in good spirit the troubles that come their way, and not to consider as blessings wicked people's prosperity and success, but rather to call them wretched. This is surely the reason he begins the psalm at the outset with the words, *Do not vie with evildoers, nor rival those committing iniquity.* Now, *Do not vie* Symmachus rendered "Do not contend," and Theodotion, "Do not fret," that is, Do not be goaded into imitation of those addicted to lawlessness on [1128] perceiving the happy lot fallen to them. To show the impermanence of the good fortune, he added at once, *Because they will quickly dry up like grass, and quickly fall like green foliage* (v. 2). Blessed Isaiah also said as much: "All flesh is grass, and all human glory like grass's flower. The grass withered and its flower fell, but the word of the Lord abides forever."[2]

(2) Blessed David said this, too. *Hope in the Lord, do good, and inhabit the earth, and you will be fed on its riches. Delight in the Lord, and he will grant you your heart's desire* (vv. 3–4). In everything he taught the benefit of hope in God: the person hoping in God,

---

1. This long psalm, an acrostic in the original and composed of generally proverbial statements, Theodoret is only vaguely interested in relating to David's life, highlighting instead his gentleness, a virtue Chrysostom also singled out for emphasis in his *Commentary*.
2. Cf. Isa 40.5–8.

he says, and fed by him will enjoy the goods supplied by him, while those who find delightful constant converse with him will most of all attain them. *Disclose your way to the Lord, hope in him, and he will act. He will highlight your righteousness like a light and your judgment like midday* (vv. 5–6). Offer up to God, he is saying, both yourself and your actions, and expect grace from him; for his part he will bring forth a just verdict like a judge, will extol you and make you famous to the extent of being known to everyone, like the light at midday.

(3) *Be subject to the Lord, and beseech him* (v. 7): aware of this, then, respond to God's governance and continue asking good things from him. *Do not vie with that one who prospers in his way, with the human being who commits lawlessness:* even if you see one choosing wickedness, and not deviating from his purpose but being borne downstream, do not be worried and concerned that no one is in control of the world. What follows clarifies this: *Refrain from rage and desist from anger; do not vie to the extent of doing evil. Because the evildoers will be wiped out* (vv. 8–9): instead of considering their prosperity, await their end, and you will see their ruin.[3] *Those who wait on the Lord will inherit the land. Yet a little while, and the sinner will not be around; you will look for his trace and not find it. The gentle, on the other hand, will inherit the land, and will find delight in the abundance of peace* (vv. 9–11): be well [1129] aware that those who depend on hope in God and choose the life of temperance will pass their days in tranquillity and peace, having purity of conscience as a steadfast delight. Those who trust in temporary prosperity, on the other hand, will undergo sudden change and will be consigned to perpetual oblivion.

(4) *The sinner will scrutinize the righteous one, and gnashes his teeth against him. But the Lord will mock him because he foresees that his day will come* (vv. 12–13). In all this he offers consolation to the wronged: he shows the lawless enraged and maddened by

---

3. It is going to be a long psalm, repetitive like many proverbial pieces, and Theodoret is most economical in his commentary; it hardly exceeds mere paraphrase, as he refuses to be tempted to gild the lily with a moralizing development of his own. A preacher with congregation before him could not resist the temptation; but Bishop Theodoret does not see this as his task here.

those who embrace the tranquil life, but the just Judge mocking their efforts from his viewpoint on their speedy end. *The wicked drew a sword and bent their bow to overthrow the poor and needy, to slaughter the upright of heart. Their sword will enter their own hearts, and their bows be broken* (vv. 14–15). This has the same sense as the preceding: he teaches that while the sinner employs a range of stratagems against those who have done him no wrong, he will be caught up in his own snares; he gave the name *sword* and *bow* to the various schemes. This resembles what was said in the seventh psalm, "He sank a pit and dug it out, and will fall into the hole he has made."[4]

(5) *Better a little for the righteous than much wealth for sinners* (v. 16). Sufficiency with righteousness, he is saying, is preferable to illegal wealth and unjust affluence. Then to show the fruit of each, he says, *Because sinners' arms shall be broken, but the Lord upholds the righteous* (v. 17). In figurative fashion he called power *arms*, because people naturally work with them. Now, it was very appropriate for him to put *upholds the righteous:* oppressed by demons and human beings but resting on divine grace, they take their stand and prevail over the difficulties besetting them.

(6) *The Lord knows the ways of the blameless, and their inheritance will last forever. They will not be put to shame in bad times, and will have their fill in times of famine* (vv. 18–19): those choosing a blameless life enjoy providence completely; even if they encounter disasters, they will emerge superior to them, and when need becomes endemic, they will receive sufficiency from God, [1132] and in addition will enjoy everlasting goods. By *famine* here I take to be suggested that which was threatened to Jews of old: "I shall bring famine on the land, not a famine of bread or thirst for water, but a famine of hearing the word of the Lord."[5]

(7) *Because sinners will perish, but the enemies of the Lord, at the time of being glorified and exalted, will truly fail like smoke* (v. 20). The

---

4. Ps 7.15.
5. Amos 8.11. Awake to the possibility of famine being spiritual, Theodoret does not make a correlative assumption made by modern commentators that "bad days" by parallelism "almost inescapably signifies drought" (Dahood), which could then equally reasonably be taken spiritually.

change of conjunction gave the impression of a difference of persons, and suggests our taking some as sinners and some as enemies of the Lord. Aquila and Symmachus, on the other hand, put "and" in place of *but*, and thus showed the same people to be both sinners and enemies of the Lord. Now, his meaning is that the people who were the object of God's hatred on account of their own lawlessness, even though for a short time flourishing and appearing to be illustrious and popular, disappeared like smoke.[6] *The sinner will borrow and not pay back, whereas the righteous has pity and gives* (v. 21). Saul was like that, ever the object of kindness at the hands of the divine David, but reluctant to repay kindness with kindness; blessed David, on the other hand, in imitation of his Lord, who makes his sun rise on wicked and good,[7] continued showing kindness. The Jews were like that, in receipt of attention of all kinds from the sacred apostles, and betraying a murderous intent, yet despite that the divine apostles kept distributing divine gifts to them with generosity.

(8) *Because those who bless him will inherit the land, whereas those who curse him will be wiped out* (v. 22). The God of all made this promise to the patriarch Abraham: "I shall bless those who bless you, and those who curse you I shall curse."[8] *A person's steps are guided by the Lord, and he will take great delight in his way. Whenever he falls, he will not be broken in pieces, because the Lord strengthens his hand* (vv. 23–24). This is surely the reason that he blesses the righteous one who blesses him while giving due recompense to that one who curses, that he guides the ways of the righteous: it is impossible for anyone to travel blamelessly the way of virtue without his grace. He works in association with those who have this intent: for the acquisition of virtue there is need of human zeal and divine assistance at one and the same time.[9] Thus, you

---

6. Theodoret establishes his Antiochene credentials here in noting the ambiguity of the conjunction δέ, which can be either adversative or simply copulative; Aquila and Symmachus cut the Gordian knot by reading καί instead. He feels confident enough to give his own ruling without having to desert the LXX.
7. Matt 5.45.
8. Cf. Gen 12.3.
9. This measured statement of the role in salvation of both divine grace and human effort, and the priority of the former, is not unprovoked. Verse

see, even if the one traveling this path should slip, he will gain divine support. Likewise, when blessed David stumbled and ran the risk of coming to grief, he was borne up by divine grace.

(9) [1133] *I have been younger and am now grown up, and have not seen a righteous one abandoned nor his offspring looking for bread. All day long the righteous one shows mercy and lends money, and his offspring will bring a blessing* (vv. 25–26): whether young or now old, it has not come to my attention that a righteous person was bereft of divine providence; the righteous Judge, to be sure, takes all care not only of them but also of their offspring. Thus despite Israel's lawlessness in this regard, he bestowed his providence on account of their forebears' virtue. Likewise, despite Solomon's impiety, he showed restraint on account of his father's piety. Now, the phrase, *All day long the righteous one shows mercy and lends money,* indicates the manifold kindnesses of the righteous, some in money, some in action, some in word and advice. By doing so, while they have mercy on the recipients, it is to their God they lend: "Whoever has mercy on the poor lends to the Lord,"[10] Scripture says, meaning that mercy and lending are the same thing.

(10) *Turn away from evil and do good, and dwell forever* (v. 27): Be aware of this, then, everyone, and learning the fruits of virtue and vice, shun the forms of vice and take the opposite path so as to enjoy the everlasting goods. *Because the Lord loves judgment, and does not abandon his holy ones, because they will be protected forever, whereas lawless people will be banished and offspring of ungodly people will be destroyed. Righteous people, on the other hand, will inherit the earth and dwell in it forever* (vv. 27–29): applying a right and just judgment, the Lord of all will make recompense befitting people's exploits, according the lovers of righteousness complete care, but rooting up those who choose the opposite.

---

22 could have given the impression that virtue prompted divine action, the commentator feels, but the following verses supplied the necessary correction—that divine blessing precedes as well as follows human initiative, both being necessary. Theodoret is here much more concerned for doctrinal accuracy than Chrysostom (as a desk theologian might be than a preacher), and therefore much less likely to lend comfort to Pelagian thinkers.

10. Prov 19.17. Theodoret's documentation of his commentary from other parts of Scripture can be thin, as in commenting on this psalm.

(11) Having shown the fruits of each in this way, he then teaches how it is possible to practice the righteousness acceptable to God. *The mouth of the righteous one utters wisdom, and his tongue will give judgment. The law of God is in his heart, and his steps will not be upset* (vv. 30–31). It is fitting, he says, to carry around the divine sayings both on one's tongue and in one's mind, and constantly give attention to them; learning in this way how to behave, the lover of virtue remains intrepid and unmoved, proof against efforts at overthrow. He said this in the first psalm as well: "But his preference is for the law of the Lord, and he will meditate on his law day and night,"[11] and so on.

(12) [1136] *The sinner scrutinizes the righteous one, and seeks to kill him. But the Lord will not abandon him into his hands, nor condemn him when he is brought to judgment* (vv. 32–33). He says the same thing in different ways, fixing it more firmly in our memory through deeper meditation. He says the Lord will not overlook the righteous when made the object of scheming by the wicked, nor join forces with those making such attempts, but will cause them to slip their nets. Abraham enjoyed this providence when on two occasions his wife was taken off;[12] Isaac had the same experience, as did Jacob when the object of ill will of brother and father-in-law, and Joseph when under attack from envy and calumny. What need is there to list every example? It is easier for the scholars, after all, both to assemble those from the past and to study the recent ones.[13] *Wait upon the Lord, and keep his way, and he will exalt you to inherit the land; you will see his destruction of sinners* (v. 34): having learned this, therefore, await

---

11. Ps 1.2.

12. Though making an initial and solitary (if ambiguous) effort to recognize an inclusive perspective in the Psalms in commenting on the first Psalm (see note 10 there), Theodoret here reproduces the sexist interpretation of Abraham's behavior and Sarah's plight in Gen 12 and 20 that Chrysostom also adopts in commenting on that book, concerned more for the patriarch than for the wife he surrendered to pharaoh and king respectively. His sympathies are likewise awry in referring to Isaac's similar treatment of Rebekah in Gen 26.

13. Theodoret is clearly not writing for a specialist readership, and out of choice or a sense of his own (real) limitations he prefers not to be exhaustive, leaving that to more studious readers of the text, the *philomatheis* of whom Chrysostom was also somewhat dismissive.

the divine verdict, and keep the laws laid down. This is the way, in fact, that you will both become the cynosure of all eyes in the present life and in the life to come will enjoy the lasting goods and see the utterly miserable end of sinners.

(13) Then, since it distresses many people not to see here and now the punishment of the unjust but their long continuance, he rightly guarantees the future on the basis of past actions. *I have seen the godless exalted and lifted up like the cedars of Lebanon. I passed by and, lo, he was no more; I searched for him, and no trace of him could be found* (vv. 35–36). The mighty David saw the end of the reign of Saul, the overthrow of Absalom's coup, the arrogance and ruin of Nahash the Ammonite, the death of the foreigner Goliath in his conceit, and in addition to these the pride and arrogance of not a few others in turn, and their overthrow. So it was right for him to liken their prosperity to the fruitless trees. Now, he said not only they but even trace of them had vanished, by this signifying the memory of them. Then in turn he introduces recommendation and advice: *Preserve innocence and take note of uprightness, because there is posterity for a peaceable person* (v. 37). Symmachus, on the other hand, put it this way, "Preserve simplicity and take note of the upright, because there is a future for a peaceable person": do not regard present vexations, he is saying, but look to the future; it is a time in which the due reward will be granted to those who employ simplicity and uprightness.

(14) [1137] *Transgressors, on the other hand, will be destroyed together; the posterity of the godless will be destroyed* (v. 38). Symmachus for his part put it this way, "But the lawless will be wiped out together, the desperate state of the lawbreakers terminated": at that time, he is saying, they too will get their just deserts and experience a common destruction. *Salvation of the righteous, by contrast, is with the Lord, and he is their protection in time of tribulation. The Lord will help them, rescue them, pluck them from sinners' clutches and save them, because they hoped in him* (vv. 39–40): those who practice righteousness, on the other hand, will enjoy divine aid and attain salvation, and by reason of placing complete hope in him will prevail over those endeavoring to wrong them.

COMMENTARY ON PSALM 38

A psalm of David, in commemoration of the Sabbath.

THE VARIETY IN CONFESSION proclaims the earnest repentance of the most divine David:[1] in many psalms he recalls the sin, unable to put up with the wound but focusing on the ailment and its cure, and thus proposing it to people as a basis for instruction. In this psalm, too, therefore, he recalls the sin and the discipline imposed with a view to curing the sin. Now, many and varied troubles were imposed on him: the killing of Amnon, Absalom's coup, the adviser Ahithophel plotting against him, the abuse from Shimei, and all the others taught by history.[2]

(2) *O Lord, do not accuse me in your anger, nor chastise me in your wrath* (v. 1). He made this beginning to the sixth psalm as well, asking to be disciplined in the manner of a surgeon, not a judge, and to be treated not with harsh remedies but with mild ones. *Because your arrows have sunk into me, and you have fastened your hand upon me* (v. 2). It is not without purpose that I make this supplication, he is saying; rather, it is because I see clouds of arrows directed at me, and your hand sorely threatening me and severely chastising me. The phrase, *you have fastened your hand upon me,* he used by analogy with those tormenting and inflicting many blows. *There is no healing in my flesh in the face of your wrath; there is no peace in* [1140] *my bones in the face of my sins* (v. 3). Pricked by punishment, he is saying, I remember the sin, and memory of it arouses in me wailing and weeping; from these things ill treatment and misery come upon me.

---

1. This is the third of the Penitential Psalms of the early Church; so Theodoret has in mind here the two others (6 and 32) his readers have already met. (He makes no comment on the reference in the title in the LXX to the Sabbath, as if to admit there is no accounting for it.)

2. Again Theodoret is rooting the psalm back (very loosely) to the stories of David's reign found in 2 Samuel.

(3) *Because my iniquities reached beyond my head, they weighed me down like a weighty burden. My scars became putrid and rotten from my stupidity. I became miserable and downcast forever, I went about with sad countenance all day long* (vv. 4–6). The weighty burden of my sin cast me down, he is saying, the stench of my putrid wounds, which I sustained when I rejected good sense and became a slave to folly, also distressed me. This is the reason that I am bereft of all satisfaction, I grieve and am constantly sorrowful, and find no change in my distress. *Because my entrails are filled with mockery, and there is no healing in my flesh* (v. 7). By reference to *entrails* he implies lust: located in them are the kidneys, through which the appetites usually are stimulated. So he means, My handling of desire not fittingly but wastefully proved the cause of these troubles. *I was afflicted and humbled to breaking point; I howled from the sighing of my heart* (v. 8). From that desire I garnered the fruit, which was my stooping to earth, he is saying, and constant bewailing on account of my heart's bitter pangs.

(4) For this reason I changed the force of desire and made it minister to the divine will. He added this, in fact, *Lord, all my desire was before you* (v. 9): since once I used it wrongly, I shall always apply it to the benefit of your commands. *And my sighing was not hidden from you. My heart was disturbed; my strength left me and the light of my eyes, and it was not with me* (vv. 9–10). Do you see my wailing and weeping, Lord, do you see me confused, deprived of strength, and bereft of accustomed light, living as though in darkness at midday? Now, by these statements he implies two things, both the extraordinary degree of depression, [1141] by which the light does not even seem to be light, and the deprivation of divine care, which he rightly called *light of my eyes*.

(5) *My friends and my neighbors took up a position against me, and those close to me kept their distance* (v. 11). Symmachus, on the other hand, rendered it this way, "My friends and my companions opposed me in my affliction." Those of my friends who perceived my affliction, he is saying, took the actions of enemies, and stood in open opposition to me, whereas those who were fearful moved away, not assisting me with support of their own. Now, he is suggesting through the former case Ahithophel, who not only moved away but also came up with deadly schemes.

Others, as is likely, did what he did—or, rather, the majority of Israel and even the very tribe of Judah waged war on Absalom's side. Immediately after the killing of the parricide, therefore, they urged one another to anticipate the other tribes and return King David to the palace. *Those seeking my life were forced out, and those seeking my harm spoke empty words, and plotted treacherous schemes all day long* (v. 12): seeing me deprived of friends, the enemies continually hatched plots, longing for my slaughter.

(6) *For my part, however, like a deaf person I did not hear, and like a mute not opening the mouth. I became like a person who does not hear and has no accusations in his mouth* (vv. 13–14). History teaches this more clearly. Even when Absalom mounted a case against his father and drew to his side those who had lost cases in judgment, blessed David was long-suffering. When Shimei berated him with voice and hand upraised, he took the abuse in silence; and he forbade Abishai to try to exact justice against the culprit in the words, "Let him curse me because the Lord bade him curse David."[3] *Because it is in you, Lord, that I hoped; you will hearken to me, O Lord my God. Because I said, May my enemies never rejoice over me; when my foot slipped, they gloated over me* (vv. 15–16). But employing this patience, he is saying, I continued to have hope in you, to entrust judgment of me to you, and to entreat that I not become an object of rejoicing to the enemy nor my defeat prove an occasion of arrogance for them.

(7) *Because I am ready for the whips, and* [1144] *my distress is ever in your sight* (v. 17). Sin made me deserve whipping, he is saying; hence I submit myself to punishment. I long for treatment at your hands, pricked as I am by the pangs of sin. *Because I declare my lawlessness, and ponder my sin* (v. 18): now, for this reason I become my own accuser, and shall give full attention to my cure. *My foes, however, are alive, and prevail over me; those who hate me unjustly, who repay me evil for good, are multiplied* (vv. 19–20). "Against you alone have I sinned, Lord," he says, "and done evil in your sight."[4] Those who often received many favors from me, however, repay me with the opposite, and gained better health than I.

---

3. Cf. 2 Sam 16.9–11.
4. Ps 51.4, the contribution of which at this point is unclear.

They calumniated me since I followed after goodness. Once again he indicates Absalom in this, calling his unjust judgments *calumniating.* Since he was a son striving to become parricide, it was right for the psalmist to add, *Though I was beloved, they rejected me, loathed like a corpse:*[5] though he should have been loved according to the laws of nature, he was disgusted with him as though a putrid corpse. Now, this is relevant also to the ungrateful people, who though beneficiary of countless kindnesses from David, and thanks to him proven victorious oftentimes over foreigners, emerged ungrateful to their benefactor.

(8) *Do not abandon me, O Lord my God, nor keep far from me. Come to my help, O Lord of my salvation* (vv. 21–22). Washed about with so many griefs, he is saying, I beseech you, my God and Lord, not to deprive me of your customary providence, but allow me to share in your grace and grant me salvation.

---

5. Though editor Schulze declares this clause to be missing from Hebrew original and Greek version, Theodoret must have found it in his form of the LXX.

COMMENTARY ON PSALM 39

To the end, for Jeduthun. A song of David.

SOME HISTORIANS ATTRIBUTED the psalm to Jeduthun, saying he wrote it. The title teaches the opposite, however, that the psalm is David's but was given over for singing to Jeduthun, because he was entrusted with the choir of singers. And "To the end" refers us forward, since it portrays the lowliness of human nature and gives us a glimpse of its end. Now, the mighty David uttered this psalm when pursued by Absalom and berated by Shimei, and it has great similarity with the preceding one.[1]

(2) [1145] *I said, I shall guard my ways so as not to sin with my tongue. I placed a guard on my mouth when the sinner took up a position against me. I kept mute and was humiliated, I made no mention of good deeds, and my grief was renewed* (vv. 1–2). When the mighty David was in flight from the coup of his parricide son, Shimei came across him, threw clods at him, and abused him personally, calling him lawbreaker and man of blood. The divine David, on the other hand, called upon his habitually sound values and not only wreaked no vengeance on him but even forbade any of his troops to fire at him, saying, "Let him be; he curses me for a reason, that the Lord told him to abuse David. Who will say to him, Why are you doing this? Hopefully the Lord may see my lowliness, and the Lord may repay me with good for his curse this day."[2]

(3) So the verses of this psalm have a close relationship with

---

1. The title prompts Theodoret to rehearse his position on authorship and the meaning of psalm titles outlined in the preface. He prefers to stay with Davidic authorship, though aware of musicians of David's time like Jeduthun (mentioned in 1 Chron 16.41). There he also states his belief that psalms can both refer to current historical events and have a wider, prospective reference. The titles belong to the psalms from the beginning, in his view, and are not liturgical directions superimposed later.

2. Cf. 2 Sam 16.5–12.

this incident: he kept a tight control on his tongue, he is saying, realizing this member is particularly liable to fail, and constantly hedging it in with a kind of wall. This was especially the case when Shimei opposed him, though in no way wronged: he called him a sinner as though unrighteous; then it was he said, *I kept mute and was humiliated, I made no mention of good deeds.* Now, this was very much like the words spoken by him in the incident, "Let him curse me, because the Lord bade him abuse David. Hopefully the Lord may see my lowliness, and may deliver me today from the hand of my foes." He says this here, too, I am like a mute, with absolutely no one to listen to me, and I humbled myself, awaiting advantage from that. *And my grief was renewed.* Abused by that fellow, he is saying, I recalled the sin brazenly committed by me and was struck by darts from that source, considering that it was on that account that I was abused, toppled by a coup, driven from the palace, and forced to flee. This, too, bears a close relationship with the incident: the phrase, "The Lord bade him abuse David," recalls the sin, since the chastisement happens on that account.

(4) *My heart became hot within me, and in my meditation fire burned* (v. 3). [1148] Symmachus rendered it this way, "My heart became hot within me, in my reflection I was burnt up with fire." Remembering my sin, he is saying, I was burning with the fire of discouragement. *I spoke with my tongue, Make known my end to me, Lord, and what is the number of my days so that I may know what is left to me* (vv. 3–4). In other words, while I made no reply to the one abusing me, I begged the Lord of all to make clear to me the end of my life, longing earnestly for death. *Lo, you made my days handbreadths, and my being is as nothing before you* (v. 5). This in turn Symmachus rendered thus, "Lo, you have given my days like a fingers' span, and my living is as nothing before you." I long for death, knowing human nature has no length of life: in comparison with your life our living seems not even to exist. You, after all, have no beginning or end, whereas our life is measured in fingers' spans and handbreadths. Now, by this means he demonstrated the brevity of human life. He says this elsewhere, too: "Because a thousand years in your eyes, Lord, are like yesterday when it is past, or a watch in the night";[3] and elsewhere in

---

3. Ps 90.4.

mentioning the heavens and the earth he said, "They will perish, but you endure; they will all wear out like a garment; you will change them like a covering, and they will be altered, whereas you remain as you are, and your years will not fail."[4]

(5) *Yet everything is futility, every living person.* And so all humankind, he is saying—the rich and the needy—are like vapor dissolving: idly and to no purpose they build, plant, amass wealth and possessions. *At any rate, man goes about like an image, worried about a nothing. He stores up treasures, and does not know for whom he is collecting them* (v. 6). Human beings in their lifetime, he is saying, are no different from paintings: both alike are naturally affected by time and fade. Despite this, they work themselves into a state by squabbling, fighting, warring, trading; all their life is full of storms, with death as their end; they amass wealth with sweat and tears, ignorant of the likely heir. Now, blessed David also wrote of this, moved about it in his own case: with the spoils of war and the tribute paid by foreigners [1149] he made the kingdom mighty and illustrious, but had no idea of his son's disloyal and lawless attitude. Then, when he saw he was in possession of the palace and was claiming for himself the riches stored there, he uttered this remarkable statement, *Worried about a nothing, he stores up treasures, and does not know for whom he is collecting them.*[5]

(6) *And now what is my expectation? Is it not the Lord? My being is from you* (v. 7): having bid farewell to all those things, I look forward to help from the Lord. Aquila, on the other hand, for *being* said "expectation," that is, I look about in expectation, awaiting your favor. Then he gives a glimpse of the cause of the sorrows: *From all my iniquities rescue me* (v. 8). Shimei likewise brings this to mind. *You gave me as an object of scorn to the fool.* This too relates closely to the words in the story, "The Lord told him to abuse David." What follows is likewise in agreement with the words. *I kept mute, I did not open my mouth, because you did it* (v. 9). It was with your concurrence, he is saying, that he got drunk: while he was like a scourge, you used it to impose chastisement. That was

4. Ps 102.26–27.
5. To an unusual degree Theodoret is warming to his theme of the brevity of human life and the transience of possessions, whether out of conviction or from the greater certainty that this is Davidic reflection on an identifiable historical incident—though he might have admitted (had it struck him) its similar occurrence in a composer like Qoheleth.

really the reason that I accepted the scourging in silence, looking beyond him to see you chastising me.

(7) Now, it was very appropriately that he added also the following: *Remove the scourge from me: I have fainted with the strength of your hand* (v. 10): so I beg and beseech you, Lord, now cease your chastisement; I am wasted with the number of the strokes. *You chastised the human being with accusations of transgression, and wasted his soul like a spider's web* (v. 11). It was not idly and to no purpose that you applied your chastisements, but to charge us with our faults, to cut us like a surgeon and draw out the hidden juices; though you waste us with the pangs from the treatment, your concern is the healing of those cut. *Every human being is worried about a nothing:* considering this within me, then, I see that human beings ought be in no way worried about passing matters.

(8) *Hearken to my prayer, O Lord, and to my request; give your ear to my weeping. Do not keep silent, because I am a stranger and* [1152] *a pilgrim like all my ancestors. Give me relief so that I may catch my breath before departing and be no more* (vv. 12–13). I beseech you, Lord, hearken to my lament and tearful supplication: I do not dwell in the land but am a stranger, and like my forebears I shall accept death after living here a short time. So grant me a brief respite so that I may live at least a few days without pain before departing this life. Once I go I shall not return: this he said, *and be no more,* that is, I shall not return to this corrupt life. Now, it is remarkable that David in his kingship, wealth, and influence called himself a *stranger* and *a pilgrim,* and was reluctant to boast of his fortunate lot. The verses, in fact, are really full of a wisdom that both understands the nature of things and for that reason despises present prosperity.[6]

6. These final verses, again about the transience of life and our pilgrim condition, make a distinct impact on Theodoret. Susceptible though the theme is of homiletic development, as biblical and ecclesiastical history confirms, our commentator refrains from applying the verses to the reader's life beyond the point of recognizing their application to David's. One feels he is suppressing a natural tendency in a pastor to expatiate on them for reason of his commitment to brevity as expressed in his preface.

COMMENTARY ON PSALM 40

To the end. A psalm of David.

OME PEOPLE APPLIED this psalm to blessed Jeremiah, others to the remarkable Daniel, since the one and the other were thrown into a pit[1] and the psalm's opening mentions a pit; they were led to that interpretation by attending to the one verse. Some, on the other hand, claimed the psalm fits the situation of the captives dwelling in Babylon. For my part, however, I believe it was written to address the events affecting David as a type, and refers to the whole human race, who receive the hope of resurrection from our God and Savior. Now, it is the divinely inspired Paul who guides us to this understanding, quoting individual verses in the Epistle to the Hebrews.[2]

(2) *I waited and waited on the Lord, and he attended to me. He hearkened to my prayer, and drew me out of a pit of wretchedness and from a miry bog* (vv. 1–2). Now, the verses bear on blessed David: they are in keeping with the previous psalm, where he said, "Hearken to my prayer, O Lord, and to my request; give your ear to my weeping. Do not keep silent; give me relief so that I may catch my breath before departing and be no more." And before that he had said, "And now what is my expectation? Is it not the Lord? My being is from you."[3] Here, on the other hand, as

---

1. Cf. Jer 38.6; Dan 6.16.
2. Theodoret has a range of commentators from both Antioch and Alexandria in mind here. Antiochene commentators, with their commitment to the literal sense of the text (arising from their wider theology), rarely concede a typological sense to biblical statement, and then only with the encouragement of Scripture itself, as here. Theodoret's further principle, that interpretations arising from consideration only of individual verses lifted from context are dubious, he himself can honor in the breach as well as the observance.
3. Cf. Ps 39.12–13, 39.7.

though the prayer had been accepted and the request granted, *I waited and waited on the Lord,* he is saying, *and he attended to me:* averting his eyes from my sin, he showed me a kindly face and hearkened to my prayer. And what did he do when he hearkened? *He drew me out of a pit of wretchedness and from a miry bog.* [1153] Now, this is the way the divine Scripture is accustomed to refer to the greatest dangers, as we remarked already.[4] After freeing you from the dangers, however, what did he grant to you in turn? *He set my feet on a rock:* he did not allow me to be driven in confusion and be unsteady, but gave me firm footing. "On this rock I shall build my Church," Scripture says, "and Hell's gates will not prevail against it."[5] *And he guided my steps:* he caused me to run the path of righteousness without obstacle, freeing me from error and giving me a glimpse of the straight way of truth.

(3) *He put into my mouth a new song, a hymn to our God* (v. 3): in place of the impious worship of the idols I was taught to sing the praises of the true God and offer a song—not an old one: a new one, suited to the new favors. I no longer make supplication in dirges, you see; instead, I sing of the favors. So this is related, as I said, to the sufferings of David as a type, and to the favors done to him. And it is related in particular to the human race, sunken to the very depths of sin and consigned to death, but retrieved through the Incarnation of our Savior and given the hope of resurrection, saying, *I waited and waited on the Lord, and he attended to me. He hearkened to me, and drew me out of a pit of wretchedness.* Now, it was proper that death be called *a pit of wretchedness,* being full of corruption, and that sin be called *a miry bog* as giving off an awful stench and impeding the steady course of human beings. *Many will see and will fear, and hope in the Lord.* Since he is recounting this in the person of those enjoying salvation, the inspired author was right in saying that those who had not yet tasted the good things would see and fear for reason of not yet having arrived, and strengthened by hope would attain salvation from God.

4. As we have remarked, Theodoret does not recognize in these terms some of the many ways the Old Testament speaks of the nether world.
5. Matt 16.18.

(4) *Blessed is the man whose hope is the name of the Lord, whose eyes were not on futilities and deceitful frenzies* (v. 4). The inspired author mentioned these *futilities* in the previous psalm as well: "Everything is futility, every living person," and again, "Worried about a nothing."[6] [1156] So here he declares blessed the one despising present realities and resting on divine hope above everything. *Many are the marvels you have performed, O Lord my God, and in your thoughts there is no one to compare with you. I proclaimed and spoke of them, they were multiplied beyond counting* (v. 5). The wonders performed by your power, he is saying, defy counting and all description: there is no one who can do the like. While your creation is great and beautiful, what you arrange time after time in your providence surpasses human praise—in Egypt, in the wilderness, in the case of Moses, in the case of Joshua, in the case of Samuel, and earlier instances than those, having to do with Abraham, Isaac, Jacob, the royalty Joseph gained through slavery, not to mention all the other cases individually.[7]

(5) Yet what has now been achieved is more wonderful than all those: you concern yourself with the salvation not of one man or of one nation but of all nations; and bringing to an end the worship prescribed by the Law, which accommodated the Jews' weakness, you gave the new grace, the worship prescribed by reason. *Sacrifice and offering you did not desire, but a body you fashioned for me. Holocausts even for sin you did not look for. Then I said, Behold, I am coming* (vv. 6–7). The apostolic exhortation sings a similar note to this, "I urge you, brethren, by the mercies of God, to present your bodies as a living sacrifice, holy, pleasing to God, the worship according to reason":[8] In place of the rites of the Law, the Lord required us to consecrate our limbs. Now, seeing your grace, he says, I offered myself to you in the words,

---

6. Ps 39.5–6. Theodoret does not advert to the use of this word by the LXX to translate Hebrew words for "idols, gods."

7. This survey of salvation history shows us Theodoret touching on true highlights, leaving aside those marginal figures like Rabshakeh and Mephibosheth that caught his fancy earlier. He proceeds to show how this pattern has been extended and transformed (even displaced, in his view) by the New Testament, especially in matters of worship, to which the psalm refers.

8. Rom 12.1.

Here I am. This statement, of course, blessed Paul applies to Christ the Lord,[9] and rightly so: he is our nature's firstfruits, and it is fitting for him in the first place to speak for us and in himself to prefigure in type what is appropriate in our case. Thus he was the first to come to baptism, giving us a glimpse of the grace of baptism; thus he washed the feet of the disciples, providing us with an archetype of humility. Hence he said to John, "Let it be just now: it becomes us to carry out all that righteousness requires."[10] So it is fitting for him also to speak for us, [1157] as head of the body,[11] as firstborn of many brethren according to the flesh.[12]

(6) *In the scroll of the book it is written of me.* Previously, he is saying, in the inspired books this was foretold of me. For *the scroll* Aquila and Symmachus said "roll"; but this is the way Jews are accustomed to handle the divine Scriptures even today.[13] *My wish was to do your will, O my God, and your law in my very innards* (v. 8). After making my approach to you, he is saying, I have utter zeal to fulfil your commandments and live according to your desire. Now, the phrase, *in my very innards,* he uttered as a metaphor for a person's good dispositions towards another and longing to enclose the beloved. This is not a reference, however, to Jeremiah, or Daniel, or blessed David: while the Law was in force, holocausts and sacrifices were offered to God. The inspired word, however, rejected all these and gave a glimpse of the sacrifice according to reason. Hence I said the psalm refers to David as a type, since even he in inspired fashion foresaw the future, and desired to live under it; in reality, on the other hand, it refers to the nations accorded salvation and freed from error.[14]

(7) *I told the good news of righteousness in a great assembly. Lo, my lips I shall not forbid; you know it, Lord. I did not conceal your righteousness in my heart, I spoke of your truth and your salvation. I did not*

---

9. Cf. Heb 10.5–10, the passage that gives Theodoret the encouragement to conduct his typological interpretation of the psalm.
10. Matt 3.15.   11. Cf. Col 1.18.
12. Cf. Rom 8.29.
13. Theodoret suggests his readers may need adverting to Jewish practice of retention and use of biblical materials.
14. The substantial use of these verses in *Hebrews* encourages Theodoret to spell out their levels of meaning, as type and as reality.

conceal your mercy and your truth from a numerous congregation (vv. 9–10). Blessed David promises to preach God's righteousness, the truth of inspired composition, the admirable salvation and immeasurable mercy in a great assembly gathered by divine grace throughout the whole world. And redeemed nature itself promises to give this response to its salvation by flocking to church, moving its lips in hymn singing, proclaiming God's righteous judgment, recounting his ineffable care, and giving a glimpse of the truth of the inspired promises. For the phrase, *from a numerous congregation,* on the other hand, Symmachus put "in a multitude," and Aquila and Theodotion, "in a great assembly" so that it might be clear that he spoke of the same assembly.

(8) *But as for you, O Lord, do not keep your pity far from me; your mercy and your truth always assisted me* (v. 11). Having gained salvation, the Church of God needs in turn the same providential assistance on account of the manifold rebellions of human beings and demons, which he mentioned in what follows. [1160] *Because evils beyond counting encompassed me, my transgressions laid hold of me, and I could not see. They became more numerous than the hairs of my head, and my heart failed me* (v. 12). Now, let no one think that these words are out of keeping with the commentary given: even the three children after attaining the summit of virtue and garlanded with the victor's crown prayed in the furnace, "We sinned, we broke the law, we did wrong, we departed from your commandments and did not keep your ordinances."[15] Likewise remarkable Daniel, likewise the divinely inspired Jeremiah, likewise the divine Isaiah, likewise the eminently wise Paul: "Christ Jesus came into the world to save sinners, of whom I am the foremost,"[16] and again, "I am not worthy to be called an apostle."[17] Likewise therefore the Church of

15. Cf. Dan 3.29 [Greek]. Theodoret forestalls a reaction from his readers to the effect that the psalm has changed course; in fact, some modern commentators would suggest it is a combination of two independent poems, of thanksgiving and lament respectively. Unable to allow for this, Theodoret turns to paradoxical Scriptural statements and the existential evidence of the Church's varied membership, having already established typological reference to the Church in the former section.
16. 1 Tim 1.15.
17. 1 Cor 15.9.

God, buffeted by billows from the godless, in its struggles is not carried away, but attributes developments to sins and failings, and begs to enjoy assistance from the Savior. In a particular way, the Church of God is not composed completely of perfect people; instead, it numbers also those addicted to sloth and inclined to the careless life, who choose to serve pleasure. Since it is one body, both features are displayed as in the case of one person.

(9) *Be pleased, O Lord, to rescue me; Lord, attend to helping me. Let those be put to shame and overturned together who seek my life to do away with it* (vv. 13–14): they wish not to wound me but to dispatch me to everlasting death. *Let them be turned back and put to shame who wish me harm:* put them to flight and make them miss the goals they aspire to; it is trouble for me they plot, after all. *Let them meet with shame from the outset who say to me, Aha, Aha* (v. 15): let shame be the fruit for those who jeer and mock at me.

(10) *May all who seek you rejoice and be glad in you, Lord, and may those who ever love your salvation say always, May the Lord be magnified* (v. 16). On the other hand, fill with constant joy, he is saying, those who seek you, who sing your praises and ever love you; may those who undergo no change in love of you undergo no change in satisfaction. He did not ask for satisfaction simply for those who love, but for those who ever and uninterruptedly have the love that deserves love. *But I am poor and needy, the Lord will be concerned for me. You are my help and my protector, Lord; do not delay* (v. 17). As he recalled his sins above, so he also calls himself poor as though in want of help and needing divine assistance; and he begs to attain it promptly. Now, this is especially applicable to blessed David: I believe that on perceiving that prophecy and the generosity of the grace, he called himself *poor and needy*, and begged to receive in his own case, too, divine providence. He asks that the predicted salvation not be delayed nor put off for a long time, but be rapidly provided to human beings.[18]

18. The commentator does not draw to his reader's attention the recurrence of vv. 13–17 later in the Psalter as Ps 70—a fact that may have escaped him.

COMMENTARY ON PSALM 41

To the end. A psalm of David.

OME ATTRIBUTED THE PRESENT psalm to David, others to Hezekiah; but the divine Gospel permits us to accept neither. In a discourse to the sacred disciples Christ the Lord added these words as well: "If you know this, blessed are you if you do it. I am not speaking about all of you; I know those I have chosen. But it is for the Scripture to be fulfilled, The one who ate bread with me lifted up his heel against me. I tell you this just now before it happens so that when it happens you may believe that I am he."[1] So since the Lord says "for the Scripture to be fulfilled," and shows the present psalm applies to him and no one else, I consider it rash and presumptuous to develop another explanation not applicable to him.

(2) *Blessed is the one who understands the poor and needy* (v. 1). The phrase *and needy* I found in some copies; but it is not in the Hebrew, or the Syriac, or the other translators.[2] He calls the Lord of all *poor*, to be sure, since "although being rich," as the divine Apostle says, "he became poor for our sake so that by his poverty we might be rich";[3] and "though he was in the form of

---

1. John 13.17–19. While we admire the reluctance of these Antiochene commentators to leave the literal sense and to find a typological sense only with the encouragement of the New Testament, that principle proves restrictive if a NT quotation is to be used to preclude any reference contemporary with the author so as to achieve an exclusively Christological meaning—especially on the basis of one verse, a practice Theodoret decried in commenting on the previous psalm (see note 2 there).

2. As we have discussed in Introduction, section 5, while it has become clear that Theodoret's grasp of Hebrew is unlikely, his native Syriac enabled him to have recourse to the version of the Bible in that language, the Peshitta; and he seems to have been able to consult other forms of the LXX than his own.

3. 2 Cor 8.9.

God, he did not regard equality with God something to be exploited, but emptied himself, taking the form of a slave."[4] And though having lordship of visible and invisible things, he had nowhere to lay his head, was born of a virgin and through lack of a bed was laid in a manger.[5] Consequently, the inspired word declares blessed the one able to understand this poverty and filled with zeal to sing the praises as far as possible of the one who accepted it. Then he shows the fruits of the blessing: [1164] *The Lord will deliver him in the evil day.* For *the evil day,* on the other hand, Symmachus said "day of trouble," hinting, I think, at the day of judgment as fearsome and troublesome to transgressors, and promising the unalloyed knowledge of that poverty will free him from the troubles of that fearsome day.

(3) *The Lord will closely guard him and give him life, and make him blessed in the land, and will not give him into the hands of his foes* (v. 2): not only will he enjoy the good things to come, but even in the present life he will attain the benefits of divine providence, proving illustrious and famous and avoiding the schemes of adversaries. And since it is likely that someone with a corruptible body should fall foul of disease, he promises also freedom from this: *The Lord will help him on his bed of pain; in his ill health you overturned all his disability* (v. 3). He will rid him of all ill health, he is saying, and change ailment into soundness. Now, he put *in his ill health you overturned disability* for "you changed."

(4) After outlining the rewards for those understanding that admirable poverty, he gives us a glimpse of the one who had it and the way he practiced it, bringing him forward to teach us and describe his own experience. *I said, Lord, have mercy on me, heal my soul because I sinned against you* (v. 4). Now, I am the one who is poor, he is saying, who embraced voluntary poverty, the Lamb of God who takes away the sin of the world, who makes my own the sufferings of human beings, who though having committed no sin offers the prayer for human nature as nature's firstfruits. It should be noted, however, that Symmachus

---

4. Phil 2.6–7.
5. Theodoret, like other Antiochenes, is much more comfortable in dwelling on the limitations that human nature imposes on the Word incarnate.

said not *because I sinned against you* but "even if I sinned against you." *My foes spoke evil against me: when will he die and his name perish?* (v. 5). He calls the Jews *foes*, showing malice and plotting his death. The narrative in the sacred Gospels also teaches this: "They conspired how to destroy him,"[6] it says.

(5) At this point he shifts the prophecy onto Judas. *He came to see me, his heart spoke idly;* [1165] *he heaped up lawlessness for himself; he went out and spoke* (v. 6). The divine evangelists also teach us to this effect, that he said to the Jews, "What do you give me in return for betraying him to you? And he began to look for an opportunity to betray him."[7] This is said also by the prophecy, *He came to see me idly, he went out and spoke:* going in and going out he plotted death with them. Then he foretells their evil conspiracy: *All my foes whispered together against me, against me they devised trouble for me; they set up a lawless plan against me* (v. 7). Now, the outcome of events testifies to these things: furtively they conversed together and looked for the way to implement the plot. Then they made a charge of overthrow, saying to Pilate, "He makes himself king and forbids us paying tribute to Caesar,"[8] which is what the prophecy says, *They set up a lawless plan against me*, that is, they leveled a charge of lawlessness against me. *Surely if I lie down, shall I not succeed in rising?* (v. 8). Even if I undergo death, he is saying, do I not rise and scatter those responsible for this? This resembles the Gospel saying, "Destroy this temple, and in three days I shall raise it up";[9] and again, "See, we are going up to Jerusalem, and the Son of Man will be given into the hands of sinners, and they will kill him, and on the third day he will rise."[10] For this very reason he was right to call death "sleep."[11]

---

6. Cf. Matt 26.4. It becomes clear how this compulsion to a Christological interpretation, based on individual verses quoted by the New Testament and thus in defiance of Theodoret's own principles, can result in a pejorative understanding of the role of the Jews, who by this kind of logic are cast in the role of "foes" of Jesus. Other NT details are also forced to corroborate the psalm text.
7. Cf. Matt 26.15–16. 8. Cf. Luke 23.2.
9. John 2.19.
10. A patchwork of various dominical sayings in the Gospels.
11. In fact, of course, the text does not speak of sleep, but the commentator has a case to mount, and details are not to be allowed to stand in the

(6) *A person at peace with me, in whom I had hope, who ate bread with me, has behaved in dastardly manner to me* (v. 9). Aquila and Theodotion said this more clearly: "A man at peace with me, in whom I had faith," whereas Symmachus said this: "But a person who kept peace with me, in whom I had faith." In other words, it was not only my enemies who devised death for me, but also an associate of mine, pretending benevolence and peace, sharing table and food with me, exposed the deceit he nourished. He gave the deceit the name of "heel,"[12] by analogy with those who are rivals for fleetness of foot, and who endeavor to trip up their fellow competitors with their heel and make them fall. [1168] Esau when deceived by Jacob also said this: "He is rightly named Jacob, for this is the second time now that he has supplanted me: he took away both my birthright and my blessing."[13]

(7) *But you, O Lord, have mercy on me, raise me up, and repay them. By this I knew that you were pleased with me, that my foe did not rejoice over me* (vv. 10–11). All this was said on the part of the nature assumed, which was involved also in the Passion. Likewise in the sacred Gospels we hear Christ the Lord praying, "Father, save me from this hour,"[14] and again, "Father, if it is possible, let this cup pass from me."[15] *But you supported me for my innocence, and confirmed me in your presence forever* (v. 12). This is also appli-

---

way. Gospel texts are quoted loosely, as though the commentator could not be bothered to check them for accuracy. The psalm speaks of a lawless plan, which is not synonymous with a charge of lawlessness. The Hebrew of v. 8 implies that rising after lying down is unlikely, whereas it is vital to Theodoret's argument that it should occur (admittedly his LXX text has already reversed the sense for him). Modern exegetes would see him engaged in an exercise of "advocacy exegesis"—if not eisegesis.

12. In fact, the word *pterna* occurs in the Gospel form of the text as quoted by Theodoret at the opening of commentary, not in the psalm verse itself in his LXX text, which is somewhat different, where the (rare) related term *pternismos* has a metaphorical meaning such as cunning, arrogance, even slander. Theodoret, with his Christological bent, is making the mistake of commenting on the NT occurrence of the text, not the OT locus.

13. Gen 27.36.
14. John 12.27.
15. Matt 26.39. Evidently by this stage, after a series of verses thought to be highlighting the indignities heaped on Jesus, Theodoret feels it is time to make again that distinction of his between the nature assumed and the nature assuming. He can then proceed to the more positive verses.

cable to the form of a slave, which God's Only-begotten assumed: "It was not with angels that he was concerned," as the divine Apostle says; "instead, he was concerned with the descendants of Abraham. Hence he had to become like his brethren in all things so as to become a merciful and faithful high priest in the service of God."[16] Since, then, the assumed nature remained free of all wickedness, it was right for him to say, *But you supported me for my innocence, and confirmed me in your presence forever:* I received a stable unity, the combining was indivisible, the glory everlasting.[17]

(8) *Blessed be the Lord, the God of Israel, from everlasting to everlasting! May it be, may it be!* (v. 13). The divinely inspired author, after foretelling these things, marveling at the ineffable lovingkindness of the Lord and understanding the voluntary poverty which was accepted, offers a hymn to him with his tongue so as to gain in his own person the blessed end. It was right that he should offer a hymn after the Passion to teach that the one who prophesied was not only human but also God eternal in his unending and immortal being.[18]

---

16. Heb 2.16–17. Again the phrase "form of a slave," quoted earlier from Phil 2.6, serves to confirm that it is "the nature assumed" speaking here.

17. Still stepping back from the graphic if imprecise language of biblical expression to the precision of dogmatic formulas, his intention as he closes the commentary is that of the Chalcedon symbol, if not its exact terminology (the council, after all, convening not long afterwards in 451).

18. Theodoret seems to have no difficulty seeing the author of these verses as both David and Jesus ("the inspired Word" being a synonym he also employs). He does not, like some modern editors, recognize in v. 13 a doxology to close the first of five Books of Psalms, a division known from the beginning of the Christian era (as he would have found in Eusebius).

COMMENTARY ON PSALM 42

To the end, for understanding for the sons of Korah.

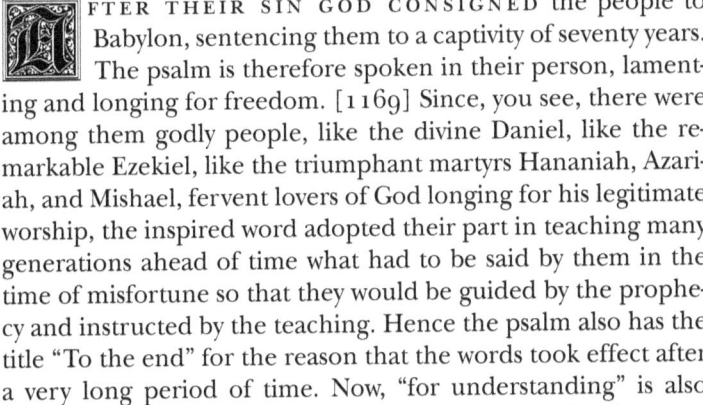FTER THEIR SIN GOD CONSIGNED the people to Babylon, sentencing them to a captivity of seventy years. The psalm is therefore spoken in their person, lamenting and longing for freedom. [1169] Since, you see, there were among them godly people, like the divine Daniel, like the remarkable Ezekiel, like the triumphant martyrs Hananiah, Azariah, and Mishael, fervent lovers of God longing for his legitimate worship, the inspired word adopted their part in teaching many generations ahead of time what had to be said by them in the time of misfortune so that they would be guided by the prophecy and instructed by the teaching. Hence the psalm also has the title "To the end" for the reason that the words took effect after a very long period of time. Now, "for understanding" is also added since that is what is particularly necessary for those encountering misfortune.[1]

(2) *As the deer pines for the springs of water, so my soul pines for you, O God* (v. 1). They say the deer eat poisonous creatures, and hence burn with an intense thirst and yearn more ardently for water. Accordingly, the above-mentioned through association with the Babylonians, men addicted to impiety and lawlessness, quite like savage reptiles, were right to say they thirsted for God like the deer, longing for liberation from there and looking for divine aid. *My soul thirsted for God, who is strong and living: when shall I come and see the face of God?* (v. 2). I am longing and thirsting for the worship of my living God, he is saying: *to see the face of*

1. We have often seen Theodoret failing to recognize the titles as liturgical directions to groups of musicians like the Sons of Korah, mentioned by the Chronicler. Reference to the conductor is taken as a hint of future application of the psalm's contents, while as with Ps 32 (see note 1 there) mention of the "maskil" genre is misread in terms of the word's roots.

God means worshipping him according to the Law, and such worship was confined to Jerusalem. Not only blessed Moses teaches this, but also the three blessed martyrs Hananiah, Azariah, and Mishael, beseeching God in the furnace. Now, very appropriately do they name God *strong and living* as they take note of the lifeless and immobile idols of the Babylonians.

(3) *My tears have become my bread day and night as they say to me each day, Where is your God? These things I remembered, and I poured out my soul* (vv. 3–4). Lamenting day and night, he is saying, I was not satisfied; instead, I make tears a kind of food, as it were, being the object of reproach on your account. My opponents mock me, in fact, representing your care as powerless, unable to match them for strength. So with this constantly in my mind, I keep weeping incessantly: the phrase, *I poured out my soul,* has this meaning, [1172] I am poured out and moved to lament. *Because I shall pass through every corner of the wonderful tabernacle as far as the house of God, with sounds of exultation and praise, a roar of celebration.* He calls God's protection *tabernacle*. After the sad events, therefore, he proclaims pleasant ones, and ahead of time teaches that they will quickly secure their recall, and with the guidance of God's grace they will return to the land of their desire and will rebuild God's house, will celebrate the customary festivals, and welcome into their ears the festive sound and spiritual melody. Blessed Isaiah also predicts that they will return with the highest honor, riding on litters of mules, shaded by parasols, diverting the sun's harm.[2] Aquila also hints at this: "I shall go in heavy shade, leading them as far as the house of God, the crowd celebrating with sound of praise and thanksgiving." Dancing and singing the praise of God the Savior, he is saying, and enjoying shade along the way, we shall thus take possession of the house of God as though making a return in some procession.

(4) On hearing this prophecy, they offer themselves consolation in the words, *Why are you disconsolate, my soul? And why do you disturb me? Hope in God, because I shall confess to him, my personal savior and my God* (v. 5). Having received these promises, O soul,

---

2. Cf. Isa 66.20.

he is saying, cease mourning and grieving, and, fortified by hope, look for the fulfillment of the prophecy; in this you will see salvation achieved, and offer hymns to the God who has saved you.[3] *My soul is confused within itself; hence I shall remember you from the land of Jordan and Hermon, from a small mountain* (v. 6). There is a kind of presentation of a soul conversing with itself: after saying, Cease your discouragement on receipt of the promises of good things, it replies to this by saying, It is not without reason that I grieve and employ words of lament; memory of the homeland prompts tears in me. He calls the promised land *land of Jordan,* and Mount Hermon *Hermon,* though by mention of the mountain and the river he indicated the whole of that land. Symmachus rendered it this way: "My soul will waste away when I remember you from Jordan's land and Hermon's smallest mountain."

(5) [1173] *Deep calls on deep to the sound of your cataracts. All your heights and your billows have passed over me* (v. 7). Now, living in that land, he is saying, I was given over to a crowd of adversaries, and became like someone drowning in the deep; he calls the ranks of soldiers *deeps,* and likens the extreme size of the crowd to immeasurable waters, and what was done by them to the flood of old which wiped out the whole world. Symmachus translated it more clearly, "Deep challenged deep with a roar of your torrents": you inflicted them, exacting of me a penalty for lawlessness.[4] *Your storms and your billows passed over me.* Having likened the army to the deep, you see, he stayed with the comparison and called the army's forays *billows* and *storms.* This is the reason I am in pain, he is saying: memory of it pricks me; yet I have your loving-kindness for consolation. He added, in fact, *By day the Lord will show his mercy, and by night his song is with me, a prayer to the God of my life* (v. 8). Ever appreciative of the mercy provided by God, he is saying, and considering it within myself by night, I sing and praise the one who shows his care for us in

---

3. The text of the verse presents difficulties for the commentator ancient and modern, and Theodoret has made a good fist of getting sense from it.

4. Is the version of Symmachus so much clearer, and is it susceptible of this interpretation? It is almost a reflex on Theodoret's part to promote this translator's effort over the LXX.

this way; I also offer supplications to him, begging to attain this loving-kindness.

(6) He then teaches the words of the prayer as well: *I shall say to God, You are my support: why have you forgotten me, and why do I go about with face downcast while the foe afflicts me? In trampling on my bones my foes reproach me by saying to me each day, Where is your God?* (vv. 9–10). Saying this to my Lord, he means, I have always been the object of your providence: why on earth do you deprive me of it now so that I mourn and grieve unceasingly at the reproaches of my adversaries? They torment me, you see, and break my bones with blows and shackles, saying to me mockingly, Where is your God? They presume I am suffering this on account of your weakness. Now, *you have forgotten me* means you have not given me a share in your providence: forgetfulness is a human weakness, whereas no such weakness belongs to God.[5]

(7) *Why are you disconsolate, my soul, and why do you disturb me? Hope in God, because* [1176] *I shall confess to him, my personal savior and my God* (v. 11). Do not despair of salvation, O soul, he is saying: you have God as savior; in him you gain sound hope. Quench your discouragement and receive consolation.[6]

---

5. We have seen Theodoret noting for his readers the figurative language of the psalms, and as an Antiochene he has to alert them to the limitations of such figures where divine transcendence is at risk.

6. In his commentary Theodoret has dispatched the psalm with customary economy, documenting it only once from elsewhere in Scripture, yet not unmoved by the plight of the sufferer (whom he takes to be one of the exiles). It is interesting to compare his conciseness with the great length to which Chrysostom goes in commenting only on the two opening verses of this psalm, commonly sung as a refrain in liturgical and paraliturgical situations, and referring his congregation repeatedly to other parts of Scripture. Theodoret does not comment on the liturgical use of the Psalms, nor their musical setting, and apart from his preface hardly acknowledges their place in his readers' spiritual lives.

COMMENTARY ON PSALM 43

A psalm of David.

ITHOUT A TITLE in the Hebrew. *Judge me, O God, and decide in my favor against a nation that is not holy; from a lawless and deceitful person rescue me* (v. 1). The psalm is without a title in the Hebrew for the reason of having a similar meaning to the preceding one.[1] Now, those who had spoken the preceding words beseech God to judge between them and the Babylonians, who were guilty of great cruelty and a ferocious attitude—hence his calling them *an unholy nation* and their king *a deceitful and lawless man*. The inspired composition of the remarkable Daniel also teaches this concerning him.

(2) *Because you, O God, are my force: why do you repulse me, and why do I go about downcast while the enemy afflicts me?* (v. 2). Again they offer the same prayer, entreating to be freed from the enemies' savagery, on account of which they were always downcast and dejected. Now, the word *why* they do not utter by way of accusation but on the part of people not sharing in the others' lawlessness and yet along with them made bereft of providence from on high; still, they make a common supplication on behalf of all.

(3) *Send forth your light and your truth; they guided me and led me to your holy mountain and your tabernacles* (v. 3). Here the Septuagint changed the tense, speaking of future events as past,[2]

---

1. Commentators remark on the similarity of the two psalms that suggests they constitute one psalm, especially for reason of the occurrence of the same verse as vv. 5 and 11 of Ps 42 (so far passing without comment by Theodoret) and v. 5 of Ps 43 (see note 5 below). The LXX does in fact have encouragement from some Hebrew manuscripts for including a title.

2. It is a further indication of Theodoret's lack of knowledge of Hebrew that he can speak of this instance of the LXX's treatment of Hebrew tenses as exceptional.

whereas the others produced a clearer translation: "Send out your light and your truth, which will guide me and lead me to your holy mountain and to your dwellings." My prayer is to enjoy divine assistance: with it I can succeed in being freed from harsh slavery, returning to the homeland, and offering the prescribed worship in the consecrated temple. He called the temple *tabernacles of God,* and Sion *holy mountain,* while he called his righteous and saving appearance *light and truth:* as he gives the name "darkness" to calamities, so *light* to freedom from them. Now, they ask for the truth along with the light in that they beg God to judge between them and the Babylonians, [1177] clearly aware that, if God employs truth and not long-suffering, he will condemn the latter and from their slavery free them.

(4) *I shall go in to the altar of God, to God who brings joy to my youth. I shall confess to you on a lyre, O God my God* (v. 4). Symmachus rendered it thus: "So that I may go in to the altar of God, to God the joy of my happiness. I shall confess to you on a harp, O God my God": I desire return, he is saying, in my longing to see your most desirable altar and through it to set eyes on you the Lord, who provides me with occasions of joy and happiness of all kinds.[3] There I shall conduct the customary hymn singing with a lyre; in Babylon, after all, "we hung up our instruments on the willows,"[4] considering worship outside of your place to be an infringement of the Law.

(5) *Why are you disconsolate, my soul, and why do you disturb me? Hope in God, because I shall confess to him, my personal savior and my God* (v. 5). From this it is clear that both psalms have the same meaning.[5] Those using them encourage themselves to have stronger hope, overcome the feeling of discouragement, and await the salvation from God that will doubtless be given them.

---

3. Again Theodoret promptly (and arbitrarily) abandons the version of the LXX for that of Symmachus, though Dahood suggests the Hebrew is susceptible of the former rendering rather than the latter.
4. Ps 137.2.
5. A cryptic comment that might have been developed for a reader (see note 1), even conceding the commentator's desire to "avoid a superfluity of words."

COMMENTARY ON PSALM 44

To the end. For the sons of Korah, for understanding.

ITH ITS PROPHECY of future events this psalm urges one to await its fulfillment. Now, "for understanding" occurs in the title so that those understanding the contents, which the inspired word prophesies, may gain benefit from them.[1] The psalm predicts the Macedonian savagery, the godless and fierce attitude of Antiochus Epiphanes, and the bravery and piety of the Maccabees.[2] The blessed and thrice-blessed Mattathias drilled his sons in divine zeal, regarding the great hordes of the Macedonians and the herds of elephants as powerless for being bereft of divine providence. With a few troops he took to the field against them and won, removed the altars of the idols, purified the divine temple, and restored the customary worship to his countrymen. Now, it was not only he but also his sons after his death who put the enemy to flight by prayer, and who by enjoying divine aid erected trophies.[3] It is in their person, then, that the inspired grace dictated the psalm, teaching ahead of time the kinds of words they needed to use in time of danger.

(2) [1180] *O God, we have heard with our ears and our fathers*

---

1. See note 1 to Ps 42.
2. Weiser remarks: "The early church fathers of the Antioch school already held that the psalm was composed at the time of the Maccabean wars during the second century BC, and have been followed by Calvin and the great majority of recent commentators." Though Theodoret is indeed referring to the reaction of the Maccabees under Mattathias to the irreligious activities of Antiochus IV, successor of Macedonian Alexander the Great's generals, he sees the psalm composed in prophetic fashion before then. Chrysostom likewise at the beginning of his commentary on this psalm says, "This is what the inspired authors are like: they traverse all times, past, present, and future."
3. The events are described in 1 Mac 1–2.

have told us the work you accomplished in their days, in the days of old (v. 1): while we were not eyewitnesses of your marvels, Lord, we learned from our fathers how great the marvels you worked in those times, fulfilling the promises made to our forebears. *Your hand utterly destroyed nations and you planted them; you afflicted peoples and drove them out. It was not by their own sword, in fact, that they inherited the land, nor their own arm that saved them; instead, it was your right hand, your arm, and the light of your countenance, because you took delight in them* (vv. 2–3). You, O Lord, he is saying, drove out from here the Canaanites along with the other nations, settling our fathers in their place: it was not by trusting in strength or depending on armor that they emerged stronger than such people, but led by your grace they felled some and took others into slavery, since you accorded them a special relationship with you—the meaning of *you took delight in them.* Now, he calls assistance *right hand,* and appearance *light of your countenance.*

(3) *You are my king and my God, commanding the salvation of Jacob* (v. 4). You are the same even now, Lord, he is saying, ruling in similar fashion, overpowering in similar fashion, exercising the same force, your nature undergoing no change. For you simply a word suffices for salvation: give the nod, and the people will enjoy it. Symmachus translated it this way: "He gives commands about the salvation of Jacob." *Through you we prevail over our foes, and through your name we bring to naught those who rise up against us* (v. 5): the horned animals received from nature the horn for weapon, whereas we have your name as horn of salvation and vanquishing weapon, and relying on it we prevail over the enemy. *Not in my bow do I hope, after all, nor will my sword save me. In fact, you saved us from those oppressing us, and put to shame those hating us* (vv. 6–7): I trust neither in bows nor in other weapons; I had experience of your power, previously dominating the adversary through you. *In God we shall rejoice all day long, and confess in your name forever* (v. 8): we always beg to enjoy your aid, and constantly to describe the great number of your favors—hence he put *all day long* in place of "always." [1181] Symmachus also, in fact, translated it this way: instead of *all day long* he put "for the whole day."

(4) *As it is, however, you rejected and shamed us, and you did not*

sally forth, God, in our forces (v. 9): so while this happened with you in previous times, in the present times we emerged deprived of your providence and live in shame without being led by your grace. The phrase, *you did not sally forth in our forces,* means "you did not lead us and provide as usual for our dominating the enemy." *You turned us back in battle with our foes, and those hating us took plunder for themselves* (v. 10): through not enjoying your providence we ran off in retreat while the foe plundered our possessions. *You gave us like sheep for eating, and scattered us among the nations* (v. 11): like sheep without a shepherd we are wasted by your enemies, and in our flight from death we are bought and sold hither and yon and forced into slavery.

(5) *You disposed of your people without charge, there was no great cost in our changing hands* (v. 12). Symmachus translated it this way: "You sold your people for a pittance, and made no great profit on them." And through the prophet Isaiah God said much the same: "What is your mother's bill of divorce, or to which creditor have I sold you? Lo, for your iniquities you were sold, and for your sins I dismissed your mother." And again, "You were sold for nothing, and you will not be bought back with money."[4] And the divine Apostle, "We know in fact that the law is spiritual, but I am of the flesh, sold under sin."[5] So here, too, the remarkable men say, You disposed of us, taking no price from the enemy: it was on account of sins you handed us over. *You set us as a reproach to our neighbors, an object of derision and mockery to those around about us* (v. 13). He gives the name *neighbors* dwelling *around about* to the foreigners, Idumeans, Moabites, Ammonites, and the others nearby, to whom they became objects of malignant joy when fighting in battle.

(6) [1184] *You have set us as a byword to the nations, a shaking of the head among the peoples* (v. 14). When describing or hearing of great calamities, we tend to shake our heads, moved to do it by our surprise. And we tend to compare feelings with feelings, saying, This person suffered what this person suffered. Here too they lament this, We have become a byword to people, they

---

4. Cf. Isa 50.1, 52.3.
5. Rom 7.14.

shake their heads at us, some gleeful, some amazed at the extraordinary turn of events. *All day long my shame is before me, and I am covered in blushes from the sound of the one blaming and slandering, from the aspect of foe and persecutor* (vv. 15–16): seeing some hostile and others mocking and ridiculing, I am completely ashamed, and am distressed all day.

(7) Then those who had escaped the snares of Antiochus and slipped the nets of impiety describe their own virtue. *All this came upon us, and we did not forget you and did not break your covenant. Our heart has not turned back* (vv. 17–18): though overwhelmed on all sides by such troubles, we did not entertain forgetfulness of your commands, or presume to transgress your Law, nor did we abandon our former resolve. *You moved our steps from your way because you humiliated us in a place of affliction and wrapped us in the darkness of death* (vv. 18–19). The phrase, *You moved our steps from your way,* Symmachus translated this way, "Our direction did not shift from your way." To convey the sense of the Septuagint, let us take it this way: You enveloped us in many griefs of all kinds sufficient even to divert us from your way; you even handed us over into slavery to impious people practicing savagery against us and inflicting deathly penalties on us (calling perils leading to death *a darkness of death*).[6]

(8) *If we forgot the name of our God, and if we spread out our hands to a foreign god, would not God find this out? After all, he knows the secrets of the heart. Because for your sake we are being put to death all day long, we are accounted as sheep* [1185] *for slaughter* (vv. 20–22). The Maccabees, those of the company of Mattathias, and the seven young men with their mother and Eleazar the priest gave evidence of this virtue:[7] they were not subdued by the torments nor bowed by the punishments; instead, they kept their reverence

---

6. Theodoret tries hard to get some consistency out of the LXX version, which unlike Symmachus has unaccountably omitted a critical negative from v. 18; but his paraphrase cannot disguise the difficulty.
7. Cf. 2 Mac 6–7. Weiser, who thinks the connection of the psalm with the Maccabees unfounded, remarks: "It cannot be proved that v. 22 refers to the religious persecution of the Jews by Antiochus IV, since the psalm nowhere speaks of religious persecution." He seems to run the risk of a fundamentalist approach to engage with the ancient commentators in this fashion.

for the true God intact, and loathed as an abomination the worship of idols. *You know this, Lord,* he is saying: not only are actions clear to you, but also movements of the mind. Now, it must be noted that the language implies two persons: after saying, *Would not God find this out? After all, he knows the secrets of the heart,* he added, *Because for your sake we are being put to death all day long.* This change in pronoun, however, the Hebrew has and also the other translators include it.[8]

(9) *Bestir yourself! Why do you sleep, Lord? Arise, and do not drive us off forever* (v. 23). He calls long-suffering *sleep:* just as the sleeping person is unaware of what is happening, so the one practicing long-suffering puts up with being belabored and abused. And he calls movement to punish *rising up.* Then he says the same thing again in a different way: *Why do you turn your face away? You have forgotten our poverty and our tribulations* (v. 24). You are ignoring what is happening to us, he is saying, and you resemble someone turning away and not seeing but forgetting and hence not caring, whereas we are suffering poverty, with no abundance of assistance. *Because our soul is brought down to the dust, our stomach is stuck fast to the ground* (v. 25): we are bowed down to the very ground so that our stomach nearly touches the ground. Now, by these expressions he implies extreme lowliness and the might of the enemies. *Rise up, O Lord, come to our aid, and redeem us for your name's sake* (v. 26): for this reason we beg you to appear, Lord, remove our problems, and make us stronger than our adversaries.

(10) Now, all this the grace of the Spirit foretold, teaching those who would experience those troubles to bear nobly what befell them and request relief from them from the God of all. Those remarkable men did exactly that: with their words they appeased God, led by him they routed the enemy, and they recovered their former freedom for their fellow citizens.

---

8. Again Theodoret displays his Antiochene credentials in picking up this morphological detail, even if he has neglected to note other such in the course of the *Commentary.*

COMMENTARY ON PSALM 45

To the end. For those to be changed. For the sons of Korah, for understanding. A song for the beloved.[1] *[1188]*

FTER PROPHESYING GRIEVOUS THINGS in the psalm before this, the inspired word now forecasts cheerful things, encouraging the downcast and teaching that they will both conquer and persevere, and will gain help from God until from their number the beloved Son shoots forth in the flesh and makes it his concern to achieve the fresh alteration for the nations. He calls the Son of God *beloved:* the divine Isaiah also speaks this way, "The beloved had a vineyard on a mound, in a fertile place."[2] This the Father himself also announced in person to the Son: "This is my Son, the beloved, with whom I am well pleased."[3] Through holy baptism he granted an alteration to the nations. Now, the psalm prophesies them, urging them to forget their ancestral gods and honor in truth the true God. Symmachus, on the other hand, called *those who will be changed* "flowers," and Aquila and Theodotion, "lilies."[4] Flowers and lilies are spring plants, and the coming of the Savior is a spiritual spring, which was a cause of joy in the inspired words of Isaiah, "The former wilderness blossomed like a

---

1. See note 1 to Ps 42 for Theodoret's reading of some of these terms. He is not prepared to settle for a mere "love song" as a further direction, but insists on finding additional theological significance.
2. Isa 5.1.
3. Matt 3.17.
4. Theodoret's LXX has committed a further solecism in rendering the title, which he is not equipped to correct. The Hebrew direction "according to the lilies (*shoshanim*)," probably a cue to a well-known melody, the LXX takes as connected with the verb *shanah,* "to change"; and, faced with the alternative versions, Theodoret proceeds at a theological level to rationalize this reading and also the alternatives, with no attempt to get behind the LXX to the language of the original.

lily."⁵ The inspired text before us prophesies in this connection, giving a glimpse of the vinedresser and farmer of all things, making changes and causing fruit to appear.⁶

(2) *My heart belched a good word* (v. 1): nourished on spiritual words, I release such belches, and utter such words.⁷ *I tell of my works to the king*. The one the title called *beloved* the opening to the psalm calls *king*. Now, the outcome of inspired discourse is the true word, which forecasts the future. So he means, I am delivering discourse about the king himself; and teaching by the use not of human but of divine words he added, *My tongue the pen of a rapid scribe*. I utter nothing of my own, he is saying, nor do I propose anything from the labors of my mind; rather, the tongue is the minister of a different faculty, imitating a pen, whereas the grace of the Spirit resembles a speedy writer, writing what it wishes through that means.⁸

(3) In this way the inspired author, having given us a glimpse of the one speaking through him, begins his prophecy thus:

---

5. Isa 35.1, a case where a comment on the alteration in tense made by the LXX (cf. note 2 to Ps 43) would be relevant if Theodoret were aware of it.

6. So, even before getting into the verses of the psalm, and simply through a misreading of elements of the title and a dependence on a faulty LXX version, which the commentator has not the skills to adjust, the reader is given a deal of material through theological rationalizing. And this despite the fact that the psalm is regarded as originally a wedding song, "the only example of a profane lyric in the Psalter" (Weiser).

7. The LXX has made a good fist of the meaning of a *hapax legomenon* in the Hebrew, and Chrysostom makes much capital of the involuntary process of belching after good food—but Theodoret does not work at that level, and quickly moves on. He does, however, like so many of the Fathers, find in this verse the occasion to outline his thinking on biblical inspiration. See my "Psalm 45: a *locus classicus* for patristic thinking on biblical inspiration."

8. Thus Theodoret emphasizes the role of the Spirit in inspired composition, a datum the Fathers generally concede. But an Antiochene like Chrysostom, sensitive always to the need also to uphold the human dimension—whether in regard to the Bible, Christology, or soteriology—will proceed to bring out as well the contribution of the human author of *propheteia,* inspired composition. Theodoret, alerting his reader even here to the limitations of the "human" figure involved, does not betray that concern, as he did not do it in speaking elsewhere of the gratuity of grace—unlike his Christological precision, which he proceeds to demonstrate.

Striking in your beauty compared with the sons of human beings. Grace was poured out on your lips; hence God blessed you forever (v. 2). You, he is saying, whom he named *king,* whom in the title he called "beloved," surpass in beauty the human race, and pour forth floods of wisdom through your tongue; [1189] this you possess not for the time being but forever. Now, it should be understood that the inspired word revealed not the divine but the human aspect of Christ the Lord: it would not have compared God the Word to human beings, nor said he received the blessing from God; after all, he is an abundant source of good things, shedding blessing on the faithful. In these words, therefore, he prophesied the human characteristics of Christ the Lord. Let no one say, however, the inspired authors are in direct contradiction with each other, when you hear Isaiah crying aloud, "We saw him, and he had no form or beauty; rather, his form was without honor, worse than the sons of human beings."[9] Those things, in fact, prefigure the Cross and the Passion, which are marked by drunken and insolent violence; hence the inspired author added, "A person abused, experienced in bearing weakness, despised, and of no account," and so on to indicate the Passion. The psalm, on the other hand, speaks of his beauty, not of body but of virtue and complete righteousness, not affected by the stain of sin, free of all defilement.

(4) *Gird your sword on your thigh, O mighty one, in your charm and your beauty. Advance, proceed, and reign* (vv. 3–4). After describing his charm and wisdom, he gives us a glimpse of both his power and his accouterments, which he used to wipe out his adversaries, teaching us the baffling character of it all. I mean, he mentions his very beauty, accouterments, and power: *Gird your sword on your thigh, O mighty one,* he says, *in your charm and your beauty;* and after saying, *Advance, proceed, and reign,* he immediately added, *For the sake of truth, gentleness, and righteousness,* teaching us clearly by this that truth, gentleness, and righteousness are his beauty and power and accouterments, and his victory. Now, you can hear the Lord himself saying, "Learn of me, because I am gentle and humble of heart, and you will find rest for

9. Cf. Isa 53.2–3.

your souls";[10] and again, "I am the way, the truth, and the life."[11] And to the divinely inspired John, "Let it be for the time being: it is proper for us in this way to fulfill all righteousness."[12] In this way he overthrew the tyranny of the avenging angel, defeated death, and procured salvation for those who believe. *Your right hand will guide you in marvelous fashion.* Since he had mentioned a sword, it was logical for him to make mention also of his right hand. Now, his *right hand* means his clever designs, by the use of which he did not suffer the assault of sin.

(5) [1192] *Your arrows are sharpened, O mighty one; peoples will fall under you in the heart of the king's foes* (v. 5). The word order is puzzling,[13] but his meaning is, By using sharp arrows against the enemy, you will strike them directly and wound their hearts, whereas you will instruct the peoples oppressed by them in the adoration of you. Your sharp arrows, in fact, O mighty one, are in the heart of the king's foes; wounded by them, peoples will fall under you, offering you the due adoration. Having foretold in this way the events having to do with the Incarnation, the prophetic word afterwards teaches the nature of God the Word incarnate himself. *Your throne, O God, is forever and ever; the rod of your kingship a rod of equity* (v. 6). Since what was said before was beneath the divine dignity—*striking in your beauty compared with the sons of human beings, hence God blessed you forever*—he is right to teach in this way that he is God and eternal king, not having had a beginning and not due to have an end. This is what *forever* suggests; hence Symmachus also foretold his being eternal, "your throne, O God, eternal." He also teaches the righteousness of his kingship: *the rod of your kingship a rod of equity.*

(6) Then in turn he moves down to the human aspect: *You loved righteousness and hated lawlessness; hence God your God anointed you with the oil of gladness beyond your partners* (v. 7)—or according to Symmachus, "beyond your companions." His partners,

---

10. Matt 11.29.   11. John 14.6.
12. Matt 3.15.
13. Like Chrysostom before him, Theodoret can see the difficulty of the sequence in the verse in the LXX, without being in a position to compare it with the original; unlike his predecessor he does not openly contest it, but in the course of commentary abandons it in effect.

however, or companions, or brothers, in human terms, are the believers; thus the divine Apostle also says, "We have become partners in Christ, after all, provided we hold firm our first confidence to the end";[14] and again, "So that he would be the firstborn among many brethren."[15] Thus he was also anointed in the all-holy Spirit, not as God but as a human being: as God he was of one being with the Spirit,[16] whereas as a human being he receives the gifts of the Spirit like a kind of anointing. Thus he *loved righteousness and hated lawlessness:* this is a matter of intentional choice, not of natural power, whereas as God he has *a rod of equity* as *the rod of his kingship.*

(7) *Myrrh, resin, and cassia from your garments, from ivory buildings, from which they delighted you; daughters of kings in your honor* (vv. 8–9). For *ivory buildings,* on the other hand, Aquila and Symmachus said "from ivory temples." [1193] Now, he calls his body a *garment,* just as the divine Apostle in the Epistle to the Hebrews also calls it a veil: "Having confidence, brethren," he says, "in our entrance into the holy places by the blood of Jesus, which he inaugurated for us as a new and living way through his veil, that is, his flesh."[17] Now, he calls the Passion *myrrh,* it being provided particularly for corpses, the fragrance from the Passion *resin and cassia,* and *ivory buildings* (or, according to Symmachus and Aquila, "ivory temples") the beautiful and illustri-

---

14. Heb 3.14.
15. Rom 8.29.
16. Theodoret continues to distinguish the human from the divine in Jesus, rejecting any suggestion of Arian subordination of the Word by invocation here of the Nicene talisman *homoousios,* which passed into the Constantinopolitan creed of 381 and encountered Arian opposition long after. While some would see a Nestorian emphasis in this insistent distinction, Theodoret is rather resisting the One Nature doctrine that made him suspicious of some of Cyril's terminology and eventually led to the summoning of the Council of Chalcedon at his request. That suspicion emerges here in his dismissal of "natural (*physike*) power"; as Kelly remarks, "The union between the Word and the humanity He assumed was the result of his free decision and loving favor towards men, and for this reason among others Theodoret objected to Cyril's description of it as 'natural' or 'hypostatic'; these terms seemed to imply some kind of necessity." Yet the mild Theodoret manages to keep a polemical edge out of this *Commentary.*
17. Heb 10.19–20.

ous churches which princes and kings built throughout land and sea. He foretells, then, that while the Passion will affect the body, it will fill the whole world with fragrance, with the result that the peoples formerly caught up in error will erect to him temples beautifully adorned and resplendent with royal ornament. After making this prophecy of the churches under the guise of bridal chambers and inner rooms, he does well to forecast the bride's adornment, charm, and type, and to offer an exhortation suited to her: *At your right hand stands a queen, clad in garments of gold, of a rich variety.*

(8) Having given us a glimpse in this way both of the magnificence of the adornment and of the high degree of her honor, by calling her queen and placing her at the right hand of such a great king, he introduces and imparts appropriate advice: *Listen, daughter, take note and incline your ear: forget your people and your father's house* (v. 10). Now, this is in no way relevant to Jews, proud of the piety of their forebears, on whose account they also enjoyed divine providence to the highest degree: Jews he bids follow in the pious ways of their fathers and urges them not to forget their fathers, whereas the Church of the nations had fathers and ancestors that served idols.[18] This Church, consequently, he advises to leave in their memory nothing of their ancestral customs; and he gives the very name *daughter* to the holy Spirit in so far as she received spiritual rebirth. Now, he promises her the king's love for keeping the counsels: *The king will long for your beauty* (v. 11).

(9) Then he teaches us her nature and the king's dignity: *Because he is your Lord, and you will bow down to him, and the daughter of Tyre with gifts* (vv. 11–12). The [1196] three other translators, in fact, bade her do the bowing: while Aquila and Theodotion rendered it, "Bow down to him," Symmachus said, "He is your Lord: bow down to him." The Septuagint, on the other hand, teaches the queen that the bridegroom is Lord not only of her but also of those presuming to oppose her; and so the daughters

---

18. This strikes one as an unusually tolerant acceptance of religious pluralism, acknowledging the value and continuing validity of Jewish religious practices, despite previous statements by Theodoret of their displacement.

of Tyre will offer gifts and will openly demonstrate submission. Now, in these ways he implied complete impiety: it is Scripture's custom to indicate the whole from a part. Likewise elsewhere he foretells by mention of Lebanon the complete cessation of superstition: Lebanon, he is saying, with its lofty heights will tumble down.[19] In what follows, however, he mentions even greater things: *The wealthy members of his people will entreat your countenance.* Now, the Lord himself is in a proper sense the Church's countenance, being head of the body: "He gave him as head of all things for the Church,"[20] Scripture says. Thereafter, the priest order also acts as the Church's countenance in being invested with greater spiritual dignity. Now, it is possible to see this prophecy also achieving its fulfillment: people abounding in wealth and being famous for the highest honors pay respect to the Church's face, so to say.[21]

(10) Since, on the other hand, he said *the queen is clad in garments of gold,* whereas disreputable attire is a feature of the athletes of virtue and for that reason they continue to use such things, he comments on the splendor of her adornment: *All the glory of the king's daughter is within, in golden tassels, clad in many colors* (vv. 13–14). Within, he is saying, she has the comeliness of virtue and is resplendent with the manifold gifts of the Holy Spirit. The operations of the divine Spirit, you see, are varied; "there are varieties of gifts, but the same Spirit: to one is given through the Spirit the utterance of wisdom, to another the utterance of knowledge according to the same Spirit, to another faith by the same Spirit, to another prophecy, to another kinds of tongues."[22] Now, the Church is composed of numbers of spiritual people who have received different gifts; so it was right for

19. That was, in fact, the way Theodoret took Ps 29.5–6. The reference in the original to Tyre is obscure, the LXX no more lucid, and Theodoret is predictably grasping at straws.
20. Eph 1.22.
21. A brief comment by this bishop on the appropriateness of respect paid to the Church's hierarchy.
22. 1 Cor 12.4, 8–10. While the comparison of tassels to charismata is fair, Theodoret can hardly claim Pauline support for this allegorical interpretation of the psalm verse.

him to liken the variety of gifts to golden tassels: tassels differ from one another, and in turn are joined together by virtue of hanging down from the same robe.

(11) [1197] *Maidens will be brought to the king after her, her neighbors will be brought to you, they will be brought in joy and gladness, they will be led to the king's temple* (vv. 14–15). In other words, since not all possess the highest perfection, he calls some *bride* for being perfect in virtue, and others *maidens* for keeping unadulterated the faith they received. Yet he also calls the latter followers of the queen, entering the royal temple along with her. This distinction the Lord taught us in the sacred Gospels, saying, "In my Father's house there are many dwelling places."[23] Blessed Paul also agreed with this when he said, "Since death came through a human being, resurrection of the dead also came through a human being; just as all die in Adam, after all, so too in Christ all will be made alive, but each in their own order."[24]

(12) *In place of your fathers your sons were born; you will set them as princes over the whole earth* (v. 16). Let Jews say which of their sons were rulers of the whole world. They could not demonstrate it, however: they neither ruled nor rule, but submit to the worst servitude, whereas the divine apostles, with the patriarchs as their fathers, even after death rule land and sea like viceroys and generals appointed by Christ, the king of all. Those following them, whom you would not be wrong to call sons of the Church—I mean the triumphant martyrs—were appointed to manage the same government, and now have everyone as subjects, some choosing to be so willingly and with desire, others under pressure of fear.

(13) *I shall remember your name in every single generation. Hence peoples will confess to you for ages of ages* (v. 17). After prophesying this, the psalmist promises to celebrate the divine name in each generation through the God-fearing people of the time. This is the version also of the three translators, in fact: "I shall celebrate your name in each generation; hence people will sing to you

---

23. John 14.2.
24. 1 Cor 15.21–23.

forever unceasingly." In other words, using music composed by me, all peoples throughout the world, learning by this means of the salvation that has been procured for them and prophesied beforehand, will continue to celebrate you as the benefactor and provider of good things.[25]

25. Despite this psalm's being "the only example of a profane lyric in the Psalter," for Theodoret it has proved fertile ground for theological development unhindered by any historical association (he has even suppressed David's name, speaking rather of "the inspired word" or at least "the psalmist"). His enthusiasm even in dealing with the many obscure verses has led him, uncharacteristically, to develop an allegorical interpretation with only the slightest of Scriptural encouragement. Though hardly prolix, he has here moved somewhat from his habitual conciseness, which preserved him from the risk of allegory.

COMMENTARY ON PSALM 46

To the end. For the sons of Korah, on the secrets.[1] *[1200]*

N FORECASTING WHAT WOULD HAPPEN a long period of time after this, the prophetic word again put "To the end" in the psalm title, urging them to await the realization of the prophecy. Now, he forecasts the uprisings, which have occurred against the Church, the assistance later provided from heaven, and the peaceful way of life that now prevails. It should be realized, however, that some suspect the present psalm refers to Gog and Magog,[2] others to Ahaz and Pekah,[3] and others to Hezekiah and the Assyrian. But comment on individual verses shows with God's guidance that the meaning of the psalm fits none of those references.

(2) *God is our refuge and power, help in the tribulations coming upon us in great number* (v. 1). After the previous psalm prophesied about the Church's being composed from godless nations and becoming a queen, and showed her sons to be made princes of the whole earth, here it gives a glimpse of the disturbances that occurred in the beginning of the preaching, with uprisings developing and opposing the believers. Then it foreshadows in word how the ranks of the persecuted would be protected by hope in God and scorn the waves crashing around them: with the God of all as strong rampart, he is saying, we shall not notice the tribulations of all kinds.

(3) *Hence we shall not fear at the shaking of the earth and the shifting of mountains in the heart of the seas* (v. 2). Some such events the

---

1. Again the LXX has confused similar Hebrew forms, *'alamoth,* "maidens" (as part of a musical cue to the singers, as in the previous psalm) for *'alam,* "to conceal." Theodoret, of course, is none the wiser, but at least this time does not try to make theological capital out of the solecism.
2. Cf. Ezek 39.
3. Cf. Isa 7.

divine Isaiah also prophesied: "Every valley will be filled in, and every hill and mound brought low; crooked things will be straight, and rough things become smooth paths."[4] He gives the name "valley" to the hollow and lowly nations, deprived of elevation, which he prophesied would be filled with the word of instruction, whereas the demons' precincts he called "hills and mounds," and foretold that their manifold and deceptive operations would be brought down and disappear without trace. So here too the prophetic word shows those believing in the Savior crying aloud, We shall admit no wave of fear in our soul when we see the earth shaken and the demons driven out to the abyss, trying to disturb those affected by them. [1201] Now, the word predicts at the same time that the impiety which of old held power over the demons will be futile, like something thrown into the deep, after rivaling the loftiness of the mountains and having had for the most part power over the world.

(4) *Their waters roared and were disturbed, the mountains were shaken by his strength* (v. 3). Now, the story of the Acts also teaches us how the cities were filled with excitement and panic when the sacred apostles traveled around the world: in Ephesus Demetrius upset the whole city, and in Lystra and Derbe the same thing happened; likewise in Philippi, Thessalonica, Athens, and Corinth, as the spirits of deceit caused these waves of disturbance. Some people affected by them cried out against the sacred apostles, "Those who have arrived here are the ones who have been upsetting the world."[5] This is what blessed Habakkuk also prophesied, "You rode your horses into the sea to disturb the mighty waters";[6] he called the sacred apostles "horses" as being a divine chariot, the Lord mounted on them and scattering the many and varied teachings of impiety like

---

4. Isa 40.4.
5. Acts 17.6.
6. Hab 3.15. Theodoret is drawing the longbow here to trace a connection among the mention of waters in the psalm verse, the apostles' effect on error throughout Asia, and Habakkuk's isolated reference to horses in the sea (an item that must have remained fresh in his mind from his *Commentary on the Minor Prophets* preceding this work). Again an allegorical reading (of both psalm and Habakkuk) has only the flimsiest of Scriptural support as he lets himself go.

waves of some sort. Here too, therefore, the prophetic word says that the waters underwent disturbance and the mountains were affected by confusion as the preaching of the Gospel passed by. Now, here he gave the name *mountains* to the column of the demons on account of the weight of their arrogance and the height of their insolence, and the name *waters* to people's attitudes, moving easily this way and that like waters, and disturbed by the winds of error.

(5) *The currents of the river gladden the city of God* (v. 4). Now, he gave the name *river* here to the preaching of the Gospel, and *city* to the way of life of God-fearing people, watered by the streams of the river to the point of fruitfulness. The three translators said this more clearly: "The branches of the river gladden the city of God": just as the spring of paradise divided into four rivers,[7] so this river of God had countless [1204] courses beyond number running to all the tribes of human beings. One ran to the Indies, one to Spain; one took hold of Egypt, and one of Greece; others had the task of watering Judea, others Syria and Cilicia, and others were charged with the cultivation of other nations. Blessed Habakkuk, at any rate, prophesied this: "The earth will be split with rivers,"[8] he says,—that is, the land is divided up into river courses under the influence of the currents of the mighty river. He called its divisions *rivers*. *The Most High sanctified his tabernacle:* to what he called *city* he gave the name *tabernacle.* "I shall dwell with them and walk about among them," Scripture says, "I shall be their God, and they will be my people, says the Lord almighty."[9] They are the same people, therefore, that he says are irrigated and sanctified by the God of all.

(6) *God is in its midst, and he will not be moved* (v. 5). This the Lord also promised in the sacred Gospels: "Lo, I am with you all the days, to the end of the age"; and "Where two or three are assembled in my name, there am I in their midst."[10] *God will help him early in the morning.* The Lord of all, he is saying, will provide rapid and prompt help to his own city, *early in the morning* being his term for rapidity and promptness. *Nations were in uproar,*

---

7. Cf. Gen 2.10–14.   8. Hab 3.9.
9. Cf. 2 Cor 6.16.   10. Matt 28.20; 18.20.

kingdoms tottered, the Most High gave his shout, the earth moved (v. 6). When divine help appeared, he is saying, the enemy turned about, and the kingdoms once ill-disposed bent their neck and submitted to the saving yoke. By employing truth, the witness of events, and the manifold wonders like some voice, God gave human beings an insight into his lofty position and filled their souls with fear.

(7) *The Lord God of hosts is with us, the God of Jacob is our supporter* (v. 7): we therefore emerged stronger than our enemies, having the assistance of the heavenly hosts of the Lord, who rendered Jacob superior to his opponents when pursued by them, and freed him from the wiles of Esau and Laban. Now, it was not idly that the prophetic word made mention of Jacob; rather, it was because he was the first to predict the calling of the nations: "A prince will not depart from Judah," he said, "and a leader from his thighs, until he comes to whom it belongs, he, the expectation of nations."[11] [1205] Since here he is prophesying the transformation of the nations, he was right in saying that the God of Jacob who foretold it had achieved it. *Come now, see the works of the Lord, portents he performed on earth, bringing wars to an end as far as the ends of the earth. He will break the bow, smash weapons, and burn shields in fire. Be at rest and know that I am God. I shall be exalted among the nations, I shall be exalted on the earth* (vv. 8–10): seeing this power of mine, then, human beings, and perceiving the sudden transformation of things—the tranquillity born of awful turmoil, cessation of hostilities, the gift of peace—learn from the events themselves that I am God of all and creator of everything, revealing the height of my power no longer to the Jews alone but in fact to all nations as well.[12] Hearing these words, the apostolic chorus utters a song of triumph against the adversaries: *The Lord God of hosts is with us, the God of Jacob is our supporter* (v. 11).

(8) Consequently, let those who applied the psalm to God, or

11. Gen 49.10.
12. At this stage in his commentary (which perhaps Theodoret feels has departed from the brevity he promised in the preface), he is content with the briefest of paraphrase. He now feels the need to proceed to a review of the possible ways of interpreting the psalm and these verses in particular.

those who claimed it was relevant to Ahaz, explain how the verse, *bringing wars to an end as far as the ends of the earth,* bears on those stories. Actually, it was not in their time that he brought all wars to a close; instead, in the time of Gog and Magog Palestine alone enjoyed peace, whereas in the time of Ahaz it was not all Palestine but one tribe, Judah, Pekah son of Remaliah suffering an assault from the Assyrians.[13] In the time of Christ the Lord, on the other hand, the prophecy took effect: firstly, local dynasties and individual kingdoms fell, on account of which people had enjoyed not even the briefest peace, every city on a war footing in fear of the outburst of sudden incursions. In the time of Christ the Savior, by contrast, the kingdom of the Romans toppled the individual kingdoms and prepared the ears of all human beings for the preachers: it was without fear that they traveled throughout one kingdom and brought the saving message to humankind. The verse, *bringing wars to an end as far as the ends of the earth. He will break the bow, smash weapons, and burn shields in fire,* was thus fulfilled in a historical sense; but if you wanted to understand it in a more figurative way, you would have regard for the cessation of hostilities against the Church and the peace provided them from God, and you would perceive the realization of the prophecy.[14]

---

13. Cf. Isa 7–8. Under Pekah Israel fell to the Assyrians in 733 BC—though in fact Judah became subservient to them at that time, too.

14. Theodoret is returning to his original principles in this closing hermeneutical review. He can be satisfied he has not devoted the bulk of his commentary to ancient history. While admitting the validity of looking for a historical application, he has not allowed this to be made exclusively of the history of the Jews but has encouraged his readers to look for another level of meaning (not κατὰ ἀναγωγήν, as Chrysostom would say, but τροπικώτερον). And as an Antiochene he recognizes in this distinction of levels of meaning in a psalm text the process of θεωρία (his final verb here being θεωρέω).

COMMENTARY ON PSALM 47

To the end. For the sons of Korah. [1208]

THIS PSALM ALSO FORETELLS the salvation of all the nations, and predicts the victory over the enemies. *All the nations, clap your hands, shout to God with a cry of gladness. Because the Lord Most High is fearsome, great king over all the earth* (vv. 1–2). While the prophetic word predicted this, it gave a glimpse of the apostolic choir urging all the nations to hymn singing. Now, clapping is typical of victory, and shouting the sound of victors. So the meaning of this psalm concurs with the previous one: that one foretold the victory indicated after the turmoil and disturbances, and this one likewise recommends those who gained the victory to offer the hymn to the provider of the victory. He is revealed to you all, he says, as king most high and fearsome. While in ancient times this was known to Jews alone, in the present time it has been made clear also to the whole human race.

(2) *He subjected peoples to us, and nations under our feet. He chose for us his inheritance, the beauty of Jacob, which he loved* (vv. 3–4). For *peoples* Symmachus said "kings," and for *the beauty of Jacob* Aquila said "the splendor of Jacob." So the apostolic chorus says that it is right for us with clapping and dancing to offer the triumphal hymn to the God of all, who subjected kings to us and gave us control of all the nations, and in addition to that entrusts the beauty and excellence of Jacob to us—not all the Jewish people, who are named for Jacob, in fact, but *the beauty of Jacob*, the excellence and the elite of Jacob, those adorned with faith, who accepted the message without delay, who submitted to the sweet yoke of the Savior. These, you see, he both *chose* and *loved*, and to them he entrusted the apostolic governance. Now, it is possible to discern with our eyes the realization of the prophecy: you

can see the believers from all the nations, prostrate before the tombs of the apostles, venerating with deep longing the small amount of dust, to the extent of gazing and at the same time singing the verse, *He subjected peoples to us, and nations under our feet.*[1]

(3) *God went up with a shout, the Lord with a sound of a trumpet* (v. 5). Now, the Lord who achieved all this, he is saying, first became human and overthrew the tyranny of the avenging demon, then went up to heaven with the heavenly hosts and angelic choirs preceding him, and those on earth [1209] crying out, "This Jesus who has been taken up from you will come in the same way as you have seen him going to heaven,"[2] while those on high urged, "Lift up your gates, O rulers, and be lifted up, eternal gates, and the king of glory will come in."[3] He called those cries *a shout* and *a sound of trumpets,* as though traveling throughout the whole earth.

(4) *Sing to our God, sing; sing to our king, sing. Because God is king of all the earth, sing with understanding. God reigned over the nations, God sits on his holy throne* (vv. 7–8): so reverence the universal king with hymns and spiritual dancing; he showed his peculiar kingship to all people, and persuaded all the nations that he is God and Lord, seated on the royal seats. Now, the verse, *God sits on his holy throne,* is consistent with the apostolic saying, "He sat down at the right hand of the Majesty on high, having become as far superior to the angels as the name he has inherited is more excellent than theirs."[4] The phrase, *sing with understanding,* was also well put, teaching us to offer hymn singing not only

---

1. We have noted that, unlike some modern commentators, Theodoret is generally not interested in the *Sitz im Leben* of the psalms or their cultic dimension even in Christian terms. Here he makes a slight exception in envisaging the psalm being sung by pilgrims to the tombs of the apostles (in Rome perhaps) and thus acquiring a fuller significance. A modern commentator like Weiser prefers to concentrate on this cultic dimension of the psalm, seeing it employed at the New Year Festival in late Judaism, when "history and eschatology become in the cultic ceremony a present reality of actual significance in which the festival congregation shares." This is not generally the perspective of Bishop Theodoret.
2. Acts 1.11.   3. Ps 24.7.
4. Heb 1.4.

with the tongue but also to raise our mind to a grasp of what it said.[5]

(5) *Rulers of peoples are gathered with the God of Abraham, because the mighty ones of God are raised to great heights over the earth* (v. 9). The promises to the patriarch Abraham, he is saying, took effect. Now, the Lord of all promised to bless all the nations in his progeny. Accordingly, both these nations and their rulers abandoned their ancestral gods and are assembled with the God of Abraham, and they call this God theirs. Now, the divine apostles were ministers of these peoples' calling, confirming the elevation of the theology with their marvels; while the Septuagint called them *mighty ones,* Aquila in fact called them "shields" instead, and Theodotion and Symmachus, "protectors." In these ways indication is given not only of their independence and invincibility but also of their protection of others: being like shields and champions of the believers, they did not allow the battle line to be broken with the onset of troubles; instead, they put the enemy to flight and urged those sharing in the faith to sing a victory song in the words, *All nations, clap hands; shout to God with a cry of gladness. Because the Lord Most High is fearsome, great king over all the earth.*

---

5. As in the case of some of the psalm titles, here the LXX does not recognize reference in *maskil* to a psalm type, but proceeds to find a point in the word's root.

COMMENTARY ON PSALM 48

A psalm for singing. For the sons of Korah.
On the second day of the week. [1 2 1 2]

HIS PSALM FORETELLS the same victory in similar fashion, and the strength of God's city.[1] *Great is the Lord, and much to be praised in the city of our God, on his holy mountain* (v. 1). We have said previously that often the divine Scripture gives the name *city* not to the building but to the way of life. Accordingly, here too he says the Lord of all was shown to be great through the things done by him in connection with his city, which the elevation of the teachings rendered illustrious as though located on a lofty and mighty hill. The Lord says, after all, "A city located on a hill cannot be hidden."[2]

(2) *Rooting it firmly in gladness of all the earth.* He built it both properly and solidly, he is saying, in joy of all the earth: he erected it, the divine Apostle says, on the foundation of the apostles and prophets, with Christ Jesus as its cornerstone.[3] The Lord himself said to blessed Peter, "And on this rock I shall build my Church, and the gates of Hades will not prevail against it."[4] So

---

1. The commentator is shrewd enough not to remark on the title: the opening phrase could hardly be other than a musical direction—an approach he has not entertained previously—and the final one (unsupported by the Hebrew, if that were a factor for him) obscure. "Where ignorance is bliss, . . ."
2. Matt 5.14. Is Theodoret being perverse in immediately dismissing the obvious sense of the verse as referring to Mount Sion, such that modern commentators remark of the psalm, "a hymn celebrating the beauty and impregnability of Zion" (Dahood)? In doing so, he has to drop David from sight, and speak again of "the prophetic word."
3. Eph 2.20.
4. Matt 16.18. From various points of view this half of the verse is "most contested" (Dahood), as Chrysostom admitted in commenting on it, citing (without benefit) original and alternatives to his LXX, whereas modern commentators tend to seek help from linguistic data. On the same reason-

rooting it means "founding it firmly" so that it would abide unshaken and unmoved. *Mountains of Sion, sides of the north, the city of the great king.* Actually, he also surrounded it with mountains so that it would escape harm from the north: "From the north troubles will be enkindled upon all the earth,"[5] Scripture says, and again, "I shall chase the north away from you."[6] The divine Apostle took the name Sion of the spiritual city: "You have come to Mount Sion," he says, "to the city of the living God, heavenly Jerusalem."[7] Now, you would be right in saying the mountains driving off the north and preserving the city intact are apostles and prophets and their manifold teachings, and in addition to them the angels set over the believers: "An angel of the Lord will encamp around those who fear him, and will rescue them,"[8] Scripture says.

(3) *God is known in its buildings whenever he supports it* (v. 3). On the one hand, there is one Church throughout all land and sea; hence [1213] we say in prayer, For the holy, single, universal, and apostolic Church,[9] from one end of the world to the other. On the other hand, it is also divided into cities, towns, and villages, which the inspired word called *buildings*. As each city is composed of different houses, and yet is called one city, so there are countless churches that defy numbering, both on islands and on continents, but all constitute one by being united in the common harmony of the true teachings. In these the God of all became apparent, he said, by offering his peculiar assistance: *God is known in its buildings whenever he supports it.*

(4) Then he forecasts the future rebellions and the transfor-

---

ing as he followed in eschewing debate on the title, Theodoret invokes no such evidence in simply adhering to his ecclesiological interpretation.

5. Cf. Jer 1.14.
6. Joel 2.20.
7. Heb 12.22. It is not quite this anagogical interpretation that Theodoret adopts for the psalm as a whole.
8. Ps 34.8.
9. Theodoret here invokes the credal article of the Constantinopolitan symbol of 381, accentuating the unity and diversity of the Church founded on right doctrine, presuming it is familiar to his readers. As a bishop, he adverts to doctrinal discord only in a minor key, and refrains from entering into polemic.

mation of the enemy: *Because, lo, the kings of the earth were assembled, they came together. On seeing it, they were amazed* (vv. 4–5): they ran in company as if about to wage war, but on perceiving the city under attack to be impregnable, they were aghast. *They were panic-stricken, staggered,* he says; *trembling took hold of them, pains there as of a woman in labor. With a violent wind you will smash ships of Tarshish* (vv. 5–7). On seeing the unbroken foundations of the Church and grasping of the verity of the prophecy, he is saying, fear and dread took hold of them, like people running the risk of the sea's swell, tossed by storms, and expecting annihilation.[10] As a result of this they put a stop to warring and attacking, and themselves proclaim the might of what they attacked, crying aloud, *As we have heard, so we have seen, in the city of the Lord of hosts, in the city of our God* (v. 8): unwilling to admit the prophecies about it, we recognized their truth from the events themselves. *God established it forever.* It is his word, after all: "On this rock I shall build my Church, and the gates of Hades shall not prevail against it."[11]

(5) Thus the prophetic word, having shown the transformation of the enemy, now foretells what kind of words those who have attained salvation use in singing of their benefactor. *We suspected, O God, your mercy in the midst of your people* (v. 9). We had an expectation, he is saying, of this assistance of yours, O Lord, knowing the certainty of your promises; you said, after all, [1216] "I am with you all days, to the end of the age."[12] *As is your name, O God, so is your praise, to the ends of the earth* (v. 10). The false gods do not have the power corresponding to their name: they are not what they are said to be. But with your name, Lord, are in keeping the works that proclaim the truth of the claim. Hence it is right that the hymn be offered to you in all the world: as you are God of all, so is a hymn raised to you by all.

---

10. The commentator's determination to give this psalm an ecclesiological interpretation is not going to be halted by going into a detail like the significance of the ships of Tarshish. Precision, evidently, is not such a fetish for this Antiochene as for Chrysostom (whose wrestling with this item, admittedly, proved fruitless).
11. Matt 16.18.
12. Matt 28.20.

Your right hand is filled with righteousness: by giving a right verdict, you scattered the enemies who rose against us. *Let Mount Sion be glad, and the daughters of Judah rejoice because of your judgments, Lord* (v. 11). He called *Mount Sion* those to whom the heights of theology were entrusted, and *daughters of Judah* the churches throughout the world, since they were founded by the apostles, who took their origin from the Jews. Now, he urges both preachers and listeners to rejoice and be glad on account of God's just judgments, which he adopted in effecting the salvation of the world.

(6) *Go around Sion, encircle it, narrate in its towers, set your hearts on its might, take its buildings one by one*[13] (vv. 12–13). Again he calls the godly form of government *Sion,* that is, the Church throughout the world, and *its towers* those devoted to virtue and imitating on earth the way of life of the angels, encircling and protecting it like towers. *Buildings* likewise, as we have said before, the churches divided among the cities, towns, and villages: he speaks of them as one and many. So the inspired word, the grace of the all-holy Spirit,[14] urges those to whom the saving message was entrusted to go around and move about, both to strengthen the towers with teaching and confirm its other force, and in addition to this to apportion care of the churches, as we have already remarked on the forty-fifth psalm.[15] He urges it here, too: *take its buildings one by one,* so that one may care for this church and another for that, [1217] and be in charge of each by way of cultivating and exercising due care.

(7) He bids this be done not once or twice but in each generation; hence he added, *So that you may tell the next generation that this is our God forever, and ever and ever. He will shepherd us forever* (vv. 13–14): each generation has to pass on to the next what we have received from the former so that the saving message may

---

13. The alternative versions make a better fist of this verse, but Theodoret is not to be distracted from his interpretation.

14. Though we have noted there are other reasons why the name of David is suppressed in this particular commentary, the alternative statements of authorship certainly confirm Theodoret's conviction of biblical inspiration.

15. Perhaps Theodoret has in mind his remarks on Ps 45.8 (the forty-fourth in his LXX text).

pass to all generations, and all people know that he is our God and Lord, good shepherd, everlasting. Since he said, *take its buildings one by one*, and entrusted to them the task of shepherding, of necessity he taught that there is one good shepherd, who laid down his life for the sheep,[16] shepherding forever, and shepherding not only the sheep but also those called pastors of the sheep.

16. John 10.11.

COMMENTARY ON PSALM 49

To the end. A psalm for the sons of Korah.

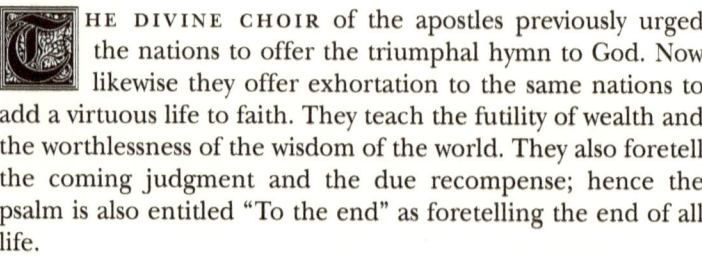HE DIVINE CHOIR of the apostles previously urged the nations to offer the triumphal hymn to God. Now likewise they offer exhortation to the same nations to add a virtuous life to faith. They teach the futility of wealth and the worthlessness of the wisdom of the world. They also foretell the coming judgment and the due recompense; hence the psalm is also entitled "To the end" as foretelling the end of all life.

(2) *Hear this, all nations, give ear, all inhabitants of the world* (v. 1). It is clear to practically everybody that the prophets offered teaching to Jews only, but here the inspired word urges the whole world to give attention. Now, this is typical of the apostolic grace: to them Christ the Lord entrusted the salvation of all the nations. "Go," he said, "make disciples of all the nations."[1] So it is clear that the words are offered by them not to Jews alone, nor to these nations or those, but to the whole human race.

(3) *Both earthborn people and human beings* (v. 2). Some called Adam and Eve *earthborn people* for being formed from earth and not coming from intercourse. But this idea is wide of the truth: he is offering exhortation not to those already dead but to those still living. [1220] He is therefore suggesting different forms of life: some people live in cities, others in towns and villages, devoting themselves to farming; some people are more refined,

---

1. Matt 28.18. Despite the content of most of the psalm, Theodoret is determined to give it a New Testament interpretation like the previous one; so David's name is not mentioned. The justification this time is the scope of the directives given: whereas inspired authors of the Old Testament, *prophetai,* had a limited public, the inspired (*prophetikos*) word in this case is universal in scope, like NT statements.

others more rustic; some live at a more intellectual level, others more at the level of wild beasts, dwelling in wildernesses; some are "wagon dwellers," others use tents for dwellings. I think the latter are called *earthborn people* for having no contact with a more intellectual life, the meaning being, All people, listen to my words, city dwellers and country people, more refined and more rustic, all in common and also individuals. This is the way Symmachus translated it, in fact: for *earthborn people and human beings* he said "humanity and as well sons of each man"—that is, Let nature in general hear my words, and each one reap the benefit for themselves. *Rich and poor alike:* let those abounding in wealth and those caught up in poverty accept the exhortation alike, the word of instruction respecting no difference between wealth and poverty.

(4) *My mouth will speak wisdom, and the pondering of my heart understanding. I shall incline my ear to a parable, I shall solve my riddle with a harp* (vv. 3–4). The words put forward by me are full of wisdom, he is saying, but I learned them by submitting my hearing to the Lord's words hidden in the depths. And what I learned through hearing I put forward through the organ of the tongue. Now, he means to say, I utter nothing of my own; rather, I am an instrument of divine grace.[2] He calls puzzling words *parables:* the Lord spoke to the crowds in the manner of parables, and offered the apostles interpretations of them privately. Hence the previous psalms also were uttered in their person. So the apostolic choir transmitted in word of mouth the wisdom of God—Christ, in other words, Christ being wisdom and power of God[3]—saying, *my mouth will speak wisdom,* since they preached, each by word of mouth, to the whole human race by giving a rational explanation of Christ. Now, the thoughts of their mind pondered nothing other than understandings. Thus their mind was concentrated on understanding so as to understand all our Savior's parables proposed in the Gospels, even before his interpretation of them. At any rate, immediately after the uttering of the

2. This verse, like Ps 45.1, provokes in Theodoret a comment on the divine inspiration of the biblical author; and, as there, his accent falls on the gratuity of that charism, not on the contribution of the human author.
3. 1 Cor 1.24.

parables the Savior questioned them in the words, "Do you understand all this?" and they replied to him, "Yes."[4] So their heart *pondered understandings.* Then, in addition, *I shall solve* [1221] *my riddle with a harp:* I whet my reasoning, he is saying, for understanding the saving parables and am able to follow the sense conveyed by them. But for those unable to do this on account of immaturity, I shall solve what is obscure and clarify the riddles and the parables; I shall do this with my harp, that is, with my bodily instrument, which, like a harp, is given to the soul dwelling within it as an instrument of the soul for hymns to be played on it to God and for stirring each sense, moving limbs and parts of the body with understanding.[5]

(5) Having covered this by way of introduction, he now begins the exhortation. *Why shall I fear on an evil day? The iniquity of my heel will encircle me* (v. 5): I fear and dread the day of retribution, on which the righteous Judge will repay everyone according to their works.[6] Now, aware of this, keep such fear before your eyes in your own case: if I am able to say, *My mouth will speak wisdom, and the pondering of my heart understanding, I shall incline my ear to a parable,* and despite that be in fear and trembling, why not you? But if you were to inquire why I am afraid, listen closely: it is an evil day, about which countless declamations are made in the inspired Scriptures. The cause of my fear is the life of lawlessness, through which I strayed from the straight and narrow: some called that way of life *heel,* whereas in my view the word refers to error, on the analogy of runners, as I have mentioned previously, who often trip up their opponents with their heel. Esau in his disappointment also taught us this in the words, "He was rightly called Jacob: this is the second time he has supplanted me; he took away my birthright, and now he has taken away my blessing."[7] Now, he called the day of judgment *an evil day* in

---

4. Matt 13.51.
5. If Theodoret seems to be unusually expansive in his commentary on these verses, it is because editor Schulze is incorporating into his text at this point excerpts from the longer form of it that occurs in the Palestinian catena. See Introduction, section 2.
6. 2 Tim 4.8.
7. Gen 27.36, where the word for "supplant" is related to "heel."

keeping with our customary way: people generally call a day evil when they accidentally encounter some troubles on it. So he is justified in using this name of it as the day for examining each one's wickedness and for inflicting punishment on the ungodly through the wrath in store for them. Hence even in saying this I tremble: *the iniquity of my heel will encircle me* on that evil day; *iniquity of my heel* refers to the path on which we pass the present life, deviation or rather [1224] error. Likewise the divine Apostle also calls it the day of judgment: "But by your hard and impenitent heart you are storing up wrath for yourself on the day of wrath, of revelation, and of right judgment of God, who will repay everyone according to their works."[8]

(6) *Those who trust in their power and boast of the abundance of their wealth* (v. 6): while I am in fear and trembling at the expected day, you in your affluence pay no heed to it, being instead puffed up with grandeur of your possessions and trusting in transient things as though permanent. *If a brother is not redeemed, will anyone be redeemed? He will not pay God a ransom for himself, or the price of redemption of his own soul* (vv. 7–8). Now, you need to understand that virtue and godliness neither of forebears or brothers is of benefit to those lacking them, nor is it possible after departure from here to buy salvation with money. It is in the present life, you see, as a sage says, "a man's own wealth is his ransom."[9]

(7) After offering this advice to those using wealth to evil ends, he shifts his attention to those who practice virtue: *He labored forever, and will live to the end. He will not see ruin when he witnesses the death of wise people* (vv. 9–10). In other words, the one who undergoes effort for godliness and righteousness and is the victim of hardship for eternal goods will have eternal life as the fruit of hardship, and will not share with the wise of this world, whom the apostolic word names fools, everlasting ruin and retribution forever. *Fool and dolt will perish together.* These people, he is saying, though called wise, find no benefit in their wisdom

8. Rom 2.5–6.
9. Prov 13.8. The brevity of the shorter form of the *Commentary* is conspicuous by contrast with the more expansive form—and thought the more authentic.

and will pay the same price of destruction as the unlearned. Symmachus, in fact, translated it this way: "Unwise and unlearned will perish together": he calls the one called wise "unwise" for not being willing to understand what should be understood, and the one uninitiated into wisdom "unlearned" for being nevertheless addicted to evil.

(8) *They will leave behind their wealth to strangers. Their graves are their homes forever, their dwelling places from generation to generation* (v. 11): bereft not only of wisdom but also of influence and all affluence, they will meet [1225] their end, dispatched from their lavish homes to graves, and forced to occupy them forever. *They bestowed their names on their lands.* They actually named their possessions after themselves, he is saying: This is such a person's house, this is such a person's land, this is such a person's houseslave; but along with their influence goes a change also in the names bestowed. Just as people become owners of what was left behind by others, so too will there be a change in the names: names will in turn be bestowed in place of the former ones. Now, in these ways the lesson we learn is not to trust in present realities, but to be concerned with the future.

(9) *Though enjoying a state of honor, man did not understand; he was comparable with brute beasts and likened to them* (v. 12). Now, he says the cause of this folly is our unwillingness to understand our own dignity and the worthiness given us by God, and instead adopting a brutish and ferocious life. *This way of theirs is a scandal for them* (v. 13). Now, they fell into irrationality, exhibiting the worst behavior from the beginning, and inclining to evil practices, calling the practices *way. And afterwards they will take delight in their mouth:* they will adopt a penitential outlook after departing from here, gaining no advantage from it then.

(10) *Like sheep they were placed in Hades; death will shepherd them* (v. 14). Symmachus translated this more clearly: "They arranged themselves like sheep of Hades, death will tend them": they acquired punishments for themselves, and preferred death to life. *The upright will dominate them in the morning, and their help will deteriorate in Hades, they were rejected from their glory:* Those who at present are wronged and despised by them will have power over them before long; bereft of all their former prosperity

these will be consigned to death. Now, the parable of the Lord bears on their situation in showing Lazarus in the bosom of Abraham while the arrogant rich man is severely punished and becomes the poor man's [1228] suppliant.[10] In thus describing the end of those people, he offers supplication to God. The one who uses such words begs not to suffer the same end as theirs, speaking this way, *But God will ransom my soul from the hand of Hades when he receives me* (v. 15).

(11) After this he provides explanation and advice for those condemned to a life of poverty and worn out through the arrogance of the rich. *Do not be afraid when one becomes rich, or when the glory of his house is magnified. Because when he dies he will not take it all, nor will his glory go down with him* (vv. 16–17). Do not consider present prosperity any great thing, he is saying: wealth that catches all eyes is not lasting; those who raise their eyebrows and are puffed up at it will shortly after leave it all behind and be dispatched to death. *Because his soul will be blessed in his lifetime* (v. 18). Some people declare the one with abundant wealth blessed while alive, he is saying, but once dead they call him thrice-miserable. *He will bless you when you do them favors.* Symmachus said this more clearly: "He will praise you if you do the right thing by them":[11] this is true praise, being famous and celebrated not only when alive but also after death. Now, the one who manages his wealth for his own benefit is deserving of such praises: beneficence to others redounds to the benefit of the benefactor.

(12) *He will go to his ancestors' generation, he will not see light forever* (v. 19). In place of *he will go* the three translators said "you will go": you will see him to whom I said, *Do not be afraid when he becomes rich,* meeting with the same death as their ancestors, and deprived of light not only here but also in eternity. *Though enjoying a state of honor, man did not understand; he was comparable to brute beasts, and likened to them* (v. 20). Now, the cause of all this is the brutish life which most people chose, repudiating the digni-

---

10. Cf. Luke 16.19–31.
11. Again Symmachus comes in for commendation, though his version seems no different from the LXX.

ty given by God: though said to be rational, they loved irrationality.[12]

12. Despite Theodoret's opening insistence on the role of the "apostolic choir" in the psalm, the content for most of its length vindicates its character as simple Wisdom material, as does his commentary. It has not elicited from him the lengthy and savage attack on the lavish expenditure on funeral monuments by wealthy contemporaries that we meet in the preacher Chrysostom's commentary on the psalm.

COMMENTARY ON PSALM 50

A psalm of Asaph.

HE WAS CONDUCTOR of another band of singers, [1129] as the story of the Chronicles informed us.[1] While the sons of Korah, appointed leaders of a different band, were entrusted with singing the contents of the forty-first psalm, they also have other psalms bearing a title of theirs, which we shall comment on should God permit. Now, the present psalm, attributed to Asaph, is in keeping with the previous psalm: it also forecasts the judgment to come and the manifestation of our God and Savior. But it forecasts as well the New Testament, showing worship according to the Law to be unacceptable to God: *The Lord God of gods spoke and summoned the earth from the rising of the sun to its setting* (v. 1). The psalm before this summoned all people to instruction, and in similar fashion this one summons all the ends of the earth: the phrase *from the rising of the sun to its setting* indicates this. The three translators, on the other hand, rendered *God of gods* differently: "Mighty God in speaking summoned the earth," whereas the Septuagint gives the name *gods* to those on whom the task of ruling fell and were entrusted with judging, something proper to God alone. The eighty-first psalm, itself bearing a title for Asaph, teaches us this: after saying, "God took his place in the assembly of gods, in their midst he passes judgment on gods," it added, "How long do you give unjust judgments, and respect the mien of sinners? Give judgment in favor of orphan and needy, render justice to

---

1. Cf. 1 Chron 25.1. Theodoret, though acknowledging Asaph's role in liturgical music, can still speak of the psalm being "attributed to Asaph," as he did in the preface. Chrysostom, too, was irked by this title, it seems, as he ignored it, perhaps for the same reason of its calling Davidic authorship into question; and in fact his extant *Commentary* does not include Psalms 73–83 that bear a similar title.

the lowly and poor."[2] Now, this belongs to priests and others to whom judgment is entrusted; even the Law is clear on this: "You shall not revile gods, and shall not speak evil of a leader of your people." It was right for those who were made in the divine image, and kept the image unsullied, to be called "gods."[3] It is their God, in fact, who assembles the whole world to judgment.

(2) *Out of Sion the comeliness of his charm* (v. 2). Now, this person, who showed his peculiar comeliness and charm in Sion and underwent the saving Passion, is the one who in the psalms commented on was called charming in his beauty beyond all human beings.[4] *God will come in an obvious manner, our God, and he will not keep silence* (v. 3). In other words, do not think the second coming will be like his first: at that time he concealed his characteristic magnificence in lowliness and poverty, [1232] whereas in this case he will reveal plainly to everyone his lordship and kingship, no longer employing long-suffering but judging justly—as he said, *he will not keep silence. A fire will burn in his presence, with a severe storm around him.* Blessed Daniel had a vision of this: "A river of fire," he says, "was flowing in front of him, his throne a fiery flame, its wheels flaming fire."[5]

(3) *He calls to heaven above and to the earth to judge his people* (v. 4). After the law-making, he bade blessed Moses assemble the people and adjure heaven and earth to give witness, as did also his song's opening, "Give heed, O heaven, and I shall speak, and let earth hear words from my mouth."[6] He calls them to witness, however, not as animate things but as inclusive of the other created things, which listen to the extent of being fearful. That was the way blessed Abraham used the seven ewe lambs as witness to his words, "This is my well." That was the way Jacob and Laban called the mound "a mound of witness."[7] *Assemble for him his holy ones, who made covenant with him by sacrifice. The heavens will announce his righteousness, because God is judge* (vv. 5–6). While by his previous words he showed his judgment to be fearsome, by these and what follows he teaches the imperfection of worship

---

2. Ps 82.1–3.
4. Cf. Ps 45.2.
6. Deut 32.1.

3. Exod 22.28.
5. Cf. Dan 7.9–10.
7. Gen 21.30, 31.48.

according to the Law and the fact that none of the victims offered were acceptable to God. He gives the name *holy ones* to Moses, Aaron, Eleazar, Phinehas,[8] and all those after them who served as priests according to the Law. Now, his purpose in bidding them be assembled was not to exact penalties, as if their views were out of keeping; the Law was his, after all, and each of those cited obeyed it in offering sacrifice. Rather, it was to show his purpose even in present realities by bringing to an end teaching appropriate to infants and proposing mature experiences. Once this happens, he is saying, the heavens will marvel at the justice of the verdict; by *the heavens* he implied heavenly powers.

(4) *Listen, my people, and I shall speak to you* (v. 7). To show which people he is addressing, he added, *Israel, and I shall testify against you.* Then he shows his own lordship: *I am God, your God, the one who freed you from slavery in Egypt,* [1233] *who gave the way through the sea, who fed you in the wilderness, who gave you that Law:* do not think I am another sort of lawgiver when you see the difference in the laws. *It is not on the score of your sacrifices that I shall censure you; your holocausts are ever before me* (v. 8). I do not accuse you of neglect of sacrifices, he is saying: you offer them continually; rather, I urge you not to confine righteousness to them. *I shall not accept young bulls from your house, or goats from your flocks, because all the wild beasts of the countryside are mine, cattle on mountains, and oxen. I know all the birds in the sky, and the charm of the countryside is from me* (vv. 9–11). I am creator and lord of everything, he is saying, both land animals and birds of the air. So do not think of meeting my needs: I gave existence to these things, and I order the fruits to be produced from earth. By *charm of the countryside*, in fact, he means the fruits of all kinds from the earth: since they were making offerings of oxen, goats, and sheep from the land animals, pigeons and doves from the winged creatures, flour, wine, and oil from the produce, and the most fragrant of odors, of necessity he made mention of them all so as to bring to an end all this kind of worship.

8. The Phinehas he has in mind emerges from Num 24.33.

(5) Then, feigning ignorance, *If I were hungry, I would not tell you: the world is mine, and all its fullness* (v. 12). If I were in need of food, he is saying, I would not need supplies from you: I am at once maker and lord of all creation. Then he teaches us his own nature's immunity from passion: *Surely I do not eat the flesh of bulls, or drink goats' blood?* (v. 13). Having thus shown their stupidity and taught it was on account of their infantile thinking that he required them of old to offer those sacrifices, he unfolds the New Testament ahead of time, and requires the sacrifice pleasing to him. *Sacrifice to God a sacrifice of praise, and pay your vows to the Most High. Call upon me in the day of your tribulation, and I shall rescue you and glorify you* (vv. 14–15). At the appropriate time he also revealed the venerable number of the holy Trinity, and bound them in the New Testament; it is with it, of course, that we also receive knowledge of the holy Trinity. His purpose, however, in distinguishing the items was not for the sake of distinguishing the operations of the indivisible and holy Trinity, but to teach the number in inspired manner to those also who would come later. He therefore says, *Sacrifice to God a sacrifice of praise, and pay your vows to the Most High.* [1236] *Call upon me in the day of your tribulation.* Now, from this we were given an understanding of three persons: it is not simply as God, or simply Most High, or recipient of a sacrifice of praise that he grants the requests: each property, God and Most High, is provider of good things. He calls hymns befitting the righteous *a sacrifice of praise,* and the promises *vows;* this is the way he speaks in the twenty-first psalm, "I shall pay my vows in the presence of those who fear him."[9]

(6) Now, after saying, *It is not on the score of your sacrifices that I shall censure you,* he now teaches the basis on which they were censured. *But to the wicked God said, Why do you outline my right*

9. Ps 22.25. As suggested in note 1, Theodoret is noncommittal about the author of this psalm, but in any case is unwilling to see him giving anything but a vague if inspired foreshadowing of Trinitarian doctrine. He takes occasion to give a brief summary of dogma on divine personal properties, the unity of divine operation, and appropriation. He briefly, if not clearly, attempts such precision on "a sacrifice of praise" at the close of the commentary.

judgments and take up my covenant in your mouth? You hated discipline and cast my words behind you (vv. 16–17). In other words, Since there are some people who blame others for their failings and remind them of the divine laws, while themselves failing to practice what they preach, it was right for him to upbraid such people in the words, Why on earth do you adopt a haughty attitude to my right judgments, and discuss the Law this way and that without drawing any benefit from it, but even treating my words with disdain? And he goes on to list the kinds of outrage. *If you saw a thief, you consorted with him, and you threw in your lot with adulterers. Your mouth was awash with wickedness, and your tongue wrapped itself around deceptions. You sat down to malign your brother, and put a stumbling block in the way of your mother's son* (vv. 18–20). Many and varied are the crimes committed by you, he is saying, speaking in the fashion of the Apostle, "Though forbidding adultery, you commit adultery,"[10] and you become accomplice and sharer with those committing such crimes. Emptying your mouth of truth, you fill it with falsehoods and wickedness; deceit gives an edge to your tongue. Hence you even despise your kin, trample down the laws of nature, secretly hatch plots against your brethren, persist in engaging in calumny, and put schemes into operation.

(7) After thus giving an outline of their lawlessness, he both teaches the long-suffering he exhibits and forecasts the punishment he will inflict. *These things you did, and I kept silence; you suspected I would be like you where iniquity is concerned* (v. 21): I saw these crimes committed by you, I practiced long-suffering, I waited for your repentance. But you took even my long-suffering as an excuse for impiety, guessing [1237] that I was pleased with your lawlessness and would not inflict punishment. Hence *I shall censure you, and bring you face to face with your sins:* since you were not cured by the mild remedy of long-suffering, I shall prepare more painful ones for you, and apply burning by censure. Now, this is in keeping with those words of the Apostle, "Do you not realize that the goodness of God leads you in the direction of repentance, but by your obduracy and unrepentant heart you store up for yourself wrath on the day of wrath, revelation, and

---

10. Rom 2.22.

just judgment of God, who will repay everyone according to their works."[11]

(8) Having thus threatened punishment, in his love he once more brings exhortation to bear. *Understand this, you who forget God, lest he ever snatch you away instead of being the one to rescue you* (v. 22). Give careful thought, he is saying, to each of my words; and you who suffer forgetfulness of God—forgetfulness of God being a source of sin—cure your wounds with the remedies of repentance before you are carried off by death, which like a lion falls upon human beings, no one capable of checking its fierce assault. Then he takes up the new lawgiving, and with it he embellishes the psalm's conclusion: *A sacrifice of praise will glorify me; that is the path by which I shall show him my salvation* (v. 23). Symmachus, on the other hand, translated this more clearly, "The one offering sacrifice for the sake of praise will glorify me, and I shall show God's salvation to the one traveling by the straight and narrow": it is necessary not only to sing to God and offer sacrifices of praise to him, but also to travel by the straight and narrow and regulate one's own life. This is the way, after all, to attain salvation from God. According to the Septuagint, by contrast, he is saying, I am pleased with the sacrifice of praise, and I consider this glory fitting, and by its means I shall give to the one offering it a glimpse of my way, which has as its end the salvation from God.[12] Now, we should take note that here, too, he made mention of two persons: *A sacrifice will praise me;* and having in this way revealed his own person, he added, *that is the path by which I shall show him my salvation.* In other words, it was necessary for the perfect instruction in the knowledge of God to be associated with the New Testament, which teaches us perfection.[13]

11. Rom 2.4–6.
12. In this case Symmachus is not given automatic preference over the Septuagint, but an attempt is made to tease out each version.
13. Is Theodoret here, in distinguishing two *prosopa*, repeating the Trinitarian precision he offered in connection with vv. 14–15? At the opening of commentary he saw the psalm dealing with "the manifestation of our God and Savior," and perhaps sees a reference to him here—unlike modern commentators, who see reference instead to "the promise of salvation, which the God-fearing members of the cult community may hope for from God" (Weiser).

COMMENTARY ON PSALM 51

*To the end. A psalm of David. [1240]
On the prophet Nathan's going in to him after he
had gone in to Bathsheba, the wife of Uriah.*

HE PSALM'S TITLE CLEARLY informs us of the occasion, and the psalm's verses suffice to teach us the depth of thinking. It is necessary to realize, however, that the psalm also contains prophecy of future events; hence it is also entitled "To the end," the word suggesting that the prophecy will have a fulfillment. But let no one be in any doubt as to whether the mighty David was accorded a prophetic grace at the time of repentance: this can be learned also in the other psalms in which he made his confession. In the sixth psalm, for example, his prophecy concerned the judgment to come: "There is no one to remember you in death," he says, "in Hades who will confess to you?" And in the thirty-first psalm he declares blessed those who received remission of sins without effort, something which the grace of baptism alone is disposed to grant.[1] In the present psalm, however, he expressly teaches us that he was not deprived of the grace of the Spirit: *Do not take your Spirit from me* (v. 2), he says. He did not in fact ask for the grace of the Spirit to be provided to him, but begged that it not be taken from him. Accordingly, enlightened by this ray and foreseeing with prophetic eyes that the people over which he reigned would fall into sins, and by way of punishment for them they would be reduced to slavery and become aliens in Babylon, he composed

---

1. Cf. Ps 6.5, 32.1–2. Theodoret situates the psalm among the Penitential Psalms of the early Church (see note 2 on Ps 6), of which it is the principal one. He also has to reconcile the forgiveness of David of which the psalm speaks with his sacramental theology (see note 2 on Ps 32), and so presents him as prophesying baptismal forgiveness as well as the correction of the people in the Babylonian captivity.

the present psalm both to heal his own wounds and to furnish an appropriate remedy for the people as well as for us all actually, in so far as we need healing in our wounded state.

(2) *Have mercy on me, O God, according to the greatness of your mercy, and according to the abundance of your compassion blot out my lawlessness* (v. 1). The present verses are relevant to the most divine David, the enslaved people, and those among us who are badly disposed. After all, the severity of wounds calls for remedies of equal intensity, the person falling victim to a serious illness needs greater care, and the one guilty of great sins requires great loving-kindness. This is surely the reason that the mighty David implores that mercy be completely poured out on him, and the whole fount of compassion be shed on the wound of sin, there being no other way to blot out the traces of sin. Now, he is right to call sin *lawlessness:* it involves double transgression of the law.

(3) [1241] *Cleanse me yet further of my iniquity, and purify me of my sin* (v. 2). You have already given me forgiveness, he is saying, through the prophet Nathan, and have brought to bear on me manifold calamities like varieties of cutting and burning. But I still need purges, giving off as I do an awful stench of sin. So wash me again, Lord, so as to remove all the filth of sin; in the words of the prophet, "The Lord shall wash away the filth of the sons and daughters of Sion by a spirit of judging and a spirit of burning."[2] *Because I know my iniquity, and my sin is always in my sight* (v. 3): even despite the forgiveness coming from you, I have not allowed myself to forget the sin; instead, I constantly see images of my wickedness and the faults committed, dreaming of them at night and imagining them by day. Now, God himself through Isaiah also bids sinners do this: "I am he," he says, "who blots out your iniquities and does not remember your crimes. For your part, on the other hand, remember, and let us come to judgment: tell your iniquities first so as to be justified."[3] And in the thirty-second psalm blessed David himself also wrote something in harmony with this: "I said, I shall admit to the Lord

---

2. Isa 4.4.
3. Isa 43.25–26.

against myself my lawlessness, and you wiped out my heart's impiety."[4]

(4) *Against you alone have I sinned, and done evil in your sight* (v. 4). Despite enjoying many wonderful gifts from you, he is saying, I repaid the gifts with the opposite, being rash enough to commit what is forbidden by the Law. By this he does not mean, I did no wrong to Uriah—in fact, he wronged Uriah and his wife—but the greatest transgression was committed against God himself, who had chosen him, who had made him king in place of shepherd, rendered him stronger than his foes, and showered on him goods of all kinds. It was proper for him to add, *and I have done evil in your sight,* history recording it: "His deed was seen to be evil in the Lord's sight,"[5] Scripture says. To take this of the people in captivity, on the other hand, *Against you only have I sinned* should be understood this way: I proved ungrateful for your gifts, and broke the laws placed on me; despite enjoying good things of all kinds, I proved unappreciative of them, whereas although I did not wrong the Babylonians, I suffered great wrong from them. *So that you were justified in your words and prevailed in judging me.* [1244] I brought troubles on myself, he is saying, whereas your righteousness is conspicuous: if the judgment of this kind passed on me by you is brought into the open, and my crimes set alongside it, you would emerge both righteous and loving, while I would appear criminal and ungrateful. Consequently, the word *so that* here does not suggest cause—the reason for either David's own sin or later the people's not being for God to be justified—but the opposite, that with the committing of sin by them God's righteousness is highlighted. After all, he bestowed complete providence on him, on them, and on all people.

(5) *For, lo, I was conceived in iniquities, and in sins my mother carried me* (v. 5). From the beginning, he is saying, and from the origins of human nature sin prevailed: the transgression of the

4. Ps 32.5.
5. 2 Sam 11.27. As with his reference to "the awful sin" of David in commenting on Ps 31 and 32, Theodoret eschews any detailed elaboration of it—an opportunity a preacher like Chrysostom (from whom we have no extant commentary on this psalm) would not have passed up.

commandment preceded Eve's conceiving; it was after the transgression, the divine sentence, and the deprivation of paradise, remember, that Adam had relations with his wife, and she conceived and gave birth to Cain.[6] So he means that, by having control over our forebears, sin effected some way or path through the offspring. This is also what blessed Paul says: "Since, you see, sin entered the world through a human being, and through sin death, because all sinned."[7] This is also what the God of all said to the remarkable Noah: "The mind of the human being is sedulously inclined to evildoing right from youth through all its days."[8] Now, we learn from all this that the force of sin is not part of nature (if this were so, after all, we would be free from punishment), but that nature tends to stumble when troubled by passions; yet victory lies with the mind-set, making use of effort to lend assistance.[9] So he is not, as some maintained, calling marriage in question, or calling the marriage relationship illicit, as some stupidly maintained in giving such an interpretation to the verse, *I was conceived in iniquities, and in sins my mother carried me;*[10] rather, he focuses on the transgression committed from

---

6. Gen 4.1. Theodoret, far from contesting an acceptance of the Fall as did the Pelagians, is concerned rather lest his reader take v. 5 to be an indictment of marriage and procreation as the source of sin. He prefers to be suitably vague about the way (or "path" or "currents") in which the sin of the first parents is transmitted to their offspring.

7. Cf. Rom 5.12. With women and particularly Eve in focus in this commentary on v. 5, it is clear that Theodoret is taking the relative ἐφ' ᾧ in a causal sense ("because, in so far as") with no reference to Adam, as is true also of his *Commentary* on that place in Paul.

8. Gen 8.21. Dahood cites this and several other places in the Old Testament, including our v. 5, to support its consensus that "all men have a congenital tendency towards evil." Theodoret, for his part, immediately proceeds to clarify what "congenital" means.

9. Theodoret steers a careful line between an Augustinian acceptance of impairment of human nature and an unwarranted Pelagian optimism: original sin (not his term) has upset a balance, and the resultant rebellion of the passions—not nature as such—is responsible for our sins. He does not see it appropriate here to sketch the role of grace in human salvation, whereas a mention of the place of human effort and the γνώμη is relevant.

10. Dualist thinking from groups like the Manichees is in Theodoret's sights here. His rebuttal is echoed by a modern commentator like Weiser: "Common sense and natural instinct as well as reverence for man's destiny as determined by creation (a reverence which the Old Testament has never

the beginning by people's forebears, and says it too became the source of these currents. After all, had they not sinned, he is saying, they would not have suffered death in punishment for sin; [1245] had they not been mortal, they would have been proof against corruption, and complete immunity from passion would have been associated with incorruption. And had immunity from passion been in force, sin would have had no place. But since they sinned, they became subject to corruption; and being corruptible, they gave birth to children like them, and on them follow closely lusts and fears, pleasures and pains, anger and envy.[11] With these and what springs from them reason is in combat, and if victorious, it is celebrated and crowned with a victor's laurels, but if defeated, it is deserving of shame and liable to punishment. In place of *carried* Symmachus, on the other hand, put "bore in the womb."

(6) *For, lo, you loved truth* (v. 6). This is what he is saying: You pass judgment, punishing some and crowning others, since you are fond of truth; but in your fondness for truth and your knowledge of the weakness of nature, give a share in pardon to those seeking remedies. *You revealed to me the uncertain and hidden things of wisdom:* I consider myself deserving of no pardon, to be sure, having proved ungrateful for such gifts: you not only put me on the royal throne, but also accorded me the grace of inspiration and revealed events due to occur much later, making what is unclear to other people clear to me so that I might teach them as well the Incarnation of your only-begotten Son, the saving Passion, the Resurrection, the salvation of the world, and the generous forgiveness of sins, the magnificent and di-

---

given up) forbid us to conclude that matrimony as such is here thought to be sinful. The poet's thought here ranges over a much wider field. It is the tragedy of man that he is born into a world full of sin."

11. The logic is ineluctable: from (original) sin follows death; from death, corruption; from corruption, (disordered) passions; from disordered passions, our own sins. To break the cycle, a firm γνώμη and sound λογισμός are required. In all this Theodoret—without prompting from earlier commentators, it seems—has departed from his professed conciseness to preserve and outline sound doctrine, whatever his traducers may have said about his orthodoxy in this area.

vine gifts of holy baptism.[12] Having been taught all this in advance by your all-holy Spirit, I beg to have a share in that grace which I am loudly prophesying to others.

(7) *Purify me with hyssop, and I shall be cleansed; wash me, and I shall be whiter than snow* (v. 7). Only the gift of baptism can achieve this cleansing. The Lord of all promised also through the prophet Isaiah to give this cleansing, saying, "Wash, make yourselves clean, remove wicked deeds from your hearts"; a little later he said, "Even should your sins be like scarlet, they will be white as snow."[13] The mighty David himself also foretells this in the sixty-seventh psalm: "When the heavenly being scatters kings, they will be snowed under on Zalmon."[14] So here, too, he is saying, [1248] I stand in need of the grace that will be given to all people: it alone can thoroughly cleanse me and give me the whiteness of snow. Now, the fact that hyssop achieves no forgiveness of sins it is easy to learn from the Mosaic writings: the Law did not cleanse the murderer or adulterer with sprinkling; rather, it subjected them to the ultimate penalty. So hyssop is a figure for other things: in Egypt by sprinkling on the doorposts the blood of a lamb with hyssop, they escaped the hands of the exterminator.[15] Now, it was a type of the salvific sufferings: there, too, were blood and saving wood and salvation accorded those approaching in faith.

(8) *Let me hear joy and gladness; bones that are humbled will rejoice* (v. 8). Fill my ears with this gladness, he is saying, by promising perfect cleansing so that satisfaction may course through all the

---

12. By conceding the scope of this charism of prophecy to David, Theodoret has no difficulty giving the psalms a Christological or generally "eschatological" (in Weiser's term), not to mention sacramental, perspective.

13. Isa 1.16, 1.18. It is interesting that Theodoret envisages forgiveness occurring through the sacrament of baptism alone, not through later approach to the sacrament of reconciliation (reflecting contemporary Church practice?).

14. Cf. Ps 68.14, a seemingly farfetched and obscure reference.

15. Cf. Exod 12.22–23. We have seen Theodoret helping his readers to appreciate language used figuratively. He is also encouraged to take this instance further as an example of typology, with the New Testament encouragement with which they would be familiar.

parts of my body, and the bones now humbled in affliction may once more flourish and recover their former strength. *Turn away your face from my sins, and wipe out all my iniquities.* Have regard not to the iniquities committed by me, he is saying, but to me lamenting them. *Create a pure heart in me, O God, and renew a right spirit in my innards* (v. 10): since I have fallen victim to the old age of sin, rejuvenate me in your loving-kindness. This is also what the Lord promised the captives in Babylon through the prophet Ezekiel: "I shall give them a new heart," he says, "and a new spirit."[16] Now, by *spirit* he means not the all-holy one but the force of reason; in other words, by disciplining you with this protracted discipline and teaching you what kinds of fruits sin engenders, I shall induce you to choose virtue. Blessed David asked this here, too, for his injured heart to be rejuvenated and his reason to be strengthened so as to tread the divine path.

(9) *Do not thrust me from your presence, and do not remove your Holy Spirit from me* (v. 11). We learn clearly from these words that he was not bereft of the grace of the all-holy Spirit: it is not as though he asks to recover it after being bereft of it; rather, he begs not to be deprived of it, nor kept far from divine care, calling care *presence* here. [1249] *Restore to me the joy of your salvation, and strengthen me with a guiding spirit* (v. 12). What he had not lost he begs to retain, that is, the grace of the Spirit. What he had rejected he asks to recover; this was joy in God. I enjoyed every satisfaction, he is saying, when I had great confidence in you, O Lord, whereas now that I am bereft of it I am deprived also of good spirits. It was slavery to pleasure, however, which robbed me of confidence. Hence I beg that my mind may recover the former guidance, and after being subject to the passions it may once more regain control over them. Again here he called the sovereign reason *guiding spirit.*

(10) *I shall teach lawless people your ways, and impious people will be converted to you* (v. 13): enjoying your loving-kindness again, I shall be a model of repentance to those who have embraced the life of crime; I shall also be a herald of your goodness, and shall persuade impious and lawless people to fly to you as suppliants.

16. Ezek 36.26.

Deliver me from bloodshed, O God of my salvation (v. 14). Constantly in his memory he mulls over the murder of Uriah; he indicated this also in the beginning, *because my sin is always in my sight.*[17]

(11) *My tongue will rejoice in your righteousness.* Symmachus translated this, "My tongue will talk about your mercy": having enjoyed forgiveness I shall not keep silence, but shall continue singing your praises and recounting your graces. *You will open my lips, O Lord, and my mouth will declare your praise* (v. 15). Sin generally checks the tongue, bars the mouth, throttles it, forces it to keep silent. So the inspired author begs to share through forgiveness in the former confidence and move his tongue in hymn singing.

(12) *Because if you had wanted sacrifice, I would have given it; you will not be pleased with holocausts* (v. 16). This is also in keeping with what was said in the previous psalm: there we heard the God of all saying, "I shall not accept young bulls from your house, or goats from your flocks."[18] The most divine David, therefore, after hearing this from the divine voice, rightly said, *Because if you had wanted sacrifice, I would have given it; you will not be pleased with holocausts:* you said the sacrifices of brute beasts are not pleasing to you—hence I shall offer worship acceptable to you. [1252] *A contrite spirit is a sacrifice for God; a contrite and humbled heart God will not despise* (v. 17). Moderation in thinking, he is saying, is worship acceptable and pleasing to you, our God; hence by deeply humbling my heart and as it were crushing and winnowing it, I shall bring the sacrifice acceptable to you. The blessed children in the furnace also used these words: "With a contrite heart and a spirit of humility," they said, "may we be received in your presence, as with holocausts of rams and rich bulls."[19] And so it is clear from here, too, that the psalm contains prophecy of what happened in Babylon and teaching relevant to it: from this those noble children also learned what was the

---

17. Though, of course, the sin—if the title is to be believed—is primarily that of adultery, on which Theodoret prefers not to dwell.
18. Ps 50.9.
19. Cf. Dan 3.39 [Greek]. We would feel this to be a slender basis for seeing the psalm, as Theodoret goes on to claim, to be referring also to the captivity.

sacrifice acceptable to God, and offered humility of mind and contriteness of heart to the Lord.

(13) *Be good, O Lord, to Sion in your good pleasure, and let the walls of Jerusalem be built. Then you will take pleasure in a sacrifice of righteousness, offering, and holocausts; then they will offer up young bulls on your altar* (vv. 18–19). From these words we are taught more clearly that the psalm is full of prophecy: the verses bear on those compelled to dwell in Babylon, longing for liberation from slavery and bewailing the desolation of the city.[20] They beg that the city be granted some pity and recover its former good fortune, with the ramparts repaired, and the liturgy performed according to the Law. As it is, he is saying, it is not possible for those living in foreign parts to offer to you the prescribed sacrifices, as the Law is clear about sacrificing in that city alone. But if we were to be granted the return and were to rebuild the Temple, then we would offer to you the prescribed sacrifices. Now, very applicable to them is the verse, *You will open my lips, O Lord, and my mouth will declare your praise:* theirs is the cry, "How shall we sing the Lord's song in a foreign land?"[21]

(14) The conclusion of this psalm contains, however, a further prophecy as well. You see, after setting forth above the gifts of the all-holy Spirit, he went on to show the God of all to be not pleased with the sacrifices according to the Law, and his prayer is for the new Sion to emerge, the heavenly Jerusalem to be built on earth, and the new way of life to be inaugurated as soon as possible, offering not irrational victims but the offering and sacrifice of righteousness, and rational and living holocausts, of which blessed Paul says, [1253] "I urge you, brethren, through the mercies of God to present your bodies as a living sacrifice, holy, pleasing to God, your rational worship."[22] The most divine

20. These final verses would seem to give Theodoret a sounder basis for arguing a further application of the psalm and David's prophetic insight. Modern commentators are divided on the origin of the verses.
21. Ps 137.4.
22. Rom 12.1. So, with New Testament encouragement, David can be seen looking even further forward. Theodoret has warmed to the theme of this most familiar of Penitential Psalms, unexceptionably attributable to David, and has devoted unusual length to explicating the various levels of meaning he has identified in it. Unlike a preacher such as Chrysostom,

David, you see, in so far as he had learned the obscure and hidden things of the wisdom of God, was aware that the New Testament contains the complete forgiveness of sins, and yearned for rapid and complete liberation from sins. And in his longing to attain in his own case the rapid and generous purification, he spoke these verses.

---

however, he has resisted the temptation to moralize about sin and repentance, obviously seeing the role of a desk commentator distinct from that of a pastor.

COMMENTARY ON PSALM 52

To the end. Of understanding for David. When Doeg the Idumean went in to him and reported to Saul, saying to him, "David went to the house of Ahimelech."

T IS CLEAR FROM THIS that Ahimelech had two names. Doeg, remember, as the first account of the Kings teaches, reported Ahimelech to Saul, and drove him [i.e., Saul] to the point of slaughter of the priests; both here and in the thirty-third psalm he calls him Ahimelech.[1] On learning the calumny directed against the priests, the divine David composed this psalm to stimulate the wronged to endurance and patience, and to teach the justice of the divine verdict. The reason, to be sure, for entitling the psalm also "To the end" and "of understanding" is that we may call on understanding and await the fulfillment in the outcome.[2] It also contains at the same time a prophecy of the frenzy of Rabshakeh, who left the company of the Hebrews, then was taken captive and learned the impiety of the Assyrians who had reduced him to slavery; he used blasphemous words against God, and tried to cheat the Jewish populace with deceptive speeches.[3] [1256] The

---

1. The events of David's visit to the priest Ahimelech, reported to Saul by Doeg and leading to the slaughter of eighty-five priests by Doeg at Saul's command, are recounted in 1 Sam 21–22. In his commentary on Ps 34 (see notes 1 and 3 there) Theodoret followed Mark 2.26 in confusing Ahimelech with his son Abiathar, observing (as here) that Scripture gave him two names.

2. We have noted often Theodoret's failure to recognize in the title to the psalm a direction to the conductor and the naming of the genre "maskil."

3. It is not immediately clear how Theodoret finds in the title a reference to that Rabshakeh mentioned in 2 Kings 18–19 (garbled here) with whom he seems to have a fascination (see note 10 to Ps 25). Comment on v. 4 provides only some slightly plausible connection.

title of the first psalm after the fiftieth suggested this explanation to us, though this inspired author personally was clearer in making his beginning this way:

(2) *Why do you boast of wickedness, you who are capable of iniquity all day long?* (v. 1). While he gives the name *capable* to Doeg as an associate of Saul, he gives it to Rabshakeh as one entrusted with command. Now, he expresses his thought in the form of a question, urging him not to be conceited in his wickedness nor devote all his time to evil; Symmachus, in fact, for *all day long* said "each day." *Your tongue gave thought to iniquity; like a sharp razor you perpetrated deceit* (v. 2). You sully your tongue with lying words, he is saying (putting *gave thought to* in place of "uttered"), and frame your speech like a sharpened razor, bringing ruin on those who believe it.

(3) *You loved evil more than goodness, iniquity in preference to speaking righteousness* (v. 3). You preferred worse things to better, he is saying, and you esteemed false words ahead of true, you embraced injustice in preference to justice. *You loved all the words involving drowning, a deceitful tongue* (v. 4). He used the phrase *words involving drowning and a deceitful tongue* for the power to sweep away completely through falsity, by analogy with those who cause drowning and are responsible for those under water drowning in the water's depths. This is what Doeg did, too: he utterly destroyed the whole city of the priests by using false words against Ahimelech. Rabshakeh also tried to do it, but was not able: he made false promises to those standing on the walls, but his prey eluded him.

(4) *May God for this reason do away with you forever; may he pluck you up and move you from your tent and your race from the land of the living* (v. 5). In making this wicked choice, he is saying, you will not escape the sentence of the God of all; he will promptly do away with you, consign you to utter destruction, mark you off from the list of the living, pluck you up by the roots, and dispatch you to death. From this, in fact, [1257] will spring the greatest benefit for those sorely troubled at the prosperity of the wicked, to see their destruction; he says, *The righteous will see and be afraid, they will laugh at him and say* (at whom? the unrighteous one [i.e., Doeg], who not only contested the truth, as did the

latter [i.e., Rabshakeh], but also raged against the priesthood; so those dedicated to God say), *Behold, the person who did not make God his helper, but hoped in the abundance of his wealth and was confirmed in his own futility* (v. 7). The ranks of the righteous, he is saying, will feel the benefit of deeper respect on perceiving the righteous judgment of God, cheered and amused at the fruitless outcome of wickedness and the result of prosperity in this world.

(5) *I, on the other hand, am like a fruitful olive tree in the house of God. I hoped in the mercy of God forever, and ever and ever* (v. 8). The mighty David says this about himself and also offers instruction to Hezekiah: both were lovers of piety, nourished by it. In the first psalm as well, he likened the champion of virtue to a tree growing on a river bank, constantly flourishing and bearing fruit in season.[4] Here, too, he spoke of the righteous as an olive tree groaning with much fruit and growing in the house of God in so far as he finds his sound hope in God, and on that account finding strength to exert himself and produce the fruits of virtue from the labors. Let no one consequently lose heart in being overtaken by contests, but take issue with them and gain credit from them in the expectation not only of being granted the crowns due him for the struggles but also of seeing in that case capture of the foes.

(6) *I shall confess to you forever for what you have done, and shall wait on your name because it is good in the sight of your holy ones* (v. 9). Now, the phrase *I shall confess to you forever* refers to the present age,[5] and *for what you have done* refers to the vindication of those believing in you. On the other hand, the phrase *I shall submit to your name* means not only that I shall persevere with great enthusiasm in the contests on your behalf, but also that you have a kingship that is good, that is, loving, and without beginning or end. *In the sight of your holy ones* means, Your help is at hand, and you will protect those striving on behalf of your name. Now, be-

---

4. Cf. Ps 1.3.
5. Theodoret, no more than Chrysostom, investigates fully the eschatology of the psalmist, being content here to utter a quick denial of an eternal perspective. It strikes the reader as a noteworthy omission. (See note 4 on Ps 6.)

ing the beneficiary of this favor, [1260] I shall always sing your praises, Lord, always longing and looking forward to the name that is desirable to those who know you, and deriving great benefit from it. God's name, in fact, is good and most desirable, not to all human beings but to those accorded knowledge of God.

COMMENTARY ON PSALM 53

To the end. On Mahalath, of understanding for David.

N MAHALATH" Theodotion rendered "On the dance," Symmachus, "by dancing" and Aquila, "in dance."[1] This psalm has the same meaning as the preceding, and likewise the thirteenth as well.[2] That is, there is one theme for both: both condemn the blasphemies of Sennacherib and Rabshakeh, and forecast the destruction happening to the impious. That was the reason it had a title about dancing, which they performed who gained salvation and sang praise to God. "To the end" is also attached on account of the prophecy reaching fulfillment at a later time. The present psalm also has this meaning in the title.

(2) Listen to what the inspired author says: *The fool has said in his heart, There is no God* (v. 1). Not only against those so-called gods, but also against the true God he directed his words, saying, "Surely the gods of the nations were unable to rescue their land from my hand (it is clear they were unable; how could they, after all, since they in no way exist?) so that the Lord will rescue Jerusalem (have regard, lawless one, to what extreme you pitch the drift of your words; it hurts you to kick against the goads).[3]

---

1. Theodoret himself eventually accepts this meaning for a term of which modern commentators are prepared to admit ignorance.

2. Theodoret does not make the bald statement of a modern commentator like Weiser on Ps 14 and 53 that "the psalm has been transmitted a second time" and so requires no comment at this place, nor, of course, on the other hand, is he able to base his reserve on evidence that "the existing variants may reflect two different dialects" and a northern and a southern edition, as does Dahood. At all events, aware that the LXX text of both is not identical, he proceeds to give another commentary. The degree to which it coheres with the more expansive former commentary (where there is evidence also of influence by Eusebius) is unclear owing to discrepancy between codices there (see notes 3 and 4 to Ps 14).

3. Cf. Acts 26.14.

Where is the god of Hamath, where the god of Arpad, where the god of the city of Sepharvaim (these gods so called by the fools likewise later provided the wretch little support)?"[4] *They became corrupt and loathsome in their transgressions.* The lawless life, he is saying, is responsible for impiety: those doing everything without a care in the world have no wish to give thought to the God who observes them, convincing themselves that no one is at the helm of creation. *There is no one who does good:* everyone, he is saying, loved the Assyrians' evil ways.

(3) All who are devotees of those gods are foolish, no matter in what eminence or obscurity they are placed; they give no heed to the fact that [1261] *God looked down from heaven on the sons of humans to see if there are any who are intelligent or seek after God* (v. 2). The God in whom they have no faith, who dwells on high and surveys the lowly, nevertheless chose to conduct an examination of their doings. *All went astray and at the same time proved useless* (all who held the same viewpoint); *there is no one who does good, there is not even one* (v. 3). He found everyone straying from the right path, he is saying, and embracing every kind of evil.

(4) *Have they no knowledge, all those who commit lawlessness?* What will they know? That the Lord God will exact vengeance? Who are they? He told in what follows: *Those who eat up my people like a meal of bread,*—clearly the non-believers. He makes their ailment more obvious in saying *they did not invoke God* (v. 4). Yet in fact through experience they will learn the penalty for wrongdoing, those who tried to consume my people like a loaf of bread and scorned the provident God. *There they will be possessed by fear where there was no fear* (v. 5): I shall make them terrified and mournful, not from fearsome apparitions but from the punishment imposed unbeknownst. Now, through this he indicates the blow inflicted on them by the angel.[5] *Because God scattered bones of those who pleased human beings; they were ashamed because God scorned them.* Aquila and Symmachus rendered *He scattered bones of those who pleased human beings* thus: "God in fact

---

4. Cf. 2 Kings 18.33–35.
5. Cf. 2 Kings 19.35.

scattered bones of those encamped around you": the deadly and destructive verdict took effect on them, and in a flash it wiped all of them out; this in fact is what is meant by *they were ashamed because God scorned them.* This is the reason, you see, he is saying, why *they will be possessed by fear where there was no fear,* since God was blasphemed by them and saw them encamped unlawfully around his city, so he consigned them to destruction, laying them out as food for vultures and wild beasts, and he scattered their bones. Now, you would not be wrong to see Rabshakeh referred to as *pleasing human beings,* since though springing from the Hebrews he hurled blasphemous words against the God of all [1264] with the intention of winning favor with the Assyrians. As some also who left God were abandoned by him—I mean in the time of Julian the Apostate, who ruled at the time.[6]

(5) *Who will give from Sion the salvation of Israel?* (v. 8). May the one who accorded us this satisfaction, he is saying, likewise provide with salvation those now held captive. At that time, remember, the ten tribes had been taken off into captivity, and many cities of Judah as well. Hence he added, *When God averts the captivity of his people, Jacob will rejoice and Israel be glad.* At that time we shall gain complete satisfaction, he is saying, when we see the other captives also enjoying their return. So we are instructed by this, according to the apostolic direction, "to weep with those who weep, and rejoice with those who rejoice," being of one mind with one another,[7] and considering our neighbor's welfare the basis of our own contentment.

6. The resurgence of paganism under Julian from 361 to 363, some of which time the emperor spent at Antioch, left an impression that is evident also in Chrysostom's commentary on Ps 111. Theodoret's reference to it is a rare comment on circumstances of the period, though before his time.

7. Cf. Rom 12.15, 15.5.

COMMENTARY ON PSALM 54

To the end. In hymns. Of understanding for David.

*On the Ziphites' coming and saying to Saul,
"Is not David in hiding among us?"*

THE PSALM'S DRIFT is clear: the mighty David sings praise to God for intervening and causing him to escape the snares of the enemies. The Ziphites feigned friendship for David, remember, but betrayed to Saul where he was trying to escape detection[1]—as even today we see some people putting on a guise of friendship while full rather of pretense than of friendship. At some point Saul gave credence to their information and took to the field against him with numerous forces; then, when he was on the point of ensnaring him unawares, he was prevented by the incursion of foreigners: he learned they were deployed against the region, and turned about to speed assistance to those under attack. Then the mighty David offered this hymn to God for accepting his petition and obviating the imminent disaster. He offered this psalm in particular as general instruction for them so that everyone under unjust attack from some people might in complete compunction offer supplication like David [1265] to the God who is able to rescue them like the inspired author from the hand of wrongdoers.[2]

(2) *Save me, O God, by your name* (v. 1). Invocation of your name, he is saying, is for me sufficient for safety. In this way, too, the divine apostles performed the great wonders: "In the name

---

1. Cf. 1 Sam 23.19.
2. Schulze's text of the commentary is drawn from various codices, some adhering to the particular story of 1 Sam 23, others wishing to apply the psalm more generally. This composite editing is visible also in the patchwork text that follows.

of Jesus Christ," Scripture says, "get up and walk."³ *And judge me in your might.* You are righteous, he is saying, and source of righteousness; so judge me and those warring unjustly. *O God, hearken to my prayer,* and not only this, but also, *give ear to the words of my mouth* (v. 2): accept my petitions with favor—to a high degree; hence he said, *Because strangers have risen up against me, and,* not only this, but also, *powerful men have sought my life* (v. 3). I need your assistance and support, O Lord, he is saying, harassed as I am by impious men trusting in their great power, human though it is and dependent on this belief in many gods, and longing to dispatch me to death. They presume to make this attempt against me, however, since they are ignorant of your providence, or rather they even despise it. In fact, he added this in the words, *They do not set God before them.*

(3) Having made his petition in this way, he loudly proclaims the assistance coming before long: *Lo, God in fact assists me, and the Lord is the support of my life. You will turn back the evils on my foes* (vv. 4–5), that is, they sank a pit and dug it out, and will fall into the hole they have made.⁴ Then he also directs his prayer to the all-holy Spirit of God in saying, *and in your truth destroy them utterly. I shall voluntarily sacrifice to you* (v. 6). But for my part, he is saying, I am instructed by your grace that you will deem me worthy of providential care, and with the troubles besetting me you will encircle those responsible for them, and will deliver a righteous verdict against them. This in fact is the meaning of *in your truth destroy them utterly. I shall voluntarily sacrifice to you:* having benefited from them, with all zeal I shall offer pleasing sacrifices to you.

(4) To teach the form of worship, he added, [1268] *I shall confess to your name, Lord, because it is good. Because you have rescued me from every tribulation, and my eye has looked down on my foes* (vv. 6–7): I shall offer you the sacrifice of praise, recounting your favors. This, in fact, is useful to me and pleasing to you (and to all helped by you). It is right for me to do this, freed as I have been from calamities of all kinds and contemplating the ruin of the

---

3. Cf. Acts 3.6.
4. Cf. Ps 7.15.

enemies. Now, that the Lord of all knows this sacrifice the blessed Paul also mentions: citing in his own case God's mercies and exhorting the beneficiaries of grace, he spoke thus, "Now, I exhort you by the mercies of God to present your bodies as a living sacrifice, holy, pleasing to God." And he mentioned what was the type of sacrifice in saying "by your rational worship."[5]

5. Rom 12.1.

COMMENTARY ON PSALM 55

To the end. In hymns. Of understanding for David.

HOUGH BLESSED DAVID spoke this psalm when pursued by Saul, turned fugitive, and forced to live in the wilderness,[1] at the same time he also forecasts the Jews' plots against the Savior, and in himself foreshadows the Lord's sufferings. I mean, in his own person he was driven out by Saul, a beneficiary of his favors, and was betrayed by some acquaintances, and with the eyes of the Spirit he foresaw the Lord suffering the same thing, betrayed by those who had been well treated, and crucified. This is surely the reason the title also refers casual readers "To the end," and exhorts them to pay attention "with understanding" to the words, as the inspired meaning is hidden and reaches its fulfillment after a time. In addition to this, however, the psalm is included among the hymns,[2] containing as it does some premonition of the Lord's sufferings: it is always right to sing the praises of the one who did not shrink from suffering for the salvation of human beings.

(2) But let no one who takes note of the lowliness of the words consider this unworthy of the Incarnation of Christ the

---

1. We have noted Theodoret's inclination, despite protestations in his preface, to look for a historical basis for psalms. In some cases, as with the preceding Ps 54, the LXX and (later) Hebrew text had acquired titles making some such connection, but none occurs in this case. Perhaps a local tradition had made it for him, as also in the many other such cases; Weiser remarks even of Ps 54 that the Syriac version relates it to an episode in David's life different from the one nominated in the title, so communities differed. Of course, misunderstanding of key terms in the title encourages him to adopt such an approach, as he goes on to reveal.

2. Theodoret seems to suggest that his church had a collection of hymns of praise for their liturgy, whether or not all biblical, and that for its Christological reference this psalm was admitted to the group (perhaps Psalms of the Righteous Sufferer).

Savior. Consider rather that he who did not shrink from gall, vinegar, nails, thorns, spittle, blows, and all kinds of drunken violence, and accepted death at the end would not have spurned lowliness of expression; after all, the terms should reflect the reality.[3] Now, his is the statement, "Learn from me because [1269] I am gentle and humble in heart, and you will find rest for your souls";[4] and again, "I accepted a command as to what to say and what to speak, and I do nothing of my own";[5] and, "My God, my God, why have you forsaken me?"[6] These and similar remarks he uttered in human fashion, both giving a glimpse of his human nature and shoring up the limitations of the Jews. So in this case the divine David both teaches the abuse committed against himself and foreshadows the abuse coming to the Lord Christ our God, congratulating himself on the sharing of sufferings, and as it were crying aloud with Paul, "I bear the marks of the Lord Jesus on my body."[7] Not only the inspired author, however, but also all who share in his sufferings for his name's sake will be glorified, as the divine Paul says, "If in fact we suffer with him so as also to be glorified with him."[8]

(3) While this is the force of the title and almost all the present psalm, the inspired author began by speaking this way: *Give ear to my prayer, O God, and do not despise my petition. Heed me, and hearken to me* (v. 1). He offers various prayers, begging that all be accepted: Do not despise my laments, he is saying, but kindly heed me and supply help. *I am annoyed by my idle talk and troubled by words of a foe and tribulation from a sinner* (vv. 2–3). Suffering re-

---

3. Here Theodoret shows his Antiochene approach both to Christology and to Scripture, and the relation between them—something more frequent in Chrysostom's *Commentary*. Thanks to his Christological "realism" he is in touch with the mysteries of Jesus' life, including those that seem to impugn divine transcendence, and likewise—and correlatively—sensitive to the inadequacies of human language to present these mysteries. He recognizes the divine purpose in both cases, and in the case of the latter expresses this as being an aid to our/the Jews' limitations. Chrysostom, of course (from whom we have no extant commentary on this psalm), would speak of this considerateness as *synkatabasis* (see my "On looking again at *synkatabasis*").

4. Matt 11.29. 5. John 12.49, paraphrased.
6. Matt 27.46. 7. Gal 6.17.
8. Rom 8.17.

proaches, he is saying, under attack from the foes who do me wrong, and pondering their manifold schemes, I am filled with deep sadness (in other words, the scheme employed against me). The divine Scripture, in fact, calls constant meditation "idle talk."[9] Symmachus, on the other hand, translates this, "While talking to myself I was brought low, and confounded by a foe's words, by trouble from the impious"; he calls the same person hostile and impious who, though the object of beneficence, brings about the killing of the benefactor. *Because iniquities have come in my direction, and in wrath they were indignant with me.* Symmachus said more clearly, "They launched attacks at me for impiety's sake, and in rage opposed me": giving vent to a wicked attitude, they plot my death.

(4) *My heart was disturbed within me, and dread of death fell upon me. Fear and trembling* [1272] *came upon me, and darkness overwhelmed me* (vv. 4–5): perceiving this impiety of theirs and the wiles of their schemes, I both tremble and dread, and await death. It was in no way surprising if David in his flight and pursuit by a great enemy feared for his life, being human and accustomed to a law-abiding way of life, and seeing from afar evangelical perfection. Christ the Lord himself, after all, although frequently foretelling and prophesying the Passion to the sacred apostles, and chastising the divinely inspired Peter for wishing it would not happen,[10] cried out at the time of the Passion, "Now my soul is troubled."[11] The divine nature allowed the human to undergo such anguish as to sweat drops of blood, on the one hand, and yet be strengthened by an angel[12] and conquer the dread, on the other. It was necessary, you see, for the nature which underwent the Passion to be revealed in this,[13] and the

---

9. A case of wishful thinking on Theodoret's part about biblical usage of *adoleschia*, it would seem, and unnecessary in view of the psalmist's thought, surely. He does not document his point, probably out of uncertainty (1 Kings 18.27 might alone have been adduced in support, other occurrences of this rare term speak to the contrary).

10. Cf. Mark 8.32.   11. John 12.27.

12. Cf. Luke 22.43–44.

13. Again Theodoret's realism regarding the humanity of Jesus (see note 3).

extraordinary longsuffering which he, in his love for us, had for our race; he underwent suffering in the flesh, wishing also in this to be involved in our salvation. At any rate, he utters all this lowliness of expression, not out of fear—perish the thought—but by way of proposing the economy of grace.

(5) *And I said, Who will give me wings like a dove's, and I shall fly and rest? Lo, I went a great distance in fleeing, and lodged in the wilderness* (vv. 6–7). This is what blessed David did: fleeing from Saul, and perceiving likewise the hostility of the foreigners in Gath,[14] he went off into the wilderness, as the first account of the Kings teaches. Christ the Lord, too, often retired to the mountain, often to the wilderness to avoid the Jews' envy. Now, it is noteworthy that the mighty David wanted to take the wings of no other bird than a dove; he clearly longed for the spiritual grace which appeared in the form of a dove.[15] *I waited patiently for God, who saves me from lack of spirit and from a tempest* (v. 8). Inundated on all sides by billows, he is saying, and as it were feeling the impact of winds or whirling gales, I await divine aid, and am buoyed up by the hope of assistance.

(6) *Drown them, O Lord, and divide their* [1273] *tongues* (v. 9): since they make use of a wicked concert, dissolve their harmony, O Lord. *Because I have seen lawlessness, and discord in the city; day and night it will encircle it on its walls* (vv. 9–10). This refers to the Assyrians, on the one hand, and the Egyptians, on the other, and even in later times the Roman Empire.[16] *Lawlessness and trouble in its midst, and also iniquity; usury and deceit were not absent from its streets* (vv. 10–11). In my view these words do not apply to blessed David: at that time Jerusalem was not occupied by the Jews, nor was any other city considered royal. Rather, he seems to be foretelling the discord and transgressions of Jerusalem

---

14. Cf. 1 Sam 22. Modern commentators recognize in these verses a resemblance to Jer 9.2, but Theodoret does not know his Bible well enough to pick up these echoes.

15. Cf. Mark 1.9; Matt 3.16; Luke 3.22. Theodoret is getting some theological mileage from his textual precision, a virtue even in one less biblically sure.

16. Theodoret rather glibly reads off historical applications of a single verse without substantiation.

and at the same time to be listing the forms of its wickedness—lawlessness, injustice, usury, deceit—which they embraced while not accepting the salutary laws of the Savior. It should be noted, however, that not only the perfection of the New Testament but also the way of life under the Law condemns *usury,* and brackets it with lawlessness, injustice, and deceit.[17]

(7) *Because if a foe reproached me, I would bear it; and if one who hated me used intemperate language to me, I would avoid his company* (v. 12). That is, if I knew the plot against me on his part, I would avoid his company. But I consider that what is done by adversaries must be endured and put up with—this is what foes and enemies do, after all—especially as it may be possible to avoid a war in the offing. *But it is you, soul mate, my leader and my friend, who took sweet meats together with me;* [1276] *in the house of God we walked in harmony* (vv. 13–14): the hardest thing of all in my view is when a man of my acquaintance and like mind, who has shared with me food and drink and things human and divine, is guilty of the actions of adversaries and enemies. Now, in these words the prophetic charism described clearly to us the traitor Judas, appointed leader by Christ the king—"You will appoint them rulers over all the earth,"[18] remember—and sharing with him table and mystical discourse, yet proving an instrument of the conspirators. While for *my leader* Symmachus read "my familiar," this is not related to blessed David: when he was pursued by Saul, none of his supporters betrayed him; neither Doeg nor the Ziphites were among his genuine friends. Instead, the inspired account concurs with the story of the Gospels: "'The one who ate bread with me lifted up his heel against me,'"[19] it says.

(8) Thus while forecasting the betrayal he also prophesies his sudden death.[20] Even up to our time it is possible to see the

---

17. A commendable attempt to be evenhanded in comparing the two dispensations.
18. Ps 45.16, in commentary on which Theodoret took the words to apply to the apostles.
19. John 13.9, quoting Ps 41.9.
20. There follows a long (and relatively obscure) comment on the verse from the more expansive version in a different codex. Schulze's text is again proving to be a patchwork of excerpts from the longer and shorter versions.

same deceit and murder abounding among some people, as the outcome of events teaches us: not only do they betray those providing them with viands despite sharing in them, but though becoming participants in the divine and ineffable mysteries they not only betray one another but even cause their deaths, oaths guaranteeing it. Paul does not cease to give witness in the whole world to "the two unchangeable things in which it is impossible [for God] to prove false"[21]—I mean an oath and faith. But I do not know how some people endeavor to change both things— or rather have changed them, maintaining due respect neither for their benefactors nor for fidelity nor for the Lord of all himself. Hence it was against them that the prophetic Spirit made a declaration in the following words.

(9) *Let death come upon them, and let them go down alive to Hades* (v. 15). He threatened them with this kind of sentence in his wish to curtail their wicked attitude. Now, Judas met with such an end to his life: tying a noose around his neck, he suffered immediate death. The Jews also encountered such calamities after the crucifixion, given over to the war against the Romans: they left this life not by the law of nature but cut down by enemies' weapons. If any of the wretches [1277] seemed to end his life with a death like others, after resurrection from death he would have a double punishment inflicted on him; Scripture says, "The sins of some people are notorious and go ahead of them to judgment, others' follow them."[22] Then he shows the justice of the punishment: *Because wickedness is in their lodgings in their midst*, that is, wickedness sprouts within them, in their very heart, and inflicts on them the deadly sentence of retribution. Now, he calls the present life *lodging* because in it we lodge, we do not find a home; blessed are those who regard the present life as a lodging, not as a home.

(10) Then, after mentioning the behavior of the lawless towards those that are wronged and yet not deprived of aid from on high, the inspired author shifts the focus of his words. *I cried to God, and the Lord hearkened to me* (v. 16). Not only the Father

21. Cf. Heb 6.18. Modern commentators would see God's promise and his oath as the two things.
22. 1 Tim 5.24.

have I learned to invoke, he is saying, but also his only-begotten Son, who out of his great loving-kindness was due a little while after me to accept the Incarnation.[23] This is the reason that *In the evening and the morning and at midday I shall tell my story and proclaim it, and he will hearken to my voice* (v. 17). When this is heard by the loving [God], *In peace he will redeem my soul from those pressing upon me, because they were with me in large numbers* (v. 18). Seeing my constant prayer, David is saying, offered by me night and day, he will free me from my enemies and grant me peace—and not only me, he is saying, but all who trust in him. Now, the phrase, *they were with me in large numbers,* indicates that the enemies were numerous; Symmachus in fact rendered it this way, "There were very many against me."

(11) *God will hearken, and will bring them down,* he is righteous, after all, and examines heart and reins,[24] *he who exists before the ages* (v. 19): on receiving my petition, the eternal God girds the schemers in weakness. *There is no change in them, in fact, because they did not fear God.* Symmachus rendered this, "They are not changed, in fact, nor do they fear God": [1280] their evil purpose will not alter, nor do they fear God; hence on seeing their unrepentant manner, he is saying, he will surround them with the aforementioned calamities.

(12) *He stretched out his hand in making retribution* (v. 20). The three translators rendered it thus, "He stretched out his hand to those who kept peace with him in it": it was not an enemy that Saul pursued but a benefactor, a familiar, an acquaintance; nor was it a foe that Judas betrayed but a Savior and provider of good things. Accordingly, the phrase, *He stretched out his hand in making retribution,* suggests that by stretching out his hand to make repayment he offered nothing good—rather, it was all full of evil. Nevertheless, Judas stretched out his hand not only in betrayal but also to get rid of the thirty pieces of silver, which, after his hanging, those who put God to death lodged in the Temple treasury.[25] What follows indicates this: *They profaned his covenant:*

---

23. Literally, "the *oikonomia* in the flesh."
24. Ps 7.9.
25. Theodoret forgets that Matt 27.6 shows the chief priests rejecting just such an option on the grounds of a prohibition in the Law.

though the divine law prescribed love for one's neighbor as for oneself,[26] they pursued the benefactor like an enemy—and not only that, but even condemned him to crucifixion.

(13) Hence he added, *They were divided in anger of their countenance, and their hearts pressed hard* (v. 21): in thrall to anger, they blamed some things while plotting others. Symmachus in fact translated it this way, "Their mouths are smoother than butter, but the heart of each of them is hostile." This accords with what follows: *Their words became softer than oil, and in fact were javelins.*[27] Now, this was what the words of Saul and Judas were like: Saul said to David, "Is that you, my son David?"[28] while Judas said, "Surely not I, Rabbi?" Many people with the same thoughts in mind put on an appearance of friendship and say to those wronged by them, Surely I did you no wrong? Likewise Judas in turn says, "Greetings, Rabbi, and kissed him."[29] While the words resemble the smoothness of oil and butter, the intentions are like sharp javelins and spears. Their javelins, in fact, were rather lances: Aquila rendered *javelins* as "lances."

(14) [1281] In this way the divine David described also what had befallen him, and after exposing the schemes against the Lord he offers advice to all people, urging them to have hope in God. *Direct your concern to the Lord, and he will sustain you* (v. 22). Not only will he glorify you here below, he is saying, but at the resurrection he will accord you the vision of God. Hence, take God as pilot and guide, and rest your affairs on that providence: this is the way you will remain unmoved and unconfused. *He will not allow the righteous to be tossed about forever:* even if he should ever allow them to encounter temptation, yet he will render prompt assistance. Now, this is really in accord with the apostolic statement, "God is faithful, and he will not allow you to be tested beyond your powers, but along with the testing he will provide also the way out so that you may be able to bear it."[30]

---

26. Cf. Lev 19.18.
27. Clearly, there is a considerable discrepancy between the ancient versions of v. 21a—though Theodoret, incapable of checking the original, seems to think Symmachus in his (more accurate) version has simply anticipated v. 21b.
28. Cf. 1 Sam 24.16.   29. Matt 26.25, 49.
30. 1 Cor 10.13.

(15) *But you, O God, will cast them down into a pit of destruction* (v. 23). Those presuming to ensnare the righteous he will consign to unending punishment. He called the unavoidable punishment *pit of destruction:* just as it is impossible for the one who falls into a pit full of slime and mud to escape destruction, so the one punished by God cannot find salvation from any other source. And listen, you fearful ones, he is saying, *Bloodthirsty and deceitful men will not live out half their days:* you will inflict a rapid death on those who have chosen addiction to murder and deceit, not allowing them to live out their allotted span. While this happens to them, I, on the contrary, says David, and all who with me await rescue from on high will be saved. He explained this more clearly, in fact, in what follows: *But I for my part shall hope in you, Lord:* knowing this power of yours and your just verdict, I await help from you.

COMMENTARY ON PSALM 56

To the end. On the people far removed from the holy ones. As an inscription for David when the foreigners in Gath seized him.

THE TITLE SIGNIFIES that the sense of the psalm is twofold, referring both to David himself and to the people in captivity forced to dwell in a foreign land, but also to many [1284] later. I mean, the phrase, "On the people hidden from the holy ones," refers to the people held captive or separated from the holy city at that time—namely, Jerusalem—or distancing themselves from God, that is, from faith in him.[1] Sufferings happened to them, after all: they were enslaved to foreign people in Babylon; and likewise this man in his flight from Saul was a sojourner among foreigners. It should be remembered, however, that he arrived in Gath twice: on the first occasion appearing to be hostile, then in danger of his life, when he simulated a disability, was dismissed and fled. But later he regained his confidence and spent time there enjoying peace.[2] He wrote the present psalm, to be sure, when exposed to the former danger.

(2) *Have mercy on me, O God, for people have trampled on me; in hostile manner they have distressed me all day long. My foes trampled on me all day long* (vv. 1–2): driven out and assaulted by various foes, and as it were trampled underfoot and constantly suffering it, O Lord, I await your loving-kindness. Symmachus, on the other hand, rendered *all day long* "the whole day," and *constantly* "unremittingly." *Because many are those warring against me from above,* that is, from their position of influence. I was not fearful, he is

---

1. Theodoret does his best with the title he finds in his LXX text, again not recognizing in this phrase (which is rendered differently by modern versions) a cue to a melody for the choir, and letting *miktam* pass as "inscription," as he had done with Ps 16 (see note 1 there).
2. Cf. 1 Sam 21 and 27.

saying, of people's affluence on which they relied to declare war on us. *Height of the day*, in fact, is the name he gave to prosperity that is present, temporary, passing, impermanent, not continuing at length.[3]

(3) Then he teaches the reason for not having to fear those carried away with prosperity. *By day I shall not fear; instead, I shall hope in you* (v. 3). I am not afraid of passing good fortune, he is saying, having as I do your support. Symmachus, on the other hand, translated this, "On whatever day I feared, I trusted in you": to fear I oppose confidence in you, he is saying. So it was good for the psalmist to put, *Instead, I shall hope in you*, that is, There is no one else, there is no one capable of rescuing those under pressure from the schemers, O Lord, except your providence alone. He clarified this further in saying, *In God I shall praise my words*[4] (v. 4). [1285] Praiseworthy, he is saying, are the prayers, which in repentance I shall unceasingly offer to him. *In God I hoped: shall I not fear what flesh will do to me?* By *flesh* he means the more materialistic people who live a life confined to the earth. In my speech, he is saying, I adorn my words with mention of God; and when attacked, I have confidence in your care and despise my attackers.

(4) *All day long they loathed my words, all their calculations of evil are against me* (v. 5). They direct every calculation towards schemes against me, he is saying, rejecting my words as false, and rebutting my defense. Now, to the present day it is possible to see many victims of this same thing whether from people or from demons. *They will stay on my heels and remain in hiding, they will watch for my weak point as though expecting to have my life* (v. 6). Symmachus rendered this more clearly: "They assembled secretly and pried on my tracks, looking forward to having my life";

---

3. If Theodoret seems to be making two attempts to explain the one phrase in his text (reproduced differently, as it happens), it is because Schulze has combined two codices here.

4. Aquila and Symmachus get closer than the LXX to the Masoretic text in reading "his word(s)"; but Dahood maintains that text is faulty, and the original should be read, "Of God do I boast, O slanderer." Theodoret would not have an opinion to offer, and is left to a commentator's last resort, rationalizing and brevity (even this muddied by his editor's recourse to two codices).

in these words he betrayed their plans, their wiles, and their schemes.

(5) *You will have no trouble in banishing them* (v. 7). It is simple and easy for you, he is saying, to banish them, lay them low, and dispatch them to death; he put *no trouble* for "without effort" and "easily." *In your wrath you will bring even peoples down, O God:* not only them but all who choose to live in lawlessness you will consign to punishment that is fraught with wrath.

(6) *I reported my life to you* (v. 8): all my doings, words, thoughts he made manifest to you. Symmachus, in fact, rendered it this way: "My secrets are listed off by you." *You laid out my tears before you, as in your promise.* You responded to my tears, he is saying, and fulfilled your promises: in decreeing your law you guaranteed to heed the wronged in their groaning. This, after all, is what he says in the Law: "He will utter laments to me, and I shall heed him, merciful as I am."[4] [1288] *My foes will turn on their heels* (v. 9): when you hear my prayer, the enemies will flee and will desist from their rash behavior. *On the day I call upon you, lo, I know you are my God:* Having received what I requested, I am persuaded from very experience how great is the care you exercise.

(7) *In God, whose word I shall praise; in the Lord, whose promise I shall praise; in God I hoped. I shall not fear what a mortal one will do to me* (v. 11). The inspired thought is beautiful here, too. How does he offer prayer that is fitting to the spotless and consubstantial Trinity? I cannot bring myself to utter it, he is saying, without invoking your assistance. Yet in proposing brief words and employing longer formulas I shall embellish them with your name, and trusting in you I shall scorn human wiles. *In me, O God, are vows of praise I shall pay to you* (v. 12). To you I shall gratefully discharge my promises, he is saying; he calls promises to God *vows,* as he does also elsewhere: "I shall pay you my vows, which my lips uttered and my mouth spoke in my tribulation."[5]

(8) Then he teaches for whom and of what kind the promises are: *Because you rescued my soul from death, my eyes from weeping,[6] and my feet from stumbling* (v. 13): after arming and securing my-

---

4 Exod 22.27.
5. Ps 66.13–14.
6. This phrase occurs in Theodoret's form of the LXX, not all.

self by all these means, and confident of having a firm trust in them, I shall perform the present song also in these terms. *I shall be pleasing to the Lord in the light of the living:* enjoying these favors and emerging superior to the various schemes, I shall give thought to your worship and choose a way of life which is pleasing to you and will win me life everlasting and that light promised to those living by your law. Now, as I said, this relates to blessed David and those held captive in Babylon. But it relates also to us, who are the object of many schemes on the part of human beings and of demons, and who by means of the divine care escape harm stemming from them.[7] [1289]

7. Conscious as he is of working as a scholar for select readers, not as a preacher to a diverse congregation, Bishop Theodoret does not direct his attention to applying the Psalms to the spiritual needs of Christians generally, and so he rarely makes even this admission of their wider relevance.

COMMENTARY ON PSALM 57

To the end. Do not destroy. As an inscription for David, when he fled before Saul into the cave.

THE MIGHTY DAVID, in flight from the first and second peril, recorded for posterity the divine beneficence as though on some pillar. "To the end" also refers the casual readers forward in both cases, since they contain a prophecy of future events: while the former forecast what happened to the people, this one prophesies the calling of the nations.[1] Now, "Do not destroy" is added to reveal to us David's thinking: though in a position to do away with Saul, dispose of his enemy by felling him, and assume control, he could not bring himself to do it, as if to say to himself, Do not destroy the virtue of forgetting injuries. "Let it be far from me to raise my hand against him," he says, "because he is the Lord's anointed."[2] It was right for him to add the phrase "Do not destroy" to the title, to teach us what thinking he followed in not doing away with his adversary.

(2) *Have mercy on me, O God, have mercy on me, because my soul trusted in you; in the shadow of your wings I shall hope until iniquity passes* (v. 1). Shut in the cave, and seeing the enemies shut in, he proclaims the divine mercy and reveals the hope he has in God. Now, he often spoke of *shadow of wings* as a name for the divine care. And the repetition of *mercy* reveals the extent of the peril. Aquila, on the other hand, rendered *until iniquity passes* more clearly as "until the plot passes," and Symmachus, "until the abuser passes." Accordingly, I shall not cease imploring, he is

---

1. As before, and specifically in the case of the previous psalm, Theodoret misreads the liturgical directions in the psalm title. In this case also, he does not pick up in the melody cue "Do not destroy" the likely reference to Moses' words in Deut 9.26, falling back on rationalizing.
2. 1 Sam 24.6.

saying, until I am free from the schemers, the Septuagint referring to the schemers as *iniquity* from their activity.

(3) *I shall cry to God the Most High, the God who did me favors* (v. 2): having the lesson of experience of divine assistance, I shall beg to enjoy it unceasingly. He calls enthusiasm of soul *cry*. *He sent from heaven and saved me; he put to shame those trampling on me* (v. 3): after according me his peculiar providence from on high, [1292] he made my adversaries appear ridiculous. History also teaches that he followed Saul when he rose, and when he was some distance away he showed him the favor done him during the night, that though having him in his power he had not dealt the blow.[3] Now, the shame was the greater for the one saved to be pursuing his savior.

(4) Hence he cries out in thanksgiving, *God sent his mercy and his truth. He rescued my soul from the midst of lion cubs* (vv. 3–4). Enjoying loving-kindness due me, he is saying, I was freed from the enemies' savagery: they fell upon me like lions in their wish to tear me apart, but you joined truth to mercy to show me the justice of loving-kindness. *I lay down all alarmed.* Theodotion rendered it this way: "I lay down with those consuming me"; Aquila, "with violent people"; and Symmachus, "with inflamed people"—that is, I lay down for all intents and purposes with consuming thoughts, biting me violently, as though almost setting my mind aflame. So it was right for me to be alarmed when forced to sleep in the midst of such people and hemmed in by the likes of them. He called Saul, you see, consuming, flaming, violent, and *lion cubs* to describe the ferocity of their attitude and their murderous way. He teaches this even more clearly in what follows: *Sons of human beings, their teeth weapons and arrows, and their tongue a sharp sword.* After calling them *lion cubs* he was right to mention their teeth, likening them to spears and arrows, and their tongue to a sharpened sword; in every way he indicates the deadly character of their intentions.

(5) *Be exalted on the heavens, O God, and let your glory be on all the earth* (v. 5). It is fitting to sing your praises in all places, supposed as you are to dwell in heaven yet filling all the earth with

---

3. Cf. 1 Sam 24.8–15.

glory. This blessed Habakkuk also said: "His virtue covered heavens, and the earth is full of his praise."[4] Now, *Be exalted* means, Show all people your exalted position.

(6) *They set a snare for my feet, and bowed my soul down. Not content with this, they dug a pit before me* [1293] *and fell in it* (v. 6). Devising traps for me, he is saying, and hatching plots, they were ensnared by us and were caught in their own snares.

(7) *My heart is ready, O God, my heart is ready; I shall praise and sing to your glory* (v. 7). Symmachus rendered it thus, "My heart is steady": seeing your manifest providence, I am no longer afraid of the foes' manifold devices; instead, I am ready and prepared to follow your words and sing of your favors. *Awake, my glory! Awake, harp and lute!* (v. 8). He then bids himself compose the divine hymn; he calls his own inspired charism *glory*, and himself *harp* and *lute* as having become an instrument of the Spirit.[5] *I shall awake at dawn. I shall confess to you among peoples, O Lord, I shall sing to you among nations* (v. 9). Not only now, he is saying, do I offer you this hymn singing; rather, also at dawning of the true light, which dissipates the long night of ignorance and gives a glimpse of the dawning of the long-awaited day, not only by his coming to us in the flesh but also through the rebirth and reshaping of washing,[6] I shall be choirmaster of all the nations and the peoples. Employing their mouths like strings, I shall sing the grateful melody of praise.

(8) O prophet, say why and by what means. *Because your mercy is magnified to the heavens, and your truth to the clouds* (v. 10): not only do heaven and the angels, who have it as their dwelling, know your mercy, but as well you have revealed your truth through the clouds. Now, the divine Scripture calls those granted divine grace *clouds;* the God of all teaches us this through the prophet Isaiah, saying in reference to Israel, "I shall leave my

---

4. Hab 3.3.
5. Theodoret accepts the imagery of the psalmist to present him as inspired by the Spirit, not passively but as a resourceful agent in composition and direction.
6. Again Theodoret likes to link the significance of the Incarnation (he speaks here of "the enfleshed one") with the sacraments in which his readers take part, especially here baptism.

vineyard untilled, and it will not be pruned or hoed," and adding, "I shall bid the clouds not to rain on it."[7] In other words, just as the cloud receives from another source the stuff of its showers, so too inspired authors and apostles were energized by divine grace and offered spiritual watering to people's souls. [1296] *Be exalted on the heavens, O God, and let your glory be on all the earth* (v. 11): through the spiritual clouds—I mean the inspired authors and apostles—the truth emerged and the Lord of all, maker of heaven and earth, was proclaimed Most High, receiving a hymn from human beings in all earth and sea.

7. Isa 5.6.

COMMENTARY ON PSALM 58

To the end. Do not destroy. As an inscription for David.

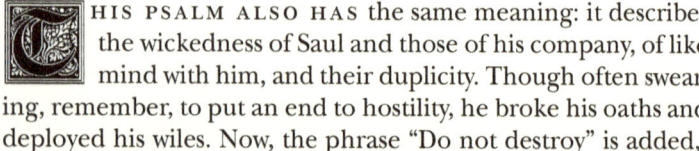HIS PSALM ALSO HAS the same meaning: it describes the wickedness of Saul and those of his company, of like mind with him, and their duplicity. Though often swearing, remember, to put an end to hostility, he broke his oaths and deployed his wiles. Now, the phrase "Do not destroy" is added,[1] since David twice had Saul in his power but could not bring himself to slay him.

(2) *Are you really delivering righteous words and upright judgment, sons of human beings?* (v. 1). He addresses this to Saul on his swearing never to pursue him and yet going on the attack in violation of his oaths. You, he is saying, become judge of what has been done by you, and relying on your judgment deliver a right and just sentence. But if you are unable to diagnose your own ailment and become a physician for it, how would you make available for others the remedy of truth? You could not, he is saying. *In your heart, in fact, you wreak crimes on the earth; your hands weave iniquity* (v. 2). Your words are those of peace, he is saying, but your purposes evil, the manifold wiles of schemers; so consider whether your deeds match your words. It was, in fact, futile of me to entrust judgment to you, unable to bring yourself to render justice.

(3) *Sinners were estranged from the womb, they went astray from birth, they spoke falsehood* (v. 3). It was long ago, he is saying, that they separated themselves from truth and embraced falsehood. Now, as was said to us before, this bears on the present in particular, *falsehood* meaning also hatred of one's neighbors. He inserted *from the womb* and *from birth* [1297] because God was aware of their behavior before their coming to be; he said so to

---

1. Cf. note 1 to Ps 57.

Jeremiah, remember: "Before my forming you in the womb, I knew you; and before you came out of the womb, I sanctified you";[2] and to Pharaoh, "This is why I vivified you, that I might demonstrate my power through you."[3] But God's foreknowledge did not make Pharaoh wicked or Jeremiah holy; rather, as God he knew ahead of time what would come to be.

(4) *They have anger in a way similar to the serpent* (v. 4). They have imitated the malice and scheming of the serpent. *Like an asp that is deaf and stops its ears, that will not hearken to the command of the charmers, drugged with drugs from a sage* (vv. 4–5). They block their ears like the asp, which is in the habit of doing this on account of its excessive malice lest it be spellbound and yield to the drug prepared by the so-called sage; he called the animal charmer here improperly *sage*, like the saying, "They are smart in evildoing, but ignorant of doing good,"[4] and, "Where is a sage? Where is a scribe?"[5] He did not really call them sages; rather, he said they gave this impression to some. You see, since blessed David had addressed many words to Saul, calling himself his slave and the other his lord and king, and showing in practice that he had no desire to slay him, and yet did not persuade him to abandon his hostility, he appropriately compared him to an asp, which is not naturally deaf but blocks its ears and prevents the onset of the charm. Symmachus, on the other hand, rendered *drugged with drugs from a sage* this way, "He is charmed with charms of a wise man," to make it clear that it was the charm he called *drug*.[6]

---

2. Jer 1.5. As westerners we may expect the commentator to see in v. 3 a reference to the Fall and original sin. Theodoret, however, though admitting the Fall in comment on Ps 51.5 (even if vague as to the mode of transmission of the sin; see note 6 there), does not advert to the subject, which is not an obsessive concern for eastern theologians.

3. Cf. Exod 9.16.　　　　　　　　4. Jer 4.22.

5. 1 Cor 1.20.

6. Theodoret is struggling here with the meaning of verses that Dahood calls "some of the most difficult phrases in the Psalter," having to have recourse to Ugaritic parallels to translate them—an option not available to Theodoret, who can only look to Symmachus for affirmation. Schulze further complicates the passage by reverting at this point to the longer version of Theodoret's text incorporating theological polemic.

(5) We were told above that in this way he makes clear the murderous intent of Saul and those of his company, in whatever position of eminence or lowliness they were placed. You would also be right, however, to take this in reference to the heretics—I mean Arians, Eunomians, Macedonians and those that seem to entertain doctrines similar to theirs: it would be fair for you to call them charmers and spellbinders.[7] Now, what makes it clear to the initiated that their mother is she who in a brief moment [1300] brings them forth reborn? You see, they are accustomed to baptize in the name of the Father and of the Son and of the Holy Spirit, and after lifting them up from the triple immersion. You who have been granted sonship know what I am saying. They impart a terrible contagion to those supposedly baptized—or rather dipped—by them, some saying, Glory to Father through Son in Holy Spirit, others Glory to Father and to Son in Holy Spirit. Thus the Godhead that is always in like manner inseparable and worshipped as Father, Son, and Holy Spirit they take as three Gods—or rather they pass them on as big, small, and smaller; and in their crazy talk they dissolve, so they believe, with the fetters of inequality the unfettered divinity of the undefiled Trinity in its one being, one kingship, one lordship, one divinity, one power, one creative activity, and whatever else is proper to its blessedness. One these wretches outrageously present as God and King, another as his Lord and minister and creature, made by him before the other things, and another as servant and minister of the Son. The inspired composition refers to them in particular: the all-holy Spirit of the inspired composition spoke not only of Saul and his company through the august tongue of the inspired author.

---

7. This extended assault on theological positions and practice of post-Nicene heretics is hardly germane to the psalm verse, not to mention its defiance of Theodoret's principle of brevity. The teaching of these groups on the status of Son and Spirit had implications for baptismal practice and validity, these Trinitarian and sacramental matters being live issues at the time; the "baptized/dipped," *baptizomenos/buthizomenos* jibe evidently figured in polemic. (The length and irrelevance of this digression from the longer form of Theodoret's text would lend support to Rondeau's preference for the shorter.)

(6) *God will smash their teeth in their mouths* (v. 6): the overseer of all things will show his schemes against us to be idle.[8] *The Lord broke the lions' molars.* In the previous psalm he called them "lion cubs," and here *lions*—hence his speaking of *teeth* and *molars.* Now, he calls the interior teeth *molars,* with which we are in the habit of grinding food. By the one and the other, therefore, he taught that the God of all will dispose of all their manifold calumnies. *They will be reduced to nothing, like water running away* (v. 7). They will be of no consequence, he is saying, like water scattered and completely useless. *He will bend his bow, and they will languish:* he will not desist from plying them with punishments until he disposes of their power, bringing about their wasting and undoing. *They will be dissolved like melting wax* (v. 8), a deadly storm of fire falling upon them, *fire fell upon them, and they did not see the sun:* they will be done away with like wax approaching fire and [1301] melting, and will be deprived of life. He said, *they did not see the sun,* because the dead are not able to see the sun's rays.

(7) *Before your thorns feel the bramble, like living things, as it were he swallows them in anger* (v. 9). Symmachus, on the other hand, rendered this more clearly, "Before your thorns grow up to become a bramble, still living, as a cyclone snatches away a dry thing." Now, what he means is this:[9] the divine Scripture calls every sin a thorn; the bramble is a thorn, though the biggest and like a tree, giving out a most lethal poison. So the prophecy delivers a threat of prompt retribution both to Saul and to his accomplices: Before your wickedness grows to be like a bramble—that is, the biggest thorn, in being the worst vice—a bolt from God will carry you off and render you helpless. This, you see, is the meaning of *he swallows them up:* just as what is ground up with the teeth's molars and is swallowed up then disappears

8. An alternative reading is "their schemes."
9. If other verses of the psalm qualify as "some of the most difficult phrases in the Psalter" in Dahood's view, here he capitulates completely before the Hebrew as "unintelligible." Theodoret, with little obvious assistance from his usual resource, Symmachus, makes a good attempt to rationalize the LXX version, loosely claiming the support of botany and Scriptural usage (perhaps with Isaiah's parable of the vineyard in mind). Brevity is permissible in an Antiochene, not capitulation.

from sight, so too will you be consigned to oblivion. This actually happened: after a short time Saul sustained a blow in battle with foreigners, and instead of adding to his wickedness he put a stop to his campaign against David, albeit unwillingly.

(8) *The righteous will rejoice on seeing vindication; he will wash his hands in the blood of the sinner* (v. 10): the student of virtue, on the other hand, will rejoice to see the evildoer punished, not to mock him but in recognition of divine providence, which is reluctant to ignore those wronged by them. Now, he *washes his hands,* not for having soiled and besmirched them with blood, but to show he is innocent and has no association with the other's wickedness; he is not, in fact, washing them in blood, as some suggested, but washing them of blood, for the reason of having nothing in common with him.[10] *Someone will say, Surely there is some benefit for the righteous; surely it is God who judges them on the earth* (v. 11). In this case *surely* is affirmative; it implies that everyone seeing the one addicted to impiety paying the penalty in this life will confess that God exists, observes what happens, governs everything wisely, and allots to the righteous fitting rewards, [1304] while inflicting penalty on those who do the opposite and imposing due retribution.

---

10. Theodoret has to contradict his own LXX text to make this plausible distinction (supported by Dahood against the NRSV and other modern versions).

COMMENTARY ON PSALM 59

To the end. Do not destroy. As an inscription for David, when Saul sent [spies] and watched his house with a view to killing him.

PREY TO ENVY, Saul plotted David's death; on one occasion when David was entertaining him he meant to fell him with his spear, but David got out of the way and escaped death. He tried again to seize him, sending some [spies] and bidding them watch the house, thus making his hostility obvious. David's wife, however, Saul's daughter, made it known to her spouse, and helped him get away through a window; she took a dummy (so the story goes) and gave it the appearance of a sleeping figure, and with clothing made it look like a sick person, showing it at a distance to those bidden to spy, saying David was indisposed with some illness. This happened at night, but when day came the ruse was exposed to Saul and his guards. So then it was that blessed David, on escaping that plot, composed this psalm.[1]

(2) He makes little reference, however, to the events of the time, forecasting instead great things after receipt of the radiance of the divine Spirit and perceiving in advance the Jews' fury against God our Savior.[2] The Jews, remember, guarded the

---

1. The events are narrated in 1 Sam 18.10–11 and 19.11–17. Despite Michal's taking the leading role in the latter episode, Theodoret allows her to go nameless—as would Chrysostom in a similar situation. It is noteworthy also that here as elsewhere he sees David as composing the psalm as a literary exercise; there is no suggestion of singing, let alone a liturgical context for its expression—though he corrects this in the last lines of the commentary.

2. Like modern commentators, Theodoret remarks that the title does not do justice to much of the psalm's content; and by implicit recourse to the mistaken clues in the title (as we have noted in connection with preceding psalms with similar titles) he feels free to find an eschatological reference.

Lord's tomb with soldiers, and at daybreak they found his garments but did not by that stage see the corpse that had been under guard: he had loosed the power of death and had risen. So blessed David, with an eye to the schemes against himself, and perceiving in advance that the God of Israel, the creator and lord of all, who came in the flesh of his own accord, would suffer harsh things at the hands of the Jews, foretells also the calling of the nations and the dispersion of the Jews.

(3) *Deliver me from my foe, O God, and redeem me from those rising up against me* (v. 1). The inspired author's request is fair: he begged to be freed from waging an unjust attack. Then he describes their purpose: *Rescue me from those who practice iniquity, and save me from men of blood* (v. 2). Bloodthirsty [1305] and lawless, he is saying, are the enemies, though I caused them no harm at all. *Because, lo, they hunted down my soul; strong men beset me* (v. 3): employing wiles of all kinds they endeavored to do away with me, trusting in their own power; yet it is fair for them to look for retribution for a prior wrong.

(4) *There was no iniquity of mine, no sin of mine, O Lord.* No trouble was caused to them on our part, he is saying; with nothing to allege against me, they plot my death. *Free of iniquity I proceeded and directed* [*my steps*] (v. 4). To be honest, these words apply not to David but to David's son and David's lord: he alone "committed no sin, nor was any sin found in his mouth."[3] No one, after all, is without sin except God alone; he in fact is the one who out of his great loving-kindness took flesh of David. Blessed David says this as a kind of type, not claiming complete freedom of sin for himself, but informing us that though he had done Saul no wrong and instead had frequently done him many favors, he becomes the butt of manifold plots. Though there was no sin, they made assaults upon him to snatch him away, guiltless though he was in their regard. Symmachus also translated it this way: "Though there was no sin, they set upon him to strike him."

(5) *Arise to meet me, and see.* On your part, he is saying, I beg you to become judge in this matter, knowing everything clearly

---

3. Cf. Isa 53.9; 1 Pet 2.22. Such Scriptural support encourages Theodoret to propose David as a type of the suffering Jesus.

as you do. *You, O Lord God of hosts, God of Israel, take the trouble to survey all the nations* (v. 5). Perceiving sinlessness to belong to him alone who came from him in the flesh, and foreseeing in the Spirit the fury directed against him by the Jews who were of the same stock, he begs the Lord of hosts and God of Israel to leave the Jews to their own devices and transfer all his providence to the nations, illuminating them with the light of the knowledge of God. Now, in announcing this to the nations, he predicts the Jews' punishment: *Have pity on none of the workers of iniquity.* Since with the eyes of inspiration he saw the cross, you see, he seemed also to hear [1308] the Lord of glory saying, "Father, forgive them their sin: they do not know what they are doing."[4] Loathing the extraordinary degree of their impiety, he prays that they enjoy no pardon.

(6) Then he prophesies the dearth of spiritual nourishment about to affect them. *In the evening they will return, they will be as hungry as dogs, and will go around the city* (v. 6). Just as dogs are in the habit of prowling around the streets of the cities at night, he is saying, forced to do it by an empty stomach, in like manner these people will be devoid of all spiritual provender; not enjoying the charism of inspiration, they will be completely bereft of high-priestly attention. Like a dog they will continue their meandering, not accorded the right to share even the scraps falling from their master's table, as the Gospel saying has it.[5]

(7) Then he teaches more clearly the cause of the punishment. *Lo, with their own mouth they will speak out, and a sword on their lips, saying, Who has heard?* (v. 7). With their tongue they cause slaughter, he is saying, giving forth their words like some dagger and sword, and events bear out their words. They crucified their Lord with their tongue, crying aloud, "Away, away with him, crucify him! His blood be on us and on our children!"[6] They put their words into action with the aid of Pilate's troops, and nailed the Savior to the gibbet. The inspired word said this, too: *With their own mouth they will speak out, and a sword on their lips, saying, Who has heard?* Because the words they utter

4. Luke 23.34.
5. Cf. Matt 15.27.
6. An (unintentional?) conflation of John 19.15 and Matt 27.25.

they use in place of swords. Now, they do this, he is saying, as though no one were watching; the phrase *saying, Who has heard?* indicates this: they are so bold as though no one were watching or listening to what happened or requiring an account. Symmachus brought out this sense, in fact: in place of *saying, Who has heard?* he put "as though no one were listening."

(8) Perceiving this attitude of theirs ahead of time, therefore, David adds the words, *You, O Lord, will mock them* (v. 8): [1309] though they are so bold, in other words, you are listening and watching and mocking their futility. *You will set all the nations at naught:* it is easy for you to prevail not only over them but over all the nations as well. The divinely inspired Isaiah said this, too, in his efforts to bring out the extraordinary degree of the divine power: "If all the nations were considered to be like a drop in the bucket, like a tilt in the scales and like spittle, and will be so considered, to what did you compare the Lord? By what comparison did you compare him?"[7]

(9) *I shall watch for you, my strength, because you are my support, O God* (v. 9). I have you as supporter and guardian of my power, he is saying; I continue to enjoy your providence. *My God, his mercy will anticipate me* (v. 10): you always anticipate my petitions, O Lord, and in an excess of loving-kindness you do not wait for supplication. *My God will show it to me among my foes.* The inspired author considers his foes to be the same as the Savior's foes. Then he predicts to them the future: *Do not kill them lest they forget your Law* (v. 11). I beg you, he is saying, not to let them undergo complete ruin: there are many among them who are being cured by the remedies of repentance. "In death there is no one to remember you, after all; in Hades who will confess to you?"[8] So what penalty does he intend to exact of them? *Scatter them in your power and bring them down, O Lord, my protector.* Scatter them throughout the whole world, he is saying, and make them exiles and refugees since they were involved in a wicked conspiracy against you.

(10) Now, what that conspiracy was he informs us: *A sin of*

---

7. Cf. Isa 40.15, 18.
8. Ps 6.5.

their mouth, a word of their lips (v. 12). This also concurs with what was said before: above he had said, *Lo, with their own mouth they will speak out, and a sword on their lips,* and here in turn he accuses them of *a sin of the mouth, a word of the lips,* teaching us in every case that they will pay [1312] a penalty for that statement which they uttered in concert, undermining Pilate's just verdict. While he intended, in fact, to release him as an innocent man, they cried aloud, "Away, away with him! Crucify him! His blood be on us and on our children." Symmachus, on the other hand, rendered this more clearly: instead of, *Scatter them in your power,* he said, "Drive them out in your power and destroy them, O Lord, our protector, in the sin of their mouths, the word of their lips." Make them fugitives, he is saying, and turn them from free men into slaves on account of the sin of their mouth and the word of their lips. Likewise in the case of the construction of the tower he dissolved their evil concert in discord, and to the ailment of the damaging harmony he applied the antidote of division of languages.[9]

(11) *Let them be caught up in their own arrogance.* Let them pay the penalty for what they perpetrated, he is saying, and for their reluctance to serve Christ who saved them, and instead embracing the rule of the emperor, let them be consigned to the emperor's servitude. *In cursing and falsehood they will be reported, in consummation, in fury of consummation, and they are not to survive* (vv. 12–13). Symmachus rendered this more clearly, "Let them be caught up with their arrogance; consume them as they give voice to cursing and falsehood; waste them in anger so that they may be no more." In other words, after they had been guilty of calumny in claiming that he had ordered them not to pay taxes to the emperor, despite hearing him urge them to give the emperor what was the emperor's and to God what was God's,[10] they

---

9. In the face of some of these obscure verses of a psalm classed by Briggs as "antique in language and style, and exceedingly difficult," Theodoret is not consistently taking refuge in brevity. Here, without obvious encouragement from the text, he finds allusions to Pilate's trial of Jesus and to the Tower of Babel in Gen 11—an unlikely pair. (The Saul of the title has dropped out of sight.)

10. Cf. Luke 23.2; 20.25.

plied him with numerous curses and insults. He said it was on account of those curses, calumnies, and *sin of the mouth* that they endured this consummation. Now, by *consummation* he means not ruin but no longer being styled God's people: they are scattered throughout the world, forced to serve the Romans as slaves, and deprived of worship according to the Law; they live far from their celebrated mother city, are bereft of royal care, no longer enjoy priestly attention, and are deprived of the charism of inspiration. So by *they do not survive* he means they no longer live as a people in their own right, dwelling in Palestine alone and styled God's People. By *consummation* [1313] he means retribution of all kinds: under Gaius, the fourth emperor, they suffered greatest perils,[11] and of course under Nero they encountered many calamities. Vespasian besieged most cities of Judea, Titus encamped around Jerusalem and plundered the city, reduced to slavery those who had escaped death, and led them off into captivity. Later they fell foul of other manifold sufferings; and likewise today in the cities where they dwell, of necessity they often suffer incurable difficulties in discharge of the penalty for the *cursing, falsehood, and sin of the mouth*. Through this they learn by experience that the crucified one is Lord and Master of all;[12] this is what the inspired author meant, *They will know that God is lord of Jacob and of the bounds of the earth*. It is in fact remarkable that before the cross he was not believed in even by the Jews, whereas after that shameful Passion the crucified One is Lord of the whole world, some willingly adoring him, others unbelieving but forced by fear to serve him.

(12) *In the evening they will return, they will be as hungry as dogs*

11. That is, Gaius Caligula, who became emperor in 37 and erected a statue of himself in the Temple. It was the emperor Nero who put Vespasian in charge of pacifying Judea before he, too, became emperor, leaving the completion of the task to his son Titus.

12. Theodoret is more dispassionate than Chrysostom in rehearsing this litany of tribulations that brought the Jews to the situation they found themselves in at his time, but quite consistent with him in his diagnosis of the cause—the crucifixion—and in finding it identified in psalms like this (though we do not have a commentary on Ps 59 from Chrysostom). We feel the commentator gets no joy from the exercise, detailed though he is; it is simply a generally held theological conviction.

and will prowl around the city (v. 14). In other words, after saying, *in fury of consummation, and they are not to survive,* he was right to employ the repetition lest anyone think the inspired author was in conflict with the phrase *scatter them in your power,* and so he says they are like dogs wasting with hunger and prowling the city at night, and will live without the benefit of any spiritual nourishment. In fact, a change of circumstances had occurred: Jews, who of old were sons, came to take the position of dogs because of their own wickedness, whereas the nations, who of old were like dogs, were accorded the honored status of sons. *They are scattered for feeding; if they are not satisfied, they will growl* (v. 15). Symmachus linked this with the preceding, putting it thus, "Let them turn about at evening time, let them make a noise like dogs prowling about the city, roaming, so as not to spend the night hungry." This is the reason, he is saying, that dogs prowl around the city at night in search of some food, so as not to spend the night hungry; for these people, in other words, every day is not only evening but also night, with the cloud of unbelief lying upon them. According to the Septuagint, on the other hand, the meaning to be taken is that these people are scattered like dogs throughout the world and search out spiritual nourishment; but not finding it [1316] on account of their unbelief in the preaching of all the inspired authors, they growl and snap, in this also giving evidence of their unresponsive attitude.[13]

(13) *But I shall sing the praises of your power, and rejoice at daybreak in your mercy* (v. 16): while, then, those who perpetrate those things shall suffer a like fate, I shall sing of your mercy. With the rising of your light upon the mind, bringing dawn to the world, I shall glorify your immeasurable compassion in all the churches. *Because you have proved to be my support and my refuge in the day of my tribulation. You are my help, I shall sing to you, because you are my support, O God, my mercy, O my God* (vv. 16–17): I have always enjoyed your assistance, and thanks to your providence I have escaped the troubles besetting me. For this reason I know

---

13. Schulze's incorporation of explication of the version of Symmachus from the longer form of Theodoret's text could obscure the preference in this case, at least in the (more authentic) shorter form, for the meaning stemming from the LXX.

you alone are God, and I call you fount of mercy and loving-kindness. Blessed David, seeing this from afar with inspired eyes, foretold the Jews' calamities and promised always to sing to the Lord; at least he fulfills the promises by offering hymn singing on the part of pious people. In other words, just as after the night everything under heaven is illuminated at daybreak with the rising of the light, so the coming of the Sun of Justice banished the darkness of sin, on the one hand, and on the other graced those believing in him with the light of the knowledge of God, and does not cease to provide it daily.

COMMENTARY ON PSALM 60

To the end. For the things that will be changed. As an inscription for David, for instruction, when he put to the flame Mesopotamia of Syria and the Syrian Zobah, and Joab returned and struck twelve thousand of Edom in the Valley of Salt.

HIS HAD HAPPENED PREVIOUSLY and is recorded in the second book of Kings.[1] The words in the title "To the end" teach us to understand that a certain prophetic statement is mingled with the history. "For the things that will be changed" is also included in the title, "change" suggesting a kind of transformation, a transformation not of past events but of things to come. For he did not say, "for the things that have been changed," but *For the things that will be changed.* "Inscription" is suggestive of victory; and at the top [1317] it is necessary to cite the theme of the prophecy. Blessed David, having won the aforementioned victories, foresaw with the eyes of the spirit the future lawlessness of the people and the captivity that would ensue because of it. He also foresaw the return from it happening through divine grace, and saw the necessity of writing up both good news and bad for the benefit of the people who would be involved in those events.[2]

(2) *O God, you repulsed us and destroyed us* (v. 1). Here he foretells the captivity, then God's righteousness and loving-kindness:

---

1. Cf. 2 Sam 8.2–13. Theodoret proceeds to pick up most of the items in the title, as usual misreading the cues they give to the musicians, including the LXX's solecism in confusing similar Hebrew forms (see note 4 to Ps 45).

2. Endowing David with this macroscopic vision enables the ancient commentator to apply the psalm to a wide range of later events, whereas a modern like Dahood—not feeling an Antiochene's burden of *akribeia*—simply concedes that "the connection between the superscription and the contents of the psalm is obscure on a number of points."

You have been angry and have had pity on us: though you have been angry at our transgressions, after the punishment you had mercy. *You have shaken the land and disturbed it* (v. 2). In this he indicated the invasions of the Assyrians and Babylonians: they completely wiped out everything like an earthquake. Then he asks for loving-kindness: *Heal its rents, for it has been shaken.* Again he describes the events. *You let the people see your harsh side* (v. 3). Namely? *You gave us wine of compunction to drink.* With the sequence of disasters, like some wine, he is saying, you instilled stupor in us, and filled our souls with pain. Aquila, in fact, translated it this way, "You gave us wine of stupor."

(3) *You gave to those who fear you a signal to flee before the bow* (v. 4). The blessed prophet Ezekiel teaches this more clearly, saying he had a vision of an angel bidden by the God of all to patrol the whole city and place a sign on the foreheads of those lamenting the people's transgressions. But those things were a type of our situation: we have received the real sign of divine grace, by using which we prove superior to the shafts of the adversary.[3] *So that your loved ones might be rescued.* With this sign, he is saying, you protect those dedicated to you, who have been thought worthy of your affection on account of their own virtue,[4] made immortal through the washing of regeneration. So the inspired author was right to add, *Save with your right hand, and listen to me* (v. 5). Turn about the disasters affecting your people, [1320] and as though with your right hand raise up those lying under your care. (May none of those believing in him doubt that his only-begotten Son is called right hand of God and Father.)[5]

(4) After offering the prayer in this way, the inspired mind receives the reply, reluctant to conceal it and instead teaching everyone. *God spoke in his holy one* (v. 6), that is, through the grace of the all-holy Spirit employing the tongue of the inspired

---

3. Ezek 9.4, a passage, which Theodoret feels able to take typologically, perhaps with the implicit encouragement of New Testament passages like Rev 7.3, 9.4, and 14.1.

4. This brief statement of the priority of human virtue to divine grace we meet more frequently in Chrysostom. The appended reference to baptism (introduced by Schulze from the longer form of the text) may have been thought to mitigate its implications.

5. Another insertion from the longer form of Theodoret's text.

author as an instrument.⁶ *I shall rejoice, and shall divide up Shechem and portion out the valley of the tents* (v. 6). Shechem is the city left by Jacob to Joseph; in it, after the division of the tribes, Ephraim fixed the kingship. *Valley of tents* means the region of the Israelites,⁷ as being a wilderness and site of shepherds' tents at that time. So the God of all promises to bring back those made captive and allot them the ancestral land, and thus fill it with inhabitants, so that those dwelling there would squabble about allotments and in the course of it make the division of the land.

(5) *Gilead is mine, Manasseh is mine, Ephraim the strength of my head* (v. 7). Gilead is the name not of a tribe but of a place, whereas Manasseh gives his name to a tribe, and from the beginning was allotted the land of Gilead. So there is reference both to the tribe and to his land as his own, and it forecasts the return and the occupation of those regions. And to Ephraim he promises to return his former strength; Symmachus, on the other hand, put "my rule" for *my head,* that is, I shall make him a champion as of old. *Judah my king.* Since the tribes remained undivided on return, except that Zerubbabel had control and sway over Judah, it was right for him to speak of Ephraim as *strength of the head,* or rule, and Judah as *king; my king* means appointed king by me and ruling over my people. Likewise in Isaiah, "Thus says the Lord: To my anointed Cyrus,"⁸ that is, to the one anointed and appointed by me.

(6) *Moab basin of my hope* (v. 8). Aquila rendered it this way, "Moab basin for my bathing," [1321] whereas the Aramaic has "dish for my washing": since in such vessels we usually wash our feet and thoroughly cleanse clothing soiled by the feet, he conveyed the subjection of Moab through the dish for washing. The basin occurs in the divine Scripture for retribution: the blessed Ezekiel teaches this, told to call Jerusalem a basin, its inhabi-

---

6. Though Theodoret may differ from other commentators in interpreting the phrase which he renders "his holy one" (NRSV "sanctuary" or "holiness"), his conviction of the divine inspiration of the biblical author is unequivocal.
7. That is, Succoth; cf. Gen 33.17–19.
8. Cf. Isa 45.1.

tants meat, the fire Babylon, and the sauce a necessary ingredient without which the meat was burnt.⁹ The blessed Jeremiah also saw a boiling pot tilted away from the north.¹⁰ So he means that Manasseh will recover their own land, Ephraim regain its former power, and Judah be renamed king of all, whereas the Moabites will be subject to them, observing their invincible strength—and not only they but also Edomites and foreigners. *I shall stretch out my shoe upon Edom; foreigners were made subject to me* (v. 10).

(7) Now, you would not be wrong to see in *basin* the divine bath punishing, burning, and removing sin, and revivifying through the divine Spirit, reshaping and rubbing away the bloodstains in the case of the uncleanness of the faults of those renewed in the bath. The phrase, *I shall stretch out my shoe upon Edom*, means, I shall not only walk on Edom, the Lord of glory to come from David is saying, but I shall proclaim the Gospel of grace by the divine apostles as though by my shoes, not in it [i.e., Edom] only but in all the nations.¹¹ In addition to the Moabites, he is saying, I shall enslave the Edomites and force the foreigners into subjection. The divine Scripture, of course, calls the Philistines *foreigners,* not as though the other nations are related, but because they are far removed from the others, not only those on their borders but also those dwelling in between. Thus Jebusites long inhabited Jerusalem, the Gibeonites Gibeon, and the Gazaites, the Ashkelonites, and the others dwelt nearby; the historical books teach this very clearly.

(8) Having in such fashion been taught this by the God of all, the inspired author longs to see the people's good fortune after the return, and says, *Who will bring me to the fortified city? Who will lead me to Edom? Is it not you, O God, who repulsed us?* (vv. 9–10). It fell to no one else, after all, to grant us such providence. He

9. Cf. Ezek 11.3–11, where in fact fire and sauce go without mention.
10. Jer 1.13. Once again, Theodoret cannot afford himself the luxury of surrender such as a modern commentator like Dahood feels obliged to concede in saying, "no rapport can now plausibly be established between the objects listed and the various nations." So, rightly or wrongly, each place name receives comment.
11. This sacramental and eschatological interpretation comes from the longer form of Theodoret's text.

calls Jerusalem *fortified city;* Symmachus rendered it "walled": as it had been razed and deprived of its walls, and after [1324] the return it regained its own fortifications, the inspired author longs to see it fortified and to travel as king as far as Edom, and see his perpetual enemies forced into slavery. Do this, O Lord, he is saying, you who have repulsed us and put us under the sway of the Babylonians.

(9) Having thus prophesied good things, his prayer turns to troublesome things: *You will not go out with our armies, O God.* You see us sorely pressed, he is saying, and you do not take command or prove our champion in your customary way. For this reason, surely, *Help us out of tribulation, where human solutions are worthless* (v. 11). By changing the conjunction, Symmachus produced a clearer translation, "Help us out of tribulation, for human solutions are worthless." Assist those in trouble, he is saying, able as you alone are to solve the problems, whereas the resources of human beings are worthless without you. Hence he was right to add, *With God we shall exercise power* (v. 12), that is, Let us turn back to him, and by worshipping him let us put him in charge of us. *And he himself will reduce our oppressors to naught.* Let us invoke his providence, he is saying, and place our confidence in it, sufficient as it alone is to remove our difficulties and abolish the sway of those warring against us.

COMMENTARY ON PSALM 61

To the end. In hymns for David.

THE INTRODUCTION OF THE PSALM follows the end of the preceding psalm: after saying, "With God we shall exercise power, and he himself will reduce our oppressors to naught," he teaches the people in captivity the kind of prayer they should offer to God. He also foretells the Incarnation of Christ the Lord our God for our sake and the conversion of the people from the nations.

(2) *Hearken, O God, to my petition; heed my prayer* (v. 1). Accept my supplication, O Lord, he is saying, and kindly listen to the words of my prayer. Now, any person at all who encountered difficulties would be right in saying this, begging in these words for supplication to be acceptable and for the granting of providence from that source. Then he teaches who are those praying: *From the ends of the earth I cried to you* (v. 2). Since Babylon was many days' journey distant from Palestine, you see, those taken captive [1325] and forced to dwell in that place suspected they were dwelling at the extremities of the world. *When my heart sank, you lifted me on a rock:* my prayer to you is that I receive guidance from you. Distressed, and lamenting the onset of calamities, I enjoyed your assistance and proved superior to the enemy. Now, this is said on the part of those taken captive from Jerusalem to Babylon and afterwards receiving the call to return; but it is applicable also to everyone taking steps through repentance towards their own salvation, no longer straying from the straight and narrow but treading the single, direct path.[1]

---

1. Three times already in the course of comment on the title and vv. 1 and 2, the longer form of Theodoret's text has shown an insistence that along with historical reference the psalmist is catering for the situation of people in difficulties generally, as if to reflect an uncertainty shown also by

(3) This is clear from what follows. *You guided me because you became my hope, a tower of strength, in the face of the foe* (v. 3): having hoped to share in your providence, I was not disappointed in my hope; you became for me both guide and strong tower. In fact, having eluded the foes' wiles thanks to your care, I will secure my return. *I shall dwell in your tent forever, find shelter under the cover of your wings* (v. 4). He calls Jerusalem God's *tent;* in it he made his appearance to them. So he means, Having secured my return, I shall be in constant attendance in your Temple, and enjoy providence at your hands; by *wings,* note, he means God's care. Now, he put *forever* to mean continually.[2]

(4) *Because you, O God, hearkened to my prayers; you gave an inheritance to those who fear your name* (v. 5): I sing to you unceasingly, since you accepted my supplications, restoring the inheritance promised to our forebears for us their progeny. Now, they say this as soon as they begin their trek. It ought to be understood, however, that the words in question contain a foreshadowing of the real inheritance; the real inheritance is eternal life, of which Christ the Lord said to the lambs on his right hand, "Come, you that are blessed by my Father, inherit the kingdom prepared for you before the foundation of the world."[3] The Lord promised to give this inheritance to those who fear him, and he restored the promised land to these people as though in a type.

(5) *Days upon days you will apportion the king,* [1328] *his years as many as the days of generation upon generation. He will remain forever before God* (vv. 6–7). After making supplication in this fashion and receiving their requests, and after giving thanks for them, they beseech God to watch in perpetuity over the king given them.[4] Now, at that time Zerubbabel was ruling over them;

---

modern commentators about the adequacy of the translation "from the ends of the earth" of the LXX and many modern versions.

2. Again Theodoret passes over what strikes us as an opportunity to compare the eschatology of the Old Testament and of the New, perhaps in view of his interpretation of the following verse.

3. Matt 25.34, which is sufficient basis for Theodoret to take the psalm verse typologically.

4. Modern commentators like Gunkel and Kraus, with their interest in classifying psalms, have had difficulty with the shift from first to third per-

but all the words of the inspired composition do not apply to him: *Days upon days you will apportion the king* apply to him, but the rest do not; instead, they apply to the one who out of great loving-kindness came of his line according to the flesh, as he himself knew. Of him, you see, were realized the words of the inspired composition, *his years as many as the days of generation upon generation. He will remain forever before God:* he had no beginning to his days, nor will he experience an end. I mean, even if he became a human being and accepted death for our sake, nevertheless, *his years are as many as the days of generation upon generation:* "he was in the beginning, and was with God, and was God."[5] Now, the phrase *before God* means always coexisting with the Father. The same inspired author, in fact, said to him in the hundred-and-first psalm, "You are the same, and your years will not have an end."[6] Do you see that the one who accepted cross and death for our sake has also an unending kingship insofar as he coexists with the Father? Zerubbabel, of course, was a type of Christ the Lord: as he was the one who led the captives from Babylon back to their ancestral land, in like manner Christ the Lord led the whole human race, who had been made captive through the transgression of the first human being,[7] back to their former nobility by rendering impotent on the cross the one who had the power of death—namely, the devil—and canceling the power of death, and thus restored life to those subject to him. From him, after all, came the statement, "I am the life and the resurrection," and "The one who eats me will live in me."[8]

---

son in these verses, and have had to presume they are a later addition. Theodoret, of course, cannot take refuge in such a critical concession; but the relative length of commentary betrays his acknowledgment of a difficulty—though Schulze has compounded this impression by several excerpts from the longer form of the text.

5. Cf. John 1.1.
6. Ps 102.27.
7. This incidental reference to the Fall is from the longer form of the text. Again Theodoret briefly concedes a typological meaning to the figure of Zerubbabel he finds in the verse.
8. Cf. John 11.25; 6.57.

(6) *Who will seek out his mercy and truth?* Who is capable, he is saying, of gaining a precise knowledge of God's just and righteous mercy? His judgments are a deep abyss, after all. *In this way I shall sing to your name forever so as to render my vows day after day* (v. 8): I shall always sing your praises, each day I shall recount your graces, and shall not be false to my promises (calling promises *vows*). [1329]

COMMENTARY ON PSALM 62

To the end. For Jeduthun. A psalm of David.

YMMACHUS, ON THE OTHER HAND, rendered it thus: "A triumphal song to David, by Jeduthun." So he indicates that the psalm was blessed David's but sung by Jeduthun: in his capacity as leader of a choir he sings to the God of all in the divine Temple, as the book of Chronicles says.[1] Now, the psalm prophesies the Macedonian invasions and the stratagems of Antiochus Epiphanes against the Maccabees, and teaches the practitioners of piety the kind of thinking they should employ in the time of adversity.

(2) *Will not my soul be subject to God?* (v. 1). Under pressure to transgress the divine Law, sacrifice to idols, and eat pork, they arouse their own thinking in the direction of piety and heighten their enthusiasm for piety. Do you not prize the service of God, O soul, ahead of everything else? Then he teaches the advantage coming from this. *From him comes my salvation; being my God and my savior, he is my support, I shall no longer be moved* (vv. 1–2): this service brings you salvation, O soul: God it is who is both provider of good things and capable of supporting those who are confused. Accordingly, by calling on his assistance I shall be rid of those trying to upset me.

(3) Having thus enkindled their thinking in regard to piety, they direct their words to their adversaries. *How long will you beset a person, will all of you seek their ruin, as though a tottering wall or toppled fence?* (v. 3). Now, the meaning of this verse is hyperbolic; it is this: What degree of cruelty do you use against us, giving no

---

1. Cf. 1 Chron 9.16, 16.41–42. As his comment on the title to Ps 39 suggests (see note 1 there), Theodoret resists any suggestion that the Psalms are not all David's, conceding to Jeduthun only his musical role—without, however, coming round to see other items in the title as liturgical directions.

consideration to our natural commonality, but instead striving to overthrow us and bring us low, like some tottering wall and fence in danger of being toppled by the wind, with such murderous thoughts in your mind? In other words, do not belabor us so severely, as though we were without strength: we have the God of all as our helper. *Yet they plotted to spurn my dignity* (v. 4). They [1332] have one end in view, he is saying, to deprive me of God's providence, on which I base all my status and good name. It is the dignity of godly people, you see, to serve God; hence the divinely inspired Paul everywhere classes himself as slave of Christ. *They pursued their course thirstily:* this scheme of theirs is no pastime; rather, acting entirely from zeal, they are thirsting to hurl me into the depths of impiety.[2] Now, he mentions what kind of wiles they employ: *They blessed with their mouth, but cursed in their heart:* they use a mere patter in an attempt to deceive, but they have destruction hidden within.

(4) Having thus revealed the others' schemes, they urge each other in turn to be staunch and await divine aid. *But be subject to God, my soul, because my endurance is from him* (v. 5): do not forsake the service of God, O soul, but since your strength has come from the aid provided by him, put up with the shafts of adversity. *Because he is my God, my savior, my support; I shall not wander far* (v. 6): knowing him to be both true God and source of salvation, I shall not bring myself to alter my contract and betake myself to a different allegiance. He put *wander far* to mean "transfer"; I shall not become a wanderer, he is saying, in thrall to impiety. *In God is my salvation and my glory; God is my help, and my hope is in God* (v. 7). Lo, once again the inspired message gives us a clearer glimpse of the persons of the Trinity, undivided, illumining, and everlasting—not to imply three Gods (perish the thought), as "God," "King," "Creator," and "All-powerful" apply to the persons, as we have often said.[3] This is surely the reason they often use the same words—God, Savior, glory, and help—to speak of the God of all, for the purpose of repelling the shafts of impiety.

---

2. Theodoret's form of the LXX comes up with this strange mention of thirst (which he has no difficulty rationalizing) apparently by a simple error of metathesis, reading *dipsi* for *pseudei,* "falsehood."

3. A rather intrusive comment from the longer form of the text.

(5) This is also the reason they urge on all other people of similar stock to the same piety, reluctant to be the only ones called victors. *Hope in him, every assembly of peoples, pour out your hearts before him,* [1333] *because God is our help* (v. 8): spurn all human beings, O fellow peoples, and confirm your hope in him and direct all your attention to him, awaiting without question help from him. The phrase, *pour out your hearts before him,* has this meaning, Consecrate all your thinking to him, and admit no ambiguity, knowing well that human beings are inconstant and unstable in all their ways,[4] and recalling the saying, "No one can serve two masters."[5] *But the sons of human beings are frivolous, the sons of human beings deceptive, tilting the balance towards wrongdoing* (v. 9). Theodotion rendered this more clearly, "But the sons of human beings are vapor, a man's sons deceitful, like a tilting balance." Nothing human is reliable, he is saying; instead, it is like vapor rising and immediately dissipated, and like a tilting balance, at one time falling, at another time rising, having nothing firm and stable about it. The version of the Septuagint is to be taken this way: Everything human is frivolous; most people trust in impermanent things as though permanent; they have no interest in equity, conforming without equity to the mind's sliding scale; they despise fairness and rejoice in what is unfair. *They themselves are likewise the fruit of frivolity:* they nonetheless reap no benefit from this, all frivolity, undergoing change in a flash. Symmachus, in fact, rendered it this way, "They are all frivolous together."[6]

(6) From this he offers advice to the adversaries who pride themselves on their wealth. *Place no hope in iniquity, and hanker not after robbery* (v. 10). Do not consider desirable, he is saying, human things of no lasting value, which are connected with iniquity. *If wealth comes your way, do not set your heart on it:* when you see wealth borne into your houses like a river, do not let your

---

4. Cf. Jas 1.8.
5. Matt 6.24.
6. It is interesting that Theodoret in commenting on this challenging verse turns not to a Scriptural locus like Isa 40.15 for clarification but to the alternative versions; from these he gets good value, teasing out also the sense of his LXX.

thinking fall under its spell. Why on earth do you give this advice and exhortation? *Once God has said this, twice I have heard it, that power belongs to God, and mercy to you, O Lord, because you repay everyone according to their works* (vv. 11–12). I have heard the God of all declaring, he is saying, that judgment is coming and reward for good and evil. Now, he put *once* to indicate not number but complete inevitability: God declared once, and there is no way it cannot happen. He says *twice:* punishment for the lawless and loving-kindness accorded the pious. [1336] On the one hand, in giving the Law God made this promise: "I the Lord your God," he says, "am a jealous God, taking recompense for parents' sin on children to the third and fourth generation of those who hate me, and having mercy on countless numbers of those who love me and observe my commandments."[7] On the other hand, in the Gospels we hear this: how the Lord of glory at his second coming from the heavens will divide them up like a shepherd, putting the sheep on his right and the goats on his left. Then he will say to those on his right, "Come, you who are blessed by my Father, inherit the kingdom prepared for you before the foundation of the world." Then to those on his left, "Depart to the darkness without, where there is weeping and gnashing of teeth."[8] On account of this declaration let everyone show zeal through purity of life and through the one true faith and on account of love for the neighbor so as to lay hold of those things "which eye has not seen nor ear heard, nor the human heart conceived, which God has prepared for those who love him."[9]

7. Exod 20.5–6.
8. Theodoret combines (confuses?) elements of the Judgment scene in Matt 25.32–41 with the fate of the unclad wedding guests in Matt 22.13.
9. 1 Cor 2.9. The hortatory style of this conclusion, unusual in this desk theologian, confirms its provenance from the longer form of the text.

COMMENTARY ON PSALM 63

A psalm for David, when he was in the wilderness of Judah.

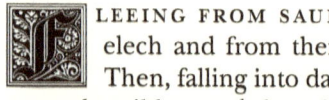LEEING FROM SAUL, the divine David reached Ahimelech and from there Achish, who was king in Gath. Then, falling into danger again and eluding it he came upon the wilderness;[1] there he wrote this psalm, both revealing the love he had for God and prophesying the overthrow of Saul. He also gave everybody who was in debt the opportunity of earnestly entreating God and awaiting help from him.[2]

(2) *O God, my God, I watch for you at break of day; my soul has thirsted for you* (v. 1). Desire for you, O Lord, he is saying, dispels even sleep and awakens me to adoration of you. *How often my flesh longs for you.* Theodotion rendered it "how many times," whereas Aquila said "was incited," and Symmachus, "yearns after." Now, I quoted all the versions to convey the idea that "how often" is not composed of two elements, "how" being separate from "often," but that it is one word, signifying the intensity of desire: the flesh is in harmony with the soul's love, and is not [1337] in conflict with its wishes.[3] It wishes to say, Both my soul and my body yearn for you and long for you, like the person thirsting for the sweetest and clearest water. *In a wilderness, inaccessible and waterless.*

(3) *Thus I appeared to you in the holy place* (v. 2): I sustained no harm from the wilderness; instead, situated in it as though in

---

1. 1 Sam 21 recounts David's time with Ahimelech and Achish; his ventures into the wilderness are mentioned in 1 Sam 22.5, 23.14, and 24.1.
2. Again the longer form of Theodoret's text characteristically gives the psalm a general application beyond the historical.
3. Against the facts, which suggest that the obvious discrepancy among the versions betrays a confusion of similar Hebrew forms (that has occurred before), Theodoret smoothes over the differences by rationalizing. *Akribeia* has its limits.

your sacred tabernacle, I offer you hymn singing in this way. The phrase *the holy place* means the tabernacle, the divine Temple not yet being built. *To see your power and your glory:* I stand in your presence, imagining your ineffable power; since your nature is beyond our grasp, I take a basis for praise from what has been done by you. The people from the nations that has come to faith would always say, *Thus I appeared to you in the holy place,* that is, in the temple where you sacrifice without sacrifice, divide without division, and consume while remaining unconsumed.[4]

(4) *Because your mercy is better than life, my lips will praise you* (v. 3): your mercy I prefer to all the life of the rich and influential, an indolent life and a busy one, a luxurious life and a careless one, and I move my lips in singing your praises. *Thus I shall praise you in my life; in your name I shall lift up my hands* (v. 4): I shall continue to do this throughout the whole of my life, singing with my tongue, reaching out my hands and begging for your loving-kindness. *Let my soul be filled as though with a rich feast* (v. 5): I take hymn singing to you as richness of soul, and think of it as rich and luxurious; meditation on your sayings is unchanging luxury and opulence. *My mouth will praise with lips of gladness:* for this reason I shall offer you the hymn with all enthusiasm, realizing the benefit coming from it.

(5) *If I remembered you on my bed, I meditated on you at daybreak. Because you proved to be my help, and in the shelter of your wings I shall rejoice* (vv. 6–7). Symmachus, on the other hand, translated it this way, "On my bed I call you to mind, at each watch I meditated on you; sheltered by your wings I praised you." He mentions the watches of the night: [1340] those entrusted with guard duty divide up the night time and perform the task in succession. Some divide it into three, some into four; the Lord came to the sacred apostles at the fourth watch of the night.[5] So the divine David means, Lying in bed I resisted the most enjoyable sleep so as to meditate on you at each watch, and I repaid with hymns the kindnesses done to me; after all, you guard me with

---

4. This final enigmatic comment comes into the text from the longer form.
5. Cf. Mark 6.48.

invincible providence as with a shelter of wings. The people that came to faith from the nations as a whole also make mention of this same thing on their bed, praising the Savior of all at daybreak.[6] *Because you in person proved to be my helper, and in the shelter of your wings I shall rejoice.* Now, one would be right to call both Old and New Testaments *wings,* being sheltered and nourished and delighted by them, and raised through the rebirth of the washing to maturity, to the measure of development of the full stature of Christ.[7]

(6) *My soul clung to you* (v. 8). Not even for a moment, he is saying, can I steal my thoughts away from remembering you; rather, inflamed by a burning potion, I am attached to your memory by desire for you as though by a kind of glue. Then he shows the fruit of the desire. *Your right hand took hold of me:* seeing me so disposed, you judge me worthy of your providence.[8]

(7) *They, on the contrary, were after my life, but in vain* (v. 9): they were anxious to do away with me, though I had done no wrong. *They shall go to the depths of the earth:* I am aware, however, that they shall be dispatched to death. Then he also prophesies the manner of their passing. *They shall be given over into the hands of the sword* (v. 10): they will suffer this at the right hand of the enemy. *They will be foxes' meals.* This fate will come to them, he is saying, not from some powerful foe but from the foreign neighbors, who sometimes attack like foxes but often, if driven off repeatedly, take to their heels. Now, the immediate interpretation is that most of those who fall in battle will not be thought worthy even of burial, but will end up as carrion for the wild beasts.

(8) *But the king will rejoice in God* (v. 11). I on the contrary, he is saying, having received kingship from you, shall take satisfaction not from their death but from your providence, thanks to

6. Comment on the verse (in a slightly different form) takes a new turn in this further excerpt from the longer form of the text. The phrase "the people that came to faith from the nations" occurs in similar excerpts on v. 2 (cf. note 4) and at the opening of the next psalm.
7. Cf. Eph 4.13.
8. Again we could imagine Chrysostom developing the implications of this thought for his more insistent views on the relation of divine grace to human effort. Theodoret does not feel he is establishing a position here.

which I escaped the various schemes of the enemy. *All who swear by him will be praised* [1341] *because the mouth of those uttering iniquity has been stopped.* In the future everyone will speak of the king with confidence and swear by his salvation,[9] no longer afraid of slanderers, whose mouth has been stopped in death. While Saul was alive, they were afraid to use that language of David; but after his death everyone then fearlessly accorded him [i.e., David] also the prerogative due the king and used the king's salvation as an oath, citing it as an honor and a basis of favor.

9. Theodoret does not concur with Dahood's belief that the LXX supports a reading of the verse in which it is by God that people swear, not by the king.

COMMENTARY ON PSALM 64

To the end. A psalm for David.

THIS PSALM HAS THE SAME theme. It describes the schemes adopted by Saul, and foretells the deliverance from them. It also foretells the prayers that should be employed by the people converted from the nations to show reverence for the Savior.

(2) *Hearken, O God, to my voice when I pray to you; rescue my soul from fear of the foe* (v. 1). Accept my petition, O Lord, he is saying, and strengthen my resolve lest I be in terror of the enemies' attacks. *Shelter me from the massing of evildoers, from the multitude of workers of iniquity* (v. 2). He gives the term *massing* to their agreement and concert in vice, to which he begs to be rendered superior, fortified by divine care as by some rampart. Then he describes their manifold wiles. *Who sharpen their tongue like a sword, bend their bow, a bitter thing, to strike down the innocent from ambush* (vv. 3–4). They devise calumnies, he is saying, in the war waged against me, whereas I have given them no cause for it. He calls the guiltless *innocent* here. Aquila, on the other hand, put "bitter word" for *bitter thing*, Theodotion, "bitter remark," and Symmachus, "They filled their bow, a bitter remark." Now, for *from ambush* Symmachus said *furtively*, that is, employing snares and traps. The psalmist teaches this also in what follows.

(3) *They will strike him down without warning, and will not be afraid.* In their trickery, he is saying, they attack suddenly, having no fear of God watching. *They confirmed their wicked plan, they talked of laying snares secretly* (v. 5). Symmachus put this more clearly: [1344] "They firmed up a wicked plan, they proceeded to lay snares secretly": hatching a deadly scheme, they plotted and planned what wiles to employ against me, and put their plans into effect. Now, they were so presumptuous because of

their belief that no one was interested in human affairs, as the following words suggest: *They said, Who will see them?* They believe, he is saying, that there is no judge of what happens. While some apply this to Absalom, Saul, and the rest, others apply it to the lawless people who from time to time devise snares and wiles against the churches of God.[1] Note what he says in the following verse.

(4) *They sought out iniquity, they wore themselves out searching searchings* (v. 6). They racked their brains, he is saying, they came up with every stratagem against me, they left no stone unturned, assailing me openly, undermining me secretly, employing spies, patrolling deserted regions, searching rocky places, on mountains and in caves and crevices hunting out the practitioners of piety, of whom the divine Paul declares, "the world was not worthy of them."[2] *Man will approach, his heart deep, and God will be exalted* (vv. 6–7). Theodotion rendered this more clearly, putting it this way, "God will shoot down a man's thought and deep heart": even if they conceal their doings countless times, these are obvious to the God who oversees everything, who gives a glimpse of his own exaltation by bringing such people to justice.

(5) *Their blows were reduced to a children's dart, their tongues lost their force against them* (vv. 7–8). Despite using such disreputable tactics, they failed in their purpose: just as the darts fired by really young children inflict no harm on their victims, so their tongues cause no harm to those affected; rather, the injury rebounds on those who cause it. *All who observed them were alarmed:* those who observed them failing in their endeavors were filled with panic and dread, and marveled at divine providence; what follows suggests this. *Every person was afraid, and reported the works of God; they understood his doings* (v. 9): coming to the realization of God's care, they were in dread of the divine judgment.

(6) [1345] *The just will rejoice in the Lord, and will hope in him* (v. 10). It is in particular those devoted to the divine laws of the Old and New Testament who are buoyed up with satisfaction and place their hope firmly in God. *All the upright in heart will be*

---

1. Again here, as in the opening comment, the longer form of Theodoret's text makes its attempt to extend the relevance of the psalm.
2. Heb 11.38.

praised: those who direct their thoughts to God and refrain from straying from the straight and narrow will also gain a good name with people. Now, you would find David and those of his time and after them living the good life; I refer to the victorious martyrs and the champions of piety.[3]

3. The longer form of the text extends the application of this closing verse as well, by the final comment and the specific mention of "Old and New Testament."

COMMENTARY ON PSALM 65

To the end. A psalm for David. A song of Jeremiah and Ezekiel, and of the people in exile when they were on the point of departing.

OW, IN SOME COPIES there occurs, "A song of Jeremiah and Ezekiel, and of the people in exile when they were on the point of departing." The Hebrew text does not have this, nor the other translators, nor the Septuagint in the Hexapla;[1] it seems likely someone added this title without heeding the psalm's meaning nor learning the history. First of all, you see, Jeremiah was not involved in captivity; instead, having the choice of living where he wanted, he chose life in his own country. Hence it is not at all relevant to those departing for captivity, but to those living in captivity: being far from their homeland and longing to sing to God, they were prevented by the Law from doing so—remember their cry, "How shall we sing the song of the Lord in a foreign land?"[2] So they said the psalm in Babylon by way of entreating God.

(2) *A hymn becomes you, O God, in Sion, and a vow will be paid you in Jerusalem. Hearken to my prayer; all flesh will come to you* (vv. 1–2). All the verses of the psalm [1348] befit those living in Babylon: longing for return, they offer this hymn singing to God. Now, with this prediction about them there is mingled as well prophecy of the salvation of the nations.[3] *A hymn becomes*

---

1. Theodoret's form of the LXX (see Introduction, section 3, for its nature) bears the extended title, which he feels free to fault for adequacy. Theodoret claims to make reference to the Hexapla, whole or in part, for noting the alternative versions and a form of the LXX, different from his.

2. Ps 137.4. Theodoret has a change of heart later, thinking even this historical reference does not do justice to the psalm's overall perspective.

3. Theodoret's wish to give the psalm a wider application emerges this time in the shorter form of the text, and this mention of the situation of the

you, O God, in Sion, and a vow will be paid you in Jerusalem. You bade us offer you the hymn in that city, he is saying; so I beg to be allowed to render it to you in that place. Now, blessed Paul said to the nations about this city, "You have come to Mount Sion and the city of the living God, the heavenly Jerusalem";[4] it was said by the Apostle about the church from the Gentile nations. *Hearken to my prayer.* Accept my request, he is saying, and free me from the bonds of captivity. While the people led into captivity from Jerusalem utter this prayer aloud, the people hastening to escape from captivity by idols also make the request; they expressed the same thing more clearly in what follows. *All flesh will come to you.* This contains a clear prediction of the nations' knowledge of God: At present our prayer is to be granted return (he is saying) and to offer the hymn in the consecrated Temple, whereas a little later the whole of humankind, rid of the error of polytheism, will run to the true God.

(3) *Lawless people's words overwhelmed us* (v. 3). Symmachus, on the other hand, [expresses it] in this way, "Lawless people's words prevailed over us": I have been forced into serving irreligious people in the grip of lawlessness, he is saying. Then he teaches the reason for the servitude: *You will have mercy on our impiety.* It was not unjust of you to condemn me to slavery, he is saying; instead, it was due to the impiety once committed by me, and from this I beg to be delivered through your [1349] lovingkindness. From this point they go on to declare blessed the life in their homeland as a mentor and provider of piety: *Blessed is the one whom you chose and adopted, who will dwell in your courts; we will be filled with the good things of your house* (v. 4). Enviable and blessed, he is saying, is the people preferred by you to the other nations: it will take its position in your sacred courts, and from there gain benefit and blessing.

(4) *Holy is your temple, wondrous in righteousness* (vv. 4–5): your temple is full of holiness, and those attending it it teaches your righteousness through your sayings. *Give ear to us, O God, our sav-*

---

converts from the nations is at once picked up and developed by the longer form.

4. Heb 12.22.

ior, hope of all the ends of the earth and of those far distant at sea. Once again at this point he foretells the salvation of the world, and recalls the prophecy of the patriarch Jacob; his words were, "A ruler shall not depart from Judah, nor a leader from his limbs, until he comes to whom it belongs, and the expectation of the nations in person."[5] Here, too, he called him *hope of all the ends of the earth and of those far distant at sea.* Now, he suggests in this way those living on the islands, those people on the continents opposite, and those assigned to inhabit the ends of the world. [1352] Give ear to us, he is saying, you who will in the near future illuminate all humankind with the light of the knowledge of God.

(5) Then he describes the power of God to the degree possible. *Preparing mountains in his strength, girt with his might. You who stir up the depths of the sea: who will bear the roar of its waves?* (vv. 6–7). Symmachus put "setting" for *preparing;* Theodotion put "soften" for *stir up.* It means, You make the mountains steady and immovable, you move the sea when you wish, and in turn cause it to rest so that there is not even a sound of it for those listening; you achieve each of these things by employing your ineffable and immeasurable power, which you wear like some belt. Since you are life, in fact, you share it with those who believe in you and arrange for those who are unmoved to be set firm.[6] Since, you see, one who is girt is better equipped for doing whatever one wishes, in figurative fashion he called God's power a belt.

(6) At this point he then goes on to lead into the achievements of the New Testament: *The nations will be disturbed* indicates the apostles' preaching, [1353] which caused disturbance and distress to people, in keeping with the Lord's statement, "I have come to set a man against his neighbor, a son against his fa-

---

5. Cf. Gen 49.10.
6. This intrusive remark from the longer form of the text seems to arise from a misreading of the original form, where there is mention of the word in the psalm text, ζώνη, "belt," evidently misread as ζωή, "life." Would that suggest that the longer form, ancient though it can be shown to be, is the work of someone (not the author) reading and developing the shorter original?

ther, a daughter against her mother, a daughter-in-law against her mother-in-law."[7] Habakkuk also foretold this in the words, "You made your horses trample the sea and disturb the mighty waters,"[8] meaning the apostles, whose riding he speaks of in the sense of their teaching of salvation. But after this he quelled the distress, and arranged for peace for everyone, saying, "My peace I give you, my peace I leave you."[9] *Those who dwell at the extremities will be in fear of your signs* (v. 8): while first came disturbance, there followed fear caused by the magnitude of the wonders, giving a lesson in piety. *You bring gladness to departures by morning and evening:* struck with fear at your marvels, people forsake their former error and enjoy knowledge of the true God, and at the beginning and close of the day they offer delightful and acceptable hymn singing to God. This meaning Symmachus conveyed, "They celebrate daybreak and evening."

(7) *You examined the earth and bedewed it; you spared nothing to enrich it* (v. 9). Symmachus, on the other hand, said it this way, "You will enrich it with abundance": not only us will you provide with spiritual watering, but the whole world you will water to satiety, sparing nothing to enrich it. *The river of God was filled with waters.* [1356] Symmachus, on the other hand, expressed the three things in the form of wishes: "You will examine the earth, give it to drink, and enrich it with abundance, with God's streams brimful of water." Now, the world, which of old was fruitless, the Lord let be seen as fruitful in abundance and variety, providing irrigation in divine rivulets. Who else would they be, these rivulets of God full of water, than the divine apostles? Christ the Lord said of them, "The one believing in me, as Scripture said, rivers of living water shall flow from his belly"; and again, "The one drinking from the water that I shall give will never be thirsty; rather, the water that I shall give will be a spring of living water gushing up to everlasting life."[10] *River of God,* in the Septuagint reading, is the grace of the Spirit, divided into rivulets, pouring the word of wisdom into one person, supplying knowledge to another, a gift of healing to another, and

7. Matt 10.35, loosely recalled.   8. Hab 3.13.
9. Cf. John 14.27.   10. Cf. John 7.38; 4.14.

kinds of tongues to another, and in these ways watering the world. *You prepared their nourishment, because this was the preparation.* Symmachus, on the other hand, put it this way, "You will bring to maturity all its seeds, you will establish it thus": ridding it of its former error and confirming it with pious teachings, you will guarantee the maturing of the fruits of virtue, which give joy to you and nourish those growing up. According to the Septuagint, you see, the fruit that is produced is nourishment for the very ones who produce it: *You prepared their nourishment,* it says, note, *because this was your preparation;* to this end you caused them to bear fruit, it is saying, so as to be nourished in this way.[11]

(8) *Bedew its furrows* (v. 10). From this it is clear that it is a prophecy of future events, not a record of the past. *Multiply its produce.* [1357] Continue, O Lord, he is saying, to water their thinking, like some furrows, and stimulate it to fertility. *In its drops it will enjoy growing up.* The drops of rain borne in due season by the teachers will give it joy and cause it to blossom. *You will bless the crown of the year of your bounty* (v. 11). *Year of bounty* is to be taken as "acceptable year of the Lord" in Isaiah's term: "The Spirit of the Lord is upon me," he says, "for which reason he anointed me and sent me to bring good news to the poor, to heal the contrite of heart, to preach freedom to captives and sight to the blind, to proclaim an acceptable year of the Lord."[12] Accordingly, he applies the term *year of bounty* to the time after the Incarnation of our Savior for reason of its providing him with one fruit, piety. The inspired word asks this blessing for this.

(9) *Your fields will be filled with richness. The beauty spots of the wilderness will be enriched, and the hills encircled with joy* (vv. 11–12). With the emergence of this bounty, the former wilderness will yield fruit in due season. The hills stained with the demons' sac-

---

11. Theodoret does seem to make heavy weather of this verse, not prepared to let it pass lightly but insisting in Antiochene fashion on wrestling with each phrase as rendered by Symmachus (primarily, as usual) and then his Septuagint. But modern commentators also differ about its interpretation, whether to see it as acknowledgment of an abundant harvest or (with Dahood) as a prayer for rain—too narrow a perspective for Theodoret, as he insists when concluding his commentary.

12. Isa 61.1–2.

rifices will welcome those who sing to the Lord constantly and embrace the angelic way of life, and will become the cynosure of all eyes. Now, events bear out these words: we see everyone making their way to those occupying the pinnacles and practicing the most exalted virtue. *The rams of the flocks were clad* (v. 13). The prophet Ezekiel also called the *rams of flocks* powerful, [1360] but accused them of consuming the good pasture and trampling underfoot the rest, of drinking the pure water and stirring up the rest with their feet.[13] Here, on the other hand, he forecasts good things even for them: he says they will be clad and clothed; the nature of the clothing the divinely inspired Paul mentions, "All you who were baptized into Christ have clothed yourselves with Christ,"[14] he says. In other words, since Christ the Lord chose those who were originally fishermen, artisans, and people living in poverty, the grace of the Spirit prophesies the salvation of both rich and powerful. Hence he says, *The rams of the flocks were clad:* not only the other sheep but also the very rams present themselves for the baptism of salvation. *The valleys will abound with grain:* those whose lot is poverty and who have chosen to practice piety will offer God their particular fruit, one thirtyfold, one sixtyfold, one a hundredfold.[15] *They will shout and sing hymns:* all the aforementioned will praise God with complete enthusiasm for bestowing upon human nature such a wonderful transformation.

(10) So we know that some historians, giving superficial consideration to what is said, claimed that each of these things happened after the return from captivity,[16] when good seasons were granted them along with their freedom, as well as such abundant rains that the Jordan overflowed, which they claimed was referred to as *river of God*. For my part, on the contrary, I discov-

13. Cf. Ezek 34.17–19. 14. Gal 3.27.
15. Cf. Matt 13.8.
16. The longer form of the text cites Origen and Eusebius in connection with this interpretation of the psalm (though our access to Origen's thinking through Eusebius's commentary on Ps 65 would not give this impression). Theodoret, we noted, is (finally—after some initial hesitation, it seems) prepared to accept a reference neither to events contemporary with the composer (like those moderns) nor to the later situation of the people, but only to the salvation of the Gentiles.

ered from history nothing of the kind happening: they lived for a long time in great need, as Ezra taught. Rather, I found in the psalm the open prophecy of the salvation of the nations: *All flesh will come to you,* it says, and *Give ear to us, O God our Savior, the hope of all the ends of the earth and of those far distant at sea;* this meaning I suspected was in keeping with those words. Those, on the other hand, who take pleasure in fairy tales, imagining the construction of Jerusalem and developing their own thoughts like dreams, claimed this did not happen but [1361] would do so after the recall of the Jews, adding this fairy tale to the corruption of the other teachings. Let us leave them to their folly and cleave to the divine sayings, crying aloud with David, "Your Law is a lamp to my feet, and a light to my paths."[17]

17. Cf. Ps 119.105.

COMMENTARY ON PSALM 66

To the end. A song of a psalm of resurrection.

HE HEBREW TEXT DOES NOT have this addition, nor do the other translators, nor the Septuagint in the Hexapla; on the contrary, it is likely some have inserted it.[1] The divine David wrote this psalm for the captives in Babylon, not still begging to be granted the return, but when they had already been granted it and were on their way. But he forecasts at the same time the salvation of the nations as well.

(2) *Shout aloud to God, all the earth, sing to his name, give glory in praise of him* (vv. 1–2). All people, he is saying, share hymn singing with us, and offer with us due reverence to God. Now, it is right that they summon all human nature to such a sharing: in [the Jews] the story of the salvation of everyone is foreshadowed. You see, just as they were freed from the slavery to the Babylonians, so all people were liberated from the harsh tyranny of the devil after the Incarnation of the God and Savior.[2] Then they teach the form hymn singing takes. *Say to God, How awesome are your deeds! In the might of your power your foes will speak falsely of you* (v. 3). Marvel, he is saying, at [1364] the marvels worked by God through his power: they are of such a kind and number that the extraordinary character of the deeds is not credited by the impious. Now, that verse, *In the might of your power your foes will speak falsely of you,* has also a different sense testified to by the truth: When you illumine the world with the light of the knowledge of God, he is saying, and bring the majority around to godliness, then those who are in the grip of the darkness of unbelief will give an impression of piety, denying

---

1. Cf. note on the similar opening to the previous psalm. Theodoret has no comment on the reason why the title should refer to resurrection.
2. This phrase, too, incorporated into the text from the longer form, makes no mention of resurrection, only incarnation.

their impiety. This we witness happening constantly: many in thrall to the pagan error are not rash enough to confess it openly, and the Jews, when pressure is brought to bear, sing of the victory of the cross, and the truth of inspired composition is displayed on all sides.[3]

(3) *Let all the earth adore and sing to you. Let them sing to your name, O Most High!* (v. 4). Symmachus said this more clearly, "All on earth adore you by giving voice, they sing to your name." Now, this is a prophecy of the present time, in which the praise of the God of all is sung by all the nations, and Christ the Lord is called Most High by everyone. *Come and see the works of God, how fearsome in his plans for the sons of human beings* (v. 5). Apply your mind, he is saying, and consider each of the things done by God, and marvel at his ineffable wisdom, through which he conducts the human race towards piety. This, in fact, is also the meaning Theodotion gave it. *Fearsome in his plans for the sons of human beings.* Symmachus, on the other hand, said, "Fearsome his designs for the sons of human beings": he employs fearsome and astounding designs for the salvation of human beings.

(4) Then he outlines what was done of old. *He turns the sea into dry land; they will cross the river on foot* (v. 6). The tense has been changed here: he spoke of the past as future,[4] [1365] whereas the others retained the tense, Symmachus saying, "He turned the sea into dry land, they crossed the river on foot." This is the God, he is saying, who will grant us salvation as well, who of old divided sea and river and bade our forebears cross without risk, and accords the nations the crossing which they make when through the washing of regeneration they are reformed. In other words, just as at that time through the hand of the mighty Moses he divided the Red Sea at this point and that, so now as well through the hand of the priest he renews the peo-

---

3. Does Theodoret seem to be conceding at several places here that conformity to Christian belief and practice on the part of pagans and Jews at his time was only forced and superficial, if gratifying for all that?

4. With rare comments like this, Theodoret could give the impression he is unaware that the LXX regularly misreads the tense of the original. It is not clear to whom he is attributing the future employed in his text here, though he suggests the alternative versions have correctly reverted to an original past tense.

ple who believe in Christ, while submerging in figure Pharaoh with his chariots—that is, the devil with his concupiscences (the initiated know what I mean). *We shall rejoice in him there,* that is, at the Jordan, like those from the nations at the divine bath: at that time the Jordan divided for the people, and today by welcoming the Maker and Creator of all the Jordan secures the salvation of human beings; our God and Savior, you see, the washing that came unnoticed on the scene for our sake, regenerated everyone by water and Spirit. Remembering this, and teaching how the ancestors crossed it,[5] they added, *We shall rejoice in him there.*

(5) *To the one ruling by his might forever* (v. 7). He has everlasting power, he is saying, and unbounded kingship. *His eyes gaze on the nations:* he not only cares for us, but exercises his providence over the whole world, and in the near future will provide all with knowledge of him. Having clearly divined this in such a fashion, the inspired composer perceived with spiritual eyes those confuting the message, and quite distinctly foretold both their unbelief and arrogance. *Let the rebellious not be exalted in their own estimation,* Theodotion calling them "deviant" and Aquila, "withdrawn"; Symmachus, on the other hand, said it more clearly: "Let the unbelieving not be exalted in their own estimation." Now, let us see also [1368] the fulfillment of this prophecy: the three or four pagans who persisted in their impiety are the very ones who have a great opinion of themselves for not being carried away with the multitude. These the inspired word admonishes, *Let the rebellious not be exalted in their own estimation:* they rebel within themselves against the just Judge, and incur his just punishment.

(6) Then, after making clear their impending retribution, the prophetic mind shifts its focus to a different aspect. *Bless our God, O nations, and make the sound of his praise be heard* (v. 8). For *make be heard* Symmachus said "ensure a hearing." They continue exhorting the nations to desist from the ancestral ways, to

5. The "it" in reference to the Jordan mentioned above betrays the expansion of the text from the longer form, which supplies a sacramental comment on the verse in two places. The author of that form of the text is aware he is using esoteric imagery, to which the baptized—"the initiated"—had privileged access.

sing the praises of their God, and to teach those ignorant of his power; he said, *make it be heard,* meaning, Teach the others. *Who has brought my soul to life, and has not let my feet slip* (v. 9): after handing me over to impious people, he did not let me stray and depart from the straight and narrow. Now, we should note that a choir of the more pious recount all this; God, you see, dispatched to them people distinguished for piety as guides in law and living, as it were, training and enlightening them, and guiding everyone towards piety. Such was David, such Ezekiel, such Hananiah, Azariah, and Mishael. It was appropriate for them and suchlike people to speak the foregoing words; in their person, after all, the grace of the Spirit composed them.

(7) *Because you have tried us, O God; you tested us in fire as silver is tested* (v. 10). You allowed us to suffer this, he is saying, in your wish to show everyone the genuineness of our piety. These very things were said in the person of those who in their time suffered for Christ or still suffer, and who won the crown. *You led us into the trap, you laid troubles on our back; you put people over our heads. We passed through fire and water, and you brought us out into refreshment* (vv. 11–12). That was what the furnace was like in which the whistling breeze cooled the athletes; *trap* is the lions' pit and an unguarded trap, yet the prophet escaped from it through divine grace.[6] It was in fact likely that they were beaten and tortured like [1369] captives and slaves by their captors; hence they also said, *You laid troubles on our back; you put people over our heads:* we were made slaves in place of being free, but we were freed from it all and gained the return, and we shall offer you the prescribed sacrifices. He added this, you see,

(8) *I shall enter your house with holocausts, I shall pay my vows to you, which my lips uttered and my mouth spoke in my tribulation* (vv. 13–14). Whatever promises I made in my pain and prayer I shall duly discharge. *I shall offer you in sacrifice holocausts of fatlings and rams, I shall offer oxen along with goats* (v. 15): what I should offer you I shall willingly slaughter. He called *fatlings* what was well-fed and fat; the Law, in fact, prescribed the offering of spotless

---

6. Cf. Dan 3 in the Greek versions, where both the lions and the "whistling breeze of dew" (Dan 3.50) caught the fancy of Fathers like Chrysostom, also.

and perfect victims, and the prophet Malachi cursed those who keep for themselves such victims and offer imperfect ones,[7] which was the beginning of those awful troubles for Cain, too.[8] And we, too, learn to celebrate the divinity with the more precious things in our possession.

(9) *Come, listen, and I shall recount to you, all you who fear God, everything he did for my soul* (v. 16). It is not without reason, he is saying, that I promise to offer these gifts; instead, I enjoyed wonderful gifts from him, which I beg you who entertain reverence for God to come to know. He spoke in this fashion also in the twenty-first psalm: "I shall pay my vows before those who fear him."[9] Now, in these ways we are taught to share with them and to recount the divine doings to them in particular: "Do not give holy things to dogs, nor cast your pearls before swine,"[10] and, "My mysteries for me and for mine."[11]

(10) *With my mouth I cried to him, and under my tongue I exalted him* (v. 17).[12] Symmachus, on the other hand, said, "I called upon him with my mouth, and my tongue was at once exalted": immediately on offering my request I received the response, and filled with joy I moved my tongue in a hymn of thanksgiving. *If I saw iniquity in my heart, let the Lord not hearken to me* (v. 18). Symmachus, on the other hand, said it this way, "If I foresaw iniquity in my heart, may [1372] the Lord not hearken." If in begging to be freed from slavery, and to be granted the return, he is saying, I imagined I would commit some iniquity after the return, let me not attain divine favor; but the facts bear witness that I am not lying.

(11) *This is the reason, you see, that the Lord hearkened to me, he attended to the sound of my petition* (v. 19): on seeing me unblemished by such thoughts, he generously accorded me his special

7. Cf. Mal 1.8.
8. A somewhat perverse reading of Gen 4.3–5.
9. Ps 22.25.
10. Matt 7.6.
11. Isa 24.16, in some Greek versions.
12. There is an obvious awkwardness with the final clause as it stands. While a modern commentator like Dahood will resolve the difficulty by reference to Ugaritic, Theodoret turns to his trusty authority, Symmachus, for an alternative reading.

gifts. This is the way the choir of pious people recounted these things, and they bring their words to a climax in a hymn: *Blessed be God, who did not reject my prayer or turn his mercy away from me* (v. 20). I shall respond to the benefactor in hymns, he is saying, both for accepting my prayer and for according me mercy. He does not cease exhorting those who believe in him to celebrate him constantly.

COMMENTARY ON PSALM 67

To the end. With hymns, a psalm of a song for David.

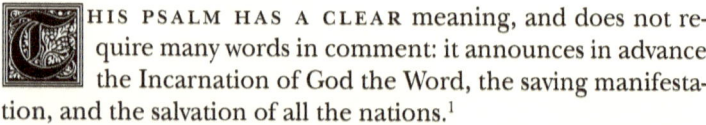HIS PSALM HAS A CLEAR meaning, and does not require many words in comment: it announces in advance the Incarnation of God the Word, the saving manifestation, and the salvation of all the nations.¹

(2) *May God have pity on us and bless us; may his face shine upon us and be merciful to us* (v. 1). Perceiving with the eyes of the spirit the salvation coming to all human beings through the divine manifestation, the inspired author begs that it be granted as soon as possible so that all may reap the blessing stemming from it. Now, he says, *May God have pity on us,* and not only this but also *bless us,* the reason being that he not only blessed us but also had mercy, having saved us by means of his coming from the Virgin; the psalmist says, *may his face shine upon us.* We saw him face to face, of course, but once made man; we saw him presenting no other form but God the Word in person immutably born of the Virgin.²

---

1. While Theodoret made clear in his preface that he would not let the "ancient history" behind any psalm predominate in his *Commentary* to the detriment of "prophecies about Christ the Lord," he made no mention of interest in the cultic setting or any other situation of the composer's time prompting the psalm beyond the historical, such as in this case the condition of crops. Here he proceeds at once to such prophecies, unlike modern commentators, who see the psalm as either thanks for a bountiful harvest or prayer for rain that would ensure it.

2. It is from the longer form of the text that this (rare) reference to the Virgin comes. The term "immutably," ἀτρέπτως, is one of the quartet that the council of Chalcedon (that "triumph of Antiochene theology," in Kelly's words; see Introduction, p. 6, n. 10) will incorporate in its carefully etched definition of the union of two natures in Christ a few years later; it occurs again at the conclusion of comment in the shorter form of the text. Both forms of the text take the Antiochene position on union; the longer alone seems to accentuate the role of Mary as Theotokos which could be seen as critical of Nestorius of Antioch.

(3) Then he teaches us this more clearly through what follows. *So as to know your way on earth* (v. 2). So that, he is saying, the earth's inhabitants may be taught the way leading to you, and be guided to it. Lest you think this is said about the land of Jews, he was right to add *your saving power in all the nations.* My prayer, he is saying, is for your face to appear so as to shed light even on the nations seated in darkness[3] and draw them to salvation.

(4) [1373] *Let peoples confess to you, O God, let all peoples confess to you. Let nations be glad and rejoice because you judge peoples with uprightness, and you guide nations on the earth* (vv. 3–4). This is the reason, to be sure, that all peoples and the nations throughout the world should rejoice and celebrate, and recount your favors: they know that no concern of theirs goes unheeded or unattended; rather, you are judge of all things, delivering righteous judgments, guiding those caught up in error towards the truth, and punishing those who refuse to believe.

(5) *Let peoples confess to you, O God, let all peoples confess to you* (v. 5). The repetition was not made idly, but to render the listeners more enthusiastic and to show that he is God and Savior of all. *Earth gave up its fruit* (v. 6). Those who spring from it are no longer in ignorance of God, who is over all and who, according to the inspired author, "found the complete way of knowledge, was afterwards seen on earth, and lived among human beings."[4] For this reason they offer him the sweetest fruit of piety.

(6) *May God, our God, bless us; may he bless us* (vv. 6–7). As twice he urged the nations to hymn singing, so twice he sought the blessing for them. It should be realized, of course, that in blessing God human beings offer him words only and are incapable of doing him any practical favors, whereas in his blessing God confirms the words in action and provides those being blessed

---

3. Cf. Luke 1.79.
4. The psalm, bereft of historical significance for Theodoret, is dispatched briefly without even Scriptural documentation, except for this significant passage from Baruch 3.36–37, which loses something in the form quoted, the original allowing for a distinction between God and the Wisdom who appears on earth. (What interests modern commentators in this verse of the psalm, whether it be thanks for rain or petition for it, is of no moment, we noted.)

with an abundance of manifold goods. Then he teaches how it is possible to attain the divine blessing: *Let all the ends of the earth fear him.* In other words, he who is well disposed to the divine laws and is fearful of the judgment to come serves God by observing them; the divine service brings the blessing.[5] The very conclusion therefore recommends not Jews but all people to have fear of God, and teaches the lesson that it is our God who is personally concerned to provide salvation for those who believe. Let the impious heretics be ashamed for not confessing him to be God of God, the only-begotten and eternal Son of the Father, who became Son of Man immutably in the last days, as we said, for the salvation of human beings.[6] [1376]

5. His mentor Chrysostom (and the Pelagians?) would be more comfortable with this admission of the role of human effort in the process of salvation after Theodoret had first carefully prioritized divine and human. It is Trinitarian and Christological heresy that he has particularly in his sight.

6. Again echoes of Constantinople's creed and foreshadowing of some elements of Chalcedon's definition (cf. note 2).

COMMENTARY ON PSALM 68

To the end. A psalm for David.

EEING THE IMPIETY THAT WAS in general practice in society and the dominion of the devil, the divine David, instructed about the manifestation of our God and Savior by the all-holy Spirit, offers supplication, begging for it to happen as soon as possible. He immediately receives revelation of the future and at the same time is instructed; and he gives instruction about the salvation of the human race, the destruction of the enemies, and in general the surprising turn of events.[1]

(2) *Let God arise, and let his enemies be scattered; let those who hate him flee from his presence* (v. 1). It is time for you to arise, O Lord, he is saying, and concern yourself with the salvation of human beings: immediately all the mass of the enemies will be put to flight, scattered by the radiance of your manifestation. Now, he calls *rising* not only the end of long-suffering, as we have often said, but also the rising of the Savior of the world in three days after willingly accepting death for us. This is also the way we are often accustomed to stir up to assistance of the wronged those judges who exercise fairness, urging them to spring to action and curb the insolence of the wrongdoers. *As smoke disappears, let them disappear; as wax melts before fire, let the sinners perish before God* (v. 2): just as the force of the winds scatters the smoke, and the wax brought close to the fire dissolves, so hostile people, O Lord, will become completely helpless in your presence. To those whom the Septuagint called *sinners* all the other transla-

---

1. While exegetes have classed this as the most difficult and obscure of all the psalms, and attempts to identify its cultic setting and genre have varied, Theodoret with his different approach and perspective admits no difficulty.

tors gave the name "ungodly," as both Hebrew and Syriac call them.[2]

(3) *Let the righteous be glad* (v. 3). When this happens, he is saying, the whole chorus of the righteous will be filled with satisfaction. *Let them rejoice before God, let them be exultant with joy.* In this he showed that he offered that supplication not against human beings but against the demons warring on human beings. When they are scattered and made helpless, the nations exult and sing the praises of the God who has saved them. [1377] *Sing praise to God,* he says, *sing to his name; make a way for him who ascends above the setting sun. Lord is his name; exult before him* (v. 4). Here the inspired word urges the sacred apostles to go in haste to the nations with dancing and hymn singing, and prepare the way for the universal king. It resembles the words spoken to them by the Lord, "Go, teach all the nations, baptizing them in the name of the Father and of the Son and of the Holy Spirit."[3] Now, through teaching of this kind and the regeneration of baptism, the rough way became smooth and was prepared for God wanting to dwell and walk with them, according to the prophet.[4] Now, he spoke of his *ascending above the setting sun* to indicate the darkness that at that time enveloped human souls. Symmachus, however, translated it this way, "Lay down a way for him who travels in an uninhabited land." Now, the wilderness is uninhabited, and the divine Scripture often called the nations wilderness: "Rejoice, thirsty wilderness," it says, and again, "The children of the desolate one will be more numerous than of the woman with a husband."[5] Upon this wilderness, uninhabited, deprived of light, and hence called *setting,* the Sun of Righteousness rose, expelled the gloom, and made the uninhabited land his own temple.

(4) *They will be panic-stricken before him, father of orphans and judge of widows* (vv. 4–5): they cannot bear his manifestation, knowing him to be a righteous Judge; after all, he made clear

---

2. While recourse to the original may not have been of help to Theodoret, Syriac and other Greek versions would shed some light for him.
3. Matt 28.19.   4. Cf. Isa 40.3–4; Matt 3.3.
5. Cf. Isa 35.1, 54.1.

the righteous character of his providence through care of widows and attention to orphans. The story of the divine Gospels, too, teaches us the panic and dread of the demons; we hear them saying, "What have you to do with us, Son of God? Have you come to torment us before time?"[6] *God is in his holy place.* Since he had said, *Let God arise,* and *Make a way for him who ascends above the setting sun,* it was right for him to add this, as if to say, Let no one think the God of all manages things by relying on change of place. It is like the saying of the Lord, "No one has ascended into heaven except the one who descended from heaven, the Son of Man, who is in heaven";[7] [1380] by this he showed the unbounded character of the divine nature, and taught that he had descended, and though living down here and associating with human beings, he was in heaven and was not separated from the Father.

(5) *God makes hermits live in a house, leading out the fettered in boldness like the embittered, those living in tombs* (v. 6). He calls *hermits* those of single purpose, who choose to be interested in virtue alone, and not choosing one thing at one time and another at another; these he says inhabit the divine dwelling. And he calls *fettered* those wrapped about with the bonds of sin, whom he predicted would be released and rendered bold. Such a person was Matthew, such James son of Alpheus, such Zacchaeus, who once freed from the bonds of iniquity waged war very boldly on the one who bound them. Not only the fettered, however, he is saying, does he render bold, but also those who have reached the heights of impiety and dwell in their own bodies like foul-smelling tombs; to these he will accord salvation along with those others.

(6) *When you ventured forth in the midst of your people, O God, when you passed through the wilderness, earth shook and the heavens sent down drops* (vv. 7–8). Symmachus rendered it thus, "O God, when you went before your people, moving through the uninhabited land, earth shook and heaven sent down drops": on the point of passing through that barren and uninhabited land,

6. Matt 8.29.
7. John 3.13.

which had not yet felt the light's ray, you disturbed the earth and shook it, and from heaven you sent down the shower of grace. Now, in the one case, this happened at the crucifixion: at that time the earth shook and the rocks broke open,[8] and all the earth was disturbed on gaining the impression that the Creator of all was hung up on the cross; in the other case, after the return to heaven: at that time the grace of the Spirit came upon the apostles, like drops of dew. Then, to teach Jews more clearly who was doing all this, he added, *at the presence of the God of Sinai, at the presence of the God of Israel.* [1381] The one who appeared to our forebears on Mount Sinai, he is saying, is the one who also shook the earth at the time of the Passion to refute our folly, and who made the gift of the Spirit.

(7) *You will allot rain without stint for your inheritance, O God* (v. 9). What he previously called drops he spoke of as a shower: grace was provided to the teachers for the needs of the learners. He calls the watering from the instruction a shower, you see, and he labeled it *without stint* on account of the voluntary attitude: you are not sprinkled by force; rather, convinced by the instruction you enjoy the grace.[9] *It was failing, but you restored it.* Not the *rain* he said was failing but the *inheritance;* he referred to the rebellions of the ungodly as *failing*. The Lord also spoke this way to Paul: "My grace is sufficient for you; my power is made perfect in weakness."[10] But as for you, in the time of rebellion affirm and strengthen the athletes: you have them for an inheritance according to the inspired words, "Ask me, and I shall give you nations for your inheritance and the ends of the earth as your possession."[11] Now, Symmachus also translated it this way, "You completed and settled it," and Aquila more clearly, "You worked on it and brought it completion": you kept it unmoved despite its troubles in the persecutions.

(8) *Your animals dwell in it* (v. 10). He calls the sacred apostles

---

8. Matt 27.51.

9. Theodoret's unwillingness to recognize the psalm as a rehearsal of historical themes (cf. note 1), plus the LXX's change of tenses, make the task of commentary that much more difficult.

10. 2 Cor 12.9.

11. Ps 2.8.

God's *animals;* he mounted them and drove out their error, and converted human beings to knowledge of God. He also spoke this way about Paul: "He is my chosen instrument for bringing my name before nations and kings and sons of Israel."[12] For this reason the divine Habakkuk called them horses: "You trampled the sea with your horses," he says, "churning the mighty waters."[13] They dwell in God's inheritance, that is, in the nations, the inspired word foretold; and they are dwelling even today, not only sanctifying with the receptacles of their bodies those who make an approach but also converting the souls of human beings by the teaching of the biblical writers. *You provided in your goodness for the poor, O God.* On account of your goodness, he is saying, you regaled poor human nature with these things.

(9) *The Lord will give a word to those bringing good news with great power* (v. 11). Those whom he named *animals* above he here calls evangelists. Since they were fishermen, [1384] tax collectors, and shoemakers, and were commissioned to be teachers of philosophers, sages, orators, and those who prided themselves on their eloquence, he rightly teaches whence they draw the streams of their teaching and offer watering. *King of the hosts of the beloved, with the charm of your house divide the spoils* (v. 12). Symmachus, on the other hand, said this: "The Lord gave sayings to those bringing good news with a mighty army. Kings of the armies were loved; they became beloved, and the dwelling of the house will divide the booty." He calls the believers a mighty army; the Apostle also speaks this way in writing to Timothy, "Fight the good fight," and, "No one serving in the army gets entangled in everyday affairs, the purpose being to please the commanding officer."[14] He called their teachers "kings of the armies," and said they were loved and beloved. The Lord calls them that, too: "You are my friends. I shall no longer call you servants but friends";[15] and the divine Apostle says the same, "The love of God urges us on,"[16] and, "Who will separate us

---

12. Acts 9.15.
13. Hab 3.15. Theodoret with this off-the-cuff citation feels no need to justify his giving this further composer an eschatological sense.
14. 1 Tim 1.18; 2 Tim 2.4.   15. John 15.14–15, loosely recalled.
16. 2 Cor 5.14.

from the love of Christ?"[17] Now, he calls "booty" those who formerly made their own limbs slaves of sin, and handed them over to the service of the devil. These he divided up among the sacred apostles, appointing one as teacher of the Romans, one of the Greeks, and making some of them heralds for the Indians, some for the Egyptians. *The charm of the house* divided up this booty for the sacred apostles. The believers, according to the divine Apostle, are house of God. *Charm of the house*, the grace of the Holy Spirit, renders it charming and resplendent with the manifold generosity of its gifts.

(10) This he taught more clearly in what follows.[18] *If you lie down among the lots, a dove's wings covered in silver, and its back, in the pallor of gold* (v. 13). He calls the grace of the Spirit *a dove's wings:* he appeared in the form of a dove at the Jordan River. He says its wings were silvered, while its back was adorned with gold: to more simple people he offers simpler and easier ideas, and the more profound to the more mature; "my mysteries are for me and mine,"[19] remember. To some, being immature, he gives milk to drink, [1385] while to others he offers solid food.[20] Now, *lots* is the word he applies to the two testaments. So he means in each instruction, Come forward and see the varied grace of the Holy Spirit, bidding them not simply come forward but be in constant attendance, describing this as *lying down,* since the person who is asleep stays still.

(11) *When heaven divides king from king on it, they will be covered in snow on Zalmon* (v. 14). Previously also he had called the apostles *kings* as heirs to the kingdom of heaven, just as in the forty-fourth psalm he called them rulers: "He appointed them rulers over all the earth."[21] He foretells, however, the visit of the all-holy Spirit, which happened on the day of Pentecost, when in their persons they received the grace of the different forms of

17. Rom 8.35.
18. Theodoret's readers would hardly find any of the comments on these verses "clear," which is not surprising, considering the renowned obscurity of the verses (not to mention the state of the original text). But he cannot allow himself to concede this lack of clarity, and proceeds quite arbitrarily and definitely to rule on the meaning of each phrase.
19. Isa 24.16, in Greek versions.   20. Cf. 1 Cor 3.2.
21. Ps 45.16.

tongues. So he means that at that time when he divides the kingdom of the world among them, bidding one have charge of these nations and another of those, he will make them famous and reveal them in a condition like snow. He also foretells the place where it will happen: he called Jerusalem *Zalmon,* the choir of the apostles living there and enjoying the grace of the all-holy Spirit.

(12) *God's mountain, fat mountain, curdled mountain, fat mountain* (v. 15). Those whom he called animals, bringers of good news, and kings he also refers to as *mountain.* Likewise the Lord also said in the sacred Gospels, "A city built on a mountain cannot be hid";[22] likewise Isaiah also cries aloud, "In the last days the Lord's mountain will be conspicuous."[23] He uses *fat* and *curdled* with the same meaning, as providing much nourishment to the flocks grazing on it, and receiving great richness from divine grace. *Why do you suspect mountains are curdled? The mountain on which God was pleased to dwell* (v. 16). Aquila, on the other hand, said, "Why do you contend, many-ridged mountains, with the mountain on which God longed to settle?" The inspired word is addressed against Jews and against the lawless assemblies of heretics, who class themselves as churches; it says, Why do you contend and claim to rival [1388] the mountain, which God has made his dwelling? *The Lord will dwell there forever:* he will not live on this mountain as he dwelt among you for a specified time, O Jews; instead, he will have an eternal dwelling in this place. This the term *forever* indicated.

(13) *God's chariotry, ten-thousandfold thousands of stalwarts* (v. 17): he will not have now, as he had among you, O Jews, but a few holy ones, on whom he descended and with whom he communicated; those worthy of the divine descent are ten-thousand times more numerous than they. The new inheritance has thousands and ten-thousands of stalwarts more numerous, who produce the fruit of godly piety, who keep to the right path, are

---

22. Matt 5.14. Theodoret must be confident his readers will not question these wild identifications—of lots with testaments, of Zalmon with Jerusalem, of mountains with apostles—which Scriptural documentation hardly supports.
23. Cf. Isa 2.2.

thought worthy of the crown, and strive after the prize of their heavenly calling. *The Lord among them, on Sinai, in the holy place.* He who appeared to our ancestors on Sinai, he is saying, will in his own person guide the latter as well; they are not different beings: "The same Lord is Lord of all," remember, "generous to all who call upon him."[24]

(14) The inspired word, having thus shown him descending and putting to flight the enemy horde, shows him ascending and granting freedom to those formerly held captive: *You ascended to the heights, taking captivity captive* (v. 18). The ascent indicates the descent; the Apostle gives testimony in the words, "When it says, He ascended, what does it mean but that he had also first descended to the lower parts of the earth? He who descended is the same one who ascended above all the heavens."[25] Now, *he took captivity captive* by taking back those formerly made captive, as though he first took them captive and then granted them their freedom. *You received gifts from among human beings.* The Apostle said "gave";[26] both things happened: accepting faith from those who made their approach, he accords them grace.[27] This is the way, in fact, the chorus of the apostles, by believing that God is of God, was declared heir of the kingdom of heaven; this is the way countless numbers of the victors and those living a holy life were glorified for devoting their words to God. *Even those resisting your dwelling.* Aquila rendered it more clearly: "Although opposed to your dwelling." You did not have regard to their former opposition, he is saying; instead, while seeing their resistance, you continued your favor until you made them your own dwelling.

(15) [1389] *Blessed be the Lord God, blessed be the Lord day after day* (v. 19). It was right for the inspired author to direct his tongue to hymn singing. You deserve to have your praises sung forever, he is saying, having practiced such wonderful lovingkindness. *The God of our salvation will make our path plain.* He who

---

24. Rom 10.12.   25. Eph 4.9–10.
26. Eph 4.11.
27. This brief comment on the relation of faith to grace, and the following similar one from the longer form of the text, reveal that Antiochene concern to uphold the role of the human in the process of salvation.

has regaled us with salvation, he is saying, will also smooth our way lest we fall short of such good things. *Our God is a God who saves* (v. 20). Now, he ensures this by being a font of salvation. *And to the Lord, the Lord, belongs escape from death:* he opened to us death's impenetrable watchtower, smashed the bronze gates, and shattered the iron bars. He indicated this by what follows.

(16) *But God will shatter heads of his foes, the hairy crown of those who cavort in their sins* (v. 21). He opened for us the gates of death, he is saying, by shattering the heads of the foes, who scrutinize people's sins and cannot bring themselves to leave unexplored even the hairs of their head. Now, by *hair* he implies the slightest failing; what he means is something like this: To sinners God allotted death as a punishment. The inquisitive devil, however, like some cruel executioner, is reluctant to overlook even the slightest detail of the life of human beings, and instead dispatches human nature to death. So on perceiving Christ the Lord to be invested with the same nature, he made his approach to find out grounds for his death; the Lord said as much, remember, in the sacred Gospels: "The prince of this world is coming, and in me he will find nothing."[28] Yet, despite finding nothing, wrongly he dispatched him to death. On the one hand, this wrong broke his power, and, on the other, it opened Hades for human beings, which is mentioned in the *Discourses on Providence* at length.[29] The divine Paul also said the devil has the power of death.[30]

(17) *The Lord said, I shall bring them back from Bashan, I shall bring them back in the depths of the sea* (v. 22). Symmachus, on the other hand, put it this way, "The Lord said, I shall bring them back from Bashan, from the depths of the sea." Now, the meaning of *Bashan* is shame, and shame is the fruit of sin; so from this

28. John 14.30, in a form that differs from our received text and yet has been defended by scholars like Boismard; it is grist to Theodoret's mill.

29. This throwaway remark is an important clue to the dating of Theodoret's extant *Ten Discourses on Providence*, which according to Quasten have been variously placed before the Council of Ephesus by some and after 435 by others on the grounds of doctrinal development. If we can date the *Psalms Commentary* between 441 and 449, there is at least a *terminus ad quem* for the *Discourses*.

30. Heb 2.14.

the God of all will bring us back, [1392] and from the depths of the sea. What *the depths of the sea* is the inspired author teaches in crying aloud, "Let me be delivered from those who hate me and from the depths of the waters. May the torrent of water not drown me, nor the deep swallow me."[31] *So that your foot may be dipped in blood, your dogs' tongue have some of it from your foes* (v. 23). Symmachus, on the other hand, put it this way: "So that your foot may be shattered with blood, and your dogs' tongue lick the blood of each of your enemies." In other words, after showing the God of all, like some hero, prevailing over the enemy and liberating those unjustly reduced to servitude, he depicts in word torrents of blood and corpses trampled on, thrown about unburied and exposed as meat for dogs. This is also the way he cries aloud in Isaiah, "I trod a winepress alone, and none of the nations was with me; I trod them in my anger and crushed them in my rage; their blood I poured on the ground, and my garments were spattered with their defeat."[32]

(18) *Your entry, O God, has been observed, the entry of my God, the king, who is in his holy place* (v. 24). He applies the term *entry of the holy one* to his dispensations, and *holy place* to the temple taken from the seed of David. Your providence became clear to everyone, he is saying, and everyone discerned your various dispensations. *At the head came rulers in the wake of singers, in the midst of young girls playing drums* (v. 25). He now teaches us at this point the joy of the churches. He calls the sacred apostles *rulers* for being appointed their master-builders, and applies the term *young girls playing drums* to those who practice virginity and offer the divine melody to God.

(19) Then he makes his words clearer: *In assemblies bless the Lord God from fountains of Israel* (v. 26). He revealed the end of the former covenant: there was one temple of the Jews, whereas here he forecasts the great number of the churches, in which from the Israelite fountains he bids hymns be sung to the Lord of all. Now, it would be right for the inspired books of the Old Testament to be called *fountains of Israel*, because from them we

---

31. Ps 69.14–15.
32. Cf. Isa 63.3.

offer hymn singing to God;[33] but since in addition to the [1393] Old Testament books he regaled us also with the apostolic fountains,[34] he is right to add, *There Benjamin despite his youth is in a trance* (v. 27). Aquila, on the other hand, has, "There little Benjamin rules over them," whereas according to Theodotion, "their mentor." Now, *Benjamin despite his youth* is blessed Paul, who came from the tribe of Benjamin—*despite his youth* on account of being called and given his name after everyone else, especially as the narrative in the Acts calls him a young man.[35] He it is who rules over the Church, gives instruction in divine matters, and guides those of good intentions towards salvation. It also happened that while in a trance he came to know that the one who was persecuted by him is in heaven, the one who was thought to be dead.[36]

(20) Since, however, it is not only blessed Paul but also the rest of the choir of the apostles who educate the believers in divine things, the inspired word was right to mention them as well: *Rulers of Judah, their leaders, rulers of Zebulun, rulers of Naphthali.* The remaining apostles took their origin from these tribes: those called brothers of the Lord had their beginnings in the tribe of Judah, whereas Peter, Andrew, James, John, and Philip were in fact from the town of Bethsaida, Matthew and James are recorded as living in Capernaum, and Simon the Zealot is called a Canaanite. Now, all these places are in Galilee, and Zebulun and Naphthali had their allotment there, too. There are two witnesses to this, the Old Testament inspired author and the evangelist, the one prophesying, the other offering testimony; they speak in these terms: "Land of Zebulun, land of Naphthali, and

---

33. Though Theodoret does not attend much to the liturgical context of the Psalms, he is ready to admit that Christian churches have adopted Old Testament themes and forms in their worship.

34. Twice in commentary on this obscure verse Theodoret makes the distinction between works and authors of Old and New Testaments—the former "inspired (*prophetikos*) books" or simply *prophetai*, the latter "apostolic books" or evangelists. As with Chrysostom, he is not thus denying the inspiration of NT authors (see my "Chrysostom's terminology for the inspired Word").

35. Cf. Acts 7.58, 13.21; Rom 11.1; Phil 3.5.

36. Cf. Acts 9.4–5.

the other inhabitants of the seacoast, across the Jordan, Galilee of the nations; the people sitting in darkness have seen a great light."[37]

(21) *Command, O God, in your might; confirm, O God, what you worked amongst us. From your temple in Jerusalem* (vv. 28–29). Symmachus, on the other hand, put it this way, "Give orders, O God, about your strength; strengthen, O God, what you did for us on account of your temple, which is above Jerusalem." [1396] Confirm the grace you accorded us, O Lord, he is saying, on account of your temple, which you assumed from us, which you set over every rule, authority, and power, above every name that is named, not only in this age but in the age to come.[38] He calls the city on high *Jerusalem,* of which blessed Paul says, "The Jerusalem on high is free; she is mother of us all."[39] So they are asking that, on account of the relationship to the temple, the grace given be confirmed, and on account of the firstfruits the whole batch enjoy the gift provided.[40] From this point he goes on to prophesy as well the change in kings: *Kings will offer you gifts:* they will cease their persecution and offer due reverence to God; and as in their person they receive tribute from their subjects, so in their own person, like slaves and subjects, they will bring you gifts. Eyes that perceive the realization of the prophecy are witnesses to this.[41]

(22) *Rebuke the wild animals of the reeds* (v. 30). Some copies, on the other hand, have "grove"; but whether grove or *reeds,* the sense intended here is sterility. Now, a habitation is had by these wild beasts, which even by divine invocation the inspired author

37. Cf. Matt 4.13–16; Isa 9.1. Theodoret's inclination to apply this verse to New Testament figures is encouraged by Matthew's quotation of Isaiah in connection with the calling of the Twelve.
38. Cf. Eph 1.21. Here, as in commentary on v. 24, Theodoret sees in mention of the temple a reference to the humanity of Jesus.
39. Cf. Gal 4.26.
40. Cf. Rom 11.16.
41. Theodoret in this psalm and almost consistently throughout the whole *Commentary* is anxious to take an eschatological and at times anagogical interpretation, seeing the psalmist's words realized at a later stage—provided the reader follows the requisite process of θεωρία (occurring here in verb form, as often) to discern that fuller sense. As in his preface, he implies here that many fail to achieve it.

teaches us to drive out. *The assembly of the bulls in the calves of the nations so as to confine those tested with silver.* He calls the throng of the Jews *bulls* on account of their habitual audacity, and gives the name *calves of the nations* to those of the Gentile nations who have come to faith, on account of their recent calling. So the inspired word foretells the rebuffs from the Jews given to the pious in the beginning of the preaching. Now, they do this, he is saying, in their wish to exclude them and deprive them of the good fortune given them, tried in the fire like silver as they are, and proven reputable. Blessed Paul also said this about them: "They make much of you, but for no good purpose; instead, they want to exclude you."[42] And since among the nations as well there were many who were in opposition and were responsible for manifold slaughter of holy ones, he is right to say also of them, *Scatter nations intent on war.*

(23) Having thus prophesied about those in opposition, he shifts his focus to those who came to faith. [1397] *Ambassadors will come from Egypt* (v. 31). Now, he made mention of Egypt first as having formerly attained the pinnacle of impiety. The Acts also mention it, describing those who were gathered together on the day of Pentecost, when the grace of the all-holy Spirit came upon the apostles.[43] *Ethiopia will take the lead in offering its hand to God.* This prophecy also had its fulfillment; the eunuch of Queen Candace of the Ethiopians is witness to it, whom Philip guided to the truth.[44] Then he calls on the kingdoms of the whole world: *Kingdoms of the earth, sing praise to God, sing to the Lord* (v. 32). Everyone in the world, he is saying, receive the light of the knowledge of God, and offer hymn singing by way of respect. *To the one who rides on the heaven of heavens at sunrise* (v. 33): Christ the Lord ascended not only to the visible heaven but also to the one above it, and took his seat at the right hand of the majesty in the upper chamber of his own dawning, emitting rays

---

42. Gal 4.17. Modern commentators are also at their wits' end endeavoring to find significance in the obscure references in this verse in particular, and are more tentative than Theodoret is prepared to allow himself to appear.
43. Cf. Acts 2.10.
44. Cf. Acts 8.26–39.

upon all human beings. *Lo, he will give his voice a sound of power.* Now, he means by this the coming of the all-holy Spirit after the assumption of our Savior; the Lord also called it *power:* "Stay in this city," he said, "until you have been clothed with power from on high." Blessed Luke also made mention of this sound in the words, "And there came a sound from heaven, like a violent wind coming, and it filled the house where they were sitting."[45]

(24) *Give glory to God* (v. 34). This resembles the edict of the Apostle, "Glorify God in your body and in your spirit, these belonging to him."[46] In other words, it is right for those enjoying such favors to glorify their benefactor in everything. *His magnificence is over Israel, and his power is on the clouds.* The sacred apostles took their origin from Israel, you see, and so gave a glimpse of God's magnificence in the wonders they worked; those who came after them, [1400] who received the gift of teaching in the manner of some clouds drawing up moisture from the sea of the Holy Spirit, bedewed human beings.

(25) *Awesome is God in his holy ones* (v. 35). All other lovers of virtue ensure the praises of God are sung, he is saying, in fidelity to the Lord's pronouncement, "Let your light shine in people's sight so that they may see your good works and glorify your father in heaven."[47] *The God of Israel will give power and might to his people.* It was not idly that he made mention of Israel here; rather, it was because Jacob, who had been afraid of Esau, was then accorded a divine vision and was encouraged, and eliminated the dread from his mind.[48] Now, the verse teaches us that the one who made that man strong and showed him to be superior to his adversaries will likewise empower his new people and render them unbeaten and unbowed.

(26) *Blessed be God!* On hearing, however, lover of learning, that God is often called God, Lord, Savior, do not get the impression of someone else: he is no one else but Father and Son and Holy Spirit—not three Gods (perish the thought), as I have

---

45. Luke 24.49; Acts 2.2. Apparently, Theodoret is unaware that he is quoting Luke in the former citation.
46. 1 Cor 6.20, in an expanded form known in Antioch.
47. Matt 5.16.
48. Cf. Gen 27–28.

often said. The names God, Lord, King, Creator, All-powerful and suchlike, in fact, are used of the undivided Trinity.[49] The conclusion fits the psalm: it was necessary for the account of such wonderful goods to finish with divine praise.

---

49. This rather peevish corrective comes from the longer form of the text, and seems out of character with Theodoret's evident wish to bring to a close a commentary that has been lengthy, more than usually expansive, and relatively fully documented from Scripture. The *monitum* delivered to the deviant scholar employs a superlative form of the *philomathes* that Chrysostom also used pejoratively of those whose studies went to extremes.

COMMENTARY ON PSALM 69

To the end. For what will be changed. A psalm for David.

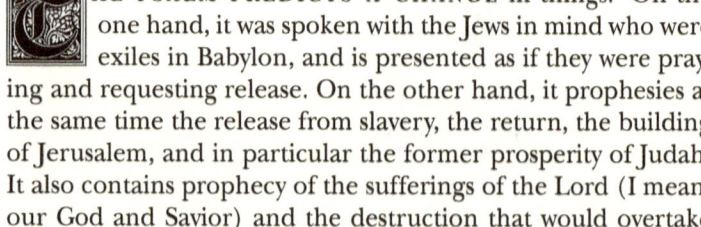HE PSALM PREDICTS A CHANGE in things.¹ On the one hand, it was spoken with the Jews in mind who were exiles in Babylon, and is presented as if they were praying and requesting release. On the other hand, it prophesies at the same time the release from slavery, the return, the building of Jerusalem, and in particular the former prosperity of Judah. It also contains prophecy of the sufferings of the Lord (I mean, our God and Savior) and the destruction that would overtake Jews on account of them.² Since, you see, what they suffered at the hands of their adversaries they had perpetrated against their benefactor and Savior, the just Judge imposed on them the verdict they called down upon their foes.

(2) [1401] *Save me, O God, because waters have impinged on my soul* (v. 1). The society of the very pious offers the supplication. The psalmist calls *waters* the vast number of calamities; on all sides, he is saying, troubles wash in upon me. *I am caught in the muddy depths, and there is no firm footing* (v. 2). Symmachus, on the other hand, says, "I am immersed in endless descents, and there is no foothold," by analogy with those falling into the depths of the sea, carried down as far as possible, and scarcely touching bottom. Now, he indicates by this the magnitude of the troubles befalling those taken off in captivity. *I reached the depths of the sea, and a tempest overwhelmed me.* He embellishes the description

---

1. In fact, Theodoret is mistakenly accepting the confusion made by the LXX of similar Hebrew forms in the psalm's title (as before: see note 4 to Ps 45), and failing to recognize there a cue for the psalm's melody.
2. Again a brief statement of theological rationale for the situation of Jews in Theodoret's world, expanded in comment on v. 25 (see note 11 below).

with various figures, not finding an image adequate for the troubles affecting him.³

(3) *I was wearied with my crying; my throat was hoarse* (v. 3). I cry aloud in constant lament, he is saying, so that even my very speech organs are affected. Now, by *cry* he means the intensity of the prayer in his mind. *My eyes failed with my hoping in God.* He used this expression by analogy with those awaiting the return from foreign parts of some friend and familiar, eyes glued to the road: I was tired out waiting for your help, he is saying.

(4) Then he goes on to teach in clearer manner what he had expressed previously in figure: *More numerous than the hairs of my head were those who hated me without cause. My foes grew strong, those who pursued me unjustly* (v. 4). Let none of the scholars get the impression, however, that this is spoken on the part of the God and Savior.⁴ It is not spoken this way: it is spoken only on the part of those taken off in captivity from Jerusalem to Babylon, as I hinted above. Now, he means, The adversaries outnumber me, they are invested with influence, they are roused to hatred against me, and all without my giving them any basis for hatred. *What I did not steal I then repaid:* I pay the penalty for wrongs I did not commit. Though no robber or wrongdoer, the people say, I am led into slavery by them on that account. *O God, you know my stupidity, and my failings are not hidden from you* (v. 5): you know everything, O Lord, and no deed escaped your notice; accordingly, you know that I did not wrong them—it was only your laws I broke. This resembles the verse, "To you only I did wrong, and committed wickedness in your sight."⁵

---

3. When not concerned to give the verses a historical or eschatological reference, Theodoret is capable of appreciating the literary artistry of the psalmist.

4. Again a jibe in the direction of over-zealous readers of the verse, as in the conclusion to the previous psalm, though here in the shorter form of Theodoret's text. "All things in moderation" is a typical Antiochene stance. His resistance to a Christological interpretation of this psalm, after Ps 22 the most frequently quoted in the New Testament, where it is taken in a messianic sense, is intriguing (see notes 9 and 11 below).

5. Ps 51.4. The pace of comment on this psalm, of similar length to the previous one but much less obscure (and textually less complicated), is clearly brisker, as the paucity of Scriptural documentation suggests.

(5) *Do not let those who wait on you, O Lord, Lord of hosts, be put to shame on my account. Do not let those who seek you, O God of Israel, be confounded on my account* (v. 6). Let me not [1404] prove an occasion of harm for others, he is saying, nor be disappointed in my hope as I wait for your salvation. Instead, let those who have knowledge of you learn from what happened to me that salvation, not shame, is the fruit you bring to those hoping in you. *Because it is for your sake that I have borne reproach, shame has covered my face* (v. 7): I am full of shame on receipt of reproaches directed at you, the enemy constantly mocking me, attributing my servitude to your weakness. *I have become alienated from my brothers, and a stranger to my mother's sons* (v. 8). He lists the occasions of the trouble to stimulate the loving God to mercy: first he mentioned the reproaches of the impious, then the separation from relatives and friends. In other words, like captives forced into slavery, they were not permitted to live with their kin.

(6) *Because zeal for your house consumed me; the reproaches of those reproaching you fell on me* (v. 9): the devastation of your holy house and the mockery of the impious were not the least cause of my trouble and distress. In fact, it was not to my fault but to your weakness that they attributed what happened to me.[6] Hence I am in torment for the blasphemies against you, being the cause of them myself. Actually, for *consumed* Symmachus instead said "wasted away." *I enveloped my soul in fasting, and it brought me reproaches. I took sackcloth for my clothing, and became a byword to them* (vv. 10–11): I am distressed by it, and waste my body with fasting; but even this proved an occasion of ridicule to them. I wear myself out, even putting on the appearance of grief with the vesture of sackcloth. The lawless took this in fact as a basis for mockery. *Those sitting at the gates gossiped about me, and in their cups they sang songs to mock me* (v. 12). In their gatherings and parties, he is saying, they hooted at my doings and made bad jokes. In former times, you see, they held gatherings at the gates.[7]

---

6. "Me" is the reading of the longer form of the text, an obvious correction of the "him" of the shorter form (movement from first to third person in the commentary admittedly being confusing).

7. A little scholarly detail is not beneath this commentator, for all his scorn for the *philomatheis*.

(7) *But as for me, my prayer is to you, O Lord* (v. 13). Symmachus, on the other hand, put it this way, "But my prayer is to you, O Lord." Despite all that has happened, he is saying, I direct my eyes to you, and await help from you. *An acceptable moment, O God*—"a moment for reconciliation," in the words of Symmachus: the punishment imposed on me has gone on long enough; it is time to bring it to a close, and let your loving-kindness come to the fore.[8] He uses *acceptable,* to imply God's good will. [1405] *In the abundance of your mercy, hearken to me, in the truth of your salvation:* measure the punishment not by my offenses but by the immeasurable mercy of your loving-kindness. On the other hand, execute your unerring and just verdict on those responsible for such awful evils against me.

(8) Then in figurative fashion he lists the calamities in an attempt to prompt his mercy by the account: *Save me from the mire lest I be stuck fast* (v. 14): I am like those who fall into a marshy pit and are expecting death; hence I beg salvation at your hands. *Let me be rescued from those who hate me and from the deep waters:* I beg to be delivered also from the enemy and from the troubles inflicted by them. To the punishments inflicted by them he applied the term *depth of waters. Do not let the watery tempest drown me, nor the depths swallow me* (v. 15). May I not be overwhelmed, he is saying, by the number and magnitude of the evils. *Nor the pit close its mouth over me.* Do not deny me salvation, Lord, he is saying, nor close the door of your loving-kindness on me: those who fall into a pity have some slight hope of release from it as long as the mouth is not closed over, whereas with it sealed up they despair of salvation.

(9) *Hearken to me, O Lord, because your mercy is good; in the abundance of your compassion cast your eye upon me* (v. 16): for the sake of your loving-kindness, not my worthiness, bring release from the evils I have outlined. Consequently, have regard to me, beset as I am by the evils, and disperse my disasters: merely an appear-

---

8. It is interesting to a translator to note that, whereas Chrysostom in commentary on this spiritual classic speaks repeatedly of God's loving-kindness, *philanthropia,* the term is relatively rare in Theodoret's script, mercy, *eleos,* being preferred by him (commentary on this psalm being something of an exception).

ance on your part is sufficient to dissipate the cloud of grievances. *Do not turn your face away from your servant* (v. 17). This, in fact, is customary for angry people to do, rejecting the supplication of those who have wronged them. *Because I am in distress, heed me promptly:* in the light of the extraordinary degree of the pain, bring me rapid consolation. *Give heed to my soul, and redeem it* (v. 18): you require but a glance to put an end to my despondency. *On account of my enemies deliver me:* while my failings are too great for pardon, yet the enemies are godless and in thrall to vice; so in view of the reproaches coming from them, let me feel the benefit of your loving-kindness, Lord. This he conveyed also, in fact, in what follows.

(10) *You in fact know my reproach, my shame, and my disgrace.* [1408] *All those distressing me are before you* (v. 19): nothing of what happened escaped you, you see everything, both their reproaches and my shame; in fact, I am both depressed and grief-stricken to be reproached by them. *My soul expected reproach and hardship; I looked for someone to grieve with me and there was no one, for comforters and I found none* (v. 20): stricken by pangs from every quarter and expecting further more grievous things, I lack any consolation. Instead, whereas those causing grief are beyond counting, there is no one to console and render the grief more bearable by sharing it.

(11) *They gave me bile for food, and offered me vinegar to drink* (v. 21). They made even my food, he is saying, vile and bitter; after all, for people who eat in pain even the sweetest food is without flavor.[9] *Let their table prove a trap before them, a retribution and a stumbling block* (v. 22): so change their joy into disasters, Lord, to beset their exploits. He called joy *table* and punishment *a trap*, note; Symmachus in fact also translated it this way, "May their table prove a trap before them, and punishment, so that they may be caught up." *Let their eyes be darkened so that they do not see*

---

9. As suggested in note 4, Theodoret's unwillingness to see a Christological reference in verses of the psalm like this seems almost perverse, considering his position on the previous psalm, for instance. Though no evangelist explicitly cites the place, the offering of the vinegar (*oxos*, as here) to Jesus is recorded in them all: Matt 27.48; Mark 15.36; Luke 23.36; John 19.29. (See note 11 below.)

(v. 23): inflict on them the dark cloud of calamities. *And completely bend their back:* condemn them to slavery, Lord, so that they may fall foul of what they do, forever stooped under burdensome toil. *Pour out your wrath upon them, and may the anger of your wrath take possession of them* (v. 24). Inflict the complete wrath of retribution on them, he is saying, and impose a prompt and adequate disaster. He suggested the promptness in the word *anger,* anger being like that, and its enduring quality in the word *wrath,* such being the nature of wrath. You see, while anger is sharp and brief, wrath is slower but more lasting; accordingly, he called the anger of wrath sharp and enduring punishment.

(12) *Let their fold be deserted, and let there be no inhabitant in their tents* (v. 25). Now, in every way he asks for the just verdict, and begs that they suffer the consequences of their own actions. Since the Chaldeans, you see, had plundered Jerusalem and the other cities of Judah, and rendered them desolate, he begs that their homeland, too, suffer this fate; and he gained his request: Babylon was made desolate, and remains so even to this day. It should be acknowledged, of course, that what the Jews begged the Babylonians should suffer for being guilty of impiety and malice against them they in their own person suffered for raging against their benefactor and savior. After all, the Babylonians rendered their food bitter, not by giving them food in that condition but by removing the natural flavor of the food through laborious servitude, whereas the Jews, far from being wronged, received favors of all kinds, and yet offered their very benefactor the gall and vinegar itself, like some pernicious vineyard.[10] This is the reason they were subjected to the same punishments, and *their table proved a trap for them, a retribution and a stumbling block:* they were condemned to slavery in place of their previous good fortune, *their eyes were darkened* for their unwillingness to see the true light, and *their back was bent* in unceasing servitude and poverty owing to their arched neck and stiff throat. *Their fold was desolate, and there was no inhabitant in the tents* of Jerusalem. So they were subjected to curses of their own making, and what they invoked upon the Babylonians for being

10. Cf. Isa 5.1–4.

wronged they suffered for doing wrong and proving ungrateful to their benefactor. This is the reason the divine apostles also used the testimonies from this place, understanding the two levels of meaning of this inspired text.[11]

(13) Let us, however, move to the next section of commentary. *Because they personally harassed the one whom you struck, and added to the distress of my wounds* (v. 26). While you, he is saying, in requiring a penalty of me for transgression, handed me over to executioners, so to speak, they enveloped me in greater troubles than you ordered, and heightened my suffering for sin. This savagery of theirs even the God of all accuses, saying, "I gave them into your hand, and you showed them no mercy; you imposed the heavy yoke on the aged, and had no mercy on the young."[12] *Add iniquity to their iniquity, and let them have no recourse to righteousness* (v. 27). The punishment imposed for sin he called *iniquity*, meaning, Impose on them a punishment appropriate to those living lawlessly; may they not attain the good things which you are accustomed to reward to the righteous.

(14) [1412] *Let them be cancelled from the book of the living, let them not be enrolled with the righteous* (v. 28). This resembles that verse, "The ungodly will not have a place to stand in judgment, nor sinners in the council of the righteous."[13] Daniel, to be sure, makes mention of these books: "A court sat in judgment, and books were opened."[14] What he means is this: Do not let them share what you give to your devotees, nor let them attain the recall which we shall enjoy, thanks to your loving-kindness. *I am poor and in pain: may the salvation from your person support me, O God* (v. 29). At this point he goes on to forecast the change in circumstances, the end of slavery, and the return of the captives—hence the psalm's title, "To the end. For what will be changed."[15] They underwent two opposite changes, in fact: for practicing repentance in Babylon they recovered their former

---

11. Finally Theodoret acknowledges the New Testament's adoption of the *testimonia* from this psalm in reference to Jesus; it is as though he cannot resist this expanded theological rationale for Jewish misfortune, "They brought it on themselves," leading him to concede two levels of meaning.
12. Cf. Isa 47.6.   13. Ps 1.5.
14. Dan 7.10.   15. See note 1.

freedom, whereas afterwards for raging against the Lord they were condemned to utter servitude. Accordingly, the present psalm foretells both outcomes, the verse, *I am poor and in pain,* signifying the former: Seeing me in poverty and testing me with many pains, you accorded me your salvation.

(15) For this reason, *I shall praise the name of my God in song, I shall magnify him with praise* (v. 30): I shall not be ungrateful for the favors, but shall return thanks with hymns, revealing to the ignorant his greatness through the account of the favors. *It will please my God more than a young bull with horns and hooves* (v. 31): the sacrifice of praise will be more satisfying to him than a young and fat bull that just recently grew hooves and horns. The transgression of the Jews is worth deploring for not wanting to understand the immaturity of the worship prescribed by the Law—namely, the captives in Babylon, who promised to sing the praises of God on return, not to offer sacrifices, the hymn singing being more satisfying to God.

(16) Let us, however, leave aside accusing them for their present behavior,[16] and proceed with the commentary. *Let the poor see and be glad* (v. 32). Let everyone, he is saying, who encounters similar problems take occasion for sound hope from us.[17] *Go in search of God, and your soul will live.* [1413] In addition to this he urges them to secure salvation through hope in God and prayer. *Because the Lord hearkened to the needy, and did not scorn those of his that are in bonds* (v. 33): he accepted our request on seeing our need, and loosed the bonds of servitude. Now, he referred to them as *in bonds* since he himself had given them into servitude.

(17) *Let heaven and earth praise him, the sea and everything crawling in it* (v. 34). I call on all creation to share in hymn singing, he is saying: the human tongue does not suffice for recounting the divine graces. *Because God will save Sion, and the cities of Judah will be built up* (v. 35): I offer this hymn to him on seeing the illustri-

---

16. Again Theodoret has to resist the temptation to dwell on the current situation of the Jews and trace it back to the psalm's obvious reference, the period of captivity.

17. Another of those rare applications of the psalm by this desk theologian, albeit bishop, to the spiritual lives of readers—a third, spiritual sense.

ous splendor of Sion and the cities of Judah, now devastated, recovering their former prosperity. Having thus prophesied the renovation of the cities, he forecasts also the great number of the inhabitants: *They will dwell there and receive it as an inheritance.* Those now captives, he is saying, once they achieve their return will build their own cities and dwell in them—not they alone, however, but their children and descendants as well. He added: *The offspring of your servants shall possess it* (v. 36).

(18) Since, however, they were due to undergo utter ruin on account of their rage against the Savior, he was right to attach a conclusion of this kind to the psalm: *Those loving your name will dwell in it.* After all, according to the divine Apostle, "not everyone from Israel is a true Israelite, nor is everyone a child of Abraham for being his descendant."[18] Now, in keeping with these words are the inspired ones from the Old Testament, "Even if the children of Israel are as numerous as the sand of the sea, the remnant will be saved."[19] This is also what blessed David means by saying, *Those loving your name will dwell in it:* after the cross and that awful frenzy those dreadful dogs were driven out, whereas by contrast the ones who love him dwelt in Sion, offering him the sacrifice of praise.

18. Rom 9.6–7. It is impossible for Theodoret to allow the psalm to close on an upbeat without taking this in an eschatological sense again, with Scriptural encouragement. The final Jewish expulsion from Jerusalem has once more to have its theological justification, their responsibility for Passion and Crucifixion—rather rabidly developed, in fact.
19. Isa 10.22.

COMMENTARY ON PSALM 70

To the end. As a reminder to David.

OR THE LORD TO SAVE ME": I found this in some copies, [1416] whereas it is neither in the Hebrew nor in the other translators. Still, it is in keeping with the sense of the psalm: the inspired author begs for salvation and for freedom from those warring against him. Now, blessed David uttered this psalm when pursued by Absalom,[1] and he is right to add "as a reminder" to the title: the memory of his sin stung him more keenly than that of the enemy. Hence he cries aloud, *O God, be prompt to help me; Lord, hasten to aid me* (v. 1). Many and varied, he is saying, are the calamities that beset me on all sides; hence I beg you to provide me with prompt assistance.

(2) *Let those who seek my soul be put to shame and routed* (v. 2). Let those hankering after my execution be disappointed, he is saying, and feel the effects of shame at it. *Let them be turned backwards, and let those bent on evil for me be confounded,* that is, not only will they be consigned to the earth, but also may those who hatch trouble for people of godly life leave this life in shame. He says as much, in fact, in what follows: *Let those saying to me, Aha, Aha, immediately be put to flight in shame* (v. 3): in addition to them let those who take satisfaction in my troubles be sent packing in shame on seeing the change in my situation.

(3) *Let all who seek you, O God, be glad and rejoice in you, and let those who love your salvation say always, God be magnified!* (v. 4).

---

1. The almost *verbatim* resemblance of this psalm to vv. 13–17 of Ps 40, so close that some modern commentators omit separate commentary, escapes Theodoret's explicit notice here as in that place, where he made no mention of this supposed *Sitz im Leben*. But he dispatches the task of commentary briskly.

The word *Lord* does not occur in the Hexapla.² [1417] Fill with complete satisfaction, he is saying, those who love you so that they may celebrate in song your kindnesses. *But I am poor and needy, O God, help me* (v. 5), that is, I am bereft of such people's righteousness, and a victim of poverty I have no wealth of virtue. *You are my helper and my deliverer:* I have benefited from your providence. *Lord, do not delay:* come to my aid as quickly as possible, and do not put off my request. It is, in fact, not only David but also the whole choir of the saints who makes this entreaty.³

2. This apparently irrelevant comment, "Lord" not appearing in the text he cites, probably arises from the fact that in some form of the LXX "Lord" occurs for "God" at this place as it did form part of the correlative verse Ps 40.16. Theodoret's footnote to this effect (as on the psalm's opening) is surely for the *philomatheis* only.

3. This final comment comes from the longer form of the text, which throughout has not been content with the brisk commentary the psalm receives.

COMMENTARY ON PSALM 71

*A psalm for David. Of the sons of Jonadab,
and the first captives.*

No title in the Hebrew.

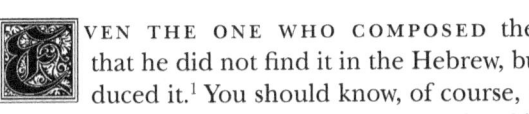VEN THE ONE WHO COMPOSED the title admitted that he did not find it in the Hebrew, but that he introduced it.[1] You should know, of course, that the sons of Jonadab were not the first to be taken captive. Blessed Jeremiah, in fact, was ordered by God to offer them wine by way of testing of the Jews' transgression: since they were unwilling to drink it on account of their forebears' recommendations, the prophet then accused the Jews of disobedience since those were observing human commands but these were transgressing divine laws.[2] Now, the psalm is spoken on the part of those in exile in Babylon, hankering for return and longing for release from slavery; blessed David wrote it, adapting the words to the group of the very pious.[3] Most of all he gives a prophecy to the sons of grace, who, freed from the abominable slavery of idols, believe in Christ [our] God and are in receipt of providence on his part.

(2) *In you, O Lord, I hoped; may I not be put to shame forever* (v. 1). May I not fall away from hope, he is saying, as I await your assistance, nor be an object of reproach to greatest extent. The for-

---

1. Theodoret has had to budge a little from his opening position on the provenance of the psalm titles as expressed in the preface.

2. The incident highlighting the exemplary abstinence of the Rechabites in fidelity to the injunction of Jonadab, son of Rechab, is recounted in Jer 35. Theodoret sees it of no relevance to the psalm contents, which he relates rather to the captivity; then the longer form of the text predictably takes it further here and below. The psalm's opening, in fact, closely resembles that of Ps 31, to which Theodoret applies a different *Sitz im Leben*.

3. We have noted that Theodoret sees the Psalms' composition as a matter of speaking and writing rather than singing.

mer offer this supplication in regard to those holding them captive, the latter in regard to the wicked demons. *In your righteousness rescue me and deliver me* (v. 2): I beg you to deliver a judgment on the Babylonians and me, and execute your verdict justly against them; this way I shall be freed from their servitude. [1420] *Incline your ear to me, and save me. Be for me a protector, God, and a secure place to save me, because you are my foundation and my refuge* (vv. 2–3). I have you as a champion, secure rampart, and safe bulwark; so receive my petition kindly. As we said before, this is said on the part of both the others, those turning away from evil afterwards up to the present and for all of life, and those being united to good. For he wishes to say this in what follows.

(3) *O my God, rescue me from the hand of a sinner, from the hand of a lawbreaker and a wrongdoer* (v. 4): I beseech you, Lord, to free me from the power of those in the grip of wickedness and impiety. *Because you, Lord, Lord, are my endurance, my hope from my youth* (v. 5). The first people[4] apply the word *youth* to the time of the great Moses, when they also enjoyed freedom even though having been enslaved to the Egyptians for the longest time. From that time, he is saying, I have had hope in you, and I await assistance from you. The new people, on the other hand, means by *youth* the renewal, which happened through the regeneration of the washing [of baptism].

(4) *Upon you I leaned from the womb, from my mother's womb you have been my shelter* (v. 6). He calls the exodus from Egypt birth and delivery. The God of all also teaches this through the most divine Ezekiel: exposing the impiety of Jerusalem and then saying, "Your father was an Amorite and your mother a Hittite," he added, "On the day your were born, your navel cord was not cut, you were not rubbed with salt or washed with water for your salvation."[5] In other words, since the navel cord is for a baby like a kind of root, through which it grows and is fed, whereas Israel

---

4. The longer form of the text, with its eschatological and sacramental viewpoint, supplies this phrase and the later comment about "the new people."

5. Theodoret is encouraged to give the verse an allegorical sense by its similarity to the expression in Ezekiel's allegory of Jerusalem, Ezek 16.3–4.

even after the exodus from Egypt had implanted within them the impiety of the Egyptians, he was right to say, "Your navel cord was not cut," because, he says, you draw nourishment from your mother's insides and persist in your former habits. So the group of the very pious then says by way of entreating God, *Because I have had hope in you before, from the very beginning, my hymn singing is ever of you.* I continue singing your praise and glory, and through your providence I became the center of attraction.

(5) *I became like a portent to many* (v. 7): [1421] after that prominence, however, I underwent a great transformation such that my situation was considered a kind of portent and sign by many. *And you are my strong helper:* yet, nevertheless, I await your help. *Let my mouth be filled with your praise so as to sing of your glory, all day long of your magnificence* (v. 8): by changing the misfortune besetting me, therefore, stir my tongue to hymn singing so that I may always offer you song. Symmachus in fact for *all day long* put "every day." *Do not cast me off in old age; when my strength fails, do not abandon me* (v. 9): I beg to enjoy even now the providence I experienced in my youth, and I ask not to be deprived of your care in old age. After all, since he called the exodus from Egypt *youth,* he used *old age* of the time of captivity, a very long period having elapsed in the meantime. *Because my foes said to me, and those protecting my soul arrived at the same decision together, saying, God has forsaken him, pursue and seize him, because there is no one to deliver him* (vv. 10–11). All my adversaries, he is saying, trample me underfoot with my calamities and surround me with troubles of all kinds, seeing me bereft of your care, and presuming me to be completely neglected and no longer likely to gain your providence.

(6) For this reason he begs, *O my God, do not keep your distance from me; O my God, have a thought for my help* (v. 12): provide me with your prompt aid, and do not keep me at length from your care. Now, it is not of God's being that he speaks of as *keeping his distance* from him—it is everywhere and is present to all—but of his providence and the operation of his assistance.[6] *Let those who*

---

6. Figurative and even (with Scriptural support) allegorical interpretation is in order—with the proviso that anthropomorphic expression is not

calumniate my soul be affected with shame and want (v. 13). Symmachus, on the other hand, put it this way, "Let those hostile to my soul be disgraced and consumed": let them fail in their familiar endeavors, and reap shame from them; let them be helpless as they unjustly plot my [1424] ruin. *Let those on the lookout for evil for me be enveloped in shame and humiliation.* Let those enveloping me in troubles of all kinds be the object of ignominy and ridicule.

(7) *I, on the contrary, shall hope in you continually* (v. 14). For seeing this happening, I shall be confirmed in my hope in you. *And I shall bring my praise of you to completion:* And I shall offer you hymn singing many times more often. *My mouth will announce your righteousness, all day long your salvation* (v. 15): I shall not cease recounting your just verdict and teaching everyone how you passed judgment on me and the enemies, and freed me from their servitude. *Because I am illiterate, I shall come under the power of the Lord* (vv. 15–16). Symmachus, on the other hand, put it this way, "I do not know how to count, in fact; I shall come under the power of the Lord." Since he promised to narrate God's righteousness and the salvation that had come to him, and yet the promise was beyond human ability, he was right to add, "Because I do not know how to count." Blessed David said this also in the thirty-ninth psalm. After saying, "You performed many marvels of yours, O Lord my God, and in your thoughts there is no one to compare with you," he added, "I proclaimed and spoke of them, they were multiplied beyond counting."[7] He says it here, too, "Because I cannot count": I was naturally incapable of writing and learning of this kind, yet I shall come under the power of the Lord and involve myself in hymn singing as far as human nature allows.

(8) *Lord, I shall recall the righteousness of you alone. O my God, you taught me from my youth* (vv. 16–17): I sing of you, O Lord, seeing the righteousness acting in my favor and recalling your commandments; for you taught me these things from infancy. From

---

allowed to go beyond due limits in speaking of God. For an Antiochene the reminder, even if rare in Theodoret's case compared, say, with Chrysostom, is necessary, especially in dealing with the lyrical language of the Psalms.

7. Ps 40.5.

this it is clear that he calls *youth* the period of the great Moses: the Law was given through him, just as also through the Incarnation of the only-begotten Son of God grace came to us, who are from the nations.[8] *And still today I shall announce your marvels; and until my mature years and old age do not abandon me, O my God* (vv. 17–18): for my part I shall teach the ignorant of your wonder-working, and for your part, as [1425] you have been called my God from the beginning, always accord me your care. *Until I proclaim your strength to every generation to come.* In inspired fashion David prophesies the future, calling the end of the Law *old age*. This happened after the coming of Christ the Lord. Now, blessed Paul teaches us more clearly in his discourse on the New Covenant. He speaks this way, "In calling it New, he made the first one obsolete; and what is obsolete and old is close to extinction."[9] So here in inspired fashion he teaches those in Babylon to say, *Until my mature years and old age do not abandon me, O God.*

(9) Then to show what kind of *old age* he speaks of, he added, *Until I proclaim your strength to every generation to come, your power, and your righteousness, O God* (vv. 18–19). Now, the *generation to come* is that following the Incarnation of the only-begotten Son of God, after which the church from the nations was formed, receiving the sacred apostles as heralds from the Jews. About this generation he speaks also in the twenty-first psalm, "The generation to come will be reported to the Lord, and will proclaim his righteousness to a people yet to be born, whom the Lord made."[10] So it is a different people from the people of the Jews, which the prophet proclaimed was not in existence but would be born. Accordingly, he says here, too, *Do not abandon me until I proclaim your strength to every generation to come, your power, and your righteousness.* Now, this resembles the prophecy of the patriarch

---

8. The longer perspective is lent to the verse by this typical comment from the longer form of the text on the Incarnation, *oikonomia*—hardly an obvious development of the verse. And in fact Theodoret goes on to draw the comparison less abruptly, with Scriptural support, employing his more usual term ἐνανθρώπησις.
9. Heb 8.13.
10. Ps 22.30–31.

Jacob: "A ruler will not depart from Judah, and a leader from his thighs, until he comes to whom it belongs—he the expectation of nations."[11] *O God, to the heights, which you made as mighty works for me.* Aquila and Symmachus, on the other hand, put it this way, "O God, on high, which you made as mighty works," that is, lofty and mighty things done by you, O Lord, sufficient to persuade everyone to name you Most High. *O God, who is like you?* No one, he is saying, can equal or be compared to you. You surpass everyone in nature, in power, and in all good things.

(10) At this point he foretells the return: *How many tribulations you revealed to me, numerous and evil; relenting, you gave me life* (v. 20). After consigning me to manifold calamities on account of the transgressions committed by me, he is saying, you then in turn brought me back to life. *And from the depths of the earth* [1428] *in former times you brought me back.* I suspect I have attained a return to life, he is saying, freed from such awful calamities, in defiance of human thinking. Now, you might say that this was also spoken on the part of human nature: he who descended into the lowest parts of the earth—namely, the God from God, who for their sake also chose to become man—brought them back from the depths of the earth.[12] God said this also through Ezekiel: "I shall open your graves, and bring you back from Babylon,"[13] that is, I shall put an end to human despair and grant you return in defiance of the enemies' expectation.

(11) *You multiplied your magnanimity in my regard, and, relenting, you consoled me and in turn brought me out from the depths of the earth* (v. 21). Symmachus, on the other hand, said, "You will increase my magnificence, and surround me with consolation." He also forecast other similar things—in other words, Your goodness will be demonstrated by your care for me. *I shall confess to you among peoples, O Lord* (v. 22): I shall not cease recounting your gifts and teaching the ignorant. Now, it should be noted that here, too, he made mention of many peoples, who after

---

11. Gen 49.10.
12. Another eschatological reference inserted by the longer form of the text (with echoes of the creed of Constantinople).
13. Ezek 37.12, conveniently misquoted.

the Incarnation of our Savior enjoyed salvation by means of the heralds from the Jews.

(12) *With musical instruments I shall sing of your truth on the harp, O God, the holy one of Israel:* I shall make use of the customary instruments to compose hymns. *My lips will rejoice because I sing to you, and my soul, which you redeemed. My tongue, too, will continue to meditate all day long on your righteousness, because those seeking troubles for me are ashamed and confounded* (vv. 23–24). According to this he forecasts the destruction of the Babylonians wrought by Cyrus the Persian and the recall of the Jews. With their destruction, he is saying, I shall attain my return; when I enjoy it, with gladness and elation I shall celebrate, singing of your favors and constantly meditating on your Law.

COMMENTARY ON PSALM 72

For Solomon.

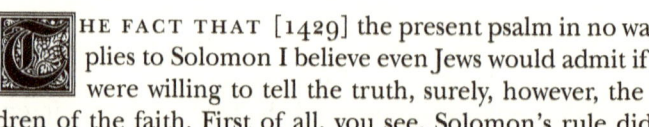THE FACT THAT [1429] the present psalm in no way applies to Solomon I believe even Jews would admit if they were willing to tell the truth, surely, however, the children of the faith. First of all, you see, Solomon's rule did not reach to the ends of the earth, nor did he receive tribute from west or east. Next, being human and living for a span in keeping with nature, he had an end to his life, and not an edifying one, either. The psalm, on the contrary, shows the person spoken of by the inspired author to be more ancient than sun and moon. Now, interpretation of the verses brings this out more clearly. The title, too, which is not inappropriate,[1] really relates to the Savior. Solomon is presented as a man of peace, and this the Chronicles clearly teach us: God says to David through Nathan, "Solomon will be his name, and I shall give peace in his days."[2] Now, this name Christ the Lord also has. Paul, the great herald of the truth, cries aloud, "He is our peace, making the two into one, and breaking down the dividing wall";[3] and the Lord himself says to the sacred apostles, "My peace I give you, my peace I leave with you."[4] Consequently, his kingship, the peace achieved by him, and the salvation of the nations is what this psalm foretells. And since he is both God and human being, being the one eternally and assuming the other for our sakes, the inspired

---

1. Theodoret, like modern commentators, is skeptical of the attribution or at least application of the psalm to Solomon (not merely by the LXX, *pace* Weiser), recognizing the hyperbolic character of some of its sentiments (as does Dahood, who unlike Theodoret can further acknowledge the antiquity of the language of the original). In this key psalm in the Epiphany liturgy he sees a messianic meaning, looking for Scriptural support for it.
2. 1 Chron 22.9.   3. Eph 2.14.
4. Cf. John 14.27.

composition teaches both: it says that as God he has authority over all, whereas also as human being he receives it from his own Father.[5]

(2) *O God, give your judgment to the king, and your righteousness to the king's son* (v. 1). Christ the Lord is king and a king's son; hence the inspired composition calls him both *king* and *king's son*. Likewise the patriarch Jacob names him both lion and a lion's cub: "Judah is a lion's cub," he says; "you have sprung from my seed, my son; lying down you rested like a lion and like a cub—who will rouse him?"[6] For he is not only king, but also a king's son. As God he was born of God the universal king, and as human being he has King David for forebear. The inspired word exhorts that righteousness to be given by God to him as human being. Then it teaches the reason: [1432] *To judge your people in righteousness, and your poor in judgment* (v. 2): those in the grip of the poverty of sin he will free from the slavery of the wicked tyrant, justly condemning him and those in his grip. *May the mountains restore peace to the people, and the hills righteousness* (v. 3). This is a literary fiction to bring out the transformation of all things. He spoke in this fashion in recounting the exodus of the people, "The mountains skipped like rams, and the hills like lambs of flocks."[7] We see the change in both the mountains and the hills: in place of the impiety that once held sway over them, those who have embraced the angelic life reap the benefit of the evangelical justice in them; acting as ambassadors for human beings, they make divine reconciliation their business.[8]

(3) *He will judge the poor of the people, save the sons of the needy, and humble a calumniator* (v. 4). Rightly is the devil called *calumniator*: he both directed calumny against God, claiming it was out of envy that God had prevented the taking from the tree, and also against Job he employed the same lies, saying, "Surely

---

5. Theodoret's comments here and below show again his carefully balanced Christology.
6. Cf. Gen 49.9.
7. Ps 114.4. A due reminder to his reader of the liberties that lyrical expression takes with language.
8. Is it the religious of his day whom Theodoret sees as having taken upon themselves this ministry of vicarious reconciliation after embracing "the angelic life"?

Job does not fear God without reason? Touch all that he has," he says, "and surely he will curse you to your face."[9] In the eighth psalm, on the other hand, he gave him the names *foe* and *avenger*,[10] whereas here, *calumniator*. But the Lord humbled and overthrew him, while according freedom and salvation to those subjected to his tyranny. *He will endure as long as the sun, and generations of generations before the moon* (v. 5). Responsible for all these things, he is saying, he has no beginning to his days, to quote the apostle, nor end to his life.[11] He was in fact born of the Father *generations of generations before the moon,* that is, in existence before the creation by generations without limit. But he also *will endure as long as the sun,* that is, he will have everlasting being, not because the sun has everlasting being, but since he did not find an adequate comparison and yet knew the sun to be remarkable and a creator of times and days; and so he compared to it the change in circumstances from darkness to light. Christ the Lord is actually given the name Sun of Justice.

(4) [1433] *He will come down like a shower on a fleece, and like a drop falling on the ground* (v. 6). Through this he gave us a clear glimpse of the human birth happening silently, very tranquilly, and secretly. Just as a fleece receives a shower without giving rise to any din, and drops of dew fall on the ground without affecting the sense of hearing, so did the Lord's conception happen, without [her] living together with any obvious suitor. Later, following the conception, he suspected some impropriety and wanted to send her away unobtrusively,[12] but through an angel was made aware that the birth was spiritual, not human.

(5) *Righteousness will arise in his days* (v. 7). The outcome bears witness to the words: human nature was freed from its former

---

9. Gen 3.5; Job 1.9, 1.11. Theodoret passes over without mention God's care of the poor and needy, a theme to which Chrysostom (had he commented on this psalm) would have warmed, one surmises. Is he not so socially sensitive, or does he think social commentary more appropriate to preachers than to desk theologians (albeit bishops)?
10. Ps 8.2.
11. Cf. Heb 7.3.
12. Cf. Matt 1.19. If Joseph is unnamed, Mary goes unmentioned. Relation of the verse to the Incarnation is encouraged by its use in Advent liturgy.

godlessness and came to learn piety. Even, however, if the life of some of the believers is not in keeping with the laws of the Gospel, nevertheless there are hordes beyond counting, in the army and in private life, in city and in country, who give close attention to virtue. *And abundance of peace until the moon is no more.* In former times, in fact, there were fiefdoms and kingdoms separated by its own race that were hard put to it through frequent wars, and so were not in a position to enjoy the gift of peace. After all, they were constantly involved in military pursuits, and many have recorded these wars of Romans and Greeks. On the other hand, the books of Kings and Maccabees teach us for what degree of trouble the fiefdoms were responsible. After the Incarnation of our God and Savior, by contrast, they came to an end, and one kingdom rules the world of ours, through which peace became the way of life and lent force to the divine preaching. Now, the phrase *until the moon is no more* means for the whole of the present life, not to mention the future, when true peace will become the way of life.

(6) *He will have dominion from sea to sea* (v. 8), that is, he will rule all the ends of the world. Since across the earth there are great and unnavigable seas, which some people call Atlantic, or western and eastern ocean, he was right to indicate that the power of the world was encircled by the seas from outside. The verse after this made it clearer: *And from rivers to the ends of the world.* He calls *river* the Jordan, in which the Lord was baptized and given testimony by the Father that he is his own beloved Son, in whom he was well pleased. Now, from that time, the evangelist says, he began to preach and say, "Repent, the kingdom of heaven is near."[13] Hence the inspired composition also says, *He will have dominion from the river to the ends of the world.*

(7) He next makes this clear in another way as well. *Ethiopians will fall down before him, and his foes lick the dust. Kings of Tarshish and the islands will offer gifts, kings from Arabia and Seba*

13. Cf. Matt 3.17, 3.2, though in this Gospel the call to repentance occurs in the Baptist's mouth. The river in this verse is usually nominated by commentators as the Euphrates, on the basis of statements about the extent of Solomon's empire such as 1 Kings 4.21—irrelevant in Theodoret's view, of course.

will bring gifts (vv. 9–10). Both blessed Isaiah and the remarkable Ezekiel give the name Tarshish to Carthage, the principal city of Libya, while *Seba* is an Ethiopian nation, whereas those called Libyans and Africans occupy the western parts of the world, Ethiopians the eastern and southern parts, Arabs the middle of the continent, and the island dwellers the middle of the sea.[14] Now, he said these people *will fall down before him,* offer adoration as to God and present gifts as to a king, whereas the foes will be subjected to the curses directed against the serpent: "Upon your breast and belly you are to go, and eat dust all the days of your life."[15] Foes of our God and Savior are the all-wicked demons, against whom he gave authority to walk on serpents and scorpions.[16]

(8) After mentioning three or four nations, however, and indicating in obscure fashion the transformation of all the nations, he makes his meaning clearer: *All the kings of the earth will adore him* (v. 11). While some are ready to do so in the present life, all will be ready after the resurrection: "We do not yet see everything subjected to him,"[17] says the divine Apostle, but at that time "every knee will bend to him, of those in heaven, on earth, and under the earth."[18] *All nations will serve him.* This is in keeping with the patriarch Jacob's prophecy, "He is the expectation of nations."[19] We also see the fulfillment of the prophecy: there is no nation, which has not heard the evangelical preaching;[20] rather, in every nation there are those who have received the radiance of the knowledge of God.

(9) *Because he rescued the poor from the powerful one, and the needy who had no helper. He will spare poor and needy, and save the souls of*

---

14. Location of these biblical places by Theodoret is probably no more accurate than modern commentators'.
15. Cf. Gen 3.14.
16. Cf. Luke 10.19.
17. Heb 2.8.
18. Phil 2.10.
19. Cf. Gen 49.10. Brisk though his pace is in commenting on this lengthy psalm, Theodoret is enjoying his work on this key piece of Church liturgy (even if, as we have seen, he has to detach it completely from its historical moorings). The degree of Scriptural documentation also suggests this.
20. A basic conviction, of course, of early ecclesiology. From our better informed standpoint, however, we may question its factual adequacy.

the needy (vv. 12–13). All will adore him, liberated from the harsh tyranny of the devil. For he named him *powerful one*, human nature, however, *poor* for being at that time bereft of God. In particular he checks the mighty with his divine laws, terrifies them with the threats of hell, and ensures they exercise some indulgence towards the needy, adding this: [1437] *He will redeem their souls from usury and injustice* (v. 14). Now, he called avarice *usury;* this is also the way the Old Law named it, "Do not take interest or profit";[21] so he will persuade those rejoicing in injustice and avarice, he is saying, to exercise mercy and loving-kindness. *His name will be honorable in their sight.* It will be an object of reverence and glory for all, he is saying.

(10) *He will live, and to him will be given some of the gold of Arabia* (v. 15). In place of *Arabia* the other translators put "Sheba": both predict offerings made to him by all, both kings and savages. He also put *will live* in place of "will abide." *They will ever pray for him, they will bless him all day long:* they will sing his praises constantly; they will also sing the praises of his Father, making him the basis of their hymn singing. The phrase *They will pray for him* resembles that apostolic direction, "I give thanks to my God through Jesus Christ,"[22] and again, "Through him we had access to the Father."[23] Through him, accordingly, all will pray to the Father and sing his praises for all the good things done for them through the Son; his praises, too, they will sing, however, as recipients of these things from him.

(11) *There will be a support in the land on the summits of the mountains* (v. 16). He himself will support and prop up those believing in him, he is saying, and render them elevated and exalted, as though placed on the very pinnacles of the mountains. The Lord, too, actually said this to his disciples, "A city placed on a mountain cannot be hidden; nor do they light a lamp and put it under the bushel basket but on the lampstand, and it gives light to everyone in the house."[24] *Their fruit will be raised above Lebanon.* Since he mentioned the lofty mountains, it was right for him to make mention also of Lebanon for being the highest

---

21. Lev 25.36.
23. Eph 2.18.
22. Rom 1.8.
24. Matt 5.14–15.

of the mountains in Palestine; his teaching and its interpreters and preachers, he says, will become more lofty and conspicuous than Lebanon. *They will blossom from a city like grass of the soil:* so, on the one hand, those believing in him will produce fruit of this kind and, on the other hand, the disbelieving Jews will be likened to grass that grows up and immediately withers. [1440]

(12) *His name will be blessed forever, his name will abide beyond the sun* (v. 17). The word *blessed* occurs in no case, neither in the Hexapla nor in the Hebrew. By *beyond* [the psalmist] shows he is older than the sun and the moon: he abides not simply before the sun but for generations of generations.[25] He put *generations of generations* to apply both to the sun and to the moon: sun and moon are the same age, being made at the same time. "God said," Scripture says, "Let there be lights in the firmament of heaven. And God made the two great lights."[26] So if before the moon for generations of generations, before the sun, too. *All the tribes of the earth will be blessed in him.* Here he recalled the promise about Abraham, Isaac, and Jacob: to the three patriarchs God promised to bless, in one case all the nations of the earth, in another the tribes of the earth.[27] He is referring in different ways to all of human nature. Blessed Paul also took this meaning in saying, "Now, the promises were made to Abraham and to his offspring." He does not say, And to offsprings, as of many, but as of one, "and to your offspring, who is Christ."[28] And of course in the Epistle to the Hebrews, "Doubtless he does not help angels."[29] The present psalm also foretells this, saying all the tribes will be blessed in him. *All the nations will declare him blessed.* The inspired word described some things as though in reference to a human being, some as though in reference to God. We find *blessed* occurring also in the case of God: "He is the blessed and

---

25. In making a comparison of variant readings here, Theodoret becomes confused: "blessed" does occur in his form of the LXX, unlike the phrase found in v. 5, "for generations of generations." The longer form of his text tries to cover his error, yet it still reads inconsistently.

26. Gen 1.14, 1.16.

27. Cf. Gen 12.3, 26.4, though these promises are not made to all three patriarchs.

28. Gal 3.16.

29. Heb 2.16—hardly a pellucid reference.

only powerful One," Scripture says, "the King of kings and Lord of lords, the only one having immortality, dwelling in unapproachable light."[30] In other words, all the nations declare him blessed, it is saying, and worthy of hymns of praise.

(13) Next the inspired author teaches more clearly his hidden divinity in adding, *Blessed be the Lord, the God of Israel, who* [1441] *alone works wonders* (v. 18). In other words, he is saying, the one who is the object of inspired discourse and due to perform the prophesied wonders is also the very God of Israel and Lord of all. *And blessed the name of his glory forever, and forever and ever* (v. 19). Hence the need for his praises to be sung by all: even if we are ignorant of his nature as inaccessible, still we have been taught his saving name. *All the earth will be filled with his glory. Amen, Amen.* What he foretold many times throughout the whole psalm he fulfilled by quoting the prophecy so as to render the prediction more definite. Now, the psalmist says he will be obvious in all the earth, is known as God and Lord of all, and receives honor from all, shining upon them with his rays of the knowledge of God. The inspired author knew this through the grace of the Spirit, and inflamed with desire he prays for it to happen and for the prophecy to take effect. Hence he adds also, *Amen, Amen,* or according to Aquila, "To be sure, to be sure," that is, the words are faultless and true, and will have a fulfillment without fail.

END OF THE HYMNS OF DAVID SON OF JESSE.[31]

---

30. 2 Tim 6.15–16.
31. As remarked of Theodoret's commentary on Ps 41.13 (see note 18 there) which closes "Book One" of the Psalms, according to an ancient division perhaps not known to him, he does not see the concluding doxology as other than a final element in the psalm as distinct from an insertion to close Book Two. At this point he makes no comment on the implications of the rubric terminating "the hymns of David," leaving to the opening of the next psalm with its title "A psalm for Asaph" a rehearsal of his views on authorship outlined in the preface.

INDICES

GENERAL INDEX

Abraham, 17, 109, 168, 227
Absalom, 14, 45, 60, 63, 77, 79, 126, 168, 192, 404
Adam, 30, 187, 190, 281, 297
agriculture, 17
Ahithophel, 77, 79, 80, 130, 193, 229
akribeia, 20, 46, 344, 357
Alexandria, 1, 15, 17, 20, 34, 204, 237
allegory, 15, 22, 23, 40, 79, 82, 145, 157, 265, 267, 407
anagogical, 73, 160, 161, 272, 277, 391
anthropomorphism, 21, 34, 69, 100, 125, 408
antigrapha, 9, 70, 159, 172, 192, 243, 364, 404
Antioch, *passim*
Apollinaris of Laodicea, 15, 18, 27, 30, 41, 118
apostolic, 19, 390
Aquila, *passim*
Aramaic, 11, 12, 346
Arius, 5, 8, 25, 26, 27, 118, 263, 333
Asaph, 5, 288, 420
Athanasius, 18, 30
Augustine of Hippo, 22, 30, 198, 297
authorship, 5, 16, 233, 279, 288, 353, 420
Azéma, Y., 2

baptism, 21, 137, 138, 154, 183, 198, 209, 240, 294, 299, 329, 373
Baptist, 19, 416
Bardy, G., 13, 32
Barthélemy, D., 8, 9

Basil of Caesarea, 18
botany, 17, 344
Boyle, L. E., v
Bouyer, L., 34, 35
Brown, R. E., 32

Calvin, J., 254
Carafa, A., 4
catechetical, 156
catena, 4
cenobite, 13
Chalcedon, 1, 6, 26, 55, 247, 263, 377, 379
Christology, *passim*
Church, 30, 31, 241, 242, 264, 265, 278
Clark, E. A., 15
classification, 20, 42, 350
clergy, 13–14, 32, 207
communicatio idiomatum, 26, 27, 246
conciseness, 5, 36, 41, 76, 77, 167, 181, 251
confirmation, 157, 209
council, 1, 6, 26, 247, 277, 377, 388
Croke, B., 3
Cross, F. M., 182
crucifixion, 32, 84, 341, 403
cursing, 217
Cyril of Alexandria, 27, 55, 263

Dahood, M., *passim*
dating, 3–4
David, *passim*
diapsalma, 9, 16, 43–44
didaskaleion, 7, 16
Didymus, 18
Diodore of Tarsus, 1, 15, 18, 23, 24, 42, 43, 45, 99, 203

GENERAL INDEX

dogma, 2, 6, 46, 50, 291
Dorival, G., 9
Drewery, B., 8

ecclesiology, 16, 30–31, 58, 277, 278, 417
eisegesis, 25, 246
Encratite, 30
Ephesus, 1, 26, 28, 388
Eranistes, 26, 27
eschatology, 16, 21, 29, 49–50, 57, 75, 112, 141, 158, 172, 299, 306, 336, 347, 384, 407
eucharist, 29, 153, 157, 207, 209
Eunomius, 5, 25, 118, 333
Eusebius of Caesarea, 8, 15, 18, 107, 113, 115, 204, 247, 308, 369
Eve, 30, 281, 297
exegesis, 1, 3, 7, 19, 22, 24

Fall, 29, 30, 85, 115, 190, 297, 332, 351
Fernandez Marcos, N., 8
fifth edition, 9, 12
flexibility, 5, 6, 24, 25, 36, 58

geography, 17, 184, 347, 417
grace, 34–35, 75, 114, 201, 224, 345, 359, 379, 387
Gregory of Nyssa, 42, 118
Guinot, J.-M., 2, 7, 9, 11, 17, 18, 30, 99, 204
Gunkel, H., 16, 350

Halton, T., 2
Hebrew, 10–12
hermeneutics, 1, 5, 17, 18–25, 36, 57, 58, 191, 272
Hexapla, 8–9, 12, 159, 172, 364, 371, 405
Hezekiah, 106, 109, 139, 141, 181, 187, 202
Hill, R. C., 1, 7, 19, 43, 315
history, 15, 16, 20, 21, 25, 41, 60, 61, 63, 80, 101, 107, 154, 172, 212, 218, 254, 314, 383
homoousios, 26, 27, 263
Huns, 3, 13, 126
hypostatic, 27, 29, 55, 116, 151, 263

Incarnation, 20, 22, 25–28, 34, 83, 85, 220, 238, 244, 298, 314, 320, 329, 371, 410
individualism, 35, 75
inspiration, 19, 43, 60, 260, 282, 346, 390
interpretation, 16, 18–25, 39, 281, 368, 391
Irenaeus, 26, 152

Jellicoe, S., 8
Jerome, 8, 9
Jews, *passim*
John Chrysostom, *passim*
Joosten, J., 11
Julian the Apostate, 13, 310

Kelly, J. N. D., 6, 27, 35, 55, 56, 75, 118, 263
Korah, 42, 288
Kraus, H.-J., 350
Krueger, D., 23

Latin, 3
Law, *passim*
lay, 13, 32, 35, 36, 166
Leroux, J.-M., 22
Letter of Aristeas, 8, 43
literalist, 21, 80, 125
liturgical, 16, 26, 40, 63, 73, 99, 157, 174, 198, 202, 233, 274, 314, 377, 390, 413
Lucian, 8

Macedonians, 5, 25, 333
male, 14–15, 48
Mandac, M., 28
Manichees, 30, 297
Marcion, 30
marriage, 30, 33, 297
Mary, 6, 26, 377, 415
maskil, 198, 248, 275, 304
McKenzie, J., 179
McNamara, K., 28
Mephibosheth, 19, 168, 172, 239
Mercati, G., 9
Michal, 15, 336
Migne, J.-P., 4, 6
monasticism, 34, 166
monophysite, 6, 26, 27

morality, 2, 32–36, 50, 168, 210
moralizing, 17, 33, 59, 61, 81, 98, 188, 303
Moses, *passim*
Mowinckel, S., 16, 169, 198
music, 11, 16, 17, 44, 63, 73, 82, 87, 145, 202, 233, 248, 267, 327, 344, 395
mystery, 87–88, 147
mystical, 34

Nestorius, 6, 26, 27, 55, 263, 377
Nicene, 26, 263, 333

O'Connell, K. G., 8
oikonomia, 87, 147, 320, 410
Olivier, J. M., 1
Origen, 8, 15, 17, 18, 22, 32, 34, 41, 369
original sin, 30, 297, 332

paleography, 12
Palestine, 4, 8, 9, 283
pastor, 2, 12–14, 197, 326
Pelagius, 29, 30, 190, 226, 297, 379
Persian, 4, 13, 126, 412
Peshitta, 10, 11, 12, 243
philomatheis, 7, 12, 14, 17, 227, 394, 396, 397, 405
Pilgrim Songs, 17
polemic, 5, 29, 205, 263, 277, 332
prayer, 64, 163
preaching, 7, 15, 17, 50, 61, 75, 166, 199
precision, 20, 46, 48, 50, 83, 135, 275, 317
priesthood, 33
propheteia, 19, 20, 39, 204, 390
providence, 2, 388

Quasten, J., 6
Qumran, 8

rabbinic, 43, 54
Rabshakeh, 19, 102, 106, 139, 168, 205, 239, 304
Rahlfs, A., 159, 192
rationalizing, 53, 68, 99, 186, 189, 259, 324, 327, 334, 354

readership, 13–14, 227, 326
Rondeau, M.-J., 2, 10, 11, 13, 15, 82, 183
sacrament, 6, 21, 23, 25, 29, 58, 153, 156, 183, 207, 220, 299, 329, 373, 407
Sarah, 15, 227
Saul, 19, 45, 62, 78, 104, 119, 174, 218, 304, 311, 336, 361
Schäublin, C., 23
Schulze, J.-L., 4, 5, 15, 39, 41, 188, 232, 283, 311, 342
Sennacherib, 19, 106, 139, 168, 181, 205, 308
Septuagint, *passim*
sexism, 15, 112, 177, 227
Sheol, 179, 188, 238
singing, 14, 36, 39, 40, 44, 109, 139, 156, 171, 175, 268, 406
Sitz im Leben, 16, 39, 181, 274, 404, 406
soteriology, 24, 25
spiritual, 19, 23, 32–36, 64, 75, 107, 168, 178, 197, 202, 220, 402
subordination, 26, 263
Symmachus, *passim*
synkatabasis, 22, 69, 100, 116, 315
Syriac, 10, 53, 243, 314, 381

text, 2, 7–12, 192, 283, 366
theology, 2, 5, 20, 25, 145, 218, 395
Theodore of Mopsuestia, 1, 15, 18, 35, 39, 41, 204
theoria, 24, 203, 391
Theotokos, 377
titles, *passim*
Torah, 43
transcendence, 22, 69, 104, 251, 315
Trinitarian, 25–28, 29, 55, 221, 291, 293, 333, 354, 379
typology, 23, 187, 191, 237, 240, 299, 337, 345, 350, 351

Ugaritic, 29, 49, 62, 67, 104, 144, 332, 375

Vaccari, A., 9, 24
Viciano, A., 27

Virgin, 6, 26, 148, 377
virtues, 78, 167, 210

Wallace-Hadrill, D. S., 8, 21, 24, 25, 31
Weiser, A., 1, 54, 64, 133, 162, 187, 254, 257, 274, 293, 297, 308, 413

Weitzman, M. P., 11
Wilken, R. L., 31
women, 14–15, 17, 46, 47–48, 51, 227

Young, F., 1, 23, 27

INDEX OF HOLY SCRIPTURE

Old Testament

Genesis
  1.6–7: 203
  1.14–15: 203, 419
  1.16–17: 135, 419
  2.10–14: 270
  3.5: 415
  3.14: 417
  3.19: 122
  4.1: 297
  4.3–5: 375
  8.21: 297
  11: 340
  12: 227
  12.3: 225, 419
  18.20–21: 109
  19.24: 100
  21.30: 289
  24.7: 209
  26: 227
  26.1: 208
  26.4: 419
  26.29: 62
  27–28: 393
  27.36: 246, 283
  31.48: 289
  32.29: 83
  48.16: 209
  49.9: 414
  49.10: 271, 366, 411, 417

Exodus
  9.16: 332
  12.23: 213, 299
  12.29: 213
  14.15: 61
  20.5–6: 356

22.27: 325
22.28: 289

Leviticus
  19.18: 321
  25.36: 418

Numbers
  6.22–26: 62
  24.33: 290

Deuteronomy
  6.1: 136
  6.5: 88, 123
  6.6–8: 49
  7.11: 136
  9.26: 327
  11.18: 49
  23.21: 152
  32.1: 289
  32.4: 47
  32.9: 57
  32.11: 121
  32.15: 149
  32.34–35: 122
  32.43: 57
  34.10: 93

1 Samuel
  2.10: 124
  16.13: 172
  18.10–11: 336
  19.11–17: 336
  21–22: 304, 317
  21: 207, 222
  21.1–6: 173
  22.5: 357
  22.9: 178, 212

22.18–19: 212
23: 311
23.14: 357
23.19–20: 178
24: 218
24.1: 357
24.8–15: 328
24.14: 214
24.16: 321
26: 218
26.1: 212
26.17–18: 214
27: 323

2 Samuel
  2.1: 172
  2.4: 172
  5.1: 173
  5.3: 172
  8.2–13: 344
  9.16: 168
  9.19: 168
  9.21: 168
  11: 199
  11.27: 296
  12: 199
  12.13: 199
  13–17: 60
  15–17: 195
  16.5–13: 195, 231
  17.23: 84
  17.27–29: 194
  22: 123

1 Kings
  4.21: 416
  17.1: 69
  18.27: 316

427

(1 Kings *continued*)
  21: 194
  24: 194

2 Kings
  2.1: 162
  2.11: 162
  6: 196
  18–19: 139, 304
  18.29–35: 106, 143, 309
  19.35: 106, 143, 213, 309
  20: 141, 187
  20.3: 190
  20.6: 190
  20.11: 191

1 Chronicles
  9.16: 353
  15.21: 73
  16.41–42: 353
  22.9: 413
  25.1: 288

Job
  1.9: 415
  1.11: 415

Psalms
  1: 19, 20, 67
  1.1: 14, 15, 46, 177
  1.2: 48, 227
  1.3: 49, 306
  1.4: 9, 50
  1.5: 10, 50, 213, 401
  1.6: 15, 51
  2: 19, 21, 60, 154
  2.1–2: 52, 53
  2.1: 20, 52
  2.3: 53
  2.4: 54
  2.5: 54
  2.6–7: 27, 55
  2.6: 55
  2.8: 56, 115, 205, 383
  2.9: 58
  2.10: 58
  2.11: 58
  2.12: 59
  3: 14, 45, 52
  3.1–2: 60
  3.2: 63
  3.3: 61
  3.4: 61
  3.5: 61
  3.6–7: 61
  3.7: 78
  3.8: 61
  4: 99, 119
  4.1: 63–64
  4.2–3: 63
  4.2: 64
  4.3: 64–65
  4.4: 65
  4.5: 65
  4.6: 66, 208
  4.7: 66
  4.8: 63, 66
  5: 11, 19
  5.1–2: 68
  5.2–3: 69
  5.4–5: 69
  5.5–6: 69
  5.7: 70
  5.8: 70
  5.9–10: 71
  5.9: 71
  5.11–12: 71
  5.11: 71
  6: 102, 229, 294, 306
  6.1: 74
  6.2–3: 74
  6.2: 74
  6.3–4: 74
  6.5: 35, 73, 74–75, 221, 294, 339
  6.6: 75
  6.7: 76
  6.8–9: 76
  6.10: 76
  7: 21
  7.1–2: 77
  7.1: 193
  7.3: 77
  7.4–5: 78, 217
  7.6: 10, 78
  7.7: 79
  7.8: 79
  7.9: 21, 79, 320
  7.11: 165
  7.12–13: 80
  7.14: 80
  7.15–16: 80
  7.15: 224, 312
  7.16: 179
  7.17: 81
  8.1: 83
  8.2: 83–84, 415
  8.3: 84
  8.4: 84
  8.5: 85
  8.6–8: 85
  8.6: 85
  9: 10
  9.1–2: 88
  9.3: 88
  9.4: 89
  9.5: 89
  9.6–7: 90
  9.6: 90
  9.7–8: 90
  9.9: 90
  9.10: 91
  9.11: 91
  9.12: 92
  9.13–14: 92
  9.13: 92
  9.15–16: 92
  9.17–18: 93
  9.19–20: 93
  10: 17
  10.1–2: 94
  10.3: 94
  10.4: 94
  10.5: 95
  10.6: 95
  10.7: 95
  10.8–9: 95
  10.8: 95
  10.10: 95
  10.11: 96
  10.12: 96
  10.13: 96
  10.14: 96
  10.15: 97
  10.16: 97
  10.17: 97
  10.18: 97
  11: 161

INDEX OF HOLY SCRIPTURE 429

11.1: 99
11.2: 99
11.3–5: 100
11.6: 100
11.7: 101
12: 73, 106
12.1: 102
12.2: 102
12.3: 102
12.4: 102
12.5: 103
12.6: 103
12.7: 103, 161
12.8: 103
13: 106
13.1: 104
13.2: 104
13.3: 105
13.4: 105
13.5: 105
13.6: 105
14: 308
14.1–3: 106
14.1: 5, 107, 110
14.2–3: 108
14.2: 205
14.4–5: 109
14.4: 16
14.5–6: 109
14.7: 110
15.1: 111
15.2–3: 111
15.2: 111
15.4–5: 112
15.4: 112
16: 19, 128, 323
16.1–2: 113
16.3: 114
16.4: 114
16.5: 17, 29, 115
16.6: 115–116
16.7: 116
16.8–11: 116
16.11: 27
17.1: 119
17.2: 119
17.3: 119, 128
17.4: 17, 120
17.5: 120
17.6–7: 120
17.6: 120

17.8–9: 120
17.8: 120
17.9–10: 121
17.11: 10, 121
17.12: 121
17.13: 121
17.14: 122
17.15: 122
18: 13
18.1–2: 123
18.2: 192
18.3: 124
18.4–5: 124
18.6: 124
18.7–8: 124–125
18.10–11: 125
18.11–12: 125
18.12–14: 3, 126
18.15: 126
18.16: 126
18.17: 126
18.18–19: 127
18.18: 126
18.20–22: 127
18.23: 127
18.24: 127
18.25–26: 128
18.27: 128
18.28: 128
18.29: 128
18.30: 128
18.31: 129
18.32: 129
18.33: 129
18.34: 129
18.35: 129
18.36: 129
18.37–38: 129
18.39: 129
18.40: 129
18.41: 130
18.42: 130
18.43–44: 130
18.43: 130
18.44–45: 130
18.46: 131
18.47–48: 131
18.49: 131
18.50: 131
19: 138, 140
19.1: 134

19.2: 134
19.3–4: 135
19.4–6: 10, 135
19.7–10: 32, 136
19.11: 137
19.12: 137
19.13–14: 137
19.13: 137
20.1–2: 139
20.3: 10, 139
20.4: 140
20.5: 140
20.6: 140
20.7–8: 140
20.10: 140
21: 161
21.1–2: 141
21.3: 141
21.4: 141
21.5: 142
21.6: 142
21.7: 142
21.8: 142
21.9–10: 142
21.9–12: 217
21.11: 143
21.12: 143
21.13: 144
22: 11, 21, 55, 87, 146, 396
22.1: 10, 146, 150
22.2: 147
22.3: 147
22.4: 147
22.6: 148
22.7–8: 148
22.9–10: 148
22.11: 148
22.12–13: 149
22.14: 149
22.14–15: 149
22.16–17: 150
22.16: 149–50
22.18: 150
22.19–21: 151
22.22: 151
22.23: 152
22.24–25: 26
22.24: 152
22.25: 152, 291, 375

(Psalms *continued*)
  22.26: 29, 153, 156
  22.27: 153
  22.28: 153
  22.29: 153, 156
  22.30–31: 154, 410
  22.30: 154
  23: 156, 157, 158
  23.1: 156
  23.2: 156
  23.3: 157
  23.4: 157
  23.5: 157
  23.6: 29, 157
  24: 9
  24.1: 159
  24.2: 159
  24.3: 23, 160
  24.4: 160
  24.5: 160
  24.6: 160
  24.7–10: 161
  24.7: 274
  25: 19, 304
  25.1–2: 163
  25.3: 163
  25.4–5: 164
  25.6–7: 164
  25.8–9: 165
  25.8: 10, 164
  25.10: 165
  25.11: 165, 169
  25.12–13: 165
  25.12: 33
  25.14: 166
  25.15: 167
  25.16: 167, 200
  25.17–18: 167
  25.19: 167
  25.20: 167
  25.21: 167
  25.22: 163, 168
  26.1: 169
  26.2: 169
  26.3: 170
  26.4–5: 170
  26.6–7: 170
  26.8–10: 170
  26.8: 175
  26.11–12: 171
  27: 11, 19, 43, 173
  27.1: 173
  27.2: 173–74
  27.3: 174
  27.4–5: 174
  27.5: 173
  27.6: 173, 175
  27.7: 173, 175
  27.8: 175
  27.9: 175–76, 200
  27.10: 176
  27.11: 10, 176
  27.12: 173, 176
  27.13: 177
  27.14: 177
  28: 180
  28.1: 29, 178
  28.2: 179
  28.3: 179
  28.4: 179
  28.5: 179
  28.6–7: 180
  28.8: 180
  28.9: 180
  29: 17, 173, 187
  29.1–2: 183
  29.1: 11, 185
  29.3: 183, 218
  29.4: 183
  29.5–6: 265
  29.5: 184
  29.6: 184
  29.7: 184
  29.8: 185
  29.9: 185
  29.10: 186
  29.11: 186
  30.1: 188
  30.2–3: 188
  30.4–5: 12, 188
  30.6: 189
  30.7: 189
  30.8–9: 190
  30.10–12: 190
  30.12: 10
  31: 9, 12, 19, 204, 296, 406
  31.1: 192
  31.2–3: 192
  31.2: 192
  31.4: 193
  31.5: 193
  31.6: 193
  31.7–8: 193
  31.7: 193
  31.9: 194
  31.10: 194
  31.11: 194
  31.12: 194
  31.13–15: 195
  31.13: 194
  31.16–17: 195
  31.16: 195
  31.17: 217
  31.18: 195
  31.19: 195
  31.20: 196
  31.21: 196
  31.22: 192, 196
  31.23: 196–97
  31.24: 197
  32: 23, 39, 198, 229, 248, 296
  32.1–2: 198, 294
  32.3: 198
  32.4: 199
  32.5: 79, 199, 296
  32.6: 13, 200
  32.7: 200
  32.8: 200
  32.9: 137, 201
  32.10: 34, 201
  32.11: 88, 201
  33.1: 202
  33.2–3: 16, 202
  33.3: 33
  33.4: 203
  33.5: 203
  33.6: 20, 22, 203, 204
  33.7: 204
  33.8–9: 204
  33.10–11: 205
  33.12: 32, 205
  33.13–14: 205
  33.15: 206
  33.16–17: 206
  33.18–19: 206
  33.20–21: 206
  33.22: 206
  34: 14, 33, 304
  34.1: 208
  34.2–3: 208

INDEX OF HOLY SCRIPTURE

34.2: 208
34.4: 208
34.5: 208
34.6: 208–9
34.7: 209
34.8: 209, 277
34.9–10: 210
34.11–12: 210
34.13–14: 210
34.14: 33
34.15: 210
34.16: 211
34.17–18: 211
34.19–20: 211
34.21–22: 211
35.1: 212
35.2–3: 212
35.4: 212
35.5: 212–13
35.6: 213
35.7: 213
35.8: 213
35.9–10: 213
35.11: 213
35.12: 214
35.13: 214
35.14: 214
35.15: 215
35.16: 215
35.17: 215
35.18: 10, 215
35.19: 215
35.20: 215, 216
35.21: 216
35.22–23: 216
35.24–25: 216
35.26: 216
35.27: 216
35.28: 216
36: 11, 19
36.1: 218
36.2: 219
36.3–4: 219
36.5–6: 219
36.7: 220
36.8: 220
36.9: 29, 220
36.10: 221
36.11–12: 221
37: 17, 18
37.1: 222

37.2: 222
37.3–4: 222
37.5–6: 223
37.7: 223
37.8–9: 223
37.9–11: 223
37.12–13: 223
37.14–15: 224
37.16: 224
37.17: 224
37.18–19: 224
37.20: 10, 20, 224
37.21: 225
37.22: 225, 226
37.23–24: 35, 225
37.23: 50, 70
37.25–26: 226
37.27–29: 226
37.27: 48, 226
37.30–31: 227
37.32–33: 7, 15, 17, 227
37.34: 227
37.35–36: 228
37.37: 228
37.38: 228
37.39–40: 228
38.1: 229
38.2: 229
38.3: 229
38.4–6: 230
38.7: 230
38.8: 230
38.9–10: 230
38.9: 230
38.11: 230
38.12: 231
38.13–14: 231
38.15–16: 231
38.17: 231
38.18: 231
38.19–20: 231
38.21–22: 232
39: 353
39.1–2: 233
39.3–4: 234
39.3: 234
39.5–6: 239
39.5: 234
39.6: 235
39.7: 235, 237

39.8: 235
39.9: 235
39.10: 236
39.11: 236
39.12–13: 236, 237
40.1–2: 237
40.3: 238
40.4: 239
40.5: 239, 409
40.6–7: 239
40.8: 240
40.9–10: 240–41
40.11: 241
40.12: 241
40.13–14: 242
40.13–17: 242, 404
40.15: 242
40.16: 242, 405
40.17: 242
41: 246
41.1: 12, 26, 243
41.2: 244
41.3: 244
41.4: 244
41.5: 245
41.6: 245
41.7: 245
41.8: 245, 246
41.9: 246, 318
41.10–11: 246
41.12: 246
41.13: 247, 420
42: 254, 259
42.1, 2: 248
42.3–4: 249
42.5: 249, 252
42.6: 250
42.7: 10, 250
42.8: 250
42.9–10: 251
42.9: 22
42.11: 251, 252
43: 11, 260
43.1: 252
43.2: 252
43.3: 252
43.4: 10, 253
43.5: 252, 253
44.1: 254–55
44.2–3: 255
44.4: 255

INDEX OF HOLY SCRIPTURE

(Psalms continued)
44.5: 255
44.6–7: 255
44.8: 255
44.9: 255–56
44.10: 256
44.11: 256
44.12: 256
44.13: 256
44.14: 256
44.15–16: 257
44.17–18: 257
44.18–19: 257
44.18: 257
44.20–22: 257
44.22: 257
44.23: 78, 258
44.24: 258
44.25: 258
44.26: 258
45: 11, 19, 43, 344, 395
45.1: 260, 282
45.2: 261, 289
45.3–4: 261
45.4: 22
45.5: 262
45.6: 28, 262
45.7: 26, 55, 262
45.8–9: 263
45.8: 279
45.10: 31, 264
45.11–12: 264
45.11: 264
45.12: 14, 33
45.13–14: 23, 265
45.14–15: 266
45.16: 266, 318, 385
45.17: 266
46: 11
46.1, 2: 268
46.3: 269
46.4: 270
46.5: 270
46.6: 270–71
46.7: 271
46.8–10: 271
46.9: 24
46.11: 271
47.1–2: 273

47.3–4: 273
47.5: 274
47.7–8: 274
47.9: 275
48: 11
48.1: 276
48.3: 30, 277
48.4–5: 278
48.5–7: 278
48.8: 278
48.9: 278
48.10: 278
48.11: 279
48.12–13: 279
48.13–14: 279
49: 13
49.1: 281
49.2: 18, 281
49.3–4: 282
49.4: 5
49.5: 283
49.6: 284
49.7–8: 284
49.9–10: 284
49.11: 285
49.12: 93, 285
49.13: 285
49.14: 285
49.15: 286
49.16–17: 286
49.18: 10, 286
49.19: 286
49.20: 286
50.1: 288
50.2: 289
50.3: 289
50.4: 289
50.5–6: 289
50.7: 290
50.8: 290
50.9–11: 290
50.9: 301
50.12: 291
50.13: 291
50.14–15: 291, 293
50.16–17: 291–92
50.18–20: 292
50.21: 292
50.22: 293
50.23: 10, 293
51–95.3: 18

51: 33
51.1: 295
51.2: 294, 295
51.3: 79, 295
51.4: 231, 296, 396
51.5: 30, 33, 35, 296, 297, 332
51.6: 298
51.7: 21, 299
51.8: 299
51.10: 300
51.11: 300
51.12: 300
51.13: 300
51.14: 301
51.15: 301
51.16: 301
51.17: 211, 301
51.18–19: 302
52: 19
52.1: 305
52.2: 305
52.3: 305
52.4: 304, 305
52.5: 305
52.7: 306
52.8: 306
52.9: 29, 306
53: 13, 107, 308
53.1: 308
53.2: 309
53.3: 309
53.4: 309
53.5: 309
53.8: 310
54: 5, 314
54.1: 311
54.2: 312
54.3: 312
54.4–5: 312
54.6–7: 312
54.6: 180, 312
55: 5, 17, 22, 25
55.1: 315
55.2–3: 315
55.4–5: 25, 316
55.6–7: 317
55.8: 317
55.9–10: 317
55.9: 317
55.10–11: 32, 317

INDEX OF HOLY SCRIPTURE 433

55.12: 318
55.13–14: 318
55.15: 319
55.16: 319
55.17: 320
55.18: 320
55.19: 320
55.20: 320
55.21: 321
55.22: 321
55.23: 322
56.1–2: 323
56.3: 324
56.4: 324
56.5: 324
56.6: 324
56.7: 325
56.8: 325
56.9: 325
56.11: 325
56.12: 325
56.13: 325
57: 331
57.1: 327
57.2: 328
57.3–4: 328
57.3: 328
57.5: 328
57.6: 329
57.7: 329
57.8: 329
57.9: 329
57.10: 329
57.11: 330
58: 17
58.1: 331
58.2: 331
58.3: 331, 332
58.4–5: 5, 25, 332
58.4: 332
58.6: 334
58.7: 334
58.8: 334
58.9: 334
58.10: 335
58.11: 335
59: 341
59.1: 15, 337
59.2: 337
59.3: 337
59.4: 337

59.5: 338
59.6: 338
59.7: 338
59.8: 339
59.9: 339
59.10: 339
59.11: 339
59.12–13: 32, 340
59.12: 339–40
59.14: 341–42
59.15: 342
59.16–17: 342
59.16: 342
60: 5, 6, 11
60.1: 344
60.2: 345
60.3: 345
60.4: 35, 345
60.5: 345
60.6: 345, 346
60.7: 346
60.8: 346
60.9–10: 347
60.10: 347
60.11: 348
60.12: 348
61.1: 349
61.2: 349
61.3: 350
61.4: 350
61.5: 23, 350
61.6–7: 350
61.8: 352
62: 5
62.1–2: 353
62.1: 353
62.3: 353
62.4: 354
62.5: 354
62.6: 354
62.7: 354
62.8: 355
62.9: 12, 355
62.10: 355
62.11–12: 356
63: 5
63.1: 357
63.2: 357, 359
63.3: 358
63.4: 358
63.5: 358

63.6–7: 358
63.8: 359
63.9: 359
63.10: 359
63.11: 359
64: 5
64.1: 361
64.2: 361
64.3–4: 361
64.5: 361
64.6–7: 362
64.6: 362
64.7–8: 362
64.9: 362
64.10: 362
65: 8, 9, 12, 369
65.1–2: 364
65.3: 365
65.4–5: 365
65.4: 365
65.6–7: 366
65.6: 6
65.8: 367
65.9: 10, 367
65.10: 368
65.11–12: 368
65.11: 368
65.13: 369
66: 6, 8, 9, 11, 12
66.1–2: 371
66.3: 31, 371
66.4: 372
66.5: 372
66.6: 372
66.7: 373
66.8: 373
66.9: 374
66.10: 374
66.11–12: 374
66.13–14: 325, 374
66.15: 374
66.16: 375
66.17: 10, 375
66.18: 375
66.19: 375
66.20: 376
67: 17
67.1: 6, 377
67.2: 378
67.3–4: 378
67.5: 378

INDEX OF HOLY SCRIPTURE

(Psalms *continued*)
67.6–7: 378
67.6: 378
68: 11, 25
68.1: 380
68.2: 12, 380
68.3: 381
68.4–5: 381
68.4: 381
68.6: 382
68.7–8: 382
68.9: 383
68.10: 383
68.11: 384
68.12: 384
68.13: 385
68.14: 299, 385
68.15: 386
68.16: 386
68.17: 386
68.18: 387
68.19: 387
68.20: 388
68.21: 2, 388
68.22: 388
68.23: 389
68.24: 389, 391
68.25: 389
68.26: 19, 389
68.27: 390
68.28–29: 391
68.30: 391
68.31: 392
68.32: 392
68.33: 392
68.34: 393
68.35: 7, 393
69: 11, 17, 396
69.1: 395
69.2: 395
69.3: 396
69.4: 7, 396
69.5: 396
69.6: 397
69.7: 397
69.8: 397
69.9: 397
69.10–11: 397
69.12: 397
69.13: 398
69.14–15: 389

69.14: 398
69.15: 398
69.16: 398
69.17: 399
69.18: 399
69.19: 399
69.20: 399
69.21: 399
69.22: 399
69.23: 399
69.24: 399
69.25: 395, 399
69.26: 401
69.27: 401
69.28: 401
69.29: 401
69.30: 402
69.31: 402
69.32: 402
69.33: 402
69.34: 402
69.35: 402
69.36: 403
70: 12, 242
70.1: 404
70.2: 404
70.3: 404
70.4: 404
70.5: 405
71: 5, 6, 12, 43, 192
71.1: 406
71.2–3: 407
71.2: 407
71.4: 407
71.5: 407
71.6: 407
71.7: 408
71.8: 408
71.9: 408
71.10–11: 408
71.12: 408
71.13: 408–9
71.14: 409
71.15–16: 409
71.15: 409
71.16–17: 409
71.17–18: 410
71.18–19: 410
71.20: 411
71.21: 411

71.22: 411
71.23–24: 412
72: 13, 413
72.1: 414
72.2: 414
72.3: 13, 414
72.4: 414
72.5: 415
72.6: 415
72.7: 415
72.8: 416
72.9–10: 416–17
72.11: 417
72.12–13: 417–18
72.14: 418
72.15: 418
72.16: 418
72.17: 419
72.18: 420
72.19: 420
73–83: 288
73: 5, 17, 42
73.18–20: 36
73.22: 10
74.3: 9
75.6: 9
75.8: 101
77.3: 88
82.1–3: 289
82.6–7: 47
83.18: 28, 56
84.1–2: 83
84.3: 83
85.1: 71
90.4: 234
101.1: 164
102.26–27: 235
102.27: 351
103.15–16: 85
105.3: 88
106.19: 184
110.1: 47
110.3: 56
111: 11, 201, 310
111.10: 108
113.1: 12
114.4: 414
115.16: 134
116.5: 165
116.9: 12
118.13: 127

119: 9
119.61: 116
119.105: 370
119.108: 180
120–134: 17
123.4: 10
127.4: 12
129: 17
132.6: 27
132.17: 128
135.7: 204
137.2: 253
137.4: 302, 364
141: 14, 45
144.4: 85
147.8: 134
148.4: 134

Proverbs
1.7: 108
13.8: 284
19.17: 226

Ecclesiastes
1.2: 160

Wisdom
1.13–14: 189

Isaiah
1.16–18: 48, 299
2.2: 386
4.4: 295
5.1–4: 82, 259, 330, 400
7: 268
7–8: 272
7.14–16: 148
9.1: 391
10.22: 403
11.10: 132
24.16: 375, 385
26.17–18: 185
35.1: 185, 260, 381
38.18: 190

40.3–4: 70, 269, 381
40.5–8: 222
40.15: 339
40.18: 339
40.22: 109
42.16: 40
43.19–20: 49
43.25–26: 295
45.1: 346
47.6: 401
50.1: 256
52.3: 256
53.2–3: 261
53.5: 147
53.9: 337
54.1: 185, 381
56.3–5: 261
58.9: 64
59.10: 58
61.1–2: 368
63.3: 389
66.20: 249

Jeremiah
1.5: 332
1.13: 347
1.14: 277
2.13: 221
2.21: 130
4.22: 332
9.24: 71
15.19: 200
25.15: 101
35: 406
38.6: 327

Baruch
3.36–37: 378

Ezekiel
11.3–11: 347
16.3–4: 407
18.23: 189
34: 156
34.17–19: 369

34.24: 130, 132
36.26: 300
37.12: 411
37.24: 411
39: 268

Daniel
2.40: 58
3.29: 241
3.39: 301
3.50: 374
6.10: 179
6.16: 237
7.9–10: 289, 401
9.23: 40

Hosea
4.16: 149
10.11: 149

Joel
2.20: 277

Amos
5.8: 204
8.11: 224

Habakkuk
3.3: 83
3.9: 270
3.13: 367
3.15: 269, 384

Zechariah
1.9: 209
11.1: 284

Malachi
1.8: 375

1 Maccabees
1–2: 254

2 Maccabees
6–7: 257

INDEX OF HOLY SCRIPTURE

New Testament

Matthew
1.1: 47, 132
1.19: 415
3.2: 416
3.3: 381
3.15: 240
3.16: 317
3.17: 183, 259, 416
4.13–16: 391
5.3: 46, 93
5.14–15: 276, 386, 418
5.16: 393
5.21–22: 93
5.27–28: 93
6.24: 355
7.2: 206
7.6: 375
7.24–25: 193
8.29: 382
10.22: 93
10.35: 367
11.29–30: 54, 262, 315
13.8: 369
13.51: 283
15.26: 150
16.18: 70, 238, 276
17.5: 152
18.20: 270
18.27: 338
21.9: 84
21.16: 84
23.37: 121
25.12: 74
25.32–41: 356
25.34: 68, 350
26.4: 245
26.15–16: 245
26.25: 321
26.49: 321
27.5: 84
27.6: 320
27.24: 170
27.25: 32, 338
27.35: 150
27.39–42: 148
27.46: 146, 315
27.48: 399
27.51: 383
28.10: 182
28.18: 281
28.19: 55, 183, 381
28.20: 270, 278

Mark
1.9: 317
2.26: 207, 304
3.6: 53
6.48: 358
8.32: 316
15.36: 399

Luke
1.76: 56
1.79: 145, 378
2.52: 116
3.5: 70
3.12–14: 166
3.22: 317
10.19: 185, 412
10.27: 88, 123
13.34: 121
16.19–31: 286
19.38: 84
20.25: 340
22.43: 116, 316
23.2: 245, 340
23.34: 338
23.36: 399
23.39: 148
24.39: 150
24.49: 184, 393

John
1.1: 204, 351
1.3: 56, 204
2.19: 245
3.13: 382
3.16: 191
4.13–14: 49, 367
5.23: 54
6.57: 351
7.37: 49
7.38: 49, 367
10.14: 156
10.16: 57
10.27–28: 115
11.25: 351
11.50: 53
12.27: 246, 316
12.28: 152
12.31: 151
12.49: 315
13.9: 318
13.17–19: 243
14.2: 266
14.6: 262
14.10: 221
14.27: 367, 413
14.30: 151, 388
15.1–2: 66, 82
15.14–15: 384
17.6: 115
17.12: 115
19.15: 58, 338
20.17: 113
20.27: 150

Acts
1.11: 274
1.15: 57
2.6: 184, 393
2.10: 392
2.29–32: 117
2.41: 57
3.6: 312
4.4: 57
4.24–30: 52
7.58: 390
8.26–39: 392
9.4–5: 390
9.15: 384
13.16: 152
13.21: 390
13.36–37: 117
14.15: 89
15.10–11: 54
17.6: 229
26.14: 308

Romans
1.8: 418
1.20: 133
2.5–6: 284
2.14: 133
2.22: 292

INDEX OF HOLY SCRIPTURE

3.10–12: 106
3.29–30: 153
5.12: 30, 297
6.5: 90
6.8: 90
7.14: 256
8.2: 133
8.16–17: 68, 315
8.28: 50
8.29: 151, 240
8.35: 385
9.6–7: 403
10.12: 387
12.1: 239, 313
12.14: 217
12.15: 111, 310
15.5: 310

1 Corinthians
1.9: 47
1.20: 332
1.24: 282
1.31: 71
2.7–8: 88
2.9: 356
2.10: 221
3.2: 385
3.15: 51, 80
5.1: 89
5.21: 147
6.20: 393
10.12: 59, 201
11.3: 47
12.3: 221
12.4: 265
12.8–10: 264
13.7–8: 123
15.6: 57
15.9: 241
15.20: 146, 188
15.21–23: 266
15.27: 86

2 Corinthians
5.14: 384
5.17: 186

6.16: 270
8.9: 243
10.17: 71, 201
12.9: 64, 383
12.10: 114

Galatians
3.1: 89
3.13: 147
3.16: 419
3.19: 133
3.27: 369
4.3–5: 91
4.7: 68
4.17: 392
4.26: 391
6.1: 201
6.17: 315

Ephesians
1.9: 72
1.21: 391
1.22: 265
2.5–6: 85
2.8: 34, 201
2.14: 413
2.18: 418
2.20: 276
3.4: 54
3.10: 162
4.9–11: 387
4.13: 359
6.1–9: 166

Philippians
2.6–7: 26, 116, 128, 247
2.9: 56
2.10–11: 154, 417
3.2: 150

Colossians
1.16: 56
1.18: 240
1.26: 88
3.18–4.1: 166

1 Timothy
1.15: 241
1.18: 384
5.24: 319
6.15: 47
6.16: 125

2 Timothy
2.4: 384
4.8: 283
6.15–16: 420

Titus
2.11–12: 90

Hebrews
1.4: 274
1.8: 55
1.14: 209
2.8–9: 86, 417
2.14: 151, 388
2.16–17: 247, 419
3.14: 263
5.5: 56
5.7–9: 112
6.18: 319
7.3: 415
8.13: 410
10.5–10: 240
10.19–20: 263
11.38: 362
12.22: 91

James
1.8: 355
5.13: 175

1 Peter
2.22: 337

Revelation
7.3: 345
9.4: 345
14.1: 345

www.ingramcontent.com/pod-product-compliance
Lightning Source LLC
Chambersburg PA
CBHW020313010526
44107CB00054B/1819